101-127

EMERGING STATES

Series in Comparative Politics and International Studies
Series editor, Christophe Jaffrelot

This series consists of translations of noteworthy manuscripts and publications in the social sciences emanating from the foremost French researchers, from Sciences Po, Paris.

The focus of the series is the transformation of politics and society by transnational and domestic factors – globalisation, migration and the post bipolar balance of power on the one hand, and ethnicity and religion on the other. States are more permeable to external influence than ever before and this phenomenon is accelerating processes of social and political change the world over. In seeking to understand and interpret these transformations, this series gives priority to social trends from below as much as to the interventions of state and non-state actors.

CHRISTOPHE JAFFRELOT

editor

Emerging States
The Wellspring of a New World Order

Translated from the French by Cynthia Schoch

Columbia University Press
New York

in association with Centre d'Etudes et de Recherches Internationales (CERI)

First published in 2008 by Presses de Sciences Po, Paris,
as *L'Enjeu Mondial. Les Pays Émergent.*

This translation published in the United States of America by
Columbia University Press
Publishers Since 1893
New York

Library of Congress Cataloging-in-Publication Data

Emerging states : the wellspring of a new world order / Christophe Jaffrelot, editor ; translated from the French by Cynthia Schoch.
    p. cm. — (Series in comparative politics and international studies)
  Includes bibliographical references.
  ISBN 978-0-231-15428-4 (cloth : alk. paper)
  1. Developing countries—Politics and government. 2. Newly independent states—Politics and government. 3. Newly independent states—Economic policy. 4. Developing countries—Economic policy. 5. World politics—21st century. 6. International economic relations. I. Jaffrelot, Christophe. II. Title. III. Series.

  JF60.E44 2009
  327.09172'4—dc22

                          2008048877

⊛
Columbia University Press books are printed on permanent and durable acid-free paper.
This book is printed on paper with recycled content.
Printed in India

c 10 9 8 7 6 5 4 3 2 1

Contents

PART 3
A NEW WORLD OUTLOOK

PART 4
PERSPECTIVES: HOPES AND HURDLES

Acknowledgements

This book inaugurates a new series of annual publications that CERI-Sciences Po will publish every autumn in French and in English on topical issues: in 2008 we have chosen to analyze the newly emerging countries; in 2009, we shall deal with migrations worldwide.

This new venture has benefited from the help of several colleagues and friends within Sciences Po and outside. At CERI, this book owes much to the work of Corinne Deloy who interacted most effectively with the authors on a regular basis. The graphs and maps were created – with a remarkable combination of rigour and imagination – by Dorian Ryser at CERI together with Benoît Martin and Patrice Mitrano at the "Atelier de cartographie" of Sciences Po. Cynthia Schoch translated the chapters from the French with her legendary skill and Miriam Périer, who is in charge of the English publications at Sciences Po, supervised the making of the present edition.

The English edition of this book, published in French by Les Presses de Sciences Po, has been made possible by a grant from the Délégation des Affaires Stratégiques where Marie André has been an active supporter of the project.

Last but not least, I wish to thank Judith Burko, who is in charge of the Publications department at CERI, for her very perceptive words of advice; Marie-Françoise Durand, who is at the helm of the "Atelier de cartographie" of Sciences Po, for her commitment to this project; and Serge Cordelier for his initial, seminal help and guidance.

But the remaining flaws of the book are naturally mine.

Christophe Jaffrelot

About the Contributors

ROLANDO AVENDANO is a Research Associate at the OECD Development Centre in Paris. He is currently working on subjects related to the macroeconomic impact of Asia in Latin America and the financial development of emerging economies.

FRANÇOIS BAFOIL, sociologist, senior research fellow with the CNRS (Conseil National de la Recherche Scientifique) at CERI-Sciences Po; Special Adviser of the OECD for the Territorial Review Poland in 2007/8. He has written *Europe centrale et orientale, Mondialisation, européanisation et changement social*, Paris: Presses de Sciences Po, 2006 [*Central and Eastern Europe: Globalization, Europeanization, and Social Change*, Basingstoke: Palgrave, forthcoming 2008]. He edited *La Pologne*, Paris: Fayard, 2007.

GEOFF BARNARD is the senior economist working on the Russia and South Africa desk for the Economics Department of the OECD. Before joining the OECD in 2007, he worked for 15 years at the IMF, including three and a half years as a resident representative in Moscow. He was educated at Cambridge University, the London School of Economics, and McGill University.

ROBERT BOYER is senior research fellow with the CNRS and teaches at the EHESS in Paris. As economist at CEPREMAP in Paris, he conducts research on economic history, institutional and historic macroeconomics and comparative analyses of capitalism in the framework of regulation theory.

JEAN COUSSY is scientific correspondent of the Centre d'Etudes et de Recherches Internationaux (Sciences Po-CERI) in France and honorary lecturer at the EHESS (Paris). His research is in international political economy (international institutions, Africa, Asia).

OLIVIER DABÈNE is professor of political science at the Sciences Po, Paris, and director of Latin American Studies (undergraduate and graduate programmes).

DOMINIQUE DARBON is professor of political science at the Institut d'Etudes Politiques in Bordeaux and chairs the scientific council of the Africa department at the French Foreign Ministry. His research focuses on public administration in the southern hemisphere countries and state-building.

JEAN-LUC DOMENACH, senior research fellow with Sciences Po-CERI, is former director of CERI and former dean of research at the Sciences Po. He is the author of several books on Asia and China, including the recent *Comprendre la Chine d'aujourd'hui* and *La Chine m'inquiète*, published by Perrin.

GILLES FAVAREL-GARRIGUES, CNRS senior research fellow with CERI (Sciences Po–CNRS) has recently published *La police des mœurs économiques de l'URSS à la Russie* (CNRS Editions, 2007).

JEAN-JACQUES GABAS, professor of economics at Paris-XI University and the Sciences Po in Paris, director of the Analysis of Economic Transformations, Information Technologies and Societies research centre at the Interdisciplinary College at Paris-XI. He is honorary president of GEMDEV.

PIERRE-NOËL GIRAUD is economics professor at the Ecole des Mines in Paris. Member of the French Académie des Technologies.

FRANÇOIS GODEMENT, a historian, teaches at the Sciences Po and is the director of its ECFR Asia Centre. His research is on changes in China and East Asian international relations.

EMMANUEL GUÉRIN graduated from the Institute of Political Studies in Paris. He heads the IDDRI's development assistance programme and coordinates activities on emerging countries there.

JÉRÔME GUILLET is an investment banker in Paris and the editor of *European Tribune*, a website focused on Europe, energy and international politics.

PIERRE HASSNER, senior research fellow emeritus with Sciences Po-CERI, currently associate researcher, has taught at many institutions, most recently the University of Quebec in Montreal and the Institut des Hautes Etudes Internationales et du Développement in Geneva.

GUY HERMET, senior research fellow emeritus, former director of CERI and Professor at the Paris Institute of Political Studies as well as Brussels, Lausanne, Geneva and Montreal Universities.

JEAN-FRANÇOIS HUCHET is currently Director of the French Centre for Research on Contemporary China based in Hong Kong (Centre d'Etudes Français sur la Chine Contemporaine, CEFC), and director of the journal *China Perspectives*.

AHMET INSEL, professor of development economics, is head of the economics department at Galatasaray University in Istanbul.

CHRISTOPHE JAFFRELOT is director of CERI (Sciences Po) and senior research fellow with the CNRS. He has recently edited *Milices armées d'Asie du Sud* (Paris: Presses de Sciences Po, 2008).

FRANÇOISE LEMOINE is economist at the CEPII and associate researcher at the Centre on Modern and Contemporary China (EHESS, Paris). She has published *L'Economie de la Chine* (Paris: La Découverte, Collection Repères, 2006).

BRUNO LOSCH is Senior Economist at the World Bank (Sustainable Development Department) and researcher at CIRAD (the Centre de Coopération Internationale en Recherche Agronomique pour le Développement).

ROLAND MARCHAL, research fellow with the CNRS at CERI-Sciences Po, works on armed conflicts in Africa. In this context he has become interested in Dubai (*Dubai, cité globale*, CNRS Editions 2001) and in the history of relations between Asia and Africa (*Afrique Asie: une autre mondialisation*, Paris: Presses de Sciences Po, 2008).

ALEXANDRA NOVOSSELOFF holds a PhD in political science from the University of Paris II and specializes in the field of international organizations, peacekeeping and the relations between the United Nations and regional organizations.

IMÈNE RAHMOUNI-ROUSSEAU is Head of the Financial Stability and Markets Division at the Banque de France, the French central bank. Her division is responsible for analyzing vulnerabilities and risks in the international financial system. She was previously employed as economist at the European Central Bank. She has written numerous articles on monetary policy implementation and financial stability, notably in the area of securitization and credit derivatives.

DAVID RECONDO is research fellow at CERI-Sciences Po/CNRS. His research focuses on the varied fortunes of participatory democracy in Latin America from a comparative perspective. He has just published *La Politique du guépard. Multi-culturalisme et démocratie au Mexique*, Paris: CERI-Karthala, "Recherches internationales", 2008.

ALAIN ROUQUIÉ, former French Ambassador to Brazil, is senior research fellow emeritus at CERI-Sciences Po and chairman of La Maison de l'Amérique Latine in Paris. He is the author of several books including *The Military and the State in Latin America* and *Le Brésil au XXe siècle*.

JOËL RUET is a senior researcher with the French CNRS, at LATTS-Ecole Nationale des Ponts et Chaussées (a College of ParisTech), and associate researcher at CERNA, Ecole des Mines de Paris (ParisTech). He teaches at the Ecole des Mines, HEC-Paris, and the University of Barcelona.

JAVIER SANTISO is director and chief economist of the OECD Development Centre. He is also the chair of the OECD emerging markets network (EMNET). Previously he was chief economist for emerging markets at BBVA (Banco Bilbao Vizcaya Argentaria) and research fellow at CERI-Sciences Po. He is the author of *Latin America's Political Economy of the Possible*, Cambridge, MA: MIT Press, 2006.

JÉRÔME SGARD holds a PhD in Economics and is a senior research fellow at CERI-Sciences Po. He has worked extensively on economic crises and reforms in Eastern Europe and in emerging countries. His most recent research addresses the relations between the law, economic development and the government of public assets.

JEAN-MARC SIROËN, professor of international economics at Paris-Dauphine University, head of the masters programme. He has published on international economic relations and the link between trade and institutions.

ANNE DE TINGUY is a professor at INALCO (Institut National des Langues et Civilisations Orientales) and CERI-Sciences Po. She has written extensively on Russian and Ukrainian foreign policy. Most recently she has edited *Moscou et le monde - L'ambition de la grandeur: une illusion?* Paris: CERI-Autrement, 2008.

LAURENCE TUBIANA is Director of the Institute for Sustainable Development and International Relations (IDDRI) and the Sustainable Development Centre of the Institute of Political Studies in Paris, and member of the China Council for International Cooperation on Environment and Development (CCIED) and the Indian Council for Sustainable Development (ICSD).

CORNELIA WOLL is a research fellow at CERI-Sciences Po. She works in the field of international political economy and has recently published *Firm Interests: How Governments Shape Business Lobbying on Global Trade* (Ithaca, NY: Cornell University Press, 2008).

ATELIER DE CARTOGRAPHIE: Created in 1995, the Sciences Po Cartography Studio offers training for students and produces graphs and charts for the institution's instructors and researchers. It has also entered into partnership agreements with press organs, publishers, public administrations, companies and museums. Part of its map database is available on its website: http://www.sciences-po.fr/cartographie.

Abbreviations

ACP: African, Caribbean and Pacific Group of States, *the 79 developing countries in these three regions. The European countries grant them preferential tariff treatment.*

AGOA: African Growth and Opportunity Act, *law passed by the US Congress to support African economies.*

ALBA: Alternativa Bolivariana para los Pueblos de Nuestra América, *Bolivarian Alternative for the People of Our America.*

ANC: African National Congress, *South African political party.*

APEC: Asia-Pacific Economic Cooperation, *forum bringing together 21 countries in the Asia-Pacific region.*

ASEAN: Association of Southeast Asian Nations *bringing together 10 countries in the region.*

ASEAN+3: *Group made up of the ASEAN countries plus China, Japan and South Korea.*

ASEM: Asia-Europe Meeting, *an informal dialogue process involving Asia-Europe, the European Union and ASEAN + 3.*

AU: African Union.

BRIC: Brazil, Russia, India and China, *acronym coined by Goldman Sachs.*

C-34: *United Nations Special Committee on Peacekeeping Operations.*

CACM: Central American Common Market grouping *Costa Rica, Guatemala, Honduras, Nicaragua and El Salvador.*

CAFTA: Central America Free Trade Agreement *grouping the United States, Costa Rica, Guatemala, Honduras, the Dominican Republic, Nicaragua and El Salvador.*

Cairns Group: *within the WTO, group of 17 non-European agriculture exporting countries.*

CAN: Andean Community of Nations *including Bolivia, Colombia, Ecuador, Peru and Venezuela.*

CCP: Chinese Communist Party.

CDM: Clean Development Mechanism. *Mechanism that enables companies in developed countries to reach their greenhouse gas emissions reduction targets by conducting projects to reduce emissions in developing countries.*

CECA: Comprehensive Economic Cooperation Agreements, *regional or bilateral agreements negotiated by India.*

CEECs: Central and Eastern European Countries.

CICID: Comité interministériel de la coopération internationale et du développement, *defines the main orientations of French development aid policy.*

CIS: Commonwealth of Independent States, *organization grouping the former USSR countries with the exception of the three Baltic states.*

CMEA: Council for Mutual Economic Assistance, *economic organization among several communist bloc countries around the USSR, dissolved in 1991. Also known as COMECON.*

Conefo: Conference of Newly Emerging Forces.

DAC: Development Assistance Committee *grouping 22 OECD member countries.*

DAG: Development Assistance Group (OEEC), *precursor of the DAC/OECD.*

DCs: Developing Countries.

DRC: Democratic Republic of the Congo.

DSF: Debt Sustainability Framework, *which aims to set a ceiling above which there is considerable risk that a country cannot repay its debt.*

ECLAC: United Nations Economic Commission for Latin America and the Caribbean.

FATF: Financial Action Task Force, *intergovernmental organization that aims to develop and promote national and international policies to fight money laundering and terrorist financing.*

FDI: Foreign Direct Investment.

FTAA: Free Trade Area of the Americas.

G4: *Group of 4 countries* (India, Brazil, Germany, Japan) *working together for their entrance into the Security Council as permanent members.*

G6: *Term used to refer to the world's six largest economies.*

G7: *Group of seven industrialized countries: Canada, France, Germany, Italy, Japan, the United Kingdom and the United States.*

G8: *G7 including Russia.*

G10: *Group of emerging countries around India and Brazil to oppose the developed countries' agenda.*

G20: *Within the WTO, group of some 20 developing countries against the trade policy of the United States and the European Union.*

G33: *Within the WTO, group of 45 developing countries that are against the total liberalization of agricultural markets.*

G77: *The largest intergovernmental organization within the United Nations, grouping together 130 developing countries.*

G90: *Group of 90 developing countries including the ACP states, the African Union states and* LDCs.

G110: *Meeting of the G20 and the G90.*

GATT: General Agreement on Tariffs and Trade.

GDP: Gross domestic product.

GNP: Gross national product.

GUAM: Georgia, Ukraine, Azerbaijan and Moldova, *cooperation organization bringing together these four countries.*

HDI: Human Development Index.

IAEA: International Atomic Energy Agency.

IBSA: *Trilateral development initiative between* India, Brazil *and* South Africa *to promote South-South exchanges and cooperation.*

ICC: International Criminal Court, *the UN's main judicial body for peaceful arbitration of disputes among states.*

IDA: International Development Association (World Bank).

IDB: Inter-American Development Bank.

IFAD: International Fund for Agricultural Development (United Nations).

IMF: International Monetary Fund.

IOC: International Olympic Committee.

IPCC: Intergovernmental Panel on Climate Change.

IT: Information technology.

LDCs: Least developed countries.

LICUS: Low Income Countries Under Stress (World Bank).

LMG: Like Minded Group, *ad-hoc coalition of developing countries voting as a bloc in international organizations such as the WTO.*

Mercosur: Southern common market, *economic community of South American countries.*

MPLA: Popular Movement for the Liberation of Angola.

NAFTA: North American Free Trade Agreement, *encompassing the United States, Canada and Mexico.*

NAM: Non-Aligned Movement.

NAMA-11: Non Agriculture Market Access-11, *group of countries organized around Brazil, India and South Africa to speed up the process of liberalizing access to the industrial products market.*

NATO: North Atlantic Treaty Organization.

NEPAD: New Partnership for Africa's Development.

NGO: Non-governmental organization.

NIC: Newly industrialized country, *expression used in the 1980s and 1990s to refer to the quick economic takeoff of certain East Asian countries (South Korea, Hong Kong, Singapore, Taiwan).*

NPT: Nuclear Non-Proliferation Treaty.

OAS: Organization of American States.

ODA: Official Development Assistance, *aid granted by industrialized countries for the economic development of developing countries.*

OECD: Organization for Economic Co-Operation and Development.

OEEC: Organization for European Economic Cooperation, *replaced by the OECD.*

OPEC: Organization of Petroleum Exporting Countries.

OSCE: Organization for Security and Co-Operation in Europe.

P3: *Meeting format for the three western permanent members of the United Nations Security Council (France, the United Kingdom, the United States).*

PAHO: Pan American Health Organization.

PAN: National Action Party, *conservative Mexican political party.*

Paris Club: *Informal group of 19 creditor countries that helps indebted nations find solutions to meet their financial obligations.*

PRC: People's Republic of China.

PRD: Party of the Democratic Revolution, *Mexican progressive political party.*

PRI: Institutional Revolutionary Party, *Mexican progressive political party.*

R&D: Research and development.

RMB: Yuan Renminbi, *currency of the People's Republic of China.*

RSA: Republic of South Africa.

SAARC: South Asian Association for Regional Cooperation.

SACU: Southern African Customs Union.

SADC: South African Development Community.

SAIDA: South African International Development Agency, *located in the South African Ministry of Foreign Affairs.*

SICA: Central American Integration System. *Intergovernmental organization made up of the seven Central American countries, with the Dominican Republic and the United States as associate members. Mexico and Taiwan participate in the capacity of observer.*

SMEs: Small and medium enterprises.

SSA: sub-Saharan Africa.

SWAPO: South West African People's Organization, *main Namibian political party.*

TRIPS: Trade-Related Aspects of Intellectual Property Rights.

UN: United Nations.

UNCTAD: United Nations Conference on Trade and Development.

UNDP: United Nations Development Programme.

USSR: Union of Soviet Socialist Republics.

WTO: World Trade Organization.

ZAPU: Zimbabwe African People's Union, *former communist political party that fought for Zimbabwe's liberation.*

Introduction[1]

Christophe Jaffrelot

U nheard of yesterday, today emerging countries are making headlines. Some observers claim that the media have invented a category devoid of any real foundation. Under such circumstances, researchers are duty-bound—unless they prefer to remain in their ivory towers—to deconstruct the object in question to examine to what extent the notion of emerging power corresponds to a reality, and what new international configuration it is likely to spawn.

The expression "emerging country" of course comes to us from the field of economics and even finance, the term "emerging market economies" being in use since the 1980s to refer to rapidly growing economies that offer investment opportunities for companies in rich countries. Twenty years later, it is still international financial organizations such as the IMF that award the "emerging market" label, or rating agencies, whose lists of emerging countries are in constant flux. They have no other "official" recognition.

In fact, emerging powers are primarily defined by their <u>economic takeoff</u>, as shown by the growing weight of some of them in the world

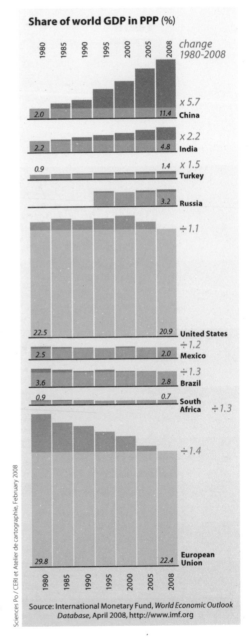

figure 1: **Distribution of world GDP, 1980-2008**

Share of world GDP in PPP (%)

Sciences Po / CERI et Atelier de cartographie, February 2008

Source: International Monetary Fund, *World Economic Outlook Database*, April 2008, http://www.imf.org

---

1   This introduction presents the issues in the order in which they are discussed by the authors of this volume.

economy. The size of China's economy multiplied by 5.7 between 1980 and 2008, and India's by 2.2, for example.

Most of them are former "developing countries", to use a term that seems very dated today—precisely because the emerging market boom has considerably outmoded it. If rapid growth constitutes the common denominator of these

figure 2: **Development of exports of goods and services, 1980-2007**

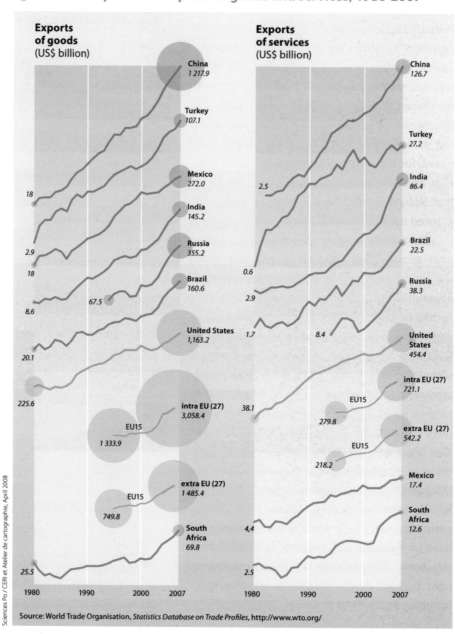

Source: World Trade Organisation, *Statistics Database on Trade Profiles*, http://www.wto.org/

Sciences Po / CERI et Atelier de cartographie, April 2008

countries, another characteristic has to do with their rapid integration into the world economy. An indication of this is the rise in their exports of both goods and services and their appeal—varying according to the country—for foreign investors since the 1990s.

Emerging powers also have in common a relative institutional stability. They have, for instance, relatively effective market regulation agencies. They may be the products of globalization, but they have built state administrations without which the growth they have enjoyed for several years would not be sustainable—yet another sign that globalization cannot do without the state. But all of them have nevertheless opted for some form of economic liberalization, and have produced variants on capitalism that Robert Boyer analyzes in the interview he granted us.

Although emerging countries all feature high growth rates, growing integration into the world economy, a stabilized institutional apparatus and some form of capitalism, the nature of their trajectories differs. Some took off before others; this is true of the Asian countries once referred to as Newly Industrialized Countries (NICs) in the 1970s-80s. These trailblazers, also known as Tigers or Dragons due to their geographical location, benefited from huge amounts of Western aid during the Cold War era, a strong state that instigated structural reforms—particularly agrarian—and growing integration into the world trade flows due to low labour costs and the welcome they gave multinationals. Many of these "emerging countries" have now arrived and are thus not the focus of this book. The present volume turns the spotlight instead on their successors—greater in numbers and in weight.

figure 3: **Inward foreign direct investment, 1980-2006**

Inward FDI, 2006 (US$ billion)

530.9 **EU (27)**	175.4 **United States**	69.5 **China**
28.7 **Russia**	20.1 **Turkey**	19.0 **Mexico**
		18.8 **Brazil**
16.9 **India**	- 0.3 **South Africa**	

Inward FDI for selected emerging countries, 1980-2006 (US$ billion)

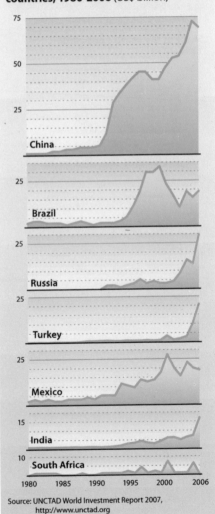

Source: UNCTAD World Investment Report 2007,
http://www.unctad.org

Sciences Po / CERI et Atelier de cartographie, February 2008

The drivers of emergence

Unlike the former NICs, emerging countries are mainly large countries with rapidly growing populations, except for Russia, and manifest new political ambitions—sometimes still tentative—based on the rise in their economic clout.

In the case of China, growth has followed the trajectory of the Tigers and Dragons, but on an entirely different scale. China, as "the world's factory", has built its expansion on an exceptional export capacity largely due to the attraction of its low labour costs for multinationals seeking to relocate, to which the country opened its doors wide after the 1978 reforms. Today it combines economic liberalization and a single party regime, and correspondingly it has invented a form of capitalism without entrepreneurs. The other Asian giant, India, readily labelled "the world's office", has taken advantage more of its middle classes' skills—from call centre employees to computer engineers—while remaining less outward-looking than China. Indian growth is moreover buoyed by the now unfettered business world since the reforms of the 1980s and '90s, and is upheld by a particularly solid democratic rule of law. With the world's two largest populations, China and India have both benefited from a considerable demographic dividend and a two-edged migratory phenomenon: although emigration at first deprived these countries of part of their workforce, the Chinese and Indian diasporas have since contributed to the development of their motherland by investing in it and returning both better trained and with a wealth of business contacts, so that there has been a shift from "brain drain" to "brain gain". Another common feature of these two "empires of billionaires" is that they are experiencing their current boom not as a new phenomenon but as a return to the heyday of the 18th century when they dominated the economy produced by an earlier era of trade globalization.

After Asia, Latin America is the subcontinent containing the largest number of emerging countries, as attested by several of them recently joining the OECD. There, too, it is sometimes

figure 4: **Demographic weight of selected emerging countries, 1950-2050**

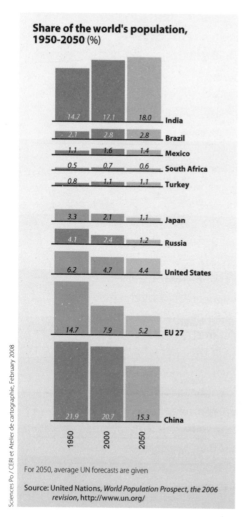

Share of the world's population, 1950-2050 (%)

	1950	2000	2050	
	14.7	17.1	18.0	India
	2.1	2.8	2.8	Brazil
	1.1	1.6	1.4	Mexico
	0.5	0.7	0.6	South Africa
	0.8	1.1	1.1	Turkey
	3.3	2.1	1.1	Japan
	4.1	2.4	1.2	Russia
	6.2	4.7	4.4	United States
	14.7	7.9	5.2	EU 27
	21.9	20.7	15.3	China

For 2050, average UN forecasts are given

Source: United Nations, *World Population Prospect, the 2006 revision*, http://www.un.org/

Sciences Po / CERI et Atelier de cartographie, February 2008

a matter of recovering past glory, but in the space of a much shorter cycle, for we only have to go back to the Brazil of the 1970s and Mexico of the 1960s-80s to find growth rates similar to what those two countries can boast today—lower than those in Asia. Both are rich in raw materials and commodities, especially energy and agricultural resources, with which Brazil is particularly well endowed. The geographical proximity to United States has also been a considerable driving force. Mexico has found there an expanding market, also for its labour: immigrant remittances have contributed to Mexico's takeoff to the extent that some speak of "development through exile".

Backing from an economically developed and politically stable entity—in this case the European Union—has also contributed to the rise of Turkey, the only Mediterranean country considered in this volume. Not only is the EU its main economic partner, but the prospect of accession—which has since faded into the distance—boosted foreign investment in the early 2000s. Turkey has moreover benefited from the entrepreneurial savvy of its business milieu and a strong demographic dividend, its population growth also fuelling a migration flow that has doubtless deprived the country of some of its youth, but from which it has received remittances to aid its growth.

South Africa appears somewhat as an isolated case, with a stark contrast between its relative prosperity and the persistent poverty throughout the rest of its region. Its wealth is relative compared to the income level of other emerging powers: it is a giant in Africa, but its emergence is only in the stage of infancy compared with China's, for instance. What if South Africa was systematically treated as an emerging country owing to the need to include a representative of Africa in this promising category, and its post-apartheid democratization further added to its aura? To some extent, if South Africa didn't exist, the international community—that indispensable fiction—would have to invent it.

Awarding an "emerging country certificate" to Russia is also a complicated affair, but for different reasons. Whereas all the other representatives of this category have an essentially young population, Russian demography is at a standstill; whereas the others' economic growth is based on rapid industrialization and/or a modern tertiary sector, Russia draws most of its wealth from its energy resources, like a rentier economy; Russia is moreover less inclined than the others to make productive investments; and, lastly and especially, whereas some emerging countries have to go back to the 18th century to accredit the notion that they are reviving their past, Russia was at the heart of one of the two superpowers of the second half of the 20th century. For all these reasons, in this book Russia is dealt with through a roundtable discussion full of worthwhile debate, rather than in a chapter.

Some countries, as noted, owe their emergence in part to a conducive regional environment. In addition to national trajectories, the area into which a country fits must also be taken into consideration. Although Africa and the Mediterranean world do not form poles of the world economy today, the EU and Asia are a whole different matter. Asia was the first to manifest the spillover capacity of a transnational investment strategy poetically called the "wild-geese-flying pattern", which unfolded in three stages: first Japanese companies set up affiliates in the NICs and in Southeast Asia where labour was cheaper; then the relocated Japanese firms—and those from the NICs—moved into China; and lastly the phenomenon spread to South Asia.

On the old continent, the rise of Central and Eastern European countries—an emerging area par excellence—owes much to the EU, not only on account of the political stability inherent in the 2004 and 2007 enlargements but also thanks to structural funds. In addition there is of course investment by companies of "the old Europe"—reinforced in their strategy by the scheduling of enlargements in the 1990s—and their strategy of outsourcing has produced a variant of the Asian "wild-geese-flying pattern", with the added benefit of an institutional framework.

In Latin America, the plethora of institutional frameworks poorly masks the slow progress of regional integration. Not only are some of these organizations in a situation of rivalry, but some are merely empty shells. Mercosur has for instance had trouble gaining in substance, owing to the wariness the Brazilian giant inspires among its neighbours, while Brasilia is in any case seeking to break loose from its region to acquire global status.

Global transformation

The emerging powers are reshuffling the cards of the international game, which probably have not been so thoroughly rearranged since 1945. Never have the dominant powers of yesterday and today had to make room for players carried by such momentum. It is all the more complicated for Europe and the United States to adapt given the fierce trade competition from emerging countries. The European Union is losing market shares in manufacturing, particularly because of outsourcing on an unforeseen scale. Beyond the trade competition that sometimes precedes the opening of Western company affiliates in emerging countries, the national firms of these countries themselves are increasingly on the offensive on the old continent and in North America. They buy up companies that are far from lame ducks thanks to liquidity generated by years of two-digit growth. The acquisitions made by Chinese and Indian multinationals are the most spectacular today, as seen in the buyout of Tetley, Corus, Jaguar and Rover by Tata and Lenovo's takeover of IBM's personal computer division.

From a geoeconomic standpoint, emerging countries also come into competition with Western states and business milieus in their traditional hunting grounds of Africa and certain Latin American countries. Their approach in this domain arises from a threefold strategy. First, they begin distributing development assistance to poor countries—from which they themselves have long benefited, but which they believe they no longer need. This aid is all the more appreciated, especially in Africa, since it is rarely associated with the conditionalities—particularly as regards governance—that are generally connected to Western aid. Secondly, emerging countries are investing more and more in Africa, whereas China is mainly establishing itself to ensure direct access to the raw materials it needs, but also to dissuade African countries from backing Taiwan in the UN. India has recently followed suit, as demonstrated by the first India-Africa summit held in April 2008 in New Delhi. The relations between the major Asian emerging countries in Latin America differ in nature, but could prefigure a third form of rivalry with the United States and the EU. China and India have in fact begun investing in Latin America, again to secure access to commodities, but Latin American firms should be able to turn this to good account, because they are more complementary than in competition with their Asian counterparts.

If emerging countries have become serious rivals for Europe and the United States, these two large entities are taking their time in making room for them in multilateral organizations. Only the IMF and the World Bank have timidly started to transfer voting rights and quotas from North to South. Enlargement of the G8 and the UN Security Council, on the other hand, is not high on their members' priorities, even if emerging countries are among the main providers of Blue Helmets and are exercising ever greater influence within the UN system. This trend is particularly salient in the WTO, where in 2003 some 20 emerging countries

figure 5: **Awards received by selected emerging countries in major international film festivals, 1990-2007**

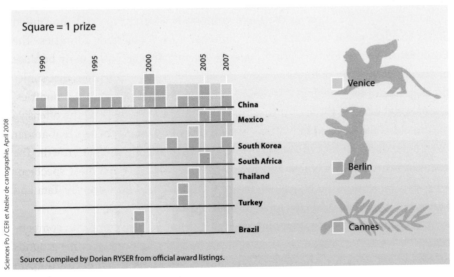

Square = 1 prize

1990 1995 2000 2005 2007

Venice

China
Mexico
South Korea
South Africa
Thailand
Turkey
Brazil

Berlin

Cannes

Sciences Po / CERI et Atelier de cartographie, April 2008

Source: Compiled by Dorian RYSER from official award listings.

7

formed a group, the G20, which has proved very resilient despite conflicting interests among some of its members. Spearheading opposition to rich countries, the G20 has managed to strike alliances with less developed countries in order to carry more weight in the Doha Round trade negotiations.

The power struggle looming in multilateral organizations reflects a shift in the world centre of gravity, in both geopolitical and cultural terms—the mounting success of emerging country literature and films attest to this.

Reference to human rights, which has worked its way into official discourse—if not reflected in deeds—throughout the 20th century, is likely to play second fiddle if the "Beijing Consensus", to use an expression coined in the West, triumphs in Asia and elsewhere. This "consensus" stresses collective discipline to attain economic achievement at the expense of political freedoms. But can China bring the rest of Asia to follow in its wake? Some of its neighbours, starting with Japan, do not adhere to the "Beijing Consensus" and are afraid of its continuing rise. The United States is banking on these countries to counterbalance the Middle Empire. They are especially counting on India's support, but that country is obviously not prepared to take sides. The future of the world will partly be decided in this new round of the Asian "Great Game". Only partly, for Pierre Hassner's convincing analysis puts back in perspective the impact of emerging powers in world affairs in this early 21st century. Nations that no one has ever catalogued in this category, such as North Korea or even Iran, may acquire the means to destabilize international relations in a more decisive manner than other more powerful but also more reasonable actors. Rather than reaching the conclusion that a new world order is in the offing, it is perhaps wiser to admit that the world has entered an era of permanent instability.

figure 6: **Main emerging country trading partners, 2006**

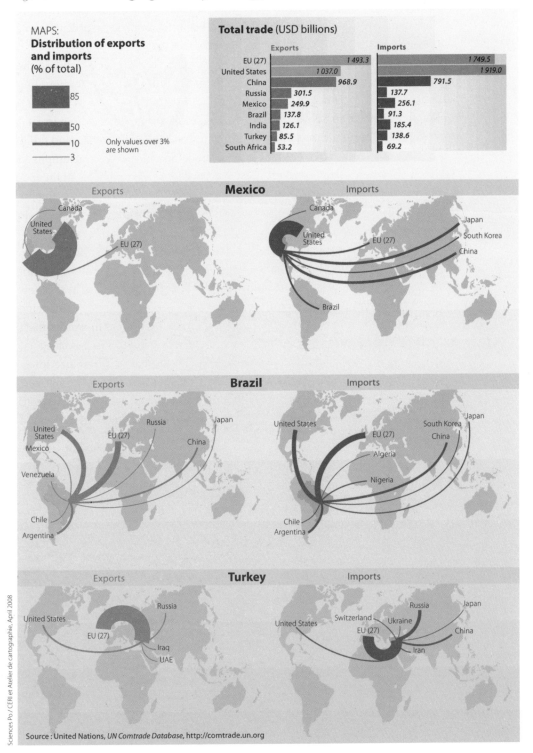

Source : United Nations, *UN Comtrade Database*, http://comtrade.un.org

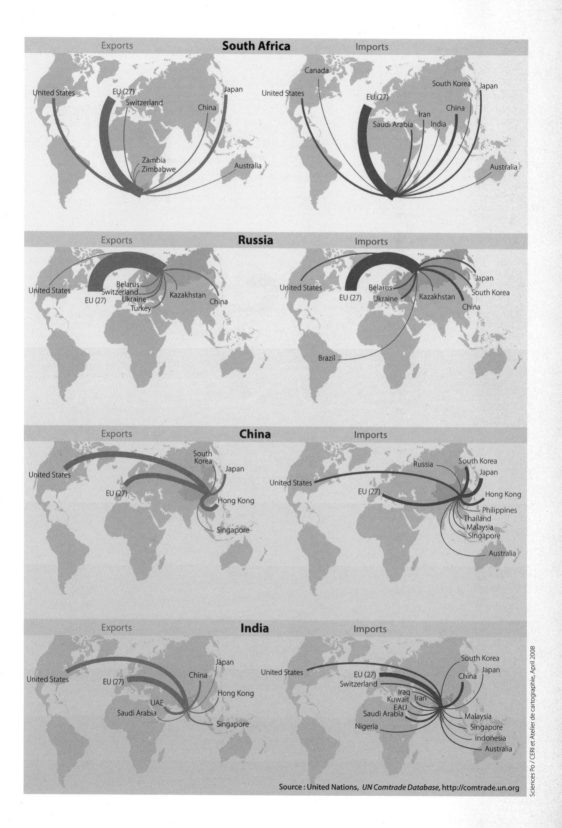

Source : United Nations, *UN Comtrade Database*, http://comtrade.un.org

Sciences Po / CERI et Atelier de cartographie, April 2008

PART 1

GENEALOGY OF A CATEGORY

Fabrications and Illusions
of Emergence

Jean-Jacques Gabas
Bruno Losch*

How is it possible to comprehend the course of a nation's development and assert that a country is "emerging"? What does emergence mean? It starts from what situation, to navigate towards what other, and on how stable a course? Since the organization of the world rests on countries that are sovereign states, usually founded on what is known as a national base, what analytical criteria should be used to describe the place these countries occupy with respect to one another and on the international level?

When one starts to look into the shifting notion of "emergence", which has no standard definition, one quickly realizes to what extent it is embedded in an implicit worldview and how much it expresses recognition of a status: waiting in the lobby to enter the "major league", the club of the most "advanced" countries that have completed their "development". This simple statement reveals the range of overtones and innuendos as well as the extreme complexity of the theme, which is mixed up with the value judgments conveyed by major international media, the academic world and the major investment bank experts.

Emergence, then, fits in with first the Eurocentric view of world history (Rist 1996), in which the trajectory of what we call developed countries today is used as an evolutionist yardstick by which changes in economies and human societies are measured. This immediately places the discussion at the heart of the field known as development economics, historically situated between the end of World War II

---

* The opinions expressed in this chapter are the authors' alone and do not necessarily reflect the views of the World Bank Group.

and the new era of globalization in the late 1970s. The point here is not of course to outline the various competing theories of development of that fairly recent period, but to provide a background by recalling the existence of two main schools of thought: the liberal-inspired modernist current influenced by evolutionist theories (Rostow) and dualist theories (Lewis, Myrdal); and a structuralist school that takes economic and social imbalances into account in suggesting Keynesian-inspired public intervention (Perroux, Kalecki, Hirschman), and which gives rise to the Latin American dependentist school (the work of CEPAL, Prebisch, Furtado).

How did the notion of emerging country grow out of this history characterized by the dilution of developmentalism into globalization?

Our first question must be, "Who is emerging?" Markets, companies, currencies, entire countries? Without dwelling too long on the question, we will identify the main approaches according to the criteria they use, for indeed there is no internationally accepted consensus on the "emerging" category, but instead only blurry contours and wavering definitions.

We will then see that the genesis of these emerging countries, contrary to what the dominant evolutionist approach would have us believe, is far from following a standardized process. The trajectories of territories and human communities are multiple. They cannot be reduced to one another, they reflect the great diversity of historic processes and combinations of factors and resources. To get beyond endogenous explanations, it is essential to understand the factors at stake, the "critical junctures" (Mahoney 2001) that determine development paths and their dependencies, as well as the interplay of national and international, domestic and external influences.

We will conclude with questions about the limits of the emergence process in a globalized world where the confrontation of levels of competitiveness due to intensified spatial interconnection leaves little room for manœuvre for countries and regions that had not begun their process of change prior to the current opening period, and where emerging countries themselves are faced with major structural challenges.

In search of the emerging country group

Although the expression "emerging country" poses no problem in everyday usage, because it is used so frequently, a variety of different criteria are taken into account to categorize the country as emerging, depending on whether the viewpoint is that of international institutions, the academic world or the world of finance.

Where does one come from when one "emerges"? Generally, the first step is that vast catch-all category known as "developing" countries (DCs). This label constitutes the most diplomatic version of the "underdeveloped" category that emerged after the Second World War, and was replaced by that of "the Third

World"—a posture of political assertions and demands in the bipolar world of the Cold War era—and then by that of "the South", more neutral politically and offering an illusion of geographical unity.

The erosion of frameworks of analysis and political models, as well as the great diversity of economic outcomes, made observers aware of the variety of national trajectories that were increasingly difficult to pigeonhole into a single category (Manor 1991, Leys 1996). These phenomena accelerated the disintegration of representations of the world, reflected in the proliferation of labels used. Thus appeared the New Industrialized Countries (NICs), the group of free market oil exporting countries, the Least Developed Countries (LDCs) and the likes of Low Income Countries under Stress (LICUS), not to mention the Central and Eastern European countries (CEECs) appearing with the end of the Soviet bloc. However, one characteristic of emerging countries is that they do not form a unified group labelled and recognized in international statistics (the United Nations, the Bretton Woods institutions or the OECD). They can be found in all four World Bank income categories: low-income economies (less than US$905 per capita) such as India and Vietnam, lower middle-income economies (between $905 and $3,595) such as Brazil and China, upper middle-income economies (between $3,595 and $11,115) such as Mexico and Russia, and lastly, high-income economies (over $11,115) such as South Korea and Israel. What type of countries are they then?

The notion of "emerging market economy" is said to have been forged in the early 1980s by analysts at the International Finance Corporation (IFC, part of the World Bank group) to characterize countries in rapid transition, undergoing industrialization, having high growth rates and presenting investment and equity opportunities

figure 7: **Different features of some emerging countries, 2006**

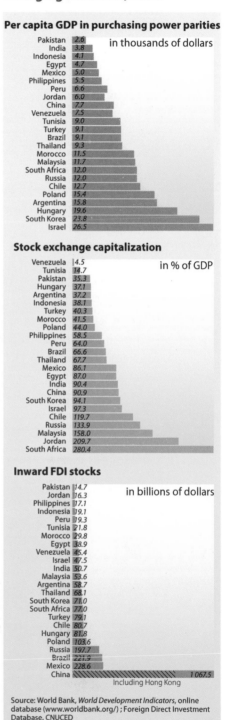

Per capita GDP in purchasing power parities

in thousands of dollars

Pakistan	2.6
India	3.8
Indonesia	4.1
Egypt	4.7
Mexico	5.0
Philippines	5.5
Peru	6.6
Jordan	6.0
China	7.7
Venezuela	7.5
Tunisia	9.0
Turkey	9.1
Brazil	9.1
Thailand	9.3
Morocco	11.5
Malaysia	11.7
South Africa	12.0
Russia	12.0
Chile	12.7
Poland	15.4
Argentina	15.8
Hungary	19.6
South Korea	23.8
Israel	26.5

Stock exchange capitalization

in % of GDP

Venezuela	4.5
Tunisia	14.7
Pakistan	35.3
Hungary	37.1
Argentina	37.2
Indonesia	38.1
Turkey	40.3
Morocco	41.5
Poland	44.0
Philippines	58.5
Peru	64.0
Brazil	66.6
Thailand	67.7
Mexico	86.1
Egypt	87.0
India	90.4
China	90.9
South Korea	94.1
Israel	97.3
Chile	119.7
Russia	133.9
Malaysia	158.0
Jordan	209.7
South Africa	280.4

Inward FDI stocks

in billions of dollars

Pakistan	14.7
Jordan	16.3
Philippines	17.1
Indonesia	19.1
Peru	19.3
Tunisia	21.8
Morocco	29.8
Egypt	38.9
Venezuela	45.4
Israel	47.5
India	50.7
Malaysia	53.6
Argentina	58.7
Thailand	68.1
South Korea	71.0
South Africa	77.0
Turkey	79.1
Chile	80.7
Hungary	81.8
Poland	103.6
Russia	197.7
Brazil	221.9
Mexico	228.6
China	1 067.5

Including Hong Kong

Source: World Bank, *World Development Indicators*, online database (www.worldbank.org/) ; Foreign Direct Investment Database, CNUCED

Sciences Po / CERI et Atelier de cartographie, February 2008

due to this growth and the development of their financial infrastructure, as well as the risks involved (with the prospect of high returns) due to their unstable economic, monetary, institutional and political environments. Today, the IMF continues to refer to "emerging markets" without this being a set category. Economies, markets, countries: the semantics are fluctuating and explain the very great variability in the number of countries to which this label is applied, depending on the viewpoint of the analyst.

For specialized financial organizations and market index makers such as Morgan Stanley Capital International and Standard & Poor's, emerging markets are defined on the basis of several criteria including market capitalization, per capita GDP, macroeconomic environment conditions, the size of the market and its companies, the economy's degree of liquidity and the level of corruption. Standard & Poor's manages a database of 33 markets considered to be emerging, to which are added 20 smaller "frontier markets". Using such an approach, the "national" characteristics of this list of emerging economies are very different and confirm the financial dimension of analyses pertaining to emergence.

The Boston Consulting Group (BCG) uses the notion of "Rapidly Developing Economies" (RDEs), which it identifies as the countries of national origin of the hundred largest companies (BCG 100) that are not subsidiaries of developed country multinational corporations (MNCs), where those countries had annual revenues of more than $1 billion in 2006, at least 10% coming from exports. Additional selection criteria were used, including other indicators related to technological expertise, research and development, etc. Among these 100 large

figure 8: **Companies in rapidly developing economies**

Source: Compiled by Jean-Jacques GABAS and Bruno LOSCH from Boston Consulting Group data, 2007

companies, 78 are based in Asia, mainly in China and India, and 22 in Latin America.

According to the CEPII (Centre d'Etudes Prospectives et d'Informations Internationales), emerging countries make their mark on the international scene first of all through the growth of their macroeconomic aggregates and adoption of policies fostering the opening-up of trade and financial sectors (Fouquin 1999). The growth rate of their GDP is higher than the world average and that of the richest countries; they stand out by their rising and diversified exports to industrialized countries, especially of high-tech products, which only fuels speculation about their future role in the international system (Hochraich 2007, Sen 2007a, Sheehan 2007). More recently, foreign exchange reserves have appeared as a new criterion of emergence: China, Taiwan, South Korea, Russia, India, Hong Kong and Singapore alone are estimated to hold 42% of international reserves. The dynamism and swiftness of the process of change constitutes the main features by which emerging economies can be identified.

Three major phenomena have reoriented discussion on these countries in a new direction. The first was the industrial surge of certain developing countries which attracted investors and financiers in a sequence that in the 1970s first produced the appearance of a group of NICs known as the "Asian Dragons" (Hong Kong, Taiwan, South Korea and Singapore), followed by a second group at the turn of the 1990s known as the "Little Dragons" or sometimes "Little Tigers", including Malaysia, Thailand, Indonesia and the Philippines. Although with less media success, the term Latin American "Jaguars" (Brazil and Mexico) has also appeared.

The fall of the Berlin Wall and then of the Soviet Union, and the arrival of Central and Eastern European countries on the international and European playing field from which they were formerly excluded, added a new dimension to the

figure 9: **Distribution of international currency reserves, 2005**

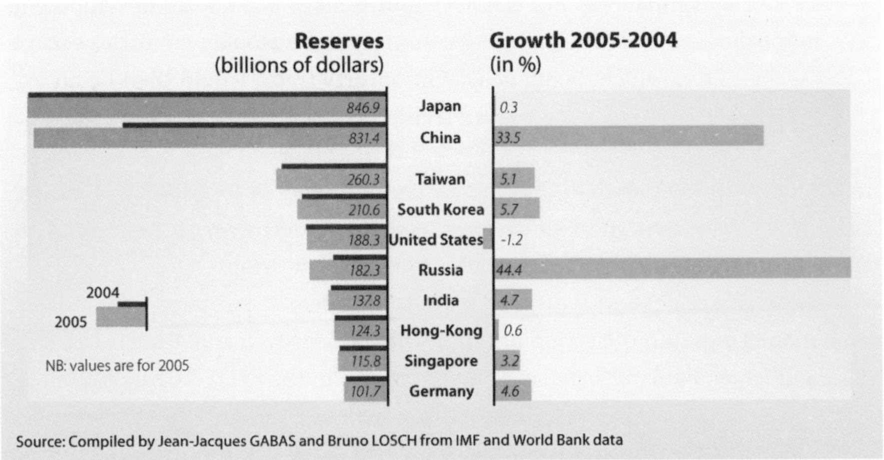

	Reserves (billions of dollars)		Growth 2005-2004 (in %)
Japan	846.9		0.3
China	831.4		33.5
Taiwan	260.3		5.1
South Korea	210.6		5.7
United States	188.3		-1.2
Russia	182.3		44.4
India	137.8		4.7
Hong-Kong	124.3		0.6
Singapore	115.8		3.2
Germany	101.7		4.6

2004
2005
NB: values are for 2005

Sciences Po / CERI et Atelier de cartographie, February 2008

Source: Compiled by Jean-Jacques GABAS and Bruno LOSCH from IMF and World Bank data

process of emergence in which political reforms and political economy reforms—here the transition towards a market economy—have become the engines of growth. This reformist dimension is essential in analyses on China and Vietnam, these two countries having the distinctive feature of dissociating political reform from economic reform.

The arrival of China in the debate in the past 15 years is no doubt the result of its booming growth due to the opening of its economy and financial markets and the rapidity of its industrialization, but a third dimension also enters into account, related to the size of its territory and especially its population, which make the country a gigantic domestic market provoking an exponential demand in raw materials and capital goods. Whereas the European Union will "lose" 40 million inhabitants, China and India, which together account for nearly 40% of the world's population, will have nearly 800 million more inhabitants between now and 2050. The rise in their standard of living will totally alter the balance of power still largely marked by the European 19th century.

This last dimension focusing on macro-aggregates seems to structure the debate today and explains the emphasis on the leading group of emerging countries: the BRICs (Brazil, Russia, India and China). This acronym, developed by the Goldman Sachs investment bank (Wilson and Purushothaman 2003), has received wide attention. It is based on the idea that reforms based on opening markets, macroeconomic stability, governance and education are decisive in the process of emergence.

To conclude, we can thus identify two major approaches to emerging countries today:

- a rather restrictive approach that would define the problematics of emergence in opposition to the G7, with a nucleus of heavyweights—the BRICs—in a position to challenge the world power order, and possibly other countries (South Africa and Mexico, for instance);
- a more encompassing and classical approach, in a catch-up development rationale, seeing all the emerging countries as developing countries except for the LDCs, which, being caught in poverty traps, would then be an exception in the global convergence trend.

The second definition enables analysts of various schools to draw up their list according to their own strategic criteria. As the figure below shows, although there is a core that few contest, their outer limits are uncertain.

FDI related to relocation of production in the immediate periphery of the European Union brings into the group not only Turkey, Morocco and Tunisia but also Jordan and Israel. Banking specialization is decisive in the case of Uruguay and El Salvador. The boom in raw materials drives growth and offers market opportunities to Bolivia, Venezuela, Saudi Arabia, Iran and Nigeria, the only sub-Saharan

figure 10: **Emerging countries seen by...**

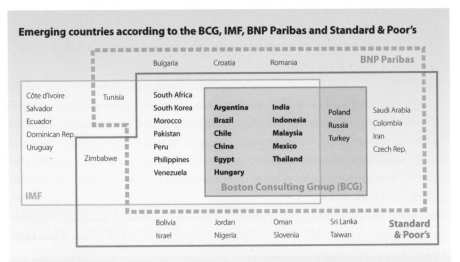

Emerging countries according to the BCG, IMF, BNP Paribas and Standard & Poor's

BNP Paribas

Bulgaria   Croatia   Romania

Côte d'Ivoire	Tunisia	South Africa		Poland	Saudi Arabia
Salvador		South Korea	**Argentina** **India**	Russia	Colombia
Ecuador		Morocco	**Brazil** **Indonesia**	Turkey	Iran
Dominican Rep.		Pakistan	**Chile** **Malaysia**		Czech Rep.
Uruguay	Zimbabwe	Peru	**China** **Mexico**		
-		Philippines	**Egypt** **Thailand**		
		Venezuela	**Hungary**		

Boston Consulting Group (BCG)

IMF

Bolivia   Jordan   Oman   Sri Lanka   **Standard**
Israel   Nigeria   Slovenia   Taiwan   **& Poor's**

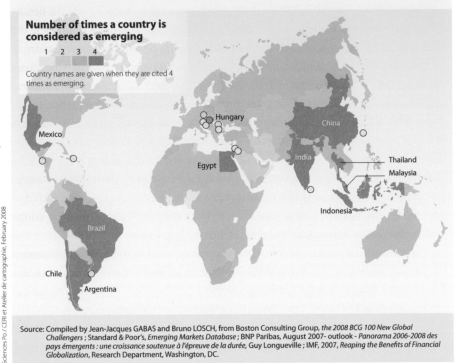

Number of times a country is considered as emerging

1 2 3 4

Country names are given when they are cited 4 times as emerging.

Mexico

Hungary

China

Egypt

India

Thailand

Malaysia

Indonesia

Brazil

Chile

Argentina

Source: Compiled by Jean-Jacques GABAS and Bruno LOSCH, from Boston Consulting Group, *the 2008 BCG 100 New Global Challengers*; Standard & Poor's, *Emerging Markets Database*; BNP Paribas, August 2007- outlook - *Panorama 2006-2008 des pays émergents : une croissance soutenue à l'épreuve de la durée*, Guy Longueville; IMF, 2007, *Reaping the Benefits of Financial Globalization*, Research Department, Washington, DC.

Sciences Po / CERI et Atelier de cartographie, February 2008

country regularly mentioned apart from South Africa. The last-named country's appeal lies in its mining and industrial sectors and the dynamism of its stock exchange. In Asia, "dragons" are more and more considered by analysts as having finished emerging, whereas the status of the "little dragons" of the 1990s appears more contrasted: that of Indonesia, Thailand and Malaysia is usually undisputed;

it is more ambiguous and qualified for the Philippines (Giri 1997) or otherwise to be confirmed in the case of Vietnam (Chaponnière et al. 2007).

Variety of emergence trajectories: the importance of the 'moment' and the role of the rest of the world

This preliminary survey of the identification of emerging countries as a group shows to what extent reference to growth and the engines of development remains central in the genealogy of emergence. These are the themes highlighted by post-war development economics, in which the idea of catching up emphasized a "big push" to escape the poverty traps of underdevelopment (Meier and Seers 1988).

An emerging country, according to this concept, is thus first a country that has "taken off". This image of economic, social and political evolution was built primarily on the work of Rostow, who based his analysis of takeoff on the example of 19th-century England, or Rosenstein-Rodan (Gabas 2007, Hugon 2006), who considered that countries had to go through "necessary stages", takeoff being a moment from which growth and physical capital investment would allow the economy to engage in a process of growth.

Yet most research in economic history considers growth processes as gradual and long-term. The history of China did not begin with Deng Xiaoping's reforms in 1978, any more than India's growth began with the reforms of 1991, even if these dates remain landmarks. The previous decades must be taken into account in order to explain today's successes or failures. Historical analyses (Maddison, Braudel, Diamond, Kennedy, Landes) do not resort to the notion of emergence. They take the long view of economic and military powers, their characteristics, successes and reversals. These views very cautiously put forward several factors such as the role of values, educational level, technical innovation, improvement of health care systems, or credit systems. But these hypotheses generally do not rank the causalities that explain a country's success at a given moment. They instead favour embedding it (Polanyi) in the historicity of each context, and criticize a simplistic representation of growth processes.

The questions of "why" and "how" largely structure the debate on development: "Why isn't the whole world developed?" asked Easterlin in 1981; "How do countries get rich?" Timmer asks us today (2006). Several country-specific mechanisms have been and still are emphasized to untangle the virtuous processes leading to emergence and exit from the "vicious circle of poverty" (Nurske). In addition to the previously mentioned factors, completion of the demographic transition, development of human capital, and more recently the establishment of effective institutions constitute essential criteria. Among these ranges of causalities, two main areas warrant special attention: the role of the state and public policy, and governance and institutions.

Much research work (Bustelo 1994, Vernières 1997, Boillot 2006) has properly analyzed these development processes in East and Southeast Asia by putting the specific and fundamental role of the state back at the heart of their studies, thus setting themselves apart from the "market friendly" view emphasized by the World Bank in its analysis of the "Asian miracle".

The role of institutions and governance sparked early attention among the precursors of development economics (Lewis). This interest was then revived by institutionalist and neo-institutionalist studies (North, Williamson), which demonstrated the existence of transaction costs and the central role of institutions and organizations in minimizing them. Institutions and organizations are diverse in nature (intersectoral, associational, private and public) and have multiple regulatory functions. Their quality then becomes the central question. Are there institutions that are favourable to growth and others that impede the development process?

This delicate and highly political question has been amply discussed from a normative standpoint in Washington Consensus circles (Acemoglu 2003, World Bank 2006, Landmann 2003). Taken up by Easterly and Collier, research on governance has sought to show that countries endowed with "good" institutions will show better economic results and that the progress observed is better explained by pro-market institutions than by levels of investment. Recently, several studies have sought to show the diversity of institutional systems in DCs and emerging countries (Ould Aoudia and Meisel 2007, Chang 2007, Lafaye de Micheaux et al. 2007). The "institutional profiles" that are taking shape do not, however, provide a single optimal institutional model that can explain emergence.

Much of the analytical effort devoted to the understanding of the engines of development and the modalities of emergence has dealt with domestic factors embedded in the economic and social fabric of each country. However, there is an intellectual challenge in reconnecting these domestic processes with the conditions prevailing in "the rest of the world". The international environment has been and remains a decisive factor in the dynamics of change, and has increasingly become one of the essential keys to comprehending the current forms of globalization (Gore 2003). The moment at which change occurs is in fact not insignificant: the modalities of the international economic and political regime, as well as the balance of power between national and international forces, decide the nature and scope of margins for manœuvre which then determine the development trajectories of each state.

The international system of reference today remains influenced by structural changes that characterized Western European countries in the 19th century and the first half of the 20th. The history of agricultural and industrial revolutions belongs to the pantheon of development, recalling the virtuous chain of events where productivity gains made possible by technological progress enabled both accumulation of capital and the freeing up of labour, thus making possible the structural transformation of economies and societies and the transition from an economy polarized on the primary sector to a tertiary polarization.

This evolutionist view at the heart of development ideology, postulating the reproducible nature of this historic process, is still very much alive in the current debate. Thus the World Bank's most recent *World Development Report* (WDR 2008), devoted to the role of agriculture in development, forcefully recalls that the benchmark path indeed remains Western Europe in the 19th century (with, as always, Britain as a precursor). It was successfully followed by the United States, Japan and then more recently by the principal emerging countries: Taiwan, South Korea, China and India, even if the situation of the two latter should be qualified, since their populations are still 65% and 60% rural respectively.

This historical perspective naturally limits the comprehension of processes and foundational moments that weigh in the final configuration, because the modalities of European emergence are of course entirely specific. They are part of that long-term evolution which is the development of merchant capitalism conceptualized by Braudel (1979) and Wallerstein (1984), and based on a set of configurations and circumstances—not the least being "the capture of America" (Grataloup 2007).

Two decisive factors of the Industrial Revolution and the European transition are largely neglected in discussions about emergence. One is the nature of the prevailing world geopolitical order during the structural change process in Europe. The 19th century was an imperial epoch during which Europe—and the country spawned by European expansion (the United States) —confirmed domination over the rest of the world. The dominance of the West provided it with captive markets to establish and supply its infant industries. It must not be forgotten that Britain's conversion to free trade and its early implementation of the theory of comparative advantages enjoyed the support of the British Army and Navy. Control of the seas, territorial expansion and coercion came to buttress technological innovations that crushed Asia's manufacturing advance and facilitated the consolidation of European industry (Bairoch 1997).

The second factor is related to the demographic adjustments that accompanied the economic transition of European countries. In fact, the labour surplus generated by agricultural modernization, the revolution in transport methods and the relative improvement of living conditions provoked massive rural depopulation— stimulated by the appeal of job demands from growing industries, although they were not in a position to absorb the overflow of labour from the poor rural areas. Thus the transition was largely facilitated by large-scale international migration (Hatton and Williamson 2005). From 1850 to 1930—the year when the flows subsided—the "white migration" towards the New World (Rygiel 2007) involved approximately 60 million Europeans. These adjustments by population transfer were an integral part of the margin for manoeuvre offered by that historical moment of European domination; they help explain both the emergence of Europe during the 19th century and how the balance of power was consolidated through to the present day.

This is why today's emergence phenomena must be analyzed from a long-term perspective, by remembering first of all that emerging countries each have specific configurations in which the economic, social and institutional legacies as well as the internal structure of their power balances have played a decisive role in inventing or reinventing their own national projects. These countries followed the self-centred policies characteristic of that period of history from the 1930s to the end of the 1970s (Giraud 1996), when the aim was to consolidate the nation-state, build and develop domestic markets and reinforce the "intersectoral linkages" (Perroux, Hirschman). These import-substitution-based national industrialization projects already characterized several Latin American countries in the inter-war period. The Asian countries made similar efforts starting in the 1950s. Everywhere, the keystone was implementation of voluntaristic public modernization policies based on state interventionism, efficient infrastructures and competitive state-owned companies. These strategies were generally implemented by authoritarian regimes—India being an exception—sometimes at the price of considerable political violence. The results were uneven: inefficiency, rent seeking and corruption, lack of returns; but also the creation of an economic and institutional fabric, organizational routines, strengthened labour skills, development of private enterprise, the appearance of national champions, etc.

These dynamics were reinforced by external support during the Cold War in the form of assistance programmes to countries considered strategic because they faced the rise of communism (South Korea, Taiwan, Singapore, as well as India). When this particular moment of the post-war world is re-situated in the long term,

figure 11: **Average annual GDP growth, 1820-2003**

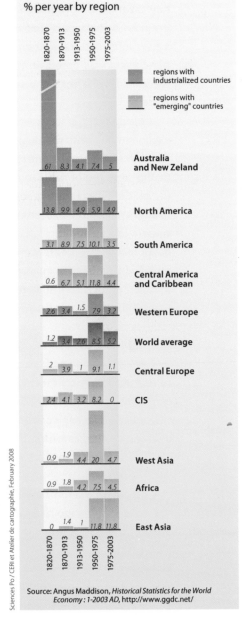

Source: Angus Maddison, *Historical Statistics for the World Economy : 1-2003 AD*, http://www.ggdc.net/

Sciences Po / CERI et Atelier de cartographie, February 2008

drawing on Maddison's work, it is striking to observe that the 25 years prior to the current wave of liberalization (1950-75) appear undoubtedly as those with the greatest economic growth for all regions of the "developing world", particularly the Asian countries.

The capacity of East and Southeast Asian countries to adapt to the swiftness of the turnaround in the late 1970s was spectacular. This reversal was directly motivated by the exhaustion of the model of mass consumerism that had previously driven growth in developed countries, and by the need of firms to seek new sources of profit in foreign markets. It was facilitated by technological progress in transport and communications, and consolidated by the spread of a new international system of reference that deliberately disregarded the prior period and was based on free trade, state withdrawal and privatization, laying the groundwork for a thorough reconfiguration of the forms of production and trade.

In this recent history, which constitutes the analytical reference of emergence, explanatory factors should be sought in a longer time period than the last 30 years devoted to the implementation of liberalization policies. In this regard, the particular situation of sub-Saharan Africa provides us with a useful contrast. In fact, the case of Africa should be analyzed in reference to a critical issue, totally absent from the common analyses that ignore the need for reconnecting domestic processes to the world timeframe: the postcolonial African states spawned by the independence of the 1960s were "caught up" by the liberalization movement when they had only been in existence for at most 20 years, far too short a time to lay the foundation for a well structured economy and an autonomous project capable of "confronting globalization".

Emergence and divergence in globalization

In this early 21st century, the panorama of new world balances of power reveals emerging economies poised to upset the old order that grew out of several centuries of European hegemony. It also points up many structural divergences between countries as well as within the group of emerging countries, especially the largest, which are subject to domestic, economic, social and territorial tensions full of implicit dangers.

First, there is a risk that growing gaps in competitiveness in a globalized world could drive some countries into a dead-end (Losch 2006). Most LDCs, and particularly the countries of sub-Saharan Africa, are indeed characterized today by their agricultural specialization, with 60% to 80% of the active population working in the primary sector. Given the productivity gaps and the new trade rules encouraged by integration processes promoted by MNCs (Reardon and Timmer 2005), there is an obvious risk of marginalization for many of these countries.

Africa will experience the world's largest demographic explosion in the next decades (one billion additional inhabitants by 2050), whereas its absorption capacities are both limited and compromised. The economic, social and political tensions inherent in such a context will result in strong migratory pressure. The difference in development trajectories in the era of globalization points up deepening inequalities that again evoke the notion of the "poverty trap", a major issue of early development economics (Geronimi 2007). Between 1820 and 1998, per capita GDP was multiplied by 20 in the United States, by 30 in Japan, by 15 in Western Europe but by only 5 in Asia and three in Africa (Maddison 2002).

figure 12: **Human development and inequalities among the main emerging countries, 2005**

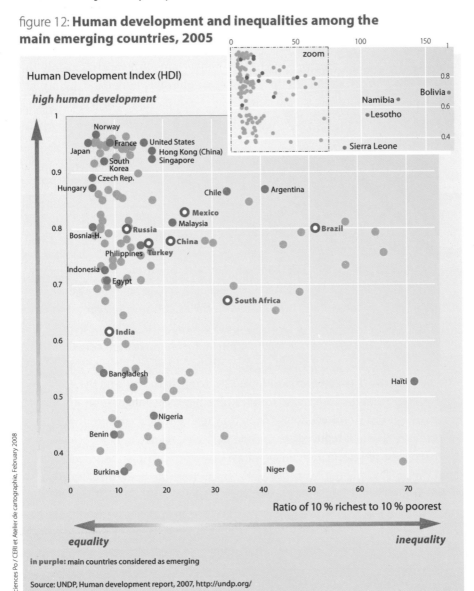

Human Development Index (HDI)

high human development

Ratio of 10 % richest to 10 % poorest

equality   inequality

in purple: main countries considered as emerging

Source: UNDP, Human development report, 2007, http://undp.org/

Sciences Po / CERI et Atelier de cartographie, February 2008

The second divergence process relates to internal imbalances in numerous emerging countries. They can be explained by the very modalities of their emergence, which most often occurs in a partial and segmented fashion because their growth is polarized and affects only a portion of their territory and their population.

Thus the main emerging countries have the highest Gini coefficients, revealing a high concentration of wealth in the upper decile. The most critical situations are in Latin America, particularly in Brazil. For most Asian countries, inequalities have deepened in the past ten years (Burton and Zanelo 2007) and reflect a real weakening of the social pact (Chung Un-Chan 2007). Russia is rising again from the collapse of the Soviet Union (Benaroya 2006), while it is faced with major structural imbalances and an ageing population. India is still experiencing a demographic explosion and will have to absorb 700 million additional people in the next 40 years. Finally, China's 10% annual growth concerns mainly the coast, and it is confronted with the crushing weight of its hinterland and its 500 million peasants; but it is also a country that in about 20 years will experience a demographic deceleration and will have to ensure the colossal cost of its ageing population.

These observations reinforce the sense that many recent emerging processes are incomplete. The modalities of their economic growth, driven by foreign investment relocated in special export zones, accentuate territorial disparities. Rather than being faced with emerging countries or integrated economies, we are instead confronted with specific territories—buffer zones, coastal areas, crossroads—whose imbalances challenge the states' redistributive capacity. This has led Sunanda Sen (2007b) to say that the term "emerging economy" is a misnomer.*

To conclude, is this image of the "emerging country", based on the conception of the nation-state forged over the past five centuries, the most relevant? Is not the current prospect rather one of a constellation of territories, large metropoles and special zones linked together via information and communication networks? This would then be closer to Braudel's original historic configuration of the "world-economy": networks of city-states—in Flanders, northern Italy and the Rhineland principalities from the 13th to the 15th century. But this configuration would then be one of a global world-economy "doped" by technological advance that enables the planet to live in a reduced space-time in which, thanks to new technologies, the movement of information and capital occurs in real time. This image would thus bring us closer to the figure of a planetary archipelago made up of little islands of wealth, and fringes trapped in lasting poverty.

Between threats of natural resource shortages and disparities in the distribution of wealth, the viability of this configuration is far from certain; it could just

---

* Sunanda Sen, Is India Really an Emerging Economy? An Assessment from the Development Perspective, oral presentation, unpublished.

as well lead to chaotic excesses as to reinforced cooperation (Wallerstein 2003). Thus, in the end, the so-called emerging countries could be merely an illusion concealing the scope of the ongoing reconfigurations in the world.

Bibliography ·····················

Braudel, F. (1979). *Civilisation materielle, économie et capitalisme (XVe-XVIIIe siècles)*, 3 volumes. Paris: Armand Colin.

Diamond, J. (1997). *Guns, Germs and Steel. The Fates of Human Societies*. New York: Norton.

Giraud, P-N. (1996). *L'inégalité du monde. Economie du monde contemporain*. Paris: Gallimard.

Landes, D.S. (1998). *The Wealth and Poverty of Nations: Why Some Are Rich and Some so Poor*. New York: Norton.

McMichael, P. (1996). *Development and Social Change. A Global Perspective*. Thousand Oaks: Pine Forge Press.

Sen, S. (2007). *Globalisation and Development*. New Delhi: National Book Trust.

Strange, S. (1988). *States and Markets*. London: Pinter.

Wallerstein, I. (1984). *Le Système du Monde du XVe siècle à nos Jours*. Two tomes. Paris: Flammarion.

What is an Emerging Country and is it an Interesting Concept for the Social Sciences?

Jérôme Sgard

The birth of emerging economies

The notion of an emerging economy or country is remarkably shifting both in public discourse and in the more specialized parlance of the social sciences. It is actually easy to identify rich economies that are no longer supposed to emerge, and others that never emerged, such as in Africa. But between the two, the dividing line is not so clear: have South Korea, Greece and Portugal finished emerging? Have Peru and Morocco joined this envied club?

The very relevance of this term, which seems to mindlessly classify countries according to whether they are in front, behind or in the middle, is indeed questionable. Obviously, an immense variety of features escape this notion, as is attested by the recently invented BRIC superclass (Brazil, Russia, India and China). Yet even if the content is uncertain, the concept sells well: billions of dollars are now placed in investment funds specializing exclusively in this group. More generally, the stocks and bonds issued by emerging countries are the asset class that has offered the highest yields in recent years. Another element of a working definition is the birth date of this category, which was invented by financiers and business consultants in the early 1990s. Three factors were particularly significant in this initial phase:

(1) Emerging countries are first the product of the liberal reforms of the 1980s, born of "structural adjustment" (1985), which would soon become the crux of the Washington Consensus, i.e. trade liberalization, privatization of state enterprises,

market deregulation, liberalization of the banking system, labour market flexibility (Williamson 1990).[1] After 1989, transition in Eastern Europe would further amplify and deepen this programme.

(2) That same year, the Brady Initiative enabled countries overburdened by debt since 1982 to obtain substantial debt relief (35% on average) (Cline 1994).[2] Its much-acclaimed success then reinforced reform and growth: its main beneficiaries still form the core members of the emerging economies club (except for Asia).[3]

(3) Lastly, capital markets were entirely reshaped by the Brady plans: once the principal was reduced, former bank loans were exchanged for freely convertible, dollar-denominated bonds, or Brady bonds - a star instrument of the 1990s. Thus, huge financial markets with both liquidity and financial depth were created almost overnight and offered a remarkable springboard for restarting North-South capital flows. Emerging markets are the offspring of the debt crisis.

figure 13: **Capital flows toward emerging economies, 1975-2005**

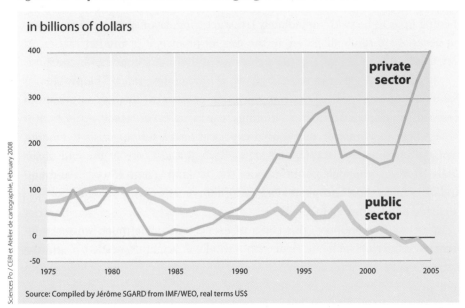

Source: Compiled by Jérôme SGARD from IMF/WEO, real terms US$

Sciences Po / CERI et Atelier de cartographie, February 2008

---

1 A distinction is generally made between macroeconomic adjustment, which has to do with the budget, currency and aggregate demand, and structural adjustment, which refers to the offer and long-term growth.

2 The "Brady Initiative" is generally used to refer to an overall strategy devised in 1989, with "Brady Plans" for each specific case. Between 1989 and 1993, 18 countries benefited from such loan reduction plans for a total of 190 billion dollars, with a total reduction of 60 billion.

3 Brady Plans were solely intended for countries with intermediate revenues, the future "emerging" economies, whereas the least advanced countries (LDCs according to the World Bank nomenclature) oddly enough benefited from a much more gradual debt reduction strategy (the so-called "Heavily Indebted Poor Countries" or HIPC Initiative). This program did not reach maturity until the early 2000s at best.

These three elements summarize what could be called "the programme of 1989". It was soon complemented by a separate, though revolutionary measure, which delivered the "programme of 1992", namely the total liberalization of short and long-term capital flows. On the one hand, international investors could now enter the domestic markets of emerging economies (stock market, public debt, banks); on the other, private actors from these countries gradually entered international capital markets (privatized utilities, regional industrial groups, financial concerns, etc). At this precise moment domestic liberalization became inextricably linked to participation in global trade and finance.

The most striking thing here is that contrary to developed countries, which took 20 to 30 years to open up their capital account (Helleiner 1994), emerging countries took this second step in three to four years in virtual silence, practically unnoticed. Many, including the International Monetary Fund (IMF), believed that it was merely a logical consequence of trade liberalization: why should a country reject the benefits of international financial exchange once it has accepted those of international commerce? This assumption soon proved to be misleading. As a rule, in the case of commodity trading, the price to pay for opening up is to be paid immediately (restructuring, layoffs, etc.), but the ensuing benefits are rarely disputed. In the case of finance, it is another matter. At first, capital flows in, redistributive conflicts are alleviated, households consume, the stock market rises and states borrow at low interest rates. The problem is that such booms repeatedly lead to declining investment quality: empty shopping centres, unoccupied office buildings, car loans never repaid. After two or three years of abundance, one should expect at best a serious crisis (which hit the Crédit Lyonnais or the United States Savings and Loans at the end of the 1980s), if not a wholesale bankruptcy of the banking system (Sweden and Finland in 1992, Eastern Europe in 1992 and 1996); or, at worst, a systemic collapse (Thailand and Indonesia in 1997).

In emerging economies, this chain of events was made much worse by ill-prepared reforms, which left them with a wholly deficient domestic oversight of markets and banks. Huge amounts of capital thus flowed in, from which the return often proved to be dismal, so that when the crash came, a rather standard banking crisis was typically compounded by a brutal, sometimes contagious foreign exchange crisis. The Mexican crisis of 1994-1995 revealed how devastating this conjunction could be. Whereas previously financial opening had happened almost unquestioned, within a few years the notion that the world economy had actually entered a completely new regime now made the headlines. In the now famous words of Michel Camdessus, then Managing Director of the IMF, this episode was widely perceived as "the first crisis of the 21st century" (Camdessus 1995). Later episodes fit within the same basic cycle of boom and bust, which reached its zenith in the autumn of 1998. After having swept three Southeast Asian countries, then South Korea and then Russia, the contagion shifted to Wall Street with the near bankruptcy of the LTCM hedge fund, which required emergency intervention from the Federal Reserve Bank in New York (Sgard 2002).[4]

At this exact moment, when the hurricane was nearing US coasts, President Bill Clinton made his famous speech about "the new international architecture" (Clinton 1998). The very term attested to the then widely shared view that capital markets could go berserk, that they might soon self-destruct, possibly carrying off the savings of millions of American families. In the face of these pressing risks, Clinton solemnly asserted that global financial markets needed rules and arbitrators, possibly sanctions and police officers. But this constructivist radicalism of the autumn of 1998 was soon forgotten: in the following years, official or private working groups regularly concluded that exercises in architectural design were pointless, or even dangerous, and that private actors would come up with effective solutions in due time.[5]

It is rather easy to see this as just another ideological proclamation, especially since the behaviour of financial operators has hardly grown more stable over the last decade: they still demonstrate a strong herd instinct and collective appetite for recklessness.[6] Yet it must also be acknowledged that since the early 2000s, financial crises in emerging economies are (almost) a thing of the past.[7] Banking systems have been solidly rebuilt; growth is high, speculative bubbles are corrected faster and cause less damage; correction phases better differentiate between more or less fragile countries, and lastly, the macroeconomic cost of market shocks is lower. The risks incurred by the boom and bust cycle did not disappear altogether, as the US-based subprime crisis has reminded us. As regards emerging economies, we are however in a third phase of development: after the boom (1989-96) and the crisis (1995, 1997-99) a degree of maturity has been reached in many countries, combining sustained growth, strong international integration and solid economic know-how.

Hence our main assumption: the greater stability of the world economy in the east and south is not merely due to stronger markets or to better international regulation. It primarily comes from states and local regulators. Learning processes, institution-building, and keener knowledge of economic dynamics have enabled countries to better protect themselves and support domestic investment and growth. In this way a more stable global order has emerged from a bottom-up

---

4   Southeast Asia (Thailand, Malaysia, Indonesia) were hit mainly in the second half of 1997, South Korea in the last two months of the same year, Russia between June and August 1998, then Brazil between October 1998 and January 1999.

5   The Enron scandal in the end had considerably greater consequences on the regulation of American markets than did the crisis in emerging markets. See Group of Ten 1997, Williamson 2000, Eichengreen 1999.

6   In early 2006, doubts about the stability of exchange rates and the banking system in Iceland (290,000 inhabitants and a GDP equal to 9% of Thailand's GDP) caused a number of markets to plunge, from Hungary to Turkey and New Zealand.

7   The Argentine crisis in 2001-2, although particularly severe, remains in many ways part of the cycle of the 1990s.

process of aggregation, in a most decentralized and differentiated fashion. The global economy is stronger, simply because the parties are more resilient. It is exactly the opposite of an international architecture that would have been designed by inspired engineers.

Greater economic regulation

Economists, IMF technocrats and bankers have already established a long list of factors to explain the new "resilience" of emerging economies. Macroeconomic policies, first of all, have in general become far more solid, confirming the triumph of the Washington Consensus: lower inflation rates, restrained budget policies, controlled public debt, etc. Secondly, current surpluses and massive accumulation of currency reserves enable them to better weather market shocks: they in fact serve as an alternative to the insurance polices of the IMF, which are now deemed costly in terms of sovereignty and of little effect in terms of results. Lastly, fixed foreign exchange policies, which have become untenable in a regime of free capital movement, have been discarded, allowing for much more flexible adjustments than in the past.

Usually, economic policy debate interprets such progress in terms of "credibility," "reputation" or "trust," words that at best refer to a set of restrictive constitutional rules—for instance the independence of central banks or the fiscal constitution of a federation. In practice, however, better economic policies also rest on often technical, specialized public institutions that were generally lacking in the 1990s. They are the actual places where collective knowledge, technical skills, rules of cooperation and operating procedures are tested and accumulated; and the capacity to regulate markets and win the trust of private agents ultimately derives from this capital.

Bank supervision, for instance, has largely been rebuilt in emerging countries after serious failings in the 1990s, with improved norms of capitalization, risk surveillance, rules of private governance, information disclosure, legal powers given to the supervisory body, etc. There is little doubt that in most countries the capacity of this agent to influence bank behaviour is now vastly superior to what it was. In short, these market institutions have become "authorities", in both the French and the English sense of the word.

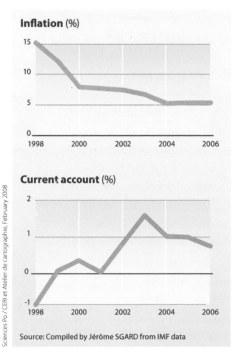

figure 14: **Inflation and current account of emerging countries, 1998-2005**

Inflation (%)

Current account (%)

Source: Compiled by Jérôme SGARD from IMF data

Sciences Po / CERI et Atelier de cartographie, February 2008

Monetary policy is another example. Most emerging countries have adopted a regime of "inflation targeting" that is mainly aimed at medium term inflation. The central bank is then judged by its capacity to reach that goal rather than by intermediate quantitative targets that may eventually drive price increases (Bernanke *et al.* 2001; Ho & McCauley 2003). With respect to the various monetary regimes of the 1990s, which were generally anchored on the exchange rate, this reflects a refocusing of monetary policies on internal anchors. In other words, today central banks are much more "on their own", whereas they previously settled for following US or German monetary policy, while acting in the most extreme cases as a glorified foreign exchange bureau. The point however is that this change necessitated a much higher level of technical skill as well as a capacity for finely-tuned interaction with economic actors, particularly financial ones. Central banks now conduct monetary policy "by instruments", as airline pilots would say, depending on their appreciation of economic trends, their intimate knowledge of financial markets and high-level macroeconomic models. And these highly professional, technocratic institutions now rule in the major emerging economies: Mexico, Chile, Brazil, Poland, South Korea, etc.

Globalization, liberalization and state-building

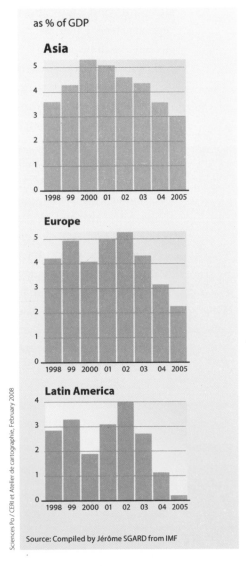

figure 15: **Budget deficits of emerging economies, 1998-2005**

as % of GDP

Asia

1998 99 2000 01 02 03 04 2005

Europe

1998 99 2000 01 02 03 04 2005

Latin America

1998 99 2000 01 02 03 04 2005

Sciences Po / CERI et Atelier de cartographie, February 2008

Source: Compiled by Jérôme SGARD from IMF

Rapid growth, solid integration into global markets and now strengthened institutional know-how... is this combination enough to define present-day emerging economies or countries? Should we content ourselves with these empirically satisfactory but nevertheless theoretically poor criteria? Like in the early 1990s, emerging economies would remain a category for "golden boys", not for social scientists. Such a conclusion would be disappointing and somewhat paradoxical, provided these countries' experiences are considered in historical perspective. They have already earned their place in economic history textbooks. These catch-up dynamics, at once powerful, very capitalistic and often brutal, take after those of the United States and Germany in the late 19th century, Japan shortly afterwards, and South Korea in the 1960s-70s. This can be seen as the large, conceptual category that the emerging countries belong to and which their specific character is to be derived from.

Capitalism, growth, inequalities, the salaried class, international division of labor, market-state relations: emerging economies raise classic, indeed defining, crucial political economy questions, though in largely new terms. Today, Adam Smith, Karl Marx and even Max Weber would necessarily be working on China, India or Brazil—at least much more than they did in their time.

What makes their present experience unique is globalization. Globalization is clearly a powerful growth accelerator, but it also implies previously unknown institutional constraints that redefine the established relationship of economic agents with rules and ultimately with public institutions. Financial supervision, intellectual property, competition law, consumer and environmental protection, direct investment: international integration and growth largely depend on the capacity of emerging economies to integrate these complex bodies of norms domestically and of course to enforce them. This is indeed where the most pressing concerns of companies opening branches in these countries are focused, as well as the thorniest political difficulties, both within these countries themselves (take for instance the issues of land and intellectual property rights in China) and on the international level – particularly at the WTO. This array of issues was much less palpable during the first globalization, between 1850 and 1914, or even during the "internationalization" phase of the 1960s to 80s (Sgard 2004).

The key point is that external demand for normalization intersects, and may also interfere, with internal efforts to build institutions, normalize economic interactions and design an increasing array of effective public policies. This is the most pressing issue that specifically defines emerging economies today: are these two internal and external demands concurrent or contradictory? How can they be coordinated or articulated?

This contribution does not attempt to answer such questions here. Instead it examines four propositions that should help us better grasp the defining relation between liberalization, globalization and the rule of law which now seem to give the emerging country experience its key features.

Globalization and liberalization are not the same thing. Ordinary language as well as the vocabulary of many researchers often confuses these two terms, whereas actually liberalization and globalization are two different phenomena. In particular, globalization is not simply the continuation of liberalization by other means. It is above all defined by the reciprocal opening up of national markets and a high degree of integration, which have very powerful effects: a convergence of relative price scales between countries, a single liquidity constraint, and investment allocation and hence division of labour across countries and sectors which are increasingly formed at the global level. The idea of a single world market is indeed the regulating concept of globalization, except that national states still impose a high degree of social and institutional fragmentation that makes governance issues particularly acute. Therein lies the historic originality of the second globalization.

Liberalism as a programme and as an ideology presents an obvious and long-standing universalistic dimension. "Market forces" have an almost irresistible propensity to extend into new countries and sectors, even if that means being subject to backlash as occurred in the 1990s in many emerging economies. That said, it is perfectly possible to construct liberalism in a single country, or simply liberalize faster on the domestic level than the external. Chile and the United Kingdom in the late 1970s are good examples of financial reforms undertaken at a time when international capital markets were still relatively undeveloped. Similarly, the Washington Consensus implied a degree of sequencing that was soon abandoned by the liberalization of the entire capital account. This amounted to combining liberalization and globalization, with their respective constraints, which theoretically was in no way necessary.

Liberalization is not a question of degree between private and public. Liberalizing is not mainly about moving from "more government" to "more market". The intellectual fault-line in the Washington Consensus stemmed from the misleading idea that opening up to markets, domestic or international, meant the retreat of the state. To stretch the point, these were seen as two measurable quantities, measurable in the same unit that could be substituted and portioned out. The model chosen by each country was, it was therefore thought, a result of collective arbitrage between social conservatism and the spirit of enterprise, or between security and appetite for risk. The inadequacy of this common belief of the 1990s is all the more striking since it was supposed to account for exceptionally complex and novel social dynamics that the actors themselves had trouble grasping.

The main issue at stake when liberalizing is not the division of a given number of goods and services between private and public producers. Nor does it boil down to a renewed assertion or sovereignty of private interests over the common good, or of one dissolving into the other. On the contrary, liberalization is characterized by a more constraining and socially tougher relationship between public and private, polarized by the relationship between autonomous private agents and universal rules, typically enforced by a state. More individualistic and competitive behaviour is observed in a publicly-instituted space, where the capacity to discipline actors should be all the more powerful since they have much more room for trading off alternative investment strategies.

The experience of transition in Eastern Europe showed that in building a market economy, the hardest thing was not to unleash an appetite for enterprise and profit. The really tough issue was to establish the authority and effectiveness of the rule of law over opportunists, oligarchs, gamblers and coalitions of gangsters. The failure of the Russian reformers in the 1990s stems from their inability to guarantee the enforcement of private contracts between the powerful and the little guys, between the *kombinats* and private SMEs, the racketeers and the innovators. The liberal experience, from both an economic and a political standpoint, is thus not defined by a supposedly free and decentralized interaction of agents, but by the central issues of rules, norms, and their underlying state guarantees. Another example is offered by the experience of "legal pluralism" observed in most developing countries, which implies the conjunction of more or less individualistic or marketized environments that will leave actors with varying capacity to trade off alternate strategies. As in Europe under the *Ancien Régime*, the state is a central actor in the extension of these "modern" norms that are a precondition for capitalist development. The experiences of Morocco and Tunisia over the past 50 years, for instance, could be compared in very contrasted terms.

In emerging countries, liberalization is state-building. If the crux of liberal reform and globalization lies in the relation to the rule of law, then the state is their main object (Bayart 2004). In particular, room for competitive interaction will have to be enlarged and protected, and there must also be an attempt to normalize it so that the results obtained are as socially acceptable or sustainable as possible. For instance, a country might confirm financial liberalization but make sure that competition among banks does not lead them to take excessive risks likely to trigger systemic crises. Public regulation will thus have to move towards rules that govern the behaviour of agents before they enter the market, hence from a distance and in an anonymous and universal fashion. Entering the market for banking or dentistry services, bans on employing children under 16, ruling on whether to allow certain chemical products on the market or not, limiting polluting gas emissions: these rules are intended to influence market outcomes (children go to school and do not work in the fields, trucks pollute less). But to be viable, they must have an effect on the agents (parents or truckers) before they take action on the market place, or on the social stage, that is, when they plan their future acts and calculate their economic options ("what will I do with my children this morning?").

This form of public action can be contrasted with intervention within the market that directly affects the outcome of competition. Examples of this are credit control, national champion preference policies, planned resource allocation, public price regulations—all things that in principle should be avoided in a liberal economy. Whereas an ex-ante perspective mainly has to do with legislation and hence universal norms applying to all market participants, intervention in the market is more of a discretionary, unilateral act of an administrative nature. Lastly, ex-post public action typically seeks to alter market results after the fact, through income redistribution or by covering private losses (crisis management or social protection). As a rule, liberalization implies a major shift toward an ex-ante perspective, which preserves or restores the freedom of private calculation and investment: common goods objectives should then be achieved indirectly, through the decentralized adjustment of agents to the enactment of a norm.

Redefining public action by making it conditional on very universal, abstract, undifferentiated rules is highly problematic from both an institutional and a political standpoint. Public action will be altogether more complex, more competence-intensive, more remote from the social sphere in its definition and also more powerful in its normative capacity. And as such, it will not easily replace the more direct, traditional form of intervention that has been dominant during the previous decades, particularly in developing countries. Unsophisticated administrations with few resources lend themselves better to "command and control" policies, market segmentation and extensive mobilization of resources. In fact, it is far easier to run monopolistic car and truck producers than to bring together all the microeconomic and institutional conditions needed in order to support privately-based development (rules of governance, credit market, competition policy, etc.). The problem of course is that in the long run, such monopolies are likely to be less innovative and less efficient.

Since the 1980s, the difficulty of redefining these modes of public action, in a market environment characterized by private rule-based competition has caused a large-scale decline or even collapse of the overall capacity to conduct public policies, which is today a defining problem for public actors. Former instruments of public action no longer function in a market economy, although acquiring new instruments is difficult: this calls for a major redefinition of the state's relation to the law, social actors and the knowledge the state has of them.

On market regulation and public policy. Globalization interferes directly with this domestic policy experience of redefining the rules of interaction between public and private. It in fact requires this effort to proceed to a large extent, by importing normative and legal apparatuses from developed countries – mainly the United States and the European Union (Berkowitz *et al.* 2003).

This echoes the experience of the "legal transplant" of entire bodies of law already observed in the 19th century in matters of civil law, corporate law and bankruptcy law, for instance. To that is now added a protean apparatus of technical protection norms, which can be statutory or regulatory, jurisprudential or professional—phytosanitary norms, food norms, consumer protection and environmental norms, etc. The *acquis communautaire*, which the new European Union member states have had to incorporate into their national legislation, is a fine example of this both domestic and external form of economic normalization. It is definitely an instrument with which to access markets and the direct benefits of trade; it is also an instrument for the modernization of both public administrations and economic regulation.

For Poland and Bulgaria today, and perhaps for Turkey and Ukraine in the future, joining the European Union and integrating its economic legislation mean access to a huge market, and possession of a powerful lever to reform the state to make it suitable to a hopefully growing market economy. This is why many countries have actually signed trade agreements with Brussels that commit them to adopting much of its normative apparatus, though without enabling them to participate in political decisions and share in the budget.

Political culture and public institutions can certainly respond vigorously to external pressures: they are malleable. The perspective of joining the European Union thus played a major role in Central Europe in the 1990s. It offered resources and a credible time frame that anchored institutional reforms and guided the restructuring strategies of firms. But very often, as we know well, ambitious reforms have not been followed through, because the rules contradict existing legislation, or the institutional means are lacking, or actors circumvent the rules and take the route of informality if they deem the costs of adjustment too high (Maloney 2004). This is where the articulation of liberal state micro-policy and the construction of rational and competent administrations of the Weberian sort takes place.

The example of technocratic central banks has shown that in order to bend private market behaviour and achieve the desired market outcomes, the regulator must be a multi-talented actor able to know, watch, measure, guarantee and also sanction private actors that will nevertheless remain free to trade off alternate economic strategies (to buy a treasury bond or not, to sell one's pesos for dollars or not). Environmental issues are an alternative example. They are generally poorly governed in comparison with currency regulation, despite huge external costs produced by high growth (soil and water deterioration, pollution, degradation of the biosphere, etc.). As a rule, these external costs are deferred to future generations, to the immediate victims or to ex-post compensatory intervention. Rather, as in financial crises, at best it is all handled by stymied public action: rare but massive mobilization of means, improvised procedures, low-level institutionalization, limited capitalization on experience. How can we ever hope to effectively treat the greenhouse effect, urban congestion or the biosphere with such low-quality ex-post action?

Social inequality offers another illustration. We know that in developing countries, social protection is usually only partial, scarcely redistributive and generally clientelistic (Van de Walle 2005). The quest for greater efficiency has led some countries to devise policies that attempt a much stronger targeting of beneficiaries (the poor) and also try to condition aid (for sending children to school). This model of policies has had profound consequences on the workings of public administrations and their relation to the population. The poor now have to be defined, counted, localized in space, their incomes are to be measured and they will have to be interviewed regularly to verify that in exchange for the money paid out, children are indeed attending school and medical checkups are made. In Brazil, the development of this type of strategy required the construction of a new administrative apparatus, alongside the older, existing Ministry for Social Development. Remarkably, the new structure works along lines that are much closer to the Weberian criteria of formal rationality: huge micro-social databases, anonymous case processing, abstract criteria for programme access, electronic transfer of monthly allocations, local disclosure of beneficiaries, and procedural rules for NGO surveillance (Janvry, Finan & Sadoulet 2006). This public policy, which has achieved considerable results,[8] is thus based on knowledge of society, particularly the "informal sector", that previously escaped the eye and hand of the state. There is indeed an anthropology of social policy.

To conclude: the specific nature of emerging economies

To sum up the story being told here : starting in the late 1980s, the main outcome of the basic liberal rules summarized in the Washington Consensus was primarily to break up corporatist or socialist regimes and open up the economic field to very individualist and competitive regulations. In Eastern Europe especially, the early period of reform was clearly dominated by revolutionary legal reforms, which had already been studied in detail by Marx and Weber, in the case of the "first transition". They positively institute private economic agents and endow them with concrete and transferable rights such as property and financial contracts. Strikingly, this phase was coupled with a radical challenging of public action and institutions, in both speech and deeds. Then, after the disasters of the 1990s—financial crises and the failure of Russian reforms—there was a reassessment of public regulation revolving around the basic institutions of currency, bank supervision, competition, intellectual property and bankruptcy procedures. Such regulation brought in tow financial stability and growth. What remains to be retrieved, beyond this minimal, almost libertarian state, is the ability and the legitimacy to produce a broader range of public goods, provision of which today is utterly limited or even absent, i.e. education, health care, the environment or the fight against poverty. As in 19th-century Europe, increasing the supply of these public goods is a condition for long-term growth as well as democratic consolidation in countries where the public good remains a much-contested notion.

This political economy of emerging countries can then be distinguished from three other models of development. First are countries that are not emerging at all, where failure of the economy and the state are usually closely linked, particularly in Africa. Second are rent-seeking economies where public funding and

---

8   From 2001 to 2005 the proportion of the indigent poor went from 15.2 to 11.4%, that of the poor from 35.1 to 30.7%.

government are not articulated on a private and competitive economy, implying a trend towards legal formalization and constitutionalized politics. The trajectory of emerging countries, lastly, differs from countries that took the liberal turn in the 1980s, but without afterwards acquiring the capacity to conduct effective rule-based policies in a competitive economy. Hence, these countries have basically remained stalled in a difficult intermediary phase marked by large-scale "deinsti-tutionalization", leading to a decline in the very notion of public action (Venezuela, Ecuador, Argentina, Russia). Here are to be found the most virulent criticisms of the liberal experience and, in addition, the strongest propensity to revive traditional forms of public intervention, which will prove less formally rational and thus less effective.

These different political economies necessarily have direct repercussions on the international stage, because in the end local regulations are more decisive than "architectural designs". In such a world, the collective ability to govern global public goods—the environment, health, security—depends on the capacity of local polities to agree collectively on the production of public goods. This is why emerging countries, through their progress or resistance, will have a decisive role to play in world affairs. Not only are the largest of them among those who write the rules of the game, but their capacity to legitimately produce more local public goods will also be decisive in increasing the production of global public goods.

Bibliography ·

Abdelal, R. (2007). *Capital Rules. The Construction of Global Finance*. Cambridge (Mass.): Harvard University Press.

Bayart, J.-F. (2004). *Le gouvernement du monde, une critique politique de la globalisation*. Paris: Fayard.

Berkowitz, D., K. Pistor and J.-F. Richard (2003). "The Transplant Effect." *The American Journal of Comparative Law*, 51 (1), pp. 163-204.

Bernanke, B., Th. Laubach, F. Mishkin and A. Posen (2001). *Inflation Targeting - Lessons from the International Experience*. Princeton: Princeton University Press.

Camdessus, Michel (1995), "Address at the UN World Summit for Social Development". Copenhagen, 7 March.

Cline, W. (1994). *International Debt Crisis Reexamined*. Washington DC Institute of International Economics.

Clinton, W. J. (1998). "Address to the Council on Foreign Relations." New York, 28 September.

Eichengreen, B. (1999). *Toward a New International Financial Architecture*, Washington: Institute for International Economics, 189p. For a good idea of the average consensus following the Asian crisis.

Group of Ten (1997). *Financial Stability in Emerging Market Economies*, Basel.

Helleiner, E. (1994). *States and the Reemergence of Global Finance*, Ithaca, NY: Cornell University Press.

Ho, C. and R. McCauley (2003). *Living with flexible exchange rates: issues and recent experience in inflation targeting emerging market economies*. Basel: Bank for International Settlements, BIS Working Papers No. 130.

Janvry, A., F. Finan F. and E. Sadoulet (2006). "Evaluating Brazil's Bolsa Escola Program: Impact of Schooling and Municipal Roles", Berkeley: University of California, mimeo, June.

Maloney, W. (2004). "Informality revisited", *World Development*, 20:10.

Rawi, A. (2007). *Capital Rules, the Construction of Global Finance*. Cambridge, MA: Harvard University Press.

Sgard, J. (2002), *L'économie de la panique, faire face aux crises financières*. Paris: La Découverte.

—— (2004), "Are there such Things as International Property Rights?" *The World Economy*, 27: 3.

Walle, D. van de (2005). *Do Services and Transfers Reach Morocco's Poor? Evidence from Poverty and Spending Map*. Washington DC: World Bank, WB Policy Research Working Paper 3478. A good example of a quantitative evaluation of the effect of social policies.

Williamson, J. (1990). "What Washington Means by Policy Reforms", in J. Williamson, *Latin American Adjustment, How much has Happened?*, Washington: Institute for International Economics, pp. 7-20.

—— (2000), "The Role of the IMF: A Guide to Reports," *International Economics Policy Briefs*, 00-5, May, Institute of International Economics.

Forms of Capitalism in Emerging Countries

Interview with Robert Boyer

In our conversation with Robert Boyer, he situates his analysis at the junction of the economic situation and the major trends of a globalized world in which emerging countries already play a leading role.

How is an emerging country defined?

The category is problematic because it refers to very different situations depending on the country. Some observers group under this label countries that have a higher growth rate than mature economies, but the term still leads to confusion if only because it was invented by external analysts, mainly financiers, who have little understanding of the countries involved. They have called "emerging" those countries in which they could make investments, carrying high risks but with potentially a high level of return due to strong growth. The category fits into the context of ever-increasing long-distance economic relations and the perspectives these open to investors. Even though overseas and overland trade already existed at the dawn of capitalism—think of the Silk Road—interpenetration is much more developed and concerns not only trade but also production methods, even lifestyles in some cases, and of course finance.

In fact, it would make sense today to analyze the duopoly formed by the United States on one side, and China and India on the other. Is it not significant that American macroeconomists themselves, who are traditionally used to reasoning in a closed economy, have realized that they could no longer analyze the United

States economy without taking into account its relations with Asia? Thus the major change in contemporary international economics is not only the extreme variety of countries that have shown an economic takeoff, but especially this bipolarization, the key to many contemporary phenomena.

Is growth the only common denominator among so-called emerging countries?

The long view of economic history shows that around 1800, all countries had practically the same standard of living and productivity level. Beginning at that time, Europe and the United States experienced a takeoff, whereas the rest of the world continued to stagnate. So-called emerging countries are those experiencing a similar process today after having been released from colonization. The characteristics of colonization, then decolonization, are what for instance explain the stark contrast between the trajectories of Latin American countries and those of Asian countries.

In Latin America, dependency theory[1] at first had some success in justifying industrialization by import substitution. It later ran into a series of crises which led to the development and then implementation of the Washington consensus, which on the contrary advocates the opening and liberalization of economies. Success was neither swift nor assured, to the point that Latin America's trajectory is associated with a form of economic failure. The introduction of modernity in fact was accompanied by several dramatic incidents, and many national institutions still bear the traces of colonization. China's history unfolded along an entirely different trajectory: an early boom of merchant institutions, later curbed by internal political conflicts and then predatory colonization which in 1949 led to assertion of a demand for national independence. Furthermore, in China but also in India, the political elite believes in its own future and that of its country, which has rarely been the case in Latin America. Argentina is emblematic of extreme wariness about a nation's future.

What, then, is the common denominator between emerging countries of yesterday and today?

The success of emerging countries is located at the junction of national political strategies—often resulting from a new awakening that grows out of serious crises—and a favourable configuration of the world economy. Poorly informed observers are tempted to attribute this coincidence, usually an unintentional one, to the virtues of a model which they see as the outcome of explicit and conscious

---

1   The theory that holds that unequal exchange mechanisms imposed by the North account for the poverty, political instability, underdevelopment and economic dependency affecting Southern countries.

strategies. But very often the synchronization of internal and external forces tends to jam, thereby producing a more serious crisis. Contemporary emerging countries are not exempt from this paradoxical sequence.

What brand of capitalism would you say characterizes emerging economies?

In fact, they do not all follow the same trajectory. The effect of opening up to the international scene has been to create considerable differences in the institutional architecture of these countries, leaving behind the rhetoric postulating that the combination of market and democracy had only one stable configuration, represented by the North American model. Suffice it, for example, to compare China with Russia and Central and Eastern Europe.

In China, personal relations continue to play an important role both in the coastal provinces and in the more remote areas. Indeed, contrary to a common interpretation, the Chinese Communist Party (CCP), far from being an obstacle to the conversion to capitalism, is a catalyst, even a key actor. It is constantly forging ties between public and private, and makes sure that the benefits of economic activity are partly redistributed in order to ensure the stability of social ties, and, consequently, the legitimacy of the Communist Party itself. We are thus a far cry from the caricatural view of the state and the market as alternative coordination mechanisms. They are basically complementary, even if tensions between politics and economics can naturally resurface. The originality of this model like no other is plain to see. Incidentally, corruption can be interpreted as the expression of transaction costs required to convert a purportedly communist structure into a typically capitalist configuration. It is sometimes the lubricant that enables seemingly collective institutions to be converted into instruments of capitalism. There are certainly flagrant instances of personal enrichment, but these then provide the government with the opportunity to announce spectacular decisions in order to show everyone that it ultimately maintains control. In most other cases, and particularly at the provincial level, corruption is actually an implicit, socially controlled and relatively well-accepted redistribution mechanism. It is thus not always or everywhere detrimental to growth and economic efficiency, whatever experts and international organizations may think, even though they make it out to be the main obstacle to development.

The Russian trajectory is radically different because, in that country, the government's logic tends to supplant that of entrepreneurs, as evidenced by the ease with which property rights can be redefined in key sectors such as energy or the media. The economy is again tending to be encompassed by the political arena, which is in keeping with a long Russian, then Soviet, then again Russian tradition. This can be seen as a consequence of the fact that struggles are mainly over the appropriation of rents. It is thus difficult for real entrepreneurs to gain a foothold, unlike what can be observed in China where, at the risk of exaggeration, the Communist Party is an incubator for seedling companies at the local level. Though the latter don't claim to innovate, they strive to place themselves at the technological frontier, which explains the very high growth in productivity. Nothing of the sort can be observed in Russia.

The Central and Eastern European countries (CEECs) are inventing still other models. Depending on the relative length of their submission to the Soviet regime and their past experience with the market and democracy, each is developing its own strategy. Government strategies are often presented as the result of a choice between the Anglo-Saxon model and the social-democrat model. It is more likely that new forms of capitalism are being created before our eyes but that the social sciences do not yet have the tools to understand the outcome of the institutional destruction/creation process that the various CEECs are undergoing.

What are the constants?

Studies on Europe, the United States and certain Asian countries that take the long view suggest that beyond a succession of growth regimes, certain common features specific to each country travel down through the ages. A number of features described by Tocqueville can still be recognized in contemporary North America. By the same token, the state's central role in initiating economic liberalization procedures seems to be a permanent feature of France. I have pointed out the particular irony of the Russian trajectory. One last example: the Danish model of flexicurity seems to many observers as the distant relative of the 1899 agreement between entrepreneurs and wage earners; however different they may be, these histories derive from a foundational compromise which then evolved into different forms depending on the world context, the type of technological paradigm or internal social changes. I might thus suggest that even during structural crises, both private and public actors draw from the repertory of coordination procedures inherited from the past and legitimated by this foundational compromise.

Do emerging countries have a notion of the international common good?

If official Chinese declarations are to be believed, the answer is affirmative. The government's official line is indeed to organize growth through autochthonous and endogenous innovation in a harmonious society that maintains peaceful relations with the rest of the world. International stability would then be a highly important public good. This position is logical for a country whose economic dynamism has partly to do with its successful integration into the world economy on which it is increasingly dependent in terms of markets as well as for raw materials and energy. Both the Chinese and the Indians have every interest in international relations being organized according to a multipolar model to prevent the dominant power, the United States, from putting their rapid development in jeopardy. In so doing, they concur with the European Union standpoint. Moreover, certain observers, probably being ironic, have put forth the idea that the obsolescence of the Washington consensus will produce another series of norms, drawn from the Chinese experience, if not proposed by the country's authorities themselves. Indeed, the pacification of international relations also requires the stabilization of social and political relations within each domestic space.

It is precisely for this reason that outside observers can harbour certain concerns. Indeed, social tensions are on the rise in China both in rural milieus and among migrants to the cities and urban dwellers. If their demands find a political outlet, as happened in South Korea in 1985, a rebalancing of the growth regime towards the domestic market might be expected, which would lower the competi-

table 1: **From the Washington to the Beijing consensus: what are the consequences?**

Characteristics	Consensus	
	Washington	Beijing
1. Vision	• Static: reforms once and for all	• Dynamic: gradual series of reforms
	• Large determinism of change	• A certain degree of unpredictability
	• Aim: attract foreign capital through finance	• Aim for social and political stability
2. Axioms	• Adopt the outdated technology of developed economies	• Cutting-edge technology reduces the cost of transition and autochthonous innovation
	• First growth, then social and political progress	• A sustainable and equitable development model
	• Accept the rules of the game set by the hegemonic powers	• Self-determination and bargaining power in defining the rules
		• National development without international tensions or war
3. Diffusion and international impact	• Via international organizations	• Chinese imports from the most advanced countries and primary exporters
	• Mainly at times of severe financial crises	• *Ad hoc* development assistance
	• Conditional development assistance	

Source: Freely adapted from Joshua Cooper Ramo, *The Beijing Consensus*, The Foreign Policy Centre, London, March 2004.

tive pressure on the rest of the world while satisfying domestic needs, especially social ones (healthcare, education, retirement, living environment, housing etc.). But the CCP's monopoly on political expression makes it difficult to satisfy these social demands.

World stability is also prey to the danger of the American authorities misjudging the threat China represents. What would happen, for instance, if the Chinese investment funds were used to acquire the finest American high-tech company on the NASDAQ stock exchange? Would Americans make a virtue of necessity as they did by allowing sovereign funds to bail out various US banks and financial institutions?

Is the confusion between public and private not another specific feature of Chinese capitalism?

Indeed, the Chinese economy serves as a remarkable example of the lack of any major antagonism between public and private. There are no fewer than 11 forms of company ownership, ranging from vestiges of the nationalized sector to multinationals. But in most of these forms, the Chinese authorities keep a rein on the instruments of control, which, although they have been loosened over time, remain firm (administrative authorizations, subsidies, access to credit, etc.). When you visit provinces far from Beijing as I have done recently, you find that companies considered private in the statistics are actually closely dependent on the political authorities for movement of people, subsidies, the prescribing of norms, permission to open branches, personnel recruitment, support in the event of difficulties, etc. In a way, contemporary China is rehabilitating a form of mixed economy.

Sociopolitical regulation seems much stronger than strictly economic regulation.

Indeed, the quality of microeconomic management seems to matter less than appropriate social regulation. There can be no doubt that capital is poorly allocated in China owing to overinvestment and constant overcapacities, but its main goal lies elsewhere—in constantly striving to improve worker productivity, a source of profits and higher standing of living. In a way, static inefficiency is offset by the quest for such dynamic efficiency. One of the major government tasks is to preserve social stability even when the dynamism of capital accumulation is eating away at former socioeconomic forms. For the Chinese political leaders, democracy is not a solution to this problem for the moment, because it is the Communist Party, permeating all strata of society, which is in charge of making the necessary arbitrages, without much concern for transparency.

Who defines the general interest? The Chinese Communist Party?

The Communist Party's explicit goal is not to directly provide the public goods needed for the current transformation phase of Chinese society. Its primary objective is stay in power as long as possible. It achieves this in part via the early detection and then reduction of the most glaring social, economic and financial imbalances. Basically, as we know, the fundamental compromise in this society rests on a tradeoff between the Communist Party's monopoly of political power and a form of economic freedom and the possibility of enrichment left to the rest of the society. In a way, economic performance is the condition for political stability.

It should also be pointed out that the central feature is the competition among the provincial authorities, which favour economic growth to better solve problems of employment and standard of living. Once again, the dynamism of growth is the result of competition in the political sphere.

Is it sustainable in the long run?

Not necessarily, because this growth regime is exposed to several tensions. First of all, if official statistics are to be believed, in the past ten years the rate of capital accumulation has gone from about 30% to nearly 45%, which amounts to over-accumulation: consumption should increase faster by bringing investment down to a more reasonable level. Secondly, the foreign trade surplus helps to restore the balance between production and demand, but this is not without posing problems with the United States and Europe in bilateral discussions of the reduction of Chinese trade surpluses. As a corollary, social tensions are rising in the rural milieu and among migrants who do not have the same social rights as urban dwellers do. Finally, the ecological limits of Chinese growth, thought to be far away on the horizon, have become pressing owing to rising raw material prices which have triggered an inflationary process, contrasting with the prior deflationary trend—not forgetting the environmental and urban planning problems pointed up by preparation for the 2008 Olympic Games.

There is another limitation that could appear on a much closer horizon, which has to do with the organization of the Chinese financial system. The authorities have started to reabsorb much of the non-performing loans made to finance risky investments. Yet we cannot bank on the resilience of the Chinese financial system, given the skyrocketing prices on the Shanghai Stock Exchange and the risks of real estate speculation. It should be remembered that the Asian countries, which had been very good pupils of industrial modernization, experienced a major crisis in 1997 due to their financial vulnerability. A similar crisis cannot be ruled out, but the authorities probably have the means to fight back quickly and effectively by mobilizing the considerable reserves of the central bank or implementing a public rescue plan for banks and financial institutions in distress.

If a major financial crisis were to occur in China, a rebound similar to the one observed in South Korea is more likely than the long stagnation and lost decade that affected Japan. Actually, the longing to consume, unmet social needs (education, health care, retirement) and the dynamism of entrepreneurs should rapidly revive a more balanced and new growth regime.

Is it a very libertarian economic model?

Not exactly, because the appearances of this economic system must not be confused with its essence. Staying on the surface of things, the Chinese economy could be considered to fit within Hayek's conception: unfettered competition would stimulate a virtuous dynamic with no conscious intervention by a government authority. It is true that competition is at the heart of this economy. On the one hand, as already noted, the provinces, cities and counties are rivals as regards the development of production capacities and the ability to attract foreign investment. On the other, the Chinese market is so promising that all multinational firms want to break in. The conjunction of these two strategies, public and private, only serves to fuel a permanent trend towards overcapacity that constantly relaunches the competitive process. Company product margins are relatively slim or eroding, as they are for multinationals. In the automobile sector for instance, profit margins, which were originally comfortable, have diminished considerably despite the strong growth in demand, because production capacities have grown even faster.

The primacy of competition does not contradict the mixed nature of the Chinese economy because at the macroeconomic level, through monetary and fiscal policy, and locally via the web of Communist Party networks, the political authorities maintain a capacity to influence the trajectory of the Chinese economy. This capacity for control may dwindle in time, with for instance a systemic crisis resulting from the gradual erosion of the tools for public intervention, under the effect *inter alia* of the affirmation of the liberal ideology embodied in new generations.

We might have expected to see fragmentation occur, with regions protecting themselves by taxes or some other means, whereas there is actually a unified market...

This danger is often mentioned by China specialists. It should probably be qualified. First of all, competition between regions and Beijing's attempt to maintain control are at the heart of both political and economic evolution in China. Next, and above all, authorities in Beijing over the centuries have managed to develop a whole series of methods to thwart any tendency towards a breakup of the country's unity. In the contemporary period, large transfers have been made to foster the takeoff of peripheral regions. Lastly, a transport infrastructure policy is aiming to unify the Chinese economic space.

What about the role of the law to codify and regulate conflicts over power, property, etc.?

Traditionally, in communist societies the law is an arm of political power. Individuals are formally granted rights, but in practice have little means of obtaining their enforcement. With economic liberalization and opening, property rights and corporate law have been strengthened. In contrast, individual rights remained embryonic and are far from being unified, since two statuses continue to coexist: that of rural dwellers whose right to own property is limited and that of urban dwellers who enjoy much broader property rights. Last, intellectual property law is very likely to develop in the coming years as it is a major stake in the plan to strengthen innovation as a vehicle for China's future growth.

What is the situation in India?

In studies of emerging countries, India is often likened to China—an entirely debatable assumption, because there are major differences between the two. First, the legacy of British colonization gave India relatively stable democratic political institutions with the development of a market economy. Secondly, if the Chinese accumulation system is based on a quest for returns on scale via mass production, India's economic dynamics are the result of a conjunction of three types of regulation. In the peasant milieu, an *Ancien Régime* form of regulation prevails, in which the main goal is to survive in the face of more or less favourable climate conditions, especially the monsoon; this logic rules over most people's lives. At another extreme, the region of Bangalore provides an example of successful adaptation to the knowledge-based economy in a highly internationalized environment. Between these two worlds is the manufacturing sector, dominated by oligopolies that have long been shielded from international competition. Indian macroeconomic dynamics result in the conjunction of these three rationales: therefore they do not have the clarity and vigour observed in China.

The singularity of India's trajectory however rests on two assets that are less salient in China. The first has to do with the swift gearing up of Indian multinational corporations, which attests to one of the essential features of globalization, that is, the emergence of new actors that are in competition with the United States and Europe. The second highlights the complementarity of India's and China's respective specializations: corporate technology services for one, the production of facilities and consumer goods related to ICT (information and communication technology) for the other.

What was Russia lacking?

Practically all the ingredients for the country to become a "market economy" and a democracy! After a phase of economic depression and a decade of experimentation during which the state's power declined steadily, the reassertion of political authority has taken the form of interventionism in all sectors of the economy. The government assumed the right to redefine property rights at any time and in any sector. Certainly, these have been allocated via a rather obscure process, perceived as unfair by a majority of the population. Separation of the economic and political spheres and a certain degree of stability in property ownership are indeed two prerequisites for establishing a capitalist economy—China being the exception. Contrary to the assertions of several American experts, Russia is not at all in transition towards a market economy and democracy.

Russia's evolution is not unrelated to the role played by the appropriation of rents in the dynamics of its economy. If financial resources come mainly from the utilization of rents, it becomes clear why appropriation of these rents is a stake in both political and economic struggles, and entrepreneurs in the literal sense are so rare in this country. Why undertake risky investments that only produce returns in the long term when it is enough to capture a rent passing in transit through the state apparatus? In short, Russia is poles apart from China and is exploring a *sui generis* model: a sort of controlled economy, no doubt different from the one prevailing under the Soviet regime, but fitting in with the long-term trajectory. Since both new and old industrialized countries have energy and raw material needs, the rise in these rents makes this atypical model viable, and this is a direct consequence of globalization that in no way implies the convergence of organizational models, but quite the contrary.

Poland has successfully managed a top-down market reform...

The Polish transition should be seen in the light of three groups of countries. At one end, continent-sized countries (the United States, China, India and Russia), by virtue of their size, have a capacity to solve most of their problems internally and if necessary transfer the attendant costs to other economies. Deepening internationalization fosters the strategy of externalizing any internal imbalances. On the other end, small open economies (the Netherlands, Denmark, Finland, Sweden) have always had to develop institutions and an economic specialization that enable them to integrate the world economy on a lasting and favourable basis. In the face of today's globalization, these countries can easily adapt their forms of organization to the new trends, for instance those of the knowledge-based economy. The position of medium-sized countries (Japan, France, Italy and to a lesser extent Germany) is more problematic in the face of globalization, because in the past the governments of these countries could attune the national situation to typically domestic objectives. With internationalization and financial globalization, their institutional configuration has been thrown off track and has to be reformed to fit in with the new international situation—a difficult and laborious task.

In this context, the case of Poland is an interesting one, because theoretically, the country belongs to the third group. But through a vigorous liberalization process, promoted by the successive governments, Poland finally found its own growth pattern. According to one interpretation, the countries of Central and Eastern Europe have enjoyed the benefits of opening up to the European and world markets. Another interpretation emphasizes how much the strategy of European Union accession facilitated the resynchronization of most economic and political institutions. The extreme uncertainty involved in structural adjustment was thus reduced, European procedures having helped to attenuate domestic conflicts before the country even benefited from the *acquis communautaire* and financial transfers provided by the European treaties. The European Union has been a remarkable vehicle for adapting to modernity and democracy. Besides, compared with the ups and downs of the Russian trajectory, the process has been to a large extent transparent. Europe should be proud of these achievements, but it is too modest and has proven incapable of protecting its model of organization as well as its model for multilateral resolution of international conflicts.

Is there an alternative model to the Washington consensus?

I have already pointed out the emergence of an implicit Beijing consensus. But it is probably in the Latin American countries that the most significant turnaround can be noted. This is not surprising since they were in the vanguard of the liberal counterrevolution, following the example of Chile. The excesses and social imbalances thus created therefore had to be corrected. With the spread of the "fair growth" ("*crecimiento con equidad*") leitmotif in Latin America, the government of Luiz Inacio Lula in Brazil and the presidencies of Nestor and then Cristina Kirchner in Argentina seem to be ushering in a new strategy to combat poverty and apply less inegalitarian social policies in order to encourage development. These policies will have to be innovative because it is impossible to import the social-democratic model and institutionalize very protective and universalistic labour laws in countries where informal labour can account for up to 70% of total employment. Other roads absolutely must be found. One example is the institution of subsidies for families so that they send their children to school, as Brazil has done. In Argentina, the informal sector has reached such a level that specific family benefits had to be created for the poorest households, because social security coverage was no longer available except to a very small minority of wage earners.

These policies concur with the recommendations made by Armatya Sen who claims that it is possible to conduct social policies that guarantee access to basic goods for the most disadvantaged populations while stimulating development. Economic and financial liberalization was devastating for many former forms of solidarity. Now corrective reforms must be undertaken to make viable societies that have become highly inegalitarian. Such is the challenge facing most Latin American countries, including Argentina—formerly reputed to be a typical middle class country.

Thus commences a new era in which international organizations such as the IMF and World Bank are no longer the only instigators of intellectual frameworks that govern development. The Indians, the Chinese and the Latin Americans are all in the process of devising strategies adapted to their own context, and national experiments are multiplying. A clear alternative to the Washington consensus may not yet have taken shape, but unilateralism in development is a thing of the past, and a much more open conception is gradually taking hold in a context of multilateral international relations.

Interview conducted by Christophe Jaffrelot and Jérôme Sgard

PART 2

EMERGING POWERS: A ONE-SIZE-FITS-ALL CATEGORY?

Emerging Countries:
An Attempt at Typology

Jean Coussy

The adjective "emerging" is affixed to a number of nouns. There are "emerging markets", "emerging countries", "emerging economies", etc. These expressions all refer to new, naturally interrelated contemporary elements that can reinforce or hamper one another. They are used by actors having diverging interests and antithetical values. Traditionally, a dividing line opposes those who mainly study the evolution of markets and those whose research primarily explores the evolution of power. In discussions today, a clear opposition in values can thus be noted between those who, like Alice H. Amsden (2001), explain the historic success of Asian economies by state intervention and protectionism, and those who insist on the consequences of the internationalization of the economy and free movement of capital and on what emerging financial markets may produce.

In this chapter, emerging countries are those displaying three characteristics. Emerging countries first of all are latecomers to development, as defined by Gershenkron (1962), Murakami (1996), Amsden (2001), etc. Secondly, they can attain very high growth rates (of about 10%). Emerging countries are, thirdly, countries whose growth challenges, even threatens, the economic situation of developed countries.

In 2003, the Goldman Sachs Group showed that GNP in four countries it called the BRICs (Brazil, Russia, India and China), which represented less than 15% of the entire GNP of the G6 countries, would surpass it in 2050. This forecast, which emphasized the weight of demographic growth in catching up, confirmed the fears developed countries had about the growth of emerging economies. The authors of the Goldman Sachs study did not, however, see in their findings any reason to apprehend—much less to criticize—the cruising speed at which emerging countries were growing.

Asian Tigers and Dragons: comparative advantages and improved financial regulation

South Korea, Hong Kong, Singapore and Taiwan, once referred to as "newly industrialized countries" or Dragons, were the first four emerging countries. Their development strategy, combining industrial policy and export promotion, was effective enough for them to become developed countries. These four countries drew inspiration from the Japanese example. Far from relying on internal dynamics and respecting the social gains (and liberalism) of developed countries, these emergences grew out of a will to challenge the international balance of power by enlisting state support. This model was taken up somewhat later by four Southeast Asian countries (Indonesia, Malaysia, the Philippines and Thailand), known as the Tigers, and to some extent influenced China and later India.

Their aim was to become part of the world economy without adhering to the rationale of comparative advantage that supposedly regulated it. The small Asian countries built new comparative advantages by protecting their infant industries (all the latecomers to development acted more or less in the same fashion) and developed an export subsidy policy. Moreover, these countries were able to take advantage of external assistance to undertake agrarian reforms that are partly responsible for the takeoff of South Korea and Taiwan. They have managed to integrate the world economy by relying on state support, developing a regulated banking system and strengthening social cohesion but without conforming to the social norms of the welfare state, at least in the first phase of their development.

This emergence raised a challenge for developed countries: a rise in imports and threats to their industries, sometimes leading to the gradual abandonment of entire industrial sectors (particularly steelmaking), a race for competitiveness, loss of jobs, threats to social compromises, gradual dismantling of the welfare state, all processes on which liberal experts generally place little emphasis. For this reason, the relations between small Asian countries and the international financial institutions quickly became complex.

As regards trade policy, the Asian countries did not respect the norm of comparative advantages taught by the World Bank and the OECD. They were sometimes criticized for this until the World Bank acknowledged the achievements of such a policy and qualified it as "respect for anticipated comparative advantages" (Balassa). As regards credit, the international financial institutions denounced the dangers of a regulated system and highlighted the considerable risk of corruption.

They did not accept that crony capitalism may have been necessary in order for the Asian countries to take off. The OECD even obliged South Korea to liberalize its credit market, and to do so by breaking into the international capital markets, which led to a liberalization of capital flows, one of the factors that triggered the East Asian monetary crisis in the late 1990s.

The Sino-Indian trajectory for pulling out of underdevelopment

China was not the first country to emerge but it has become the largest, the most influential and the most emblematic of emerging countries. It typifies countries that have emerged by breaking the vicious circles of underdevelopment and challenging the longstanding positions of developed countries. Twenty-five years ago, the country was in fact locked into three vicious circles: between population growth and low per capita income, between small GNP and weak capital formation, and, lastly, between disarticulation of the economy and low level of overall productivity.

Today, on the contrary, forecasts regarding China's future (particularly those made by Goldman-Sachs) view demographic dynamism as a primary growth factor (which, depending on the forecast, is expected to fuel growth in the country for the next four decades, even more in the case of India). China, where the age pyramid is imbalanced because of the single child rule, is nevertheless experiencing population problems in its rural areas. The current gross capital formation rate (40% of the GNP) is another important growth factor. The very high level of investment, however, may jeopardize its effectiveness and the rise in productivity is still debatable.

China's capacity to challenge the achievements of developed countries arises first of all from its very size, its territorial and linguistic unity and the concentration of political power in a few hands. This is a far cry from the "dependentist" theories holding forth about the inevitable reproduction of international economic and political inequalities. Secondly, China has implemented a voluntaristic development model (investment rate, driving role of the state, purposely low salaries and deliberately low consumption rate). This development was accelerated by the mobilization of long unutilized resources (the jobless population, income from Chinese abroad, undeveloped areas, etc.). It is based on industry that imports a large share of its inputs and exports its output. It is on the offensive abroad (searching for trade surpluses, conquering markets and raw material supplies). There is a whiff of mercantilism in its quest for monetary holdings and in its determination to use its economic relations for purposes of political and military power (including use of financial investments in developed countries and political and sometimes military intervention in countries to secure supply of strategic products). Chinese development is viewed as aggressive when it systematically focuses on markets that are already occupied by foreign countries; it is considered brutal when it does not accompany its offensives with forms of compensation (for development, the environment, the fight against poverty, etc.).

This emergence has shaken up the world economy. Developed countries have seen their relative weight diminish, they have recorded considerable job losses and have seen their industrial or service sectors disappear to the benefit of emerging countries. They have sometimes had to give up well-established social norms and are sometimes tempted not to respect international norms. Protectionism is finding newfound legitimacy today because of threats against capital assets and the multiplication of company buyouts in developed countries by emerging countries. The slow return to protectionism against Chinese products is explained by the fact that transnational companies have been able to anticipate and even sometimes provoke the emergence of Chinese exports (Michalet), upstream through direct investment and technological support and downstream through imports of goods.

India has long been considered as the other typical case of a country caught up in vicious circles of underdevelopment. Growth in particular was thwarted by demographic, geographic and social imbalances. Poverty stemmed from high population growth: rural depopulation was fairly low in relative terms (the result being aggravated pressure on land) but too high in absolute value to be absorbed by the cities.

Until the early 1990s, India maintained limited relations with the outside world. The country borrowed from the Soviet strategy of planned development and was wary of capitalist imperialism. Institutionally, this era enabled the "meta-institutions" of democracy, the rule of law, press freedom and a civil service to be introduced in India, which helped to save the country from the crises that some other developing countries went through (Rodrik and Subramanian 2004).

Domestically, growth prevented sudden changes and drastic decisions, thanks to democratic procedures (out of a fear of conflict) and to a capacity for resistance—not always very democratic—on the part of economic, political and regional actors. Major economic innovations, for instance the Green Revolution, have always been the object of debate, the land tenure system has undergone few modifications, the caste system has continued to function even as it has changed (Jaffrelot 2005). India has not undertaken to regulate the rural-urban drift, which would have allowed it to reduce pressure on the land, or to regulate urban growth in order to avoid overpopulation of poor neighbourhoods and megalopoles. In what was sometimes an abuse of democracy, India's states maintained their prerogatives, even if this came at considerable cost (and still does today), and discouraged foreign investors who were concerned about the plurality of public decision-makers. All these distinctive traits of the Indian economy, still present in emergent India today, have led to relative stagnation with respect to other Asian countries.

Starting in 1991, India chose to open up its trade, appeal to foreign direct investment, and resort to financial capital incentives for Indians living abroad to repatriate their savings. It accepted the "reform" suggested by the various international institutions and Western countries. Today, the country has a growth rate that nearly matches China's, and it constitutes the second largest emerging power in the world. The China-India comparison has become a central theme of many studies on emergence (G. Etienne 2007).

Such studies explore the different effects of China's and India's emergence trajectories on third countries. The impact of population growth in India (later and lower than China's) could become greater than in China. China intentionally planned the single child policy, and India currently has a window of demographic opportunity: the ratio of under 14 and over 65 to the total population is at its lowest, which favours economic takeoff. India's macroeconomic strategy is not as harsh as China's (the national savings rate represents 24.8% of the GNP, compared to 47.9% in China) and is less aggressive from a trade standpoint (in India the total current balance is 0.6% of GNP, compared to 2.9% in China) but also less open to foreign direct investment (total FDI is less than one-tenth of the Chinese total).

Developed countries feel less threatened by India's specialization in services than by China's in industry. Moreover, in recent years Indian industrial groups, Tata being a perfect symbol, have developed internationally on a large scale through corporate mergers and acquisitions even in Western countries. In the long run, the country should represent a major challenge for developed countries: the size of the working population should in fact grow by 180 million by 2020, whereas China's should drop by 10 million and the growth rate of India's GNP should exceed China's after 2015.

The oligopolistic strategies of oil and mineral-rich countries

Oil and mineral-rich countries are for the most part rentier economies, often affected by the "resource curse", corruption and capital flight. Some observers have moreover contrasted small emerging Asian countries and states with natural resources (Chaponnière 1985, Judet 1993). However, certain oil-producing countries and those with other raw materials (particularly mineral ores) have gradually been classified among emerging countries. For instance, Russia is named as part of the BRICs by the famous Goldman Sachs report (Wilson and Purushothaman 2003).

Growth spawned by raw materials has created a whole different dynamic from that which is characteristic of emerging countries where labour costs are low. Raw material producing countries drive world prices up instead of lowering them. In this way, they do not intensify competition but reduce it. Emerging countries thus become responsible for both the rise in energy costs and the fall in labour costs. As for developed countries, they must simultaneously face a rise in the cost of their energy imports and a drop in prices of their industrial exports.

The price of raw materials also weighs on emerging countries' relations among themselves, as their interests sometimes diverge. The rise in demand on international markets gives countries that have raw material deposits the hope of getting out of the vicious circles of underdevelopment and guarantees them diplomatic influence.

Rentier countries have learned from emerging countries and now copy their strategy for international expansion; the countries of the Middle East and Russia are developing financial and real estate investment in developed countries at a faster pace and take part in corporate mergers and acquisitions.

In Africa: economic or diplomatic emergence?

The "emerging country" label has now spread to all continents, including Africa. The expression is in vogue and is used by some countries to attract capital and political support and mobilize economic actors. Several African countries are indeed showing signs of economic emergence as they have begun to instrumentalize emerging country coalitions in the diplomatic sphere.

South Africa has long displayed certain characteristics that are attributed to emerging countries: competitiveness, capital accumulation, control of its development, undisputed progress beyond a rentier economy, spillover effects (as well as domination) on the other African economies, the existence of an institutionalized financial market, the capacity for negotiation with developed countries, etc. This emergence has not prevented large pockets of poverty from persisting inside the country. The South African economy has not experienced a takeoff similar to those in the emerging countries of Asia or Latin America, but it has real economic power from which it derives diplomatic power, which will be examined further on.

In the 1990s and 2000s, the growth rates of African countries revealed the existence of a growing but limited number of countries (Botswana, Uganda, Ghana, etc.) that had embarked on a strong growth pattern respecting the norms of financial management defined by international financial institutions. These states have acquired a financial credibility that they had heretofore been lacking, even if, since 2004, the rise in growth rates, over 6%, comes primarily from oil-producing countries (OECD 2006).

The rise in exports to Asia has also become a decisive factor in the growth of African countries, which is likely to foster a return to the rationale of rentier economies. It is also known that China accompanies its ever-increasing purchases in Africa with aid packages granted on criteria that are sometimes poles apart from those of the international financial institutions (Sudan, Angola, countries along the Gulf of Guinea, Zimbabwe, etc.). Of course it cannot be ruled out that part of the volume of exports and aid will eventually be committed to productive investment, as happened in Asian countries as a consequence of Chinese demand.

The liberalization of international trade has produced more calls for projects for competitive commercial activities: new crops (flowers, for example) or industrial products (textiles). Although the former have sometimes succeeded, the textile industry did not survive liberalization. In Northern Africa (Tunisia, Morocco) and in South Africa, competitive companies were founded and then had to close because of Asian competition.

In Africa, at least four major phenomena are affecting financial markets. First of all, banking and financial institutions are draining an increasingly abundant slice of local savings. Remittances sent by migrants are on the rise. "Africa is in the process of becoming the new frontier for emerging market investors... flows of investment into the entire continent are gathering pace, to countries like Kenya, Ghana and Botswana" (Santiso 2007). Lastly, capital exports from certain African countries are growing, a phenomenon sometimes considered to be a symptom of Africa's takeoff. It should not be forgotten, however, that these capital flows are not recent in Africa and that such exports contribute to the low level of investment on the continent.

South Africa is recognized as an emerging country by all diplomatic bodies and has—or assumes—real representational power for the entire African continent, which until recent years instead attempted, emphasizing its difficulties, to exercise over developed countries what has been called "the soft power of poverty".

South Africa has a leading role in African bodies (SACU, SADC, NEPAD) that has been confirmed by its recognition by the G8 and European institutions and rumours about Africa being granted a permanent seat on the UN Security Council. The country's diplomatic fate is thereby tied to that of the coalition of emerging countries in international bodies, in whose name it claims to speak.

South Africa has also turned out to be an excellent interpreter of the complexity and multiculturalism of emerging countries, as well as an advocate of alliances between emerging countries and the poorest countries remaining in Africa. As it is itself characterized by the coexistence of two worlds within its own borders, its discourse reflects a dualism that is often neglected by other countries.

Lastly, South Africa is striving to be an example and a necessary instrument, although often forgotten, for any emerging country coalition. In many emerging countries there is a real plurality of cultures that is sometimes at the root of tension. Pretoria's multicultural discourse is on the other hand well received in international organizations and has always had a place of honour in calls for unity among the three formerly colonized continents. In official South African discourse the opportunity is never missed to recall the common history and age-old relations between Africa and India (sometimes presented in peace-oriented reinterpretations).

Different modes of international integration

The diversity of emerging country trajectories suggests a typology of these countries according to their modes of integration into the international political economy. These determine their relations with countries that were forerunners of development, as well as their mutual relations. The structural similarities between emerging countries foreshadow possible economic coalitions and other diplomatic alliances but also probable antagonisms and risks of rivalry. Dissimilarities can create divergent interests containing the seeds of conflict over how the fruits of common growth are to be shared.

Countries that export labour-intensive products have taken the most spectacular trajectory, the one most likely to modify the international economic and political order. It is the most characteristic measure in the current phase of globalization. In developed countries it has lowered prices, slowed inflation, exerted pressure on wages, threatened jobs, etc. Emerging countries placed in competition by countries with low wages are also undergoing this process: China's entry into the WTO was a shock for the textile industries in the small emerging countries of the North and South of Africa which had hoped to take advantage of the liberalization of international trade.

Countries exporting on competitive markets create a race to competitiveness among emerging countries. Countries that are better endowed with natural resources, low wages or technical progress (as in the case of African agricultural exports competing with Asian exports) can win this game. But subsidies and state protection can also make them competitive. Such measures have also been practiced by small Asian countries in both agriculture and industry.

Countries selling in monopoly or oligopoly markets can raise the prices of their exports at the expense of consumer countries. Oil exporting countries have managed to increase their power in the oil oligopoly by which they felt exploited up until 1973. After this date, they increased their revenue, but many have become rentier economies with revenue that does not derive from production activities. They were unable to diversify, or in some cases even to create states. All were threatened with regression due to what has been called the resource curse. Today, after considerable price fluctuation, the decisive rise in payments to producer countries has given them financing capacities that have spawned new emergences (and reemergence in the case of Russia), with investment enabling them to diversify production, strengthen states and finance international, economic and political alliances. All oil economies are no longer only rentier economies.

Importing emerging countries represent a growing proportion of world demand, particularly through their purchases from other emerging countries. The increase in South-South trade has been evidenced by the annual UNCTAD reports. Complementarities have arisen between African countries that produce raw materials and Latin American agricultural countries and industrial Asian countries. Sometimes complementarities are regional, for instance around China (less frequently around India). They can create a vertical division of labour between the upstream and downstream phases of the productive process (a recent World Bank report on relations between Africa and Asia used the timber industry to illustrate the model of Afro-Asian affiliates). It is however obvious that all these complementarities, whether existing or potential, lead to conflicts between emerging countries over terms of exchange, specializations with a promising future and technology transfer.

Foreign direct investment in emerging countries encounters principled refusal less often now than in the past. There is even competition among emerging countries to attract private investors. These, on the other hand, are hampered—to different degrees depending on the country—by increased national savings, the unalienable character of certain property rights (especially land tenure), administrative and regional resistance, and multinational corporations whose contribution is more in markets, services and technologies than in investment. Short-term capital inflows from the 1980s until the 2000s led to multiple financial and monetary crises on different scales depending on the continent. The appearance of emerging financial markets did not do much to erase the traces of these different experiences. The Asian countries reacted to their crisis of 1997 by putting their credit in order; Latin America learned to regulate its macroeconomic imbalances without depending on international financial institutions.

Capital exports from emerging countries are high (this is what is called the "original sin" of the emerging economies). Their effects have been diversified as allocations have changed: real estate investments by elites and the traditional portfolio investments have been replaced by corporate mergers and acquisitions, increasing Western apprehensions about emerging countries.

The growth of monetary holdings, lastly, has enabled China to become the main partner of the United States in world financial regulation: in increasing its trade surplus, the accumulation of dollar denominated monetary reserves which are not productive, China has been able to avoid a revaluation of the renminbi, which remains competitive, thereby contributing to the increase in the United States debt. Beijing has become the arbiter of the evolution of the dollar and the financial situation of the United States. A single emerging country has attained the ultimate achievement of upsetting power relations.

The different emerging countries currently experiencing the crisis

The world economy today is threatened by the conjunction of three crises (fuel, food, financial) creating a risk of stagflation. The local structure of each country has determined its experience of the crisis and the repercussions. China, for instance, has been able to import the fuel and meat that it demands, thanks to its increasing purchasing power. By doing so, China has accelerated the rise in the cost of fuel and food in the rest of the world.

Petroleum-producing countries (Russia and the Middle East) have used the considerable increase in their incomes to offset the price of food and increase their foreign investments. In the short term, they have slowed the banking and financial crisis of developed countries. However, in the long term, this also threatens the sovereignty of developed countries, particularly through the control of sovereign funds.

In India, there is a risk of the crisis aggravating urban poverty through the consequent hike in the cost of necessities. There is also a malign effect on rural poverty, a paradox that can be observed in unbalanced economies. Agricultural producers can find themselves even more isolated from their markets, a situation that can threaten internal political equilibrium, particularly when elections are looming.

A few African countries with petroleum and mining industries have seen their incomes rise thanks to global demand and international investments (most notably from Asia). Nevertheless, food shortages in the cities – aggravated by the international crisis – have failed to benefit local agricultural producers. Despite experiencing a period of positive economic growth, the absence of political regulation and the failure to distribute supplies have caused hunger riots and urban violence.

Paradoxically, in Latin America, the crisis has had the effect of accelerating emerging countries' development. Some countries have disclosed the discovery of petroleum resources or affirmed their intention to mobilize their resources economically and politically. Furthermore, Brazil's success in the production of biofuels has established it as predominant within BRIC.

Bibliography ·

Amsden, A. H. (2001). *The Rise of "the Rest," Challenges to the West from Late-Industrializing Economies.* Oxford: Oxford University Press.

Boillot, J.-J. (2006). *L'économie de l'Inde.* Paris: La Découverte.

Chaponnière, J.-R. (1985). *La Puce et le riz. Croissance dans le Sud Est asiatique.* Paris: Armand Colin.

Enderwick, P. (2007). *Understanding Emerging Markets. China and India.* New York and London: Routledge.

Hochraich, D. (2007). *Pourquoi l'Inde et la Chine ne domineront pas le monde de demain.* Paris: Ellipses.

Lemoine, F. (2003). *L'économie chinoise.* Paris: La Découverte.

Murakami, Y. (1996). *An Anticlassical Political Analysis.* Stanford, CA: Stanford University Press.

Pacek, N. and D. Thornley (2007). *Emerging Markets.* London: Profile Books for The Economist.

Can We Speak of an Emerging Chinese Power?

Jean-Luc Domenach

E vents in China regularly give rise to commonplaces that are readily taken to be self-evident. In the early 20th century, China seemed to be finally subjugated. In the 1960s, it was relaunching the world revolution. Today, it appears as a power on a path of rapid emergence. What is really the case? A critical examination first reveals that this last commonplace is less mistaken than the preceding ones, although China's current progress is largely the result of its prior stagnation.

Catching up and economic progress

Even if the broad-scale revolutionary movement that pervaded in China throughout the 20th century imposed the idea that economic progress was necessary and possible, as of 1949 its communist incarnation was incapable of achieving anything but a predatory and brutal caricature. The exhausted and impoverished population, which had accumulated terrible destitution over three decades, was aware that capitalist countries were progressing in their own right. So when a credible alternative was offered by an equally credible man, Deng Xiaoping, immense hope sprung forth. This alternative was officially summarized in a programme known as the "four modernizations" (industry, agriculture, science and defence). It was actually a policy that gave priority to economic progress, whose methods gradually became clear: relaxation of collective constraints, reinstatement of profit and opening up to foreign countries.

Popular confidence was primarily what drove the economic development that followed: an average annual GDP growth of 9% since 1979. The population settled down to work. But this development was for a long time merely catching up: modernization of agriculture and industry, urban development, overhaul of the educational system and social infrastructures. In this first phase, China essentially settled for coming into the world, increasing its number of friends and developing its trade and scientific exchanges. The influences unleashed by this opening-up, however, contributed to the divisions between reformists and conservatives that were to bring about the democratic explosion of the spring of 1989.

figure 16: **China's participation in the main Asian regional organizations, 2008**

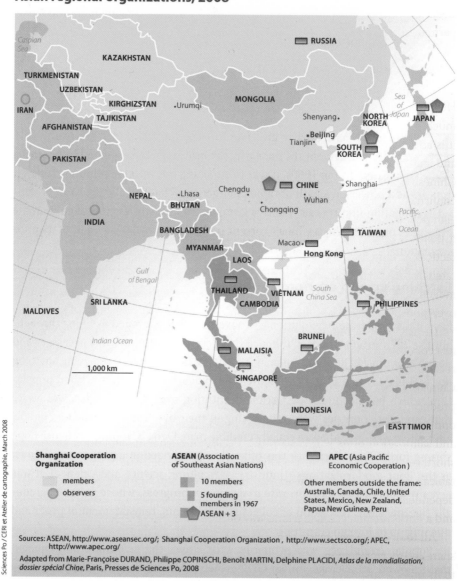

Sciences Po / CERI et Atelier de cartographie, March 2008

Sources: ASEAN, http://www.aseansec.org/; Shanghai Cooperation Organization, http://www.sectsco.org/; APEC, http://www.apec.org/

Adapted from Marie-Françoise DURAND, Philippe COPINSCHI, Benoît MARTIN, Delphine PLACIDI, *Atlas de la mondialisation, dossier spécial Chine*, Paris, Presses de Sciences Po, 2008

Post-Maoist China then entered a new phase. Furious at the boycott capitalist countries declared against the country in the aftermath of the Tiananmen massacre, Chinese leaders gradually devised a new policy. It involved intensifying the shift towards state-supervised capitalism and an economic strategy based on foreign trade, but in order to make China emerge as both an economic and a political power. It is noteworthy that in 2003 China officially endorsed the concept of "peaceful emergence" and discarded this notion the following year, partly owing to displeasure among nationalists who did not want their hands tied with respect to Taiwan. In fact, today, Beijing no longer hesitates to emphasize the weight of its economy, which has become the third largest in the world, and to wield its influence in major world issues—for instance by denying India and Japan permanent membership of the UN Security Council.

An exaggerated 'yearning for China'

However real China's achievements may be, they prompt undue praise that is much more emphatic than what greeted Japan's emergence in the 1960s. In fact, it is as if there was a sort of "yearning for China" in world society. Exaggeration and ignorance have always made fine bedfellows, and the imperial practices of the Chinese leadership make an impression on the world: these two explanations are confirmed by the behaviour of many heads of state visiting Beijing. Chinese foreign policy has also proved capable of fostering economic growth and then giving it political weight by striking a remarkable balance between the evolution of its tactical machinery and its diplomatic discourse. Its action has also been facilitated by the very widely shared view that only an ancient empire like China, which indeed now appears as a new power, might one day legitimately compete with an over-powerful America whose reputation George Bush has compromised.

Clearly, world opinion exaggerates the emergence of China. In the first place, its economic growth, based on foreign trade and chronic overinvestment, is both risky and costly in terms of raw materials as well as natural resources. Admirers of Chinese growth often forget that it depends massively on the huge trade surplus produced by exports to the American market. They also forget that China's development is based on an unprecedented environmental catastrophe: desertification and salinization of its soil, devastating floods and droughts, pollution and water shortages, acid rain, lung diseases—nothing has been left out of this catastrophic tableau. China should orient itself towards a less rapid growth path that is less dependent on cheap exports and more qualitative, based on productivity gains and a domestic market. It is a long way off.

All told, China has made enormous progress, but it has not yet recovered the share in the world economy that it had in the 18th century or one proportionate to its population, about 20% of the world's total. Although it is true that its coastal areas boast an increasingly internationalized and competitive avant-garde, three-quarters of the country remains more or less underdeveloped, and the per capita GDP (in purchasing power parity) does not exceed $7,500 per year. China has certainly developed, but it remains far from being a modern economic and social power.

Moreover, it will be difficult to "upscale" its economy because, first of all, the country does not have a business culture and must fashion one from scratch. Its companies today largely live off the orders made, protection provided and exemptions granted by the Chinese party-state. Many of them have trouble distinguishing

figure 17: **Per capita GDP and main Chinese population centres, 2005**

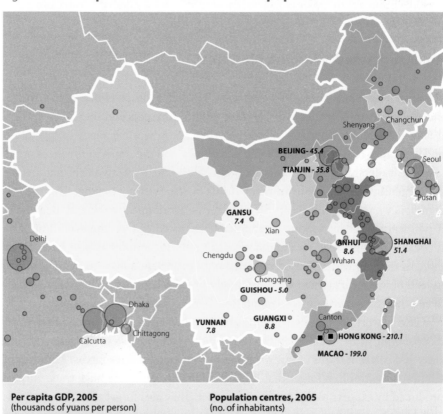

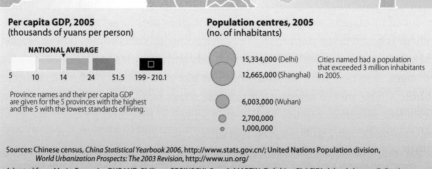

Per capita GDP, 2005
(thousands of yuans per person)

NATIONAL AVERAGE

5 10 14 24 51.5 199 - 210.1

Province names and their per capita GDP are given for the 5 provinces with the highest and the 5 with the lowest standards of living.

Population centres, 2005
(no. of inhabitants)

15,334,000 (Delhi)
12,665,000 (Shanghai)

Cities named had a population that exceeded 3 million inhabitants in 2005.

6,003,000 (Wuhan)

2,700,000
1,000,000

Sources: Chinese census, *China Statistical Yearbook 2006*, http://www.stats.gov.cn/; United Nations Population division, *World Urbanization Prospects: The 2003 Revision*, http://www.un.org/

Adapted from Marie-Françoise DURAND, Philippe COPINSCHI, Benoît MARTIN, Delphine PLACIDI, *Atlas de la mondialisation, dossier spécial Chine*, Paris, Presses de Sciences Po, 2008

Sciences Po / CERI et Atelier de cartographie, March 2008

between predation and production, exploitation and profit, schemes and opportunity assessment. Their international culture is weak, which exposes them to frequent mishaps. In addition, despite real progress, Beijing does not have the intellectual and scientific elite of a country like India even if the number of post-graduate students has been increasing since 2000. To achieve that, it would need to invest financially and politically in research over the long term. The Chinese leadership is reluctant to do this because it remains communist—refusing to give intelligence an entirely free rein—and because it has also become capitalist and is therefore primarily interested in rapid gains that counterfeiting and industrial espionage seem surer ways to achieve. Furthermore, contrary to the leaders' claims, they are unable to recover more than a slim proportion of their US-trained researchers, and not the best ones either.

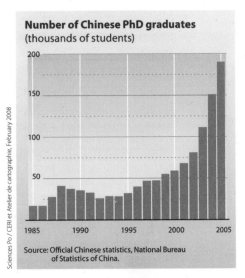

figure 18: **Chinese graduate students, 1985-2005**

Number of Chinese PhD graduates (thousands of students)

Source: Official Chinese statistics, National Bureau of Statistics of China.

Sciences Po / CERI et Atelier de cartographie, February 2008

The Chinese army reflects another aspect of the situation. China has nuclear weapons and certain missiles capable of reaching North America or destroying a satellite. Moreover, it has downsized its army and modernized its navy, aviation corps and certain elite corps, including electronic defence and attack—but it still remains very scarred by its political, peasant and bureaucratic past. No one knows how it would behave in combat.

In short, to understand where the country really stands, it is essential to gain a grasp on three things: that China has the wherewithal to reach the level of Western powers, that it has still not achieved this, and, lastly, that it is exhausting itself today in a still insufficient attempt to catch up.

Hu Jintao's new strategy

The Chinese authorities are acutely aware of the situation. Since Hu Jintao's arrival in power in 2002, they have devised a clever strategy to salvage the situation, and this without glorifying themselves, which in itself is a new sign of lucidity. The strategy involves promoting both a technological shift in the Chinese economy and the building of a domestic market, partly through social policies. In the first place, the aim is to impose an economic slowdown to bring an end to overheating, and to terminate a strategy based exclusively on exports and the waste of natural resources.

But this attempt runs up against three huge obstacles. The first is the mute but resolute opposition of provincial and local authorities, often linked to veritable mafias, who believe wholeheartedly in pursuing the unbridled and costly growth rate of over 11% per year, from which they derive financial benefits. They have protectors at the highest level: members of the "Shanghai Group" who are allies of former President Jiang Zemin. During the 17th CCP Congress in October 2007, Hu Jintao's political line was ratified and his power reinforced at the highest level. But we still do not know to what extent, because he was forced to compromise on his successor, Xi Jinping, who comes from Shanghai. And it remains to be seen if he will want or be able to make the provincial governments' voices heard.

The second obstacle has to do with the price to pay for this new policy. For in order to ensure political stability and encourage the creation of a domestic market, the leaders have made considerable promises that boil down to producing the results of a democracy without democracy: strong public policies in social, cultural, transportation and environmental protection matters. But in depressed demographic conditions, a dwindling active population will have to pay more and more dearly for an elderly population increasing in size.

Furthermore, measures aimed at ensuring a technological shift will be extremely costly in political terms: it is clear for instance that the Chinese authorities will have to relinquish control over information, culture and their universities if they really want to revive scientific research. It is true that the human rights situation has somewhat improved—violations have become more rare and more targeted, and political prisoners probably number only a few thousand. Social rights are what pose the most substantial problems. Nevertheless, the regime remains authoritarian and its leaders will have difficulty resigning themselves to swifter detente.

That is because they fully understand the meaning of the dozens of thousands of incidents of social unrest that occur every year. These do not threaten the regime's power as long as it remains unified and its means to police the population remain intact, but they remind them of its limits. The same leaders are despised for their past excesses and their present corruption, and the population only puts up with the severe social and geographic inequalities—greater even than those in US society—engendered by the economic strategy on condition that economic growth continues. China is a country in which peasants on the outermost desert fringes and consumers in Shanghai have almost nothing in common, any more than the migrant worker from the countryside and the university-educated engineer. Nothing, except the hope that things will be better tomorrow and that everyone will be able to enjoy, as the authorities promise, "a little bit of prosperity".

Now, and this is the third obstacle, it is hard to see by what miracle the country will be able to maintain the very rapid growth rate demanded by the population. No serious observer rules out critical incidents, either in trade or finance. Inflation is looming and the Chinese stock exchanges have created a dangerous bubble. And all admit that the wage, social and environmental costs, added to the inevitable evolution towards a more qualitative growth, will force the growth rate to slow to around 5% to 7%, perhaps even less. What will happen then? No one knows. What appears certain is that in any event, while China has only just pulled off a costly catching up, the true test lies ahead, and it will be more costly still.

Uneven deployment

Currently the somewhat lopsided economic situation largely explains the very uneven deployment of China's power throughout the world. China certainly carries more weight than before, essentially through a mass effect, but it is not of much consequence in any of the three areas where power is formed. Indeed it has no financial power, military advance or "normative" power—it submits to cultural trends rather than inspiring them. Chinese leaders are perfectly aware of this and therefore demonstrate considerable envy of American power, an envy which is reflected, depending on the case, either in a discreet follow-my-leader attitude or in nationalist tensions.

This explains the peculiar situation where China universally inspires fear and admiration throughout the world, but on the whole has rather little influence, except when it focuses all its means (for instance in relations with Taiwan and Japan) or when it is subject to the concentrated attention of its international partners (as in the Darfur question).

Two spectacular examples of this state of affairs can be seen in the relations China has with the United States and East Asia. The United States, once called "imperialist" and today only "unilateral", is the object of a policy that seems intelligent only on paper. For what are the billions of dollars of Chinese trade surplus worth when they are mostly reinvested in US treasury bonds? A pressure on the American economy, certainly, but at a time when another pressure is weighing much more heavily on China's future: the intellectual and moral attraction of a civilization that represents an absolute ideal for Chinese elites.

The same goes for East Asia. The focus of American policy on antiterrorism has accentuated a phenomenon that was germinating in the Chinese-American reconciliation of the 1970s: a curbing of American activities in zones neighbouring China. At certain times, the United States produces the impression that it is conceding China a certain hegemony in the region. Yet on closer inspection, the advantages for Beijing are negligible. The growth of the Chinese economy probably tends to cast Taiwan's economy in a provincial light, but with its turbulence and its oddities, the renegade island does not seem solidly anchored in a specific historical trajectory. Moreover, recent efforts to marginalize Japan have reached their limits: Beijing has thus resigned itself to renewing courtesies. Even if it is true that China played its hand cleverly in the Korean affair, it is to the United States' advantage that a settlement of the nuclear problem seems to be on the horizon. Finally, in this region Beijing makes progress only with respect to the weak: Mongolia, which is having trouble moving on from the post-communism situation; Vietnam, not yet recovered from having been bled white in the 30 years that followed the Second World War; the ASEAN countries, which never really imagined banding together and are now flooded with Chinese trinkets; and the Central Asian members of the Shanghai Organization, which Moscow also has a close eye on, and which are influenced by perilous trends either towards Islamism or towards democracy. Also, certain small partners are giving China grief as well: North Korea, which suddenly seems to have emancipated itself to deal directly with the United States and its southern neighbour, and Burma, where the junta, grappling with social unrest, refuses to listen to its Chinese godfather's advice to use moderation and modernize. With regard to India, which knows much better what it wants, Chinese policy is infinitely more cautious, and less dazzling.

These reservations mean that the effects of the Chinese economic boom are less significant than what is often believed, but not that they are nonexistent. In certain spheres there is tangible, if not definitive progress. For instance, China, in its relations with Europe, has largely taken advantage of its leaders' naïveté and the rivalry they permit themselves. Despite Angela Merkel's and Nicolas Sarkozy's coming to power, which portend more difficult relations in the future, China has not yet exhausted all its advantages. In Africa, the offensive launched in 2004 created a sensation. In fact, it has enabled Beijing to secure new sources of oil supply and other raw materials through cooperation agreements that are at the same time political initiatives. This offensive undeniably ranks among the newest geopolitical developments in recent years, even if it has encountered a number of unexpected complications. For instance, support for the Sudanese regime, making China an accessory to atrocious abuse in Darfur, brings in oil, but also additional financial engagements and more threats to the hosting of the Olympic Games in Beijing in 2008.

To become a world power...

All told, a mixed assessment is in order. Although it is difficult to consider that China has become a real world superpower, it must be acknowledged that for the first time in its modern history it is in a position to hope to become one. Its leaders are currently pondering the transition and in their wake the Chinese media are solemnly meditating on the rise and fall of great powers. But this highly uncertain transition will depend on two major conditions, one external and the other internal.

The first requirement is that there should be no complete turnaround in the international economic outlook of which Beijing has taken advantage for over 30 years. Abundant investments, distractedly generous cooperation agreements, massive imports: these advantages could be dissipated at least in part if China ceases to be a hub for labour-intensive industries and instead becomes a competitor in high technology. Similarly, should it become less trade-oriented, more political and tackle others' truly exclusive domains, the Chinese offensive in the world is likely to encounter more substantial difficulties and lead to greater costs. If China's leaders should prove tempted to force open the Taiwan question, they would risk alienating much of the capital of sympathy they have already accumulated.

But the most important condition is obviously domestic. The question of whether China deserves to become a world power has been resolved: its leaders indisputably have the calibre required to make it one. But other things are at stake here: first of all the aptitude of the CCP, including the mafiosi and bureaucrats, to line up in battle formation behind its central leaders; secondly, and especially, the capacity of the party, little liked and little respected by the people, to make them nevertheless accept the need to reduce the pace and change the nature of growth. And a final question is whether anyone can say exactly what role should China play in the world.

Bibliography ·······································

Cabestan, J.P. (2007). "La montée en puissance de la diplomatie chinoise", in Sophie Boisseau du Rocher (ed.). *Asie dix ans aprés la crise*. Paris: La documentation française: 57-80.

Domenach, J.L. (2002). *Où va la Chine?* Paris: Fayard.

—— (2008). *La Chine m'inquiète*. Paris: Perrin.

Naughton, B. (2006). *The Chinese Economy. Transitions and Growth*. Cambridge (Mass.): The MIT Press.

Pei, M. (2006). *China's Trapped Transition. The Limits of Developmental Autocracy*. Cambridge (Mass.): Harvard University Press.

Shirk, S. (2007). *China, Fragile Superpower*. Oxford: Oxford University Press.

Wo-Lap Lam, W. (2006). *Chinese Politics in the Hu Jintao Era*. Armonk (N.Y.): ME Sharpe.

India, an Emerging Power, But How Far?

Christophe Jaffrelot

Not so long ago India was still perceived as a poor country and readily acted as spokesman for the Third World in multilateral organization meetings. In 1991 it was on the verge of bankruptcy, with reserves in its coffers to cover only three weeks of imports. Today it declines international aid—even flying to the rescue of its neighbours after the 2004 tsunami—and displays many of the attributes of power. In January 2007, Goldman Sachs predicted it would be the world's third largest economy in 2025,[1] after China and the United States. In military matters, India has declared itself a nuclear power and is willing to play the role of policeman in the Indian Ocean.

This expansion has been built on the economic foundations constructed over decades, starting with the Nehru years. It differs from that of China, first because industry and exports have played only a secondary role in India's recent trajectory, and second because it does not draw only on assets that can be measured in terms of hard power, but also on an above-average power of influence and attraction by comparison with other emerging countries. However, India's breakthrough remains limited and certain obstacles stand in the way of the ongoing dynamic.

An atypical emergence in Asia

The Nehru dynasty foundation

It is very fashionable today in India to downplay the contribution of the 1950s and 1960s when the government of Jawaharlal Nehru set up a specific development

---

1   T. Poddar and E. Yi, "India's Rising Growth Potential," *Global Economics Paper* 152, 22 January 2007, p. 5.

pattern to which the present successes of the Indian economy owe much. Politically, this is the time when democracy and the rule of law took root in society; the regime was to remain more stable in India than in any other Asian country, Japan excepted. The national question was also largely solved by the implementation of an accomodating federal system that defused most of the separatist forces, except in Kashmir. Economically, in addition to very substantial industrial achievements, the land reform, though limited, and the Green Revolution implemented by Indira Gandhi, Nehru's daughter, enabled India to gain food self-sufficiency. The elite institutions initiated by Nehru—especially the Indian Institutes of Technology (IITs)—trained scientists who were to be responsible for India's performances in IT. Simultaneously, state-sponsored institutions endowed the country with remarkable engineers in the fields of nuclear and space technology.

Economic reform and capitalist underpinnings

Perfectly aware of the limitations of the statist model initiated by Nehru, Indira Gandhi and then her son, Rajiv, started to reform it in the 1980s. This policy took a more radical turn in 1991 when India had to accept IMF recommendations. The country did not adopt the export-oriented Asian pattern at the time. Certainly, the measures that were taken aimed at integrating India into the global market: customs tariffs began to drop steadily and the main obstacles to admitting foreign MNCs on its soil were gradually lifted. But that brand of liberalization did not change much in the short run. India's integration into world trade remained very tentative and foreign investors were not rushing in. The aspect of the reform that primarily accounted for acceleration of growth in India was purely domestic;

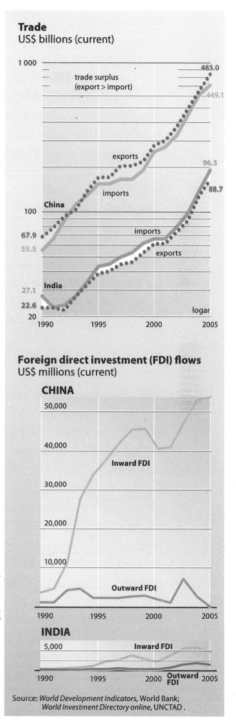

figure 19: **International trade and FDI flows from India and China, 1990-2005**

Source: *World Development Indicators*, World Bank; *World Investment Directory online*, UNCTAD.

Sciences Po / CERI et Atelier de cartographie, February 2008

the country adopted a supply-side policy which turned out to be so successful because it was also stimulated by the middle class' eagerness to consume.

In 1991 India gave up maintaining the private sector under its control via the License Raj, a bureaucratic straitjacket through which every company had to request administrative authorization to increase or diversify its production, since the Nehruvian state was supposed to ensure the optimal allocation of resources. The License Raj had already been relaxed somewhat in the 1980s, when Indian growth in fact began to accelerate; now it was entirely dismantled. This supply-side approach, which involved measures such as the lowering of corporate taxes and taxes on the higher income brackets, gave the economy a boost because India was able to rely on a very rich entrepreneurial substratum.

Unlike China, which annihilated its middle class after the revolution, India settled for closely monitoring a business community that was heir to a long capitalist history. Some families that still dominated the business world in the 1980s and 1990s—the Tatas, the Birlas and the Bajajs, for instance—had learned how to manage a company way back in the late 19th or early 20th century. Coming from merchant communities such as the Parsis and the Jains or merchant castes such as the Marwaris, they were infused with excellent business sense that they continued to cultivate by earning MBAs in the United States. In the 1980s and even more in 1991, the state thus liberated long-bridled and specifically national energies.

The new Indian middle class and the 'demographic dividend'

This economic dynamic has been primarily supported by the domestic market. The middle class is largely responsible for the increasing level of consumption, whose rise is attested by the savings rate—26% in 2005 as against 40% in China.

In India the middle class is an old concept that for decades has been associated with the role of the state in the economy, given the huge number of civil servants in the bureaucracy as well as in publicly-owned industry. Even today, a majority of the white collar workers—and of salaried people generally—are in the public sector. In the 1990s, this middle class displayed a vigorous interest in the products that the private sector began to put on the market (finally!), the dynamism of the corporate sector itself contributing to the growth of a new, market-oriented middle class through job creation and wage increases. Fifteen years after the 1991 reform, in its survey of 240 million Indian households, the National Council of Applied Economic Research (NCAER) identified four social categories, including a large middle class. 5 million of them, the elite group, earned at least 46,600 euros a year in purchasing power parity; 75 million, the middle class, earned 28,100 to 46,600 euros a year; 82 million, the labouring masses, earned 7,200 to 28,100 euros and 78 million, the poor and the destitute, less than 4,000 euros. In terms of percentage the middle class remains a minority, but in absolute terms, it represents a huge market. These figures, indeed, bear testimony to a demographic dynamism which has been another factor of India's emergence.

India's population growth was long perceived as a handicap. It remains one in rural areas where unemployment is endemic. But the youth of India's population has proven to be an undeniable advantage in recent years. Not only has the country escaped the decline in activity that accompanies the ageing of a population in any society, but the active minority has not had to bear the weight of its inactive population. India has in fact reaped the benefits of a strong "demographic dividend". This term refers to the difference between the working and the nonworking population in a given society: the population growth rate among people aged 15 to 59 is significantly higher than that of the total population since the late 1990s, the ratio of working age to dependent people having reached 62% in 2000. This ratio has fostered an accumulation of abundant savings, which has financed increasingly large investments: these grew at 6% per year in the early 2000s.

India's population mass has moreover contributed to maintaining labour costs at a much lower level than elsewhere, including China, where a growing labour shortage should lead to higher prices in the short term. Many foreign investors have thus been dissuaded from opening branches in the "world's workshop" to relocate more in India, even if the country's main attraction among foreign MNCs has to do with its consumer market, itself due to its population mass. This new situation contributes to higher growth rates in industry, which in 2006-7, for the first time since 1991, rivalled the growth rate in services, reaching up to 11% per year.

The brainpower of the 'world's office'

The emergence of India is especially atypical in Asia because it has been primarily supported by the services sector, especially back office activities for which the country has offered remarkably attractive opportunities because of the sophistication of relatively inexpensive IT engineers. The country's assets in this field can first be explained by the excellence and number of its scientists and engineers. This undoubtedly has its roots in cultural features specific to the upper caste ethos: the Brahmins—a caste of scholars and the most prestigious caste in the Hindu world—value knowledge acquired through study, not only in literary fields but also in scientific ones such as mathematics, in which India played a pioneer role. These elective affinities—to use Max Weber's terms—were fostered by the higher education policy implemented by Nehru in the 1950s, of which the IITs are still the cream of the crop; but there are other institutions, including the very prestigious Indian Institutes of Management (IIMs).

The information technology sector was the first to benefit from this brainpower in a highly favourable context. First, economic liberalization enabled new

figure 20: **Number of engineering schools in India, 1997-2007**

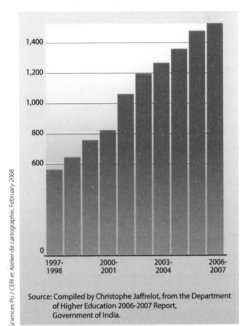

Source: Compiled by Christophe Jaffrelot, from the Department of Higher Education 2006-2007 Report, Government of India.

Sciences Po / CERI et Atelier de cartographie, February 2008

companies to be formed (Infosys was founded by a handful of engineers in 1981) and older ones to retool (Wipro went into computing at the instigation of Azim Premji). Secondly, India put computer services and software on the market at an excellent quality-price ratio that could be exported—here the external variable plays an important role—via telephone lines, the only infrastructure India is relatively well endowed with. The world would discover India's comparative advantage in computer technology on the occasion of the "year 2000 bug" when American corporations called on the talents of Indian engineers in great numbers, India's time difference enabling them to work by day when it was night over in the United States.

India also earned its reputation in the 1990s in other high added-value sectors such as pharmaceuticals, first with generic drugs developed by small companies, later to become multinationals such as Ranbaxy or Dr. Reddy, copying molecules from the major Western firms before making the needed investments in R and D to have their own licenses registered. The weight of high-tech in India's economic boom explains why the services sector has gradually gained an edge over the others, to end up accounting for over half the country's GDP with a growth rate

table 2: **The Indian Population in the United States in 2006**

		Indian community	US Population
Demographics	Total population	2,482,141	299,398,485
	% of 18-34 year-olds	33.1	23.2
Education (% of 25 years and over)	High school graduates	90.3	84.1
	Bachelor's degree	68.6	27
	Graduate and professional school	36.5	9.9
Resources	Per capita income in dollars	34,895	25,267
	% of people below poverty threshold	8.2	13.3

Source : 2006 American Community Survey, U.S. Census Bureau

of over 10% since the 1980s; services are driving India's growth, ironically making India a post-industrial economy before having been an industrial one.

Exile as a path to development

The brain drain has long been perceived in India as a dead loss. But it has also proven to be a long-term investment. Once again India's specificity derives from its very particular elite made up of highly educated upper caste individuals, who yet have no other than intellectual capital. Many of them chose emigration because of the lack of job opportunities (in southern India, due to a policy of positive discrimination towards the lower castes) and the appeal of the West, especially since US immigration policy was relaxed in 1965. Indians have also met remarkable success in North America where they numbered over 2 million in the early 2000s.

The United States Census in the year 2000 show them to be a model minority with a per capita income substantially above the national average and with exceptional education levels. Indian students moreover make up the largest contingent of foreigners on American university campuses, with a strong presence in information technology, especially in Silicon Valley. These high-achieving immigrants were to contribute to the boom of Indian firms working in this field by placing orders with them and making technology transfers—if only by returning to the country or setting up subsidiaries there.

The massive exodus of millions of Indians has also contributed to the country's boom, through the funds they send their families from abroad. The above-mentioned elites are not the only ones to make remittances, because unskilled workers who since the oil crises of the 1970s have found industrial or domestic jobs in the Middle East or elsewhere in the world also bring in considerable sums to the country. These remittances are on the rise each year, so that India is the country that since 1994 has received the most funds from its emigrants in the world,

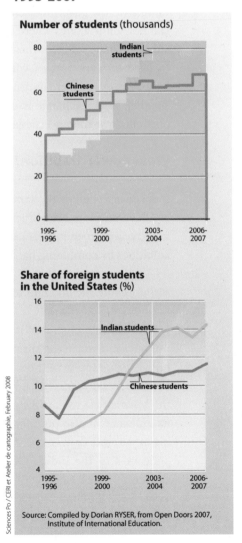

figure 21: **Indian and Chinese students in the United States, 1995-2007**

Number of students (thousands)

Share of foreign students in the United States (%)

Sciences Po / CERI et Atelier de cartographie, February 2008

Source: Compiled by Dorian RYSER, from Open Doors 2007, Institute of International Education.

and its 25 million strong diaspora has become a significant foreign investor in the country, with $27 billion of investment in 2007.

Multinationals are back

The diaspora is no longer the main source of FDI today, even though its contribution remains significant. The multinationals that Indira Gandhi had expelled in the 1960s-70s in keeping with her anti-imperialist agenda—Coca Cola and IBM had to leave India at the time—are back. After a long "wait and see" period in the 1990s, the big firms eventually admitted that post-1991 India was a country they could no longer ignore because of its expanding domestic market and its potential as a hub for manufacturing products to be exported elsewhere in Asia—all the more so as the government (drawing its inspiration from China) has created Special Economic Zones where taxes are low and labour laws more flexible. As a result, foreign direct investment, which was very low until the early 2000s, is flowing in. High-tech enterprises, which had been the first ones to set up R and D centres, have been joined by manufacturing firms, including car-makers. Furthermore, the Bombay stock exchange is experiencing an unprecedented rate of growth, and portfolio investments established new records until 2007.

What power ambition?

India does not enjoy the same recognition for its place on the international scene as China does. Its economic power is not comparable and, unlike China, it does not have a permanent seat on the UN Security Council, which triggered its power ambitions by combining hard power and soft power.

Military effort and quest for strategic partners

New Delhi demonstrated its desire to play in the major league by conducting five nuclear tests in the spring of 1998. India is developing an ambitious ballistic missile programme in the same spirit. The Agni III missile it has been developing for several years with a range of 3,000 km will give it a radius of action from the Middle East to East Asia, covering the area over which it intends to exercise its influence. It also purchased six Scorpene submarines. From Russia it is buying an aircraft carrier currently under restoration in order to assert its role of policeman in the Indian Ocean. The country's military expenditure has risen constantly since 1994, with a defence budget increasing from $12.2 billion in 1994 to $23.9 billion in 2006. India moreover plans to acquire 126 fighter planes to modernize its air capability in the coming years—one of the largest contracts of its kind ever signed.

At the same time, India indicates that it knows its limits and remains true to parts of its Third Worldist past. It has joined hands with other emerging countries in the WTO and with Brazil and South Africa in the framework of the IBSA forum, a grouping formed in 2003 in order to ostensibly gather together three major market-oriented democracies of three continents. India even projects itself as spokesperson for poor countries—a category of which it claims to be part of when that suits its purposes—by arguing, for instance, that it is not rich enough to implement environmental norms.

Besides, India continues to feel the need for strategic partnerships with bigger countries, all the more so as the country is very isolated in her own region. In the 1970s and 1980s, India strayed from its nonalignment policy and moved closer to the USSR—while remaining refractory to alliances and jealously guarding its national independence—to earn protection from a superpower whose Indian leaders to some extent shared its worldview and economic model. The same type of scenario is seen today in the Indian-American rapprochement. After the collapse of the Soviet bloc, India found itself isolated and sought to build stronger ties with the United States, whose capitalist mode of development seemed moreover better suited to Indian needs. The country thus asserted its emerging power not in the shadow of the United States—it is far too attached to its national sovereignty for that—but at least with its aid. Washington is counting on New Delhi to act as a counterweight to China and to isolate Iran, an old friend of India's against which it has voted twice in the IAEA since the beginning of the nuclear crisis. In exchange, India convinced the United States to allow Israel to sell it military equipment, such as the Phalcon radar system, under American license, and to give it access to American civilian

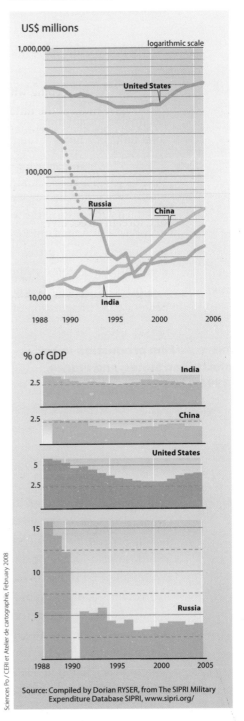

figure 22: **Military expenditure in the United States, China, Russia and India, 1998-2006**

US$ millions

logarithmic scale

1,000,000

United States

100,000

Russia

China

10,000

India

1988   1990   1995   2000   2006

% of GDP

India

2.5

China

2.5

United States

5

2.5

15

10

Russia

5

1988   1990   1995   2000   2005

Source: Compiled by Dorian RYSER, from The SIPRI Military Expenditure Database SIPRI, www.sipri.org/

Sciences Po / CERI et Atelier de cartographie, February 2008

nuclear technology, a concession that sparked opposition from the right as well as the left in India, both being anxious to preserve the national independence of the country. The exceptional treatment India enjoys in this way in this very sensitive nuclear issue is explained partly by the effectiveness of its soft power.

On the art of wielding 'soft power'

If India has a growing weight in the affairs of the world, it is not because, like China, it inspires fear, but because it exercises a power of attraction and even fascination—something the 2008 Olympic games may have given China. Its cultural influence flows through many channels. It is first of all a great civilization with which pacifist values have readily been associated since the time of Mahatma Gandhi and the granting of asylum to the Dalai Lama in 1959. But this idealized image, which had its heyday in the 1960s, has been entirely renovated since the 1980s. First, because of the world impact of its remarkably inventive literature: Salman Rushdie, Arundathi Roy, Lahiri, Mistry, Seth, and Naipaul have all snatched up Western literary prizes. Even when they no longer live in India or were not even born there, these authors speak about their country of origin with a talent that makes it familiar to the rest of the world. To make a society and its culture penetrate the imagination of others is already to exercise power over them. On a less elitist register, Bollywood produces a record number of films that finds an audience abroad—particularly in countries that host a strong Indian immigrant population. Although this brand of cinema cannot compete with products of the American majors, it exports better than the seventh art of many European countries.

The fact that India is a democracy and a constitutional state is naturally a significant resource in terms of soft power. The country exploits this vein all the more readily since the Bush administration put "regime change" in the Middle East and elsewhere on the top of its priorities in the 2000s. India makes use of this whenever the opportunity arises. For instance, it put forward its democratic qualities to justify its demand for special treatment in nuclear affairs, and the West acquiesced: if India enjoys particular goodwill even if it is not a signatory to the NPT, and if Iran on the contrary awakens great suspicion although it is, this is because one is a democracy

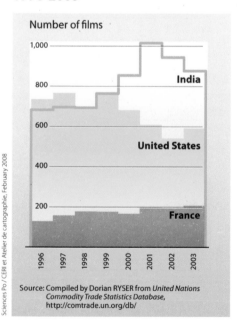

figure 23: **Film production in India, the United States, and France, 1996-2003**

Number of films

1,000

800 — India

600

United States

400

200

France

1996 1997 1998 1999 2000 2001 2002 2003

Source: Compiled by Dorian RYSER from *United Nations Commodity Trade Statistics Database,* http://comtrade.un.org/db/

Sciences Po / CERI et Atelier de cartographie, February 2008

figure 24: **American, French, and Indian film imports, 2006**

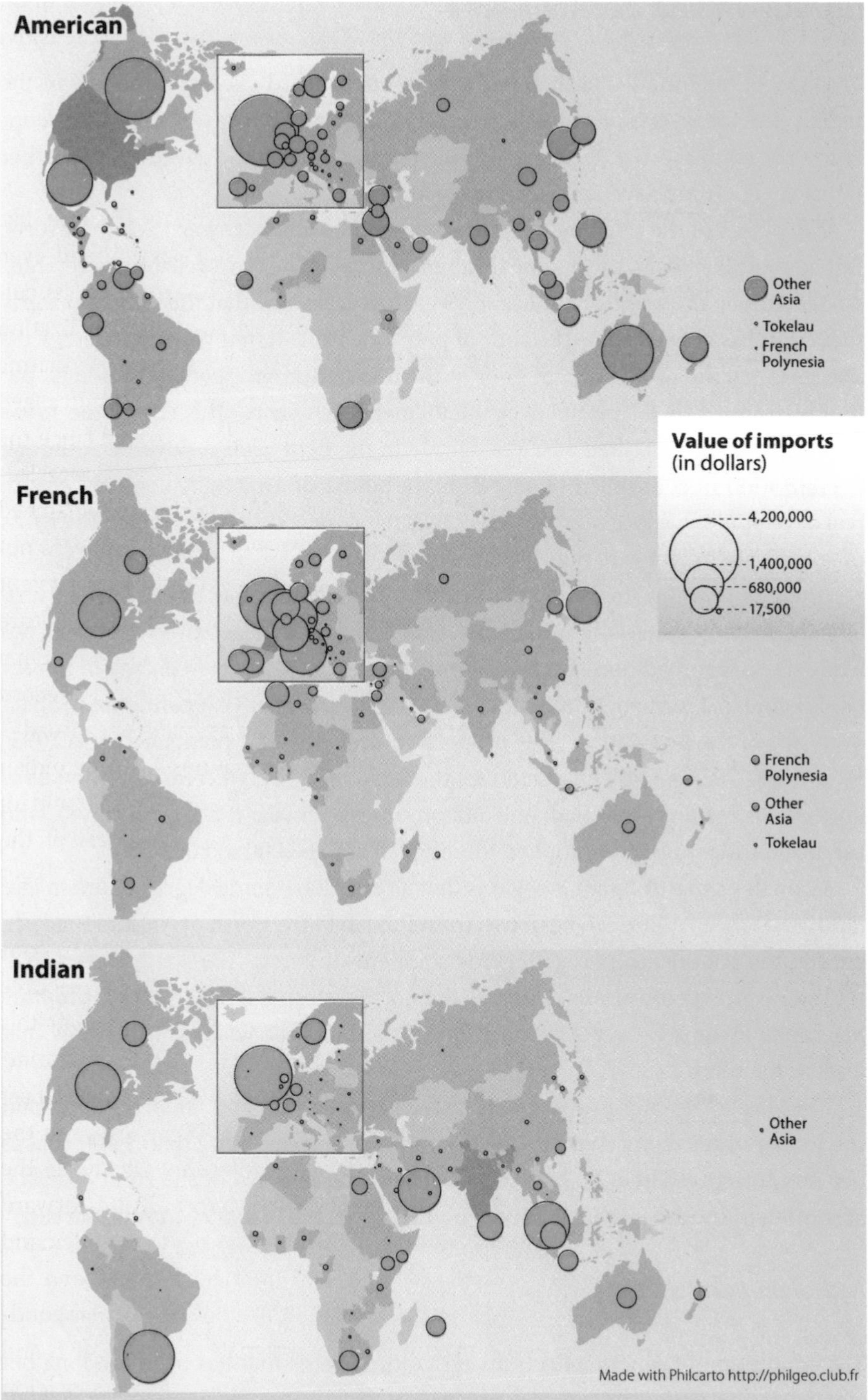

American

Other Asia
Tokelau
French Polynesia

Value of imports
(in dollars)

4,200,000
1,400,000
680,000
17,500

French

French Polynesia
Other Asia
Tokelau

Indian

Other Asia

Made with Philcarto http://philgeo.club.fr

Source: United Nations Commodity Trade Statistics Database, http://comtrade.un.org/db/

Sciences Po / CERI et Atelier de cartographie, February 2008

and the other is not.

Growth without development?

"The sky is the limit" is probably the most often heard cliché on the lips of the Indian elite today, even among the urban middle class. But several obstacles jeopardize the country's rise in power—to the point of raising the question of whether India can continue developing at such a pace.

Advocates of the ongoing liberalization see it as the best way to stem poverty. But figures taken from the National Sample Survey—the most reliable survey conducted among thousands of households each year—show that the pace of poverty reduction has slowed since the shift of policy in 1991. In ten years, between 1983 and 1993-94, the proportion of poor in the population dropped by 11 points, but it only dropped by 6.7 points over the following ten years. This is why the 1990s have often been described as a lost decade in the fight against poverty. Although liberalization may have led to several extra points of growth, it does not ensure real development, especially because it fails to create jobs in rural areas. The fruits of growth are in fact very poorly distributed.

There is nothing surprising about this: liberalization has enabled those who already owned capital—be it financial, social and or intellectual—to grow richer while those who had none (or not as much) stagnated. The percentage of households living on less than 90,000 rupees (i.e. 1,800 euros) per year continues to affect over 70% of the population. This proportion dropped by 7 points between 1995-96 and 2001-02, but still characterizes the large majority, whereas the number of households earning more than one million rupees per year (i.e. 20,000 euros), who can be considered rich, multiplied threefold, from 268,000 to 807,000.

Growth primarily benefits regions that already have some degree of urban and industrial fabric. A line can be drawn from Punjab to the north of Andhra Pradesh, cutting the country in two as regards standard of living. The southwestern half represents prosperous India, whereas the northeastern half lags behind. Monthly per capita income is over 22,000 rupees in the first area whereas it is below that level in the second.

The disparities are also growing larger between city and countryside within the Indian states themselves. In 2004-5, those who spent more than 1,100 rupees per month represented 38.3% of city dwellers and only 6% of the rural dwellers, according to the most reliable source on this issue, the National Sample Survey.

Agriculture in crisis

The condition of farmers reflects an agricultural crisis that has been too long neglected. In the 1980s, the average annual growth rate of primary agricultural product was 4%. It dropped to 3.5% in the 1990s and 2% in 2000-7, at a time when the secondary and tertiary sectors were experiencing growth rates of over 9%. The Planning Commission today foresees that the country's food security requires an agricultural product growth rate of 4% to 4.5% per year. This relative decline is largely explained by the steady drop in agricultural prices since 1991, and more generally, by the state's growing disinterest in the agricultural sector. Fertilizer subsidies fell by 20.18% between 2000-1 and 2004-5. Subsidies to ensure the supply of electricity—vital for running irrigation pumps—dropped by 21.3% in 2002-3, bringing them below their 1996-97 level.

Widening gaps could prompt more farmers to adopt revolutionary tactics promoted by the Naxalites. This Maoist movement takes its name from the Bengali city of Naxalbari where the first insurrection broke out in 1966. It experienced an upsurge in activity in the early 2000s in a regional context marked by the success of the Maobhadis in Nepal, but also, especially, an international context dominated by the pauperization of rural areas. For millions of farmers overburdened with debt—to the extent that they have committed suicide by the thousands—in a number of districts the Naxalite discourse is finally the only one that makes sense to them. The Naxalite landslide coming from Bengal and Bihar today flows through Jharkhand, Chhattisgarh, Madhya Pradesh, Orissa, Andhra Pradesh and even Karnataka. In 2006, for the first time attacks on police stations and other ambushes, claimed more victims than the Kashmiri guerrilla war.

Bottlenecks

Infrastructure is one of the traditional weaknesses of the Indian economy. The roads and railways are in such a bad shape that the average speed, for passengers as well as freight, is less than 20 km per hour (so far as roads are concerned, this is also due to the remains of the old octroi system). Modernization of these two means of transport should be boosted soon by the "Golden Quadrilateral" project, which is planned to create a new network of roads and railways connecting Delhi-Calcutta-Chennai-Mumbai-Delhi. The 5,846 km of motorway under construction should allow cars to reach 80 km/h.

The dearth of energy resources may present another of the greatest predicaments India will have to overcome in the coming decades. With a strong annual rise in growth rate and population, the country's energy consumption is bound to explode—its electricity needs are expected to increase 3.5 times by 2025. Its coal consumption should go from 311 million tons in 1997 to 540-690 million tons; depending on the scenario, oil consumption is likely to go from 83 million to 195-245 million tons; and gas consumption from 21.5 billion to 65-71 billion cubic metres—and this when its production is expected to develop very little. Unless there is an unlikely discovery of a particularly rich oil field, India will see its black gold self-sufficiency rate, which was 59% in 1990, drop to 13% in 2020. As a result, the lowest estimates—banking on an average yearly economic growth of 6%—predict that the share of energy in the country's imports should rise from 16% in 1990 to 33%-38%, depending on whether the country optimizes its energy use or not. The upper figure in this bracket would mean that the country had to devote $39,500 million per year to its energy bill, which would amount to between one-fifth and one-fourth of its export revenue.

These forecasts will be proved wrong, however, if India reforms its system of electricity production and distribution. Its State Electricity Boards are well known for their nepotism, low productivity and populism—which explains why peasants do not pay for the power they use. Political parties might have the courage to change this, but it is a very touchy issue.

India's trajectory is thus different from that of other emerging countries of Asia. Today's growth relies on an exceptional "demographic dividend" and a capitalist milieu which is long-standing but which has been reactivated by the recent reforms. It owes much to the dynamism of domestic consumption supported by an expanding middle class, and to the services sector which is very well integrated into the global market because of the skill of relatively cheap IT engineers and the diaspora. Yet, massive investment in industry—from both foreign and Indian firms—will boost India's position in areas where China dominates, largely because its labour will gradually become cheaper than Chinese labour.

Emergence, but how far?

India's emergence is also atypical from the point of view of international relations. The country asserts itself in the world because of its military-strategic assets, but also in terms of soft power. Secondly, India is jealous of its national independence, but has found a new partner (after the demise of the USSR) in the US, who is likely to help it find short cuts to power—even though Washington may not get much in return. Thirdly, India is trying to obtain a global status—by knocking at the door of the UN Security Council, for instance—without being a regional power first, a rather unusual strategy but a logical one given the fact that the country is isolated in South Asia, a region where it is so much bigger than its neighbours that they cannot accept its leadership without considerable apprehension.

As an emerging power, India may join hands with its peers at the WTO within the IBSA group, but it often reverts to its Nehru legacy to become once again the spokesperson of the poor countries that it was at Bandung. Behind the apparent contradictions of the Indian trajectory, one constant can be found: a strong nationalist sentiment which is fostered today by new economic assertiveness. As a result, like China, India sees its emergence as a return to the position it occupied in the 18th century and as revenge over the West. In that sense, India's emergence is truly postcolonial and breaks from the Nehruvian universalist perspective. Moreover, India is tending to forget the message it had for the world thanks to Nehru—and Gandhi—*just when* it is acquiring the influence it once lacked to impose that message. India's mindset is so nationalistic that its foreign policy may only consist today in a quest for power *per se*, a policy where even its soft power attributes are supposed to support a Realpolitik striving for respect and international status.

India has not arrived, though. Its growth is affected by major bottlenecks and generates dramatic inequalities. The informal sector—90% of the working population—offers no social security. The state's investments in health and education remain low. At the receiving end, poor peasants might be tempted by revolutionary movements, while some Muslim youth, victims of discrimination, might be tempted by Islamist groups.

Besides, India is under great ecological threat. India's rising consumption of fossil fuels not only poses a balance of payments problem. It also raises a burningly topical environmental question. If nothing is done to reduce CO_2 emissions, they will double in 20 years to go from 11.33 million to 22.32 million tons between 1997 and 2020. The Indian authorities have demonstrated their ability to react in this area as soon as the problem is brought before the Supreme Court: the judges for instance made the use of Compressed Natural Gas mandatory for the highest polluting vehicles in Delhi, buses and taxis. The obvious lack of ecological awareness demonstrated by the political class is, precisely, such that most of the pressure will have to come from the country's legal apparatus and NGOs, which may not be sufficient.

Bibliography ·

Cohen, S. (2002). *India. Emerging Power*, Oxford: Oxford University Press.

Engardio, P. (ed.) (2006). *Chindia: How China and India are Revolutionizing Global Business*, McGraw Hill.

Jaffrelot, C. (ed.) (2008). *New Delhi et le monde. Une puissance émergente entre realpolitik et soft power*, Paris: Autrement.

Jaffrelot, C. and P. van der Veer (eds) (2008). *Patterns of Middle Class Consumption in China and India*, New Delhi: Sage.

Meredith, R. (2007). *The Elephant and the Dragon: The Rise of India and China and What It Means for All of Us*, W.V. Norton and Co.

Mukherji, R. (ed.) (2007). *India's Economic Transition. The Politics of Reforms*, Oxford: Oxford University Press.

Smith, D. (2007). *The Dragon and the Elephant: China, India and the New World Order*, Profile Books.

Winters, L. A. and S. Yusuf (2007). *Dancing with Giants: China, India and the Global Economy*, World Bank Publications.

Brazil, a South American State Among the Key Players

Alain Rouquié

razil, 1985. After twenty-one years of dictatorship, democracy is restored. The difficult task of reconstructing stable political institutions against a backdrop of soaring inflation and economic recession occupies centre stage. Diplomatic ambition and dreams of grandeur are not a priority of this continent-sized country. Hard hit by the debt crisis, Brazil, in spite of its size and resources, still seems—as a spiteful cliché would have it—like an "eternal country of the future".

Two decades later, the leaders of the G7 member countries suggest including it among this club of "rich countries". Bankers rank Brazil among the major emerging markets of the BRICs along with China, India and Russia. Indeed, its GDP is now on a par with the latter two. What is more, the most reliable forecasters anticipate that before 2050, Brazil will be the world's fourth largest economy. Conscious of the country's position and role, and with the support of several other countries, its leaders are demanding a permanent member seat on the United Nations Security Council, as are Germany, Japan and India. At the dawn of the 21st century, Brazil's status appears to have truly changed—as if the giant has awakened or at least that the eternal country of the future has finally embraced the present.

How did the biggest country of Latin America, known for its cyclical prosperity and its glaring "contrasts", become a major emerging country? What were the contributing factors to this rise in power? Are we witnessing a new economic cycle, one that is by nature transitory, or a promotion into the international arena that is bound to last?

'A country of the future': resources and driving forces

Brazilians are well aware that nature has blessed their country. In fact, historical as much as geographical factors helped to preserve the unity of the huge Portuguese colony. The flat expanse of space unbroken by any natural barrier, a central monarchical power and the huge and menacing presence of slave labour together saved 19th-century Brazil from breaking up into independent republics like Spanish America.

The "largest tropical country in the world" is also endowed with exceptional natural resources. Fertile soils, sunshine and abundant water supply enabled it to achieve high agricultural yields with low production costs. If we add to that an "agricultural border" of around 90 million hectares (not counting the forests) and highly capable agronomical research structures, thanks to which it has been able to cultivate shrubby savannas and scrub thorn deserts, it is easy to see how Brazil has become one of the world's leading agricultural powers.

Brazil has long been known for its coffee, which between 1880 and 1929 accounted for up to 70% of its exports. Today it represents only a very meagre share of its trade. However, Brazil is still the world's leading coffee producer and exporter. But the country is now also in the lead or among the top ranks for production and export of many other agricultural products: sugar, soya beans, citrus fruit, orange juice, beef, maize, tobacco, cotton, cellulose. And its wealth is not limited to agriculture. Brazil is also the leading exporter of iron ore, the fourth or fifth for tin and aluminium.

What is more, while during the 1970s nearly half of its trade revenue went to paying its oil bill, Brazil has become practically self-sufficient in hydrocarbon resources largely thanks to its state-owned company's technological capabilities in deep water extraction. Another reason is a bold experiment in fuel substitution that began with the first oil crisis; the country is also a leading world producer of ethanol, and its biofuels, produced mostly from sugar cane, enjoy competitive

figure 25: **Biofuel production in Brazil, 1990-2008**

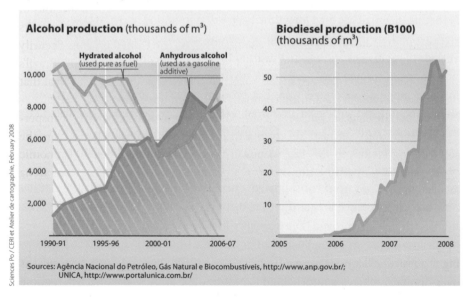

Sources: Agência Nacional do Petróleo, Gás Natural e Biocombustíveis, http://www.anp.gov.br/;
UNICA, http://www.portalunica.com.br/

Sciences Po / CERI et Atelier de cartographie, February 2008

costs without jeopardizing the country's food security. With huge, partly unexploited hydraulic capacity, and major offshore and biomass oil resources, Brazil has an enormous energy potential.

But this agricultural power is also an industrialized country. Sixty per cent of its foreign trade is made up of manufactured or semi-finished goods. Since the year 2000, transport equipment and metallurgical products have accounted for a quarter of its exports. Its state-owned aeronautical company Embraer, the fourth largest aircraft manufacturer in the world, is the country's largest exporter. Brazil has a production capacity of 3 million motor vehicles. Moerover, most of those on the market today have two fuel engines (flex-fuel) designed using local technology—because this country, with R&D expenditure on a level with that of some developed countries, boasts quality research institutes and universities whose work has never been affected by the vicissitudes of its political life.

Lastly, the importance of cultural factors in Brazil's rising trajectory must not be underestimated. Brazil's geographical vastness and the abundance of its natural resources represent a source of pride and hope for Brazilians, largely explaining their inveterate optimism. It is true that owing to its immensity, its initially small population and the absence of any major pre-Columbian civilization on its territory, Brazil really is a new country, a space waiting to be occupied. This "American nation" in constant transformation does not dwell on its past. Eighty per cent urban, it has proved its dynamism by creating several *ex-nihilo* cities in the 20th century. Brasilia, a monumental "capital of hope", has become Brazil's most accomplished symbol in less than fifty years.

The political aspects of Brazil's international advancement

Nonetheless Brazil has for a long time been a disappointing hope. Its takeoff lacked stamina and steadfastness. Sudden recessions followed periods of high growth. Periods of rapid expansion were thwarted by bouts of inflation. This seesaw evolution has been termed the "permanent myth of Sisyphus". The political conditions for long-range development were not brought together, and economic volatility went hand in hand with a succession of weak governments and frequent military interventions. And the 21 years of the military regime that began in 1964 were no more successful at establishing ongoing development despite the triumphal years of the "economic miracle."

Democracy has been consolidated since it was re-established in 1985. It has now been in existence longer than the dictatorship. Political institutions in post-military Brazil have proved their strength: first by overcoming the crisis provoked by the impeachment of President Collor de Melo in 1992, then, in 2003, by allowing a political change of power (from centre to left) that was both dreaded and over-dramatized. This unprecedented constitutional stability enabled Brazil to put its economy and finances somewhat back in order. From 1994 with the *Real Plan*, inflation was stemmed and the country, until then very closed, began to open up to improve its competitiveness.

Fernando Henrique Cardoso and Luiz Inacio Lula da Silva, two successive presidents from rival parties and with opposite political tendencies, have since 1995 pursued macroeconomic policies based on similar models. Above and beyond election promises, both administrations have carried out rigorous management policies aimed at reducing the exterior vulnerability of a country that exported little and was heavily in debt. The rise in exports even became the main economic goal of President Lula, who, moreover, never called into question his predecessor's opening-up of the economy and state reforms. While at the end of the 1990s Brazil struggled to pass the 60-billion-dollar mark for exports, by 2005 its foreign trade had doubled, reaching $138 billion. This was low compared to its GDP (less than 15%) or compared to other states on the continent, but it still signifies a huge qualitative transformation for an economy that was long focused on its domestic market.

A decade of financial restraint and export incentives has given Brazil a new standing, that of a country which offers satisfactory conditions of political stability and continuity. This new image is largely responsible for attracting a considerable flow of foreign direct investment, which has reached as much as $30 billion per year. But other aspects have probably contributed to Brazil's renewed appeal and expansion, the first being the particular prestige of its last two presidents.

Fernando Henrique Cardoso and Luiz Inacio da Silva, who have successively governed the country since 1995, are two very contrasting characters who have both enjoyed considerable popularity outside Brazil. Cardoso is an academic, a sociologist of international renown who comes from an old family. Lula is the son of poor peasants from the arid Nordeste. A metal worker and then a trade union leader, he was a founding member of the Workers' Party.

Both these presidents, each outstanding in his own way, have taken a very similar approach to foreign policy, albeit with very different styles. For Cardoso, Brazil's main goal was to achieve competitive integration into the international market. As for Lula, he wants to "change the world's trade map", in other words to take things even further in the same direction in order for Brazil to take its rightful place in the concert of nations. Both of them in fact speak out against the asymmetry of the international order and the inequalities among states.

In the pursuit of these goals, the role of Brazil's diplomacy must not be underestimated. Officials with Itamaraty, the Brazilian Foreign Relations Ministry, are reputed for their quality and worth. The competence of this meritocratic elite is no small asset for the country's foreign policy. It should also be noted that, since 1995, the Foreign Relations Minister portfolio has been held by career diplomats for ten out of the past twelve years.

Brazil, an unrivalled regional power

The largest of the sub-continental countries (nearly four times the size of Argentina), Brazil has common borders with all the South American states except Chile and Ecuador. This geopolitical location defined democratic Brazil's primary sphere of foreign activity. Strengthened ties, even reconciliation with neighbouring countries, was essential following twenty years of a military dictatorship suspected of expansionist goals.

Brazil's first move was therefore to establish a "strategic alliance" with its historic rival, Argentina. The two countries have converging interests. Their recently re-established democratic institutions are still fragile. This lends them solidarity, and hence it was urgent for them to normalize relations to avoid any bilateral tension that might destabilize them both. The two governments first reached an agreement on particular confidence measures in the nuclear arena, each country suspecting the other of using nuclear power for military purposes. In 1988 they signed a free trade agreement, the first step towards the creation of Mercosur, together with Uruguay and Paraguay, through the 1991 Treaty of Asunción.

The process of regional integration at first appeared an economic success. Between 1991 and 1998, gradually liberalized "intrazone" trade increased five-fold. In 1996-97, Brazil became Argentina's principal customer, selling it twice the amount that it sold to the United States and as much as to the entire European Union. The regional market absorbed over 15% of Brazil's exports, mainly high added-value manufactured goods.

But in 2000, Mercosur experienced a crisis. This was partly the result of the severe financial crisis in Argentina due to an unworkable fixed exchange rate mechanism, and partly of the sudden, unanticipated devaluation of the Brazilian currency. As Mercosur had no institutional mechanism able, if not to ensure a minimum of macroeconomic convergence, at least to facilitate the conciliation of diverging interests, the integration process began to back-pedal. Mercosur functions on a strictly inter-governmental level, Brazil being particularly reticent, despite what its leaders claim, about any supranational mechanism.

Furthermore, the organization's partners and associated countries that could become partners (Chile in particular) fear Brazil's unilateralism. They are not far from considering that, even if Brazil claims "Mercosur is its destiny", the South American giant does not intend to share decision-making powers with its "humble" neighbours. It seems, on the contrary inclined to "seek maximum profit with minimum commitment".

Moreover, in face of the Mercosur crisis, Brazil seems to have chosen headlong flight. As it cannot envisage a deepening of the integration process, expansion has become its chief goal. It is as if the organization had been merely one step in a major strategic project of South American integration conceived and carried out by Brasilia.

On 1 September 2000, President Cardoso invited the South American heads of state to Brasilia for their first summit. A second one took place at Guayaquil in Ecuador in July 2002. These presidential conferences had at least three goals: to assert a regional identity, launch an infrastructure integration programme and finally gain international recognition of Brazil's irreplaceable regional role.

The organizer of the sub-continental gathering also appears to have been its main beneficiary. The initiative for the Regional Infrastructure Integration programme (IIRSA), at the centre of discussions in Guayaquil, is the implementation of Brazil's historic project for an overland link between the two oceans. Programmes to build roads, pipelines and electric networks form a network of which Brazil occupies the hub, and which basically extends the main priorities of Brazil's indicative planning. Brazil thus seems intent on organizing the South American space in concentric circles with itself at the centre.

While Mercosur, an incomplete customs union and incomplete free trade area, was cracking apart, Brazil under Lula pursued its continental strategy. In December 2004, in Cuzco in Peru, the South American Community of Nations was created. It united Mercosur and the Andean Community (CAN) countries, with a view to merging them as well as three countries from the region that did not belong to either of those organizations.

The Mercosur partners did not show much enthusiasm for this expansion. The first summit of the new body, which took place in Brasilia in September 2005, was only a partial success. Some heads of state appeared to suspect Brazil of acting only in its own interest and twisting their arms. A continental integration process initiated and organized by the most powerful country was, however, not likely to go ahead without arousing some unease.

Some neighbouring countries fear this will get them into a North-South type of relationship with Brazil, in which heavyweight Brazil would play the role of the industrial North, buyer of raw materials and sensitive assets (in particular in the energy field). This is especially true of a de-industrialized Argentina for which such a regional division of labour is very menacing. As for the leaders of Bolivia, Brazil's main gas supplier, they speak out against what they deem asymmetrical, even neo-colonial relations. President Evo Morales' "nationalization" of hydrocarbon resources on 1 May 2007, declared symbolically at facilities of the Brazilian company Petrobras, says a lot about the strife and resentment that separates these two neighbouring countries.

This is the reason why the Argentine and Uruguayan governments in particular have supported Venezuela's request for membership of Mercosur even while Hugo Chávez's diplomatic goals are very far from the trade rationale of the Treaty of Asunción. They are counting on the oil-rich state to rebalance the grossly inegalitarian regional organization. Beyond these speculations about Brazil's ulterior motives, the prevailing sentiment in the region is that Brazil, driven by its global ambitions, is also gradually moving away from Latin America.

A hesitant global player

With the end of the Cold War and the era of globalization, Brazil suddenly became aware of its isolation, the legacy of two decades of military rule. The country, cut off from the outside world for far too long, had to start increasing its presence abroad in order to have a say in major international decisions. A Brazil hoping to become a "global trader" can only guarantee its autonomy and defend its interests by taking part in international organizations and sitting at the negotiating table.

The most emblematic decision of this new state of affairs came in 1997 when Brazil joined the Treaty on the Non-Proliferation of Nuclear Weapons (NPT), which for thirty years it had deemed grossly unfair and unacceptable. Having ratified the Treaty of Tlatelolco for the prohibition of nuclear weapons on the continent and renounced, with its 1988 Constitution, use of the atom for military purposes, to refuse to join the NTP and other similar multilateral conventions could no longer be justified. However, Brasilia remains opposed to an NPT that allows the five major nuclear powers to keep their nuclear weapons, and insists on the total elimination of all other countries' existing arsenals. Brazilian diplomacy works towards equality between nations and a reconsideration of the international status quo. This revisionism, it must be said, is expressed in a non-aggressive and non-confrontational manner. The tone may have changed and become more adamant with Lula's arrival in power, but Brazil's excellent relationship with the United States is proof that the traditional cordiality remains unaltered.

However, Brazilian foreign policy now aims to be a stronger and more visible force. And this means embarking on a strategy that looks beyond the regional sphere. Brazil's first move, in 2003, was to demand a permanent seat on the United Nations Security Council. The Brazilian leaders in fact believe that theirs is the only Latin American state that has the qualities and skills necessary to gain access to the club of key players on the Security Council, not as the representative of a regional group but in its own right. They asked their neighbours and friends to back their claim. By contributing the largest military contingent to peacekeeping operations in Haiti (MINUSTAH), Brazil aimed to prove that it was now able to assume its global responsibilities.

But it is probably Brazil's role in the World Trade Organization (WTO) that has really shown the world its newfound determination and its diplomatic ambitions. Because all member countries are on an equal level and because trade problems, in particular the liberalization of agricultural trade, are one of its priorities, Brazil has been very active in the WTO. This was the case, in particular, at the opening of a new round of multilateral trade negotiations in Doha in November 2001. It is in this context that in August 2003 in Cancún, Brazil led a group of emerging countries, the G20, to lobby against a minimalist compromise on the agricultural subsidies issue that grew out of a bargain reached between the United States and the European Union. Since then, Brazil has been one of the five major players (alongside the European Union, the United States, Japan and India) likely to organize the revival of the Doha Round of negotiations.

That Brazil (with Argentina's help this time) managed to block the North American project for the Free Trade Area of the Americas (FTAA-ALCA) is no less symbolic of the determination of its diplomacy to defend its national interests. This process was due to reach completion at the beginning of 2005, but the United States wanted to push the agricultural issues off the negotiating table. According to Washington these issues fall within the scope of the WTO. Brazil, a major actor in agribusiness, acted likewise regarding all the sensitive issues for its own economy (services, intellectual property, public procurement) that might be referred to the WTO. The Monterrey Summit of the Americas in January 2004 ratified a minimal agreement between the United States and Brazil, making the American strategy obsolete. In November 2005 in Mar del Plata, President Bush acknowledged that the FTAA—even a downscaled version—had little chance of succeeding. Without Brazil, a Free Trade Zone of the Americas cannot exist. It is interesting to note in this respect that Brazil, in its own way an "indispensable nation", barely took into consideration the expectations and wishes of those countries of the continent in favour of the US project. Indeed the formation of G20 at Cancún did not mobilize all of the Latin American countries; neither Columbia nor Uruguay cared to be a part of it.

Brazilian foreign policy aims to form new alliances with countries of the South beyond its continent alone. Its critics even see in this a resurgence of outdated Third-Worldism, even of the spirit of Bandung. It is in accordance with this South-South approach that Itamaraty managed to make the G20 a durable entity. Most recent Brazilian diplomatic initiatives follow this trend. The strengthening of ties with India and South Africa in a three-way discussion forum, the first Arab-South American summit held in Brasilia in May 2005, the much publicized exchanges of presidential visits with China, and the desire for an active presence in sub-Saharan Africa, are all signs of a determined policy of "peripheral solidarity".

It is not easy to understand the true significance of this diplomatic activism. Does Brazil want to play the role of global actor in order to ensure there is absolutely no doubt as to its regional leadership? Or conversely, is it aspiring to establish itself as indisputable leader of Latin America in order to gain recognition of its status as one of the "new key players"? Maybe it is simply at a crossroads, searching for a role and a status in a global order that promises to remain destructured for a long time to come.

An uncertain power

Brazil is the fifth largest country in the world in terms of size and population. But it ranks only 30th in participation in world trade (at barely 1%). What is more, the tenth largest world economy has been relegated to 64th place on the Human Development Index (HDI), while two-thirds of the world's countries have a lower per capita income than Brazil does. Indeed, despite recent progress in this country of incredible natural wealth, Brazil still has a high poverty rate. Nearly 50 million Brazilians live below the poverty line, a proportion three times higher than that of countries with similar incomes.

These are just a few statistical markers that set the framework for, and the limitations to, Brazil's promotion onto the international stage. It is true that "incon-

figure 26: **Per capita GDP in Brazil, 2005**

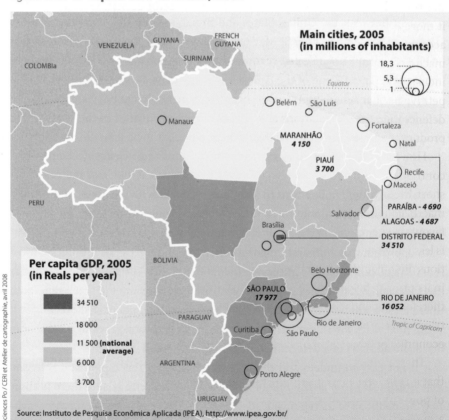

Source: Instituto de Pesquisa Econômica Aplicada (IPEA), http://www.ipea.gov.br/

Sciences Po / CERI et Atelier de cartographie, avril 2008

gruence of status" is common to all of the main emerging countries, especially the BRICs. But for Brazil, this giant with feet of clay, the challenges are accumulating. Severe regional disparities, age-old social inequalities, and the inefficiency, even obsolescence of its road, port and air transport infrastructure are all factors that significantly hamper its development.

What is more, the country has for the last twenty years been showing poor growth rates: 2.5% compared to 8.7% in the 1970s. Even during the boom years, its performance ranked lower than the Latin American average (4.3% in 2004 compared to 5.4% for the whole the continent). This is a far cry from the dynamism of the Asian economies.

And yet Brazil has benefited hugely from the vertiginous rise of India and China. In 2003, China increased its imports from Brazil by 80%. Over four years, trade with China has grown fourfold and has accounted for 6% of Brazil's exports. In 2004, China became Brazil's third biggest customer, after the United States and Argentina. It is not certain, however, that this strengthening of relations between the "world's workshop" and the "world's breadbasket" is entirely positive for the latter. China, insatiable consumer of raw materials and the world's leading importer of soya beans, does little to help diversify the Brazilian economy. On the contrary this trade encourages it to slip back to a primary sector economy, thereby making it more vulnerable. Indeed, commodities (soya, cellulose, iron ore, orange juice) account for over 75% of Brazil's trade with China, while Brazil mainly purchases machines and chemical products from China. The structures of the two countries' industrial exports may not be identical, but that does not make them any less competitive in many sectors of third-party markets. And it is not certain that Brazil's defence mechanisms will be able to resist the huge wave of Chinese manufactured products from low technology sectors for long.

However, even if there is no doubt that increased worldwide demand has contributed to Brazil's growing strength, this growth is not just the result of a short-lived windfall. Democratic stability, financial stabilization and realistic macroeconomic management have all enabled the country to make the most of a favourable economic situation. Brazil, which in 2006 invested $26 billion abroad, is less vulnerable to external financial crises today than it was ten years ago. Ambitious diplomacy has done the rest, without actually achieving truly decisive results in its priority fields (UN, WTO, regional integration). Brazil's international status therefore depends as much on the fortunes of the other "major peripheral countries" and the development of world markets as on the virtuous continuity of its economic policy.

There is one crucial difference, however, between Brazil and its "counterparts": that it is an "unarmed" giant. Brazil is indeed lacking one of the major instruments of power that each of its BRIC peers possesses: nuclear weapons. The pacifism of a nuclear-weapons-free Brazil is written into its Constitution. Not only has the

figure 27: **Inward and outward FDI in Brazil, 1970-2007**

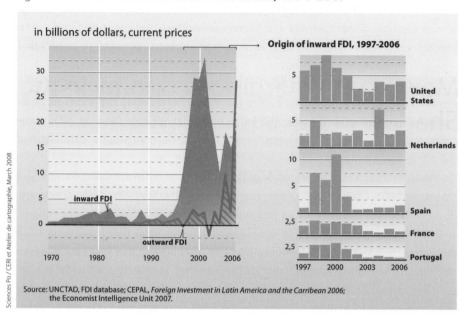

Source: UNCTAD, FDI database; CEPAL, *Foreign Investment in Latin America and the Carribean 2006*; the Economist Intelligence Unit 2007.

country abandoned all claim to military use of nuclear power; it does not have the capacity to deploy its conventional armed forces abroad. Not having had to face any threat, it has reduced its military budget and armed forces and therefore cannot pursue a hegemonic policy. It is through the tranquil strength and confidence inspired by its "constructive moderation" that this cooperative state, preferring to oppose "power politics" and form coalitions, will maintain its role as a global player.

Bibliography •

Benassar, B. and R. Marin (2000). *Histoire du Brésil*. Paris: Fayard.

Droulers, M. (2001). *Brésil, une géohistoire*. Paris: PUF.

Lamounier, B. and R. Figueiredo (eds) (2002). *A Gra FHC*. Sao Paulo: Cultura Editures.

Rouquié, A. (2006). *Le Brésil au XXIe siècle. Naissance d'un nouveau grand*. Paris: Fayard.

Thery, H. (2000). *Le Brésil*. Paris: Armand Colin.

Van Eewen, D. et al. (2006). *Le nouveau Brésil de Lula: dynamique des paradoxes*. La Tour d'Aigues: Editions de l'Aube.

Mexico, an Emerging Economy in the Shadow of the Superpower

David Recondo

"Poor Mexico, so far from God and so close to the United States," exclaimed the Mexican President Porfirio Diaz, early in the 20th century, alluding to the unequal balance of power between Mexico and its northern neighbour. Although exaggerated and dated, reflecting the era of US interference in Mexico's trade, politics and military affairs, Diaz's remark is revealing in that it highlights Mexico's fundamental identity as a frontier land. This state with a population of 107 million has a unique geopolitical and geocultural position which conditions its emergence. Geographically, Mexico is considered as part of North America, but historically and culturally it is linked to Latin America. As a frontier land it is both the meeting point and the buffer zone between the developing "Indo-Afro-Latin" South, which is also home to Asian and Arab minorities ass a result of transcontinental migration, and the hyper-developed North, home to the world's biggest economic and military power, to which it is inextricably connected by a land border of 3,300 kilometres.

Apart from this geographical specificity, Mexico shares a number of characteristics with the other emerging countries: stable political institutions, a diversified export-led economy albeit dependent on the North's growth (essentially that of the United States), and a highly unequal distribution of wealth, with around 25% of the population living below the poverty threshold. Beyond these shared traits Mexico has two major differences from the other emerging economies: the key role of drug trafficking, and the phenomenon of migration towards the North.

The three drivers for emergence:
the state, regional integration and exile

Mexico owes its emergence to three fundamental factors. Firstly, the political will of the post-revolutionary governments from the 1930s played a crucial part in diversifying Mexico's economic activities and enabling the country to become heavily industrialized. Within a few decades, Mexico progressed from being an essentially agricultural economy, with some export crops (coffee, sisal, tropical fruit), to an industrialized economy from as early as the 1940s. The late 1930s also saw the nationalization of oil (21 March 1938) and the establishment of the state-owned company PEMEX (Petróleos Mexicanos). The oil boom was to finance the country's industrialization on the "import substitution" principle developed as a model by the Economic Commission for Latin America and the Caribbean (ECLAC) in the 1950s under the guidance of the economist Raul Prebisch.

However, since Miguel de la Madrid's government (1982-88), the Mexican state has come to play a more modest role in the national economy which is beset by falling oil prices and a huge debt. Nonetheless, in the eyes of the other countries in the region, Mexico remains the leading promoter of economic development. Privatization of some sectors (banks, airline companies, road infrastructures, food industry, etc.) is relatively limited compared to that of other Latin American countries, starting with Brazil and Argentina; but the Mexican state does continue to support agricultural and industrial export activities, particularly through fiscal incentives and subsidies towards energy consumption. It also has a monopoly on the extraction, conversion and commercialization of hydrocarbons.

The second factor helping the Mexican economy become part of the global market is its integration into the North American market in 1994. Overall, the impact of the North-American Free Trade Agreement (NAFTA, signed in 1993 and inaugurated on 1 January 1994) has been good for the Mexican economy. The assembly industry and its associated activities saw strong development during the first decade of integration. The Agreement not only stimulated US industry relocations; domestic industry and the services sector also benefited from the removal of tariffs and other trade barriers. Exports of manufactured goods and agricultural produce and raw materials to Mexico's two northern neighbours increased

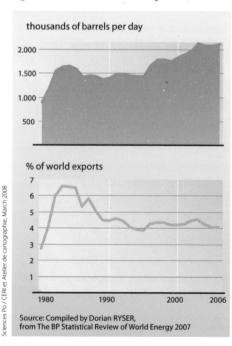

figure 28: **Mexico's oil exports, 2006**

thousands of barrels per day

2.000
1.500
1.000
500

% of world exports

7
6
5
4
3
2
1

1980   1990   2000   2006

Source: Compiled by Dorian RYSER,
from The BP Statistical Review of World Energy 2007

Sciences Po / CERI et Atelier de cartographie, March 2008

exponentially. The figures seemed to contradict the doom-mongers who, after the neo-Zapatista uprising of January 1994 and the ensuing political and economic crisis, claimed that Mexico's entry into the "first world" was merely a trick on the part of President Carlos Salinas de Gortari (1989-94) and his gang of "Chicago boys".

The country entered the 21ˢᵗ century with public finance in a healthier state (the public debt is much lower than Brazil's, around 25% of GDP as against 50% for the giant of the Southern Cone), a steadily decreasing foreign debt and an increasingly diversified economy. The OECD considers Mexico to be a middle-income country, with a GDP of $10,700 per capita in 2007. However, there are two factors that tarnish the image of this success: on the one hand, Mexico remains one of the most inegalitarian countries in the world, with a Gini coefficient barely lower than that of Brazil (50.9 as against 56.7; that of the United States being 45), and with 26.3% of the population living on less than two dollars a day, according the World Bank data. On the other hand, the products which have driven growth since NAFTA came into force (textiles, toys, household appliances, etc.) are encountering fierce competition from the Asian countries. Mexico's prosperity has pushed up labour costs and allowed China to flood the local market and that of the USA with cheap goods. Beijing has superseded Mexico as the USA's second trade partner. And so Mexico now finds itself having to develop activities with a high added value and requiring a much greater investment in capital and training than has been made to date. The other side of the coin is Mexico's growing dependence on the US economy. At present, 80% of Mexico's trade is with its northern neighbour, further bearing out the old adage: "When America sneezes, Mexico catches a cold!" The slowdown of the American economy these last two years is probably largely responsible for the crisis hitting the Mexican economy, whose growth

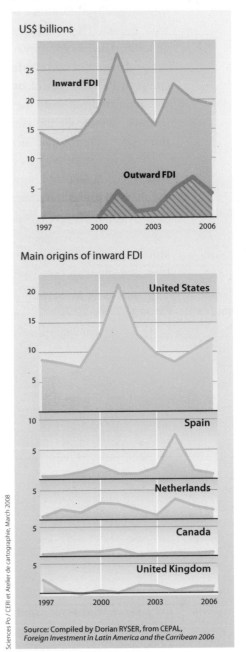

figure 29: **Foreign direct investment (FDI) in Mexico, 1997-2006**

US$ billions

Inward FDI

Outward FDI

Main origins of inward FDI

United States

Spain

Netherlands

Canada

United Kingdom

Sciences Po / CERI et Atelier de cartographie, March 2008

Source: Compiled by Dorian RYSER, from CEPAL,
Foreign Investment in Latin America and the Carribean 2006

figure 30: **Trade between Mexico and the United States, 1990-2006**

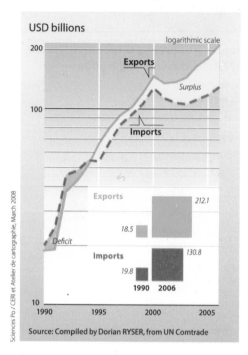

Source: Compiled by Dorian RYSER, from UN Comtrade

figure 31: **Remittances of Mexican migrants abroad, 2001-2006**

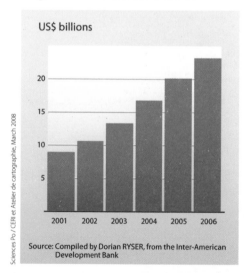

Source: Compiled by Dorian RYSER, from the Inter-American Development Bank

rate in 2007 (2%) was three times lower than the average for the rest of Latin America (6%).

Last but not least, the third driver for Mexico's emergence is migration, which is a well-established phenomenon since the first "*bracero*" labour programmes signed between the United States and Mexican governments, dating back to World War II. A more or less temporary northward displacement of the Mexican population rose to reach exceptional proportions within less than twenty years. According to official estimates, each year around one million people attempt to cross the border clandestinely, and half succeed. There are nearly 20 million US inhabitants of Mexican origin, more than 58% of America's Hispanic population.

The economic impact of this modern-day exodus is an acknowledged fact: nearly 25 billion dollars of remittances (*remesas*) were sent in 2007, the equivalent of half the value of the country's oil exports.

Millions of Mexicans rely more on these transfers from relatives working "on the other side" than on welfare assistance. This is a particularly significant case of "development through exile", with all the ambivalence such a notion implies. By guaranteeing a certain level of consumption and savings, the financial transfers make a major contribution to the emergence of the Mexican economy, while the mobility of surplus labour is a safety net that defuses the social and political tensions created by poverty. On the other hand, it is likely that over time the family and community ties will loosen and the transfers will end up being reinvested in the US market. Furthermore, a close sociodemographic analysis tends to show that the migrants are not necessarily from the poorest sectors of Mexican society. On the contrary, those who leave are the people who have a certain material and cultural capital which the Mexican economy partly loses to its two northern neighbours. More than ever, the symbiosis of Mexican and US societies is challenging the idea of Mexico as an independent power. Perhaps we will soon be speaking of the emergence of a "Mexamerican" power rather than seeking south of the Rio Grande a rival power to its uncomfortably close northern neighbour.

Democratic pluralism at the centre, authoritarian enclaves on the fringes

Although the Mexican economy experienced ups and downs in the 1980s and 1990s, the country's political stability has always distinguished Mexico from its southern neighbours. The transition from a regime led by one dominant party to competitive multiparty politics was smooth, almost without violence. And yet, the presidential election of 2 July 2006, with its extended post-electoral conflict, called into question the idea of Mexico as a fully-fledged democracy. For the first time in ten years, the institutions responsible for organizing the ballot and resolving disputes were seriously called into question. The left-wing opposition's accusation of widespread fraud is reminiscent of the dark years of election rigging by the Institutional Revolutionary Party (PRI), the dominant party from the 1930s until the transition years between 1977 and 1994. However, since the electoral reform of 1996 and the establishment of the Federal Electoral Institute (IFE) and the Electoral Tribunal of the Judicial Branch of the Federation (TEPJF), the elections have become genuinely competitive. This has enabled the right-wing opposition (National Action Party, PAN) and the left (Party of the Democratic Revolution, PRD) to win some ballots, first of all in the federal states and in the Federal District, then at federal level (in 2000 the PAN candidate, Vicente Fox, won the presidential election after 71 years of PRI rule). The extraordinarily close result of the 2006 presidential election (Felipe Calderón (PAN) with a 0.58% lead over Andrés Manuel Lopez Obrador (PRD), i.e. less than 235,000 votes out of 50 million) and the IFE's inefficiency led to mobilization of the left-wing candidate and his supporters, convinced that they were victims of election rigging. Andrés Manuel Lopez Obrador remained intransigent, driven by a messianic fervour; he refused to accept the results and proclaimed himself president. The credibility of the electoral institutions was seriously damaged; the opposition parties (including the PRI) did their utmost to obtain the resignation of the members of the IFE board and appoint their own members to this independent administrative authority, looking ahead to the federal legislative elections of 2009 and the presidential election of 2012!

However, generally speaking, the Mexican political regime remains stable and the election controversy has not jeopardized the democratic order. Democracy is well and truly established after a very long transition from the regime of the dominant party, which had come to power in the late 1920s, to the multiparty system, which has only been in operation since the legislative elections of 1997, when the PRI lost its majority in the Chamber of Deputies and the PRD won the election for Mayor of Mexico City. Gradually, cohabitation between a government and a parliamentary majority of opposite tendencies is becoming a tradition after the presidential handover of 2000. Today, Congress is truly independent, the debates are lively and the agreements on proposed laws vary in nature. In short, the separation of powers is no longer a mere façade. Political debate and negotiation have also become a reality in most of Mexico's 31 states. The PRI continues to govern in more than half the states but only has a relative majority in some of them. The remaining states are divided between the PAN and the PRD, creating a geographically differentiated pattern of party support: in the south and in the centre-south of the country the PRI and the PRD dominate the electoral scene (except in Yucatán in the Maya peninsula), while the PRI and the PAN control the north and centre-north (except for Baja California South, which is governed by the PRD). However, the electoral landscape becomes much more complicated at municipal level: the PAN governs most cities, in both north and south of the country, in contrast to the early 1990s, when it was established predominantly in the cities in the north. The pendulum swing with each changeover is unquestionably the best sign that democracy is well and truly established in Mexico. In 2005, the PRI regained the industrial northeast state of Nuevo León on the US border, after more than a decade of the PAN being in power. The same thing happened in Yucatán in 2007.

One of the knock-on effects of the transition, in particular the swings in the north and north-west states in the late 1980s (Chihuahua, Baja California, Nuevo León, Guanajuato and Jalisco), and of the PRI losing its majority in Congress in 1997, has been the consolidation of the governors' power. As part of the decentralization process the state governments received financial injections from the Federation. Furthermore, the heads of the executive of the 31 states and of the Federal District are no longer controlled by an all-powerful president. In the past, the president had the power to dismiss them at any time. Now they are key political actors, often managing vast resources, not always lawful (some, including Roberto Madrazo, Governor of Tabasco from 1994 to 2000, and Mario Villanueva, Governor of Quintana Roo from 1993 to 1999, have been accused of accepting funding from drug cartels). Some observers see this consolidation of gubernatorial power as the sign of a return to the political order that prevailed from 1910 into the 1920s, when the revolutionary *caudillos* were the bosses and no one was strong enough to stand up to them, not even from Mexico City. The political crises like the one in Oaxaca in 2006 (violent repression of a protest movement led by the primary school teachers' union) reveal the strength of authoritarian enclaves beyond the federal government's reach. Even if political pluralism and guarantees of fundamental rights are becoming established at the national level, democracy is still very precarious on the fringes of the country.

Growing inequalities

The signs of an improved macroeconomic balance barely conceal a structural trend: the widening of social and territorial inequalities. Generally, the indicators show the extent to which a minority has been able to take advantage of the opportunities offered by the increase in trade with the United States. The assembly industry boom in the centre and the north of the country (*maquiladoras*) has harnessed a mainly urban population with a low literacy level, while the rural population has been hit harder by the lack of competitiveness of its agricultural produce compared with imports from North America. Furthermore, NAFTA puts Mexican products at a disadvantage, while the hefty subsidies the US government gives its own farmers have contributed to the deterioration of living conditions in the Mexican countryside. Additionally, the setting up of monopolies in some activity sectors (telecommunications, retail distribution) has contributed to the concentration of wealth in the hands of a few big groups and their employees, to the detriment of small and medium-sized businesses which have felt the impact of the lifting of trade restrictions. This has resulted in a two-speed development,

figure 32: **Per capita GDP of Mexican states and major urban agglomerations, 2006**

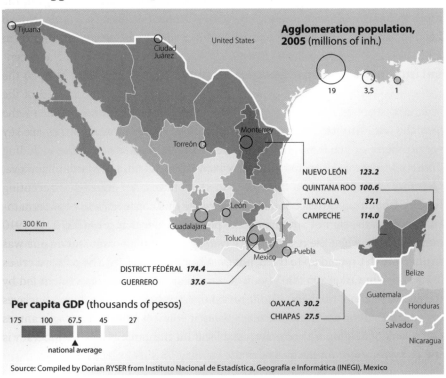

Sciences Po / CERI et Atelier de cartographie, March 2008

Source: Compiled by Dorian RYSER from Instituto Nacional de Estadística, Geografía e Informática (INEGI), Mexico

with "enclaves" that have succeeded in joining the global economy, and other parts that are lagging behind. This disparity is reflected geographically in a particularly graphic manner, with the country literally divided down the middle: the industrial north and centre have a GDP well above the national average (Aguascalientes, Queretaro, Mexico state and the Federal District), while in the south, all the indicators show a GDP more akin to that of Central America, except for the Maya peninsula (Campeche, Yucatán and Quintana Roo), which is boosted by domestic and international tourism.

At the same time, in the big cities (Tijuana, Monterrey, Guadalajara, Mexico City and the metropolitan region), opulence and consumption of luxury goods exist side by side with extreme poverty. The latest models of American cars and "intelligent" buildings in the business districts contrast sharply with the ragged children selling chewing gum at traffic lights. But in these same towns, the territorial disparity is greater, with ghettos forming: the wealthy districts, on the one hand, surrounded by walls and barbed wire and guarded by private security firms; on the other, the "disreputable" districts or the "new towns", mostly with solid buildings, but lacking in basic infrastructure (asphalt roads, electricity, running water, etc.). This scenario, familiar in other emerging countries, is relatively recent in Mexico (twenty years at most), where for a long time the post-revolutionary state ensured a certain social mix, and by promoting state education and industrialization, helped create a large middle class. Until the 1980s, only the very rich lived in exclusive districts. Now, the impoverishment of the middle classes goes hand in hand with the spread of poverty in the country's cities.

Oil income: a poorly managed resource

The Mexican state nationalized the oil industry in March 1938. Within seventy years, PEMEX has become the world's ninth biggest oil company, the third largest producer of crude oil and the twelfth biggest refiner of oil. Some 80% of crude oil exports are to the United States, Mexico being the second supplier after Canada.

The other side of the coin is that while 40% of state revenues come from oil, proven reserves will be exhausted within less than a decade. PEMEX, a real cash cow for the Mexican state, has not invested sufficiently in exploration to ensure further proven reserves and a reassessment of probable and potential reserves. With sales of nearly $100 billion in 2007, this oil giant does not have the resources to finance its modernization alone, because of the high taxes to which it is subjected. Furthermore, most of the potential new reserves lie deep under the waters of the Gulf of Mexico, where costs of exploration and exploitation are higher, and the company does not have the financial means for this in its present state. The main problem is the fact that PEMEX is run like an administrative department and not like a public company allowed a minimum of independence in planning its spending and defining and implementing its development strategies. The result of this fiscal and managerial servitude is not only a drop in PEMEX's output, but also the underdevelopment of its refinery and petrochemicals activities, whose products have a much higher added value than that of crude oil. As a result, Mexico is increasingly dependent on the United States, from which it imports nearly 25% of its domestic consumption of refined products.

Over the last decade, the steadily rising price per barrel has only aggravated the situation, since it more than makes up for the drop in production. The fiscal reform of 2007 is not sufficient to remove the constraints that prevent PEMEX from increasing and diversifying its investments. Moreover, the constitution still prohibits any strategic alliance between nationalized industries and private companies (national or international) in any sector of the oil industry, from exploration to petrochemicals. But the nationalization of 1938 is such a potent symbol of the sovereignty of the Mexican nation in the face of interference from foreign powers, and of the state's determination to encourage industrialization by exploiting raw materials directly, that this issue is a political taboo. Since that date, any endeavour to open up the hydrocarbons sector to private investment is seen by public opinion as an attempt at privatization. The opposition—especially Andrés Manuel Lopez Obrador's PRD party—made the battle against privatization its key campaign issue, once the post-electoral conflict of 2006 was over. However, in April 2008, boosted by support of the PRI, President Felipe Calderón put before Congress a proposal seeking to allow PEMEX to enter into partnerships with private companies, for exploration, transport or refinery, but not allowing them a share in the risks or profits or a stake in the reserves. It is not certain whether that would be enough to make PEMEX a profitable company, nor even whether private companies want to take on all the risks with no stake in the hydrocarbon reserves. But even if such a reform were to be introduced, the state's dependency on oil revenues would still not be reduced. The illusion of a significant increase in reserves in the medium term prevents successive governments from seeking to diversify fiscal revenues and from reinvesting energy sector profits in the development of high-added-value sectors or in supporting other economic activity sectors.

figure 33: **Destination of Mexican oil exports, 2006**

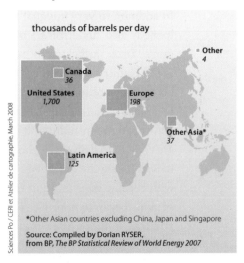

thousands of barrels per day

Other
4

Canada
36

United States
1,700

Europe
198

Other Asia*
37

Latin America
125

*Other Asian countries excluding China, Japan and Singapore

Source: Compiled by Dorian RYSER,
from BP, *The BP Statistical Review of World Energy 2007*

Sciences Po / CERI et Atelier de cartographie, March 2008

Drug cartels: the power in the shadows

In addition to very unequal social and territorial development, Mexico's government is also undermined by the increasingly menacing presence of organized crime. Drug trafficking in particular has reached an unparalleled scale. Not only is the country the main route for drugs destined for the North American market (chiefly cocaine from Colombia but also cannabis, its derivatives, and, more recently, synthetic drugs), but for nearly a decade the Mexican cartels have directly controlled the introduction of drugs into the US market. The Colombian cartels are content to deliver the goods to the Mexicans and are seeking alternative outlets in Europe, via the Caribbean and West Africa. Mexico itself is also a major market, with cocaine consumption rising steadily since 1997, the year when the standard of living began to improve. The impact of trafficking is not only economic but also political. In this matter, the end of the dominant PRI regime was a determining factor. Effectively, the political influence of the drug barons, still barely visible in the 1980s, has been very much in evidence since the cocaine boom. However, unlike Colombia during this same period, a sort of non-interference pact between the executive and the main cartel bosses (mainly the Sinaloa cartel in the north Pacific) made it possible to prevent the mafias from infiltrating the state and federal government to a greater extent until the beginning of the 21st century. It is highly likely that in the drug producing federal states and/or drug trafficking hubs, narcodollars helped finance political life in the 1970s and 1980s. It is also likely that since the 1980s, presidential campaigns have been funded by dirty money. The immediate entourage of President Carlos Salinas de Gortari (1988-94) was accused of benefiting from laundered drug money. However, never have the cartels attempted, as in Colombia, to control entire sections of the national territory or to place their own men in Congress or within the Presidential cabinet. Contact has always been indirect and covert.

The change of president and the dismantling of the pyramidal, centralized political system constituted by the dominant PRI régime led to a sharp break in the relations between the cartels and the state powers. Evidence of the drug barons' growing political influence began to appear at the end of the 1990s. The increased independence of the judiciary, the introduction of an anti-corruption policy and the end of the law of silence guaranteed by the PRI's power monopoly also revealed the connivance between politicians and drug bosses. But it was above all the end of the non-interference pact and the proliferation of the cartels, and the rivalry between them, that helped to make drug trafficking visible and to push the war on narcotics to the top of the political agenda. The first president of the new regime, Vicente Fox (2000-6), sparked things off when he attacked the various drug trafficking operations in the Gulf head-on while treating those of the Pacific Coast more circumspectly. The outcome of this policy, carried out without first stopping to weigh up the situation, was a resurgence of turf wars between drug gangs vying to control the trade routes and the local markets. In 2006, Felipe Calderón took on all the cartels—those of the Pacific as well as the Gulf. This was a priority issue for him, and he entrusted the task to the army. The confrontation resulted in pitched battles in the northwest and northeast of the country (Michoacán, Sinaloa, Baja California, Nuevo León, Tamaulipas). A large number of soldiers and civilians were killed, and the government's policy of challenging the drug cartels head-on was strongly criticized by the political class and a section of the public. But the war between the organized crime gangs to control the drug trade caused more deaths than the army's operation. The hierarchy of the past, which allowed one cartel (chiefly the Sinaloa cartel) to rule, persisted for a long time; now the Gulf organizations were fighting those of the Pacific with commando forces (the *Zetas*), sometimes better equipped and trained than the army itself. The "cartel war" has claimed thousands of victims during the last five years.

The most optimistic view portrays the present government as keeping up deliberate ongoing harassment of the drug organizations while stoking their intrinsic rivalries in order to re-establish the monopolistic balance of the past, but the other way around (Gulf *versus* Pacific). Meanwhile, Mexico's cooperation with the United States' government with a view to halting arms dealing—which takes place mainly on the other side of the Rio Bravo—and to deal with the problem by trying to halt demand, has produced few results to date.

Translated by Ros Schwartz

Bibliography

Modoux, M. (2006). *Fédéralisme and démocratie au Mexique (1989-2000)*. Paris: CERI-Karthala, Recherches internationales.

Musset, A. (1998). *Le Mexique entre deux Amériques*. Paris: Ellipses.

Recondo, D. (2007). "Oaxaca: la périphérie autocratique de la démocratie mexicaine". *Problèmes d'Amérique Latine*, 64, Spring, pp. 73-90.

—— (2008). *La Politique du Guépard. Multiculturalisme et Démocratie au Mexique*. Paris: Sciences Po/ CERI-Karthala.

Turkey: A Dynamic Economy Confronted With Political Uncertainty

Ahmet Insel

Turkey is an atypical emerging country. It is a longstanding member of Western institutions in the club of developed countries: the Council of Europe since 1949, NATO (1951) and the OECD (1960); it is connected with the European Union by an Association Agreement since 1963, superseded by a Customs Union in 1995, and official European Union accession talks were launched in 2005. Compared with its degree of institutional integration in the developed world, Turkey's level of economic and social development is seriously out of step. Its economic takeoff was late, slow and most of all chaotic. The weight of its socio-political problems long inhibited its growth potential. And although the impact of these problems has dwindled in recent years, they continue to weigh on the future of the Turkish economy.

Turkey is close to mature markets (the former European Union of 15) as well as growth markets (Russia, the Middle East, South East Europe). As a neighbour of the Balkans as well as the Middle East and the Caucasus, controlling the straits that give fleets in the Black Sea access to the Mediterranean, it possesses a considerable geostrategic resource. It also enjoys an extensive and dynamic domestic market. Its population is estimated at 72 million inhabitants and—another strong point—its demographic growth is experiencing a rapid deceleration. Above all, Turkey currently has a demographic window of opportunity. The population dependency rate (the ratio of under 14 and over 65 to the total population) is on a downward slide; it fell from 82% in 1975 to 55% in 2000. According to demographic forecasts, it will continue to decrease in coming years to reach 31% in 2025. Such a population structure is generally considered to be a favourable condition for a quick takeoff; South Korea in the 1970s is an illustration.

EU oriented dynamism

Turkey began its emergence process in the 1980s. The economic liberalization programme implemented in the wake of the 1980 military coup espoused the structural adjustment policies recommended by the international financial institutions. By deploying a monetarist policy and a liberalization policy accompanied by direct export incentive measures, Turgut Ozal's government encouraged companies, which had developed in the shadow of import substitution policies, to seek markets abroad. The liberalization policies of the 1980s made a reality of the emergence potential, accumulated during decades of protectionism and state development policies. Turkish companies, integrated as they were into a fairly diversified industrial fabric with a certain level of know-how and production capacities, were able to penetrate the markets of Arab oil-exporting countries in the 1980s and those of the CIS in the 1990s. When the Customs Union with Brussels came into effect, Turkish foreign trade made its second leap forward and the European Union became its main trading partner (over half its exports and imports).

Turkish society's dynamism, both regarding population movements (immigration to Europe, emigration from the country to the city and from east to west) and in economic terms, accelerated in the 1990s. Taking advantage of an available supply of cheap labour, SMEs went after surrounding foreign markets, new industrial and financial groups appeared on the Turkish economic scene, and certain provincial cities became industrial clusters. The dampening of employee bargaining power by the new labour code, the greater flexibility granted employers in their recruitment practices, and a public policy allowing the informal sector to develop have made Turkish companies much more competitive. The main accelerating factor of Turkey's emergence was its engagement in a fairly deregulated

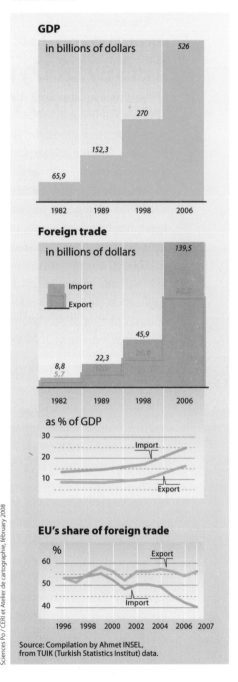

figure 34: **Turkey's foreign trade, 1982-2006**

Source: Compilation by Ahmet INSEL, from TUIK (Turkish Statistics Institut) data.

Sciences Po / CERI et Atelier de cartographie, février 2008

market economy. The same factor was also responsible for the repeated financial crises in the 1990s.

The most patent sign of Turkey's entering the emergence process was the sudden rise in its foreign trade. The volume of foreign trade has multiplied 15-fold in the past 25 years and it has considerably changed in make-up. Turkey went from being an exporter of agricultural and mining products in the early 1980s (57% of its exports came from agricultural products and livestock) to a supplier of industrial products (90% of Turkish exports now include textiles and clothing, semi-processed goods, durable consumer goods including cars and household appliances). Despite this performance, Turkey still has a trade deficit (another atypical situation among emerging countries) due to its concentration of imports in energy, semi-finished manufactured goods and investment credits. Exports cover about 60% of imports. Growth is structurally dependent on imports. On the other hand, finished consumer goods occupy a minor place in imports, and Turkey remains to a large extent self-sufficient in food.

Foreign direct investment (FDI), starting at a very moderate level in the 1980s, followed this opening up but with a lag of nearly a decade. Acceptance of Turkey's application to the European Union at the Helsinki conference in 1999 and the official opening of accession talks in 2005 prompted a rise in FDI. The volume of FDI actually made in 2006 was equivalent to the amount received in the six years between 2000 and 2005 and much higher than the sum of FDI received between 1980 and 2000. In reaction to this overture, Turkish companies began investing in CIS countries, in the Middle East and more and more in the European Union. In 2006 the stock of Turkish company investments abroad nevertheless remain fairly low ($8 billion, 60% of which was in the 25 EU member countries), while the stock of inward FDI entering Turkey was $88 billion.

Since currency exchange restrictions were lifted and the Turkish lira became a convertible currency in 1989, Istanbul has gradually become a prominent financial centre among emerging countries. Offering among the highest positive real interest rates in the world, Turkey has attracted a large flow of portfolio investments whose stock amounted to nearly that of FDI in 2006. This foreign exchange resource enables it to cover the growing current transactions deficit (equivalent to 7.5% of GDP). The structural vola-

figure 35: **Inward FDI flows to Turkey, 1980-2007**

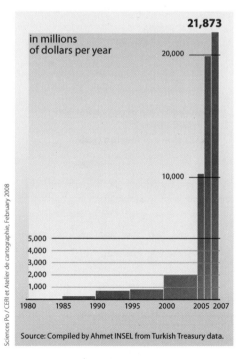

Source: Compiled by Ahmet INSEL from Turkish Treasury data.

Sciences Po / CERI et Atelier de cartographie, February 2008

tility of portfolio investments has made the economy more vulnerable to financial and political crises. Nevertheless, in 2007, during international financial tremors and domestic political crises, capital flight was minimal and the Turkish lira resisted. The dollar crisis and real interest rates among the highest in the world, together with investments denominated in Turkish lira, have reinforced stability. The backlash of this latter fact is the cost of public debt: in 2007, servicing the debt continued to mobilize 32% of Turkey's budget resources, compared to 78% in 2000.

Insufficient investments for progress

The Turkish economy, after stagnating for a long time in the lower bracket of the group of intermediate income countries, manage to pull off its second takeoff, enabling it to surpass the threshold of $5,000 per capita GDP in 2005. Expressed in purchasing power parity, the per capita GDP has gone from $6,550 in 2002 to $8,400 in 2006. The economic results of the 1990s, marred by recurrent financial crises and an annual inflation rate wavering between 50 and 100%, were very mediocre indeed. On emerging from the last crisis in 2001 (a 9% drop in GDP), the Turkish economy recovered its 1994 level of per capita income. Implementation of an austere budget policy with a primary budget surplus (before interest was paid) amounting to 6.5% of GDP, and the stabilization of the banking system helped to break the vicious circle of the 1990s. Since 2002, the Turkish economy has entered a cycle of sustained growth, accompanied by gradual disinflation, which has enabled it to increase the volume of its GDP by 40% in six years. During that same timeframe, the annual inflation rate fell from 80-100 % to 8-10%.

This exceptional growth (18 successive quarters with a growth rate of over 3%) took the emergence of the Turkish economy one step higher. This was achieved by additional buttressing of the Turkish economy against the European Union (hence the acceleration of FDI), a spectacular leap forward in labour productivity,

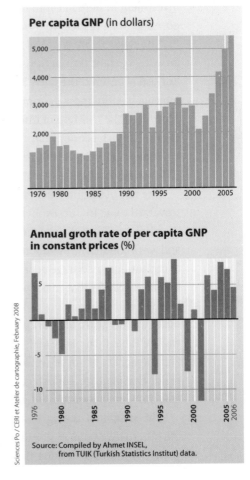

figure 36: **Turkey's Gross National Product (GNP), 1976-2006**

Per capita GNP (in dollars)

Annual groth rate of per capita GNP in constant prices (%)

Sciences Po / CERI et Atelier de cartographie, February 2008

Source: Compiled by Ahmet INSEL,
from TUIK (Turkish Statistics Institut) data.

and renewed political stability after the end of 2002. However, growth has not been backed by a substantial investment effort. The per capita level of investment has remained practically unchanged over the past ten years (1,450 euros in 2005 compared to 1,375 euros in 1997). Here we find one of the long-term weaknesses of the Turkish economy. Without a significant resumption of investments, labour productivity gains are likely to dry up quickly, particularly because of delays accumulated in education and health care.

According to UNPD data, Turkey has come down about 20 pegs on the world Human Development Index (HDI) with respect to its rank in terms of per capita GDP expressed in purchasing power parity (among 177 countries, 84th in the first case and 66th in the second). This downgrading is basically due to the low percentage of children attending school. Despite the youth of its population, the country devotes only about 4% of its GDP to education. By comparison with the achievements of other emerging countries, the average length of education (six years) remains low and the education available, quantitatively insufficient and elitist, remains particularly deficient at the secondary education level. Low average investment in human capital is likely to cripple the competitiveness of the Turkish economy with respect to other emerging economies in the years to come.

The overvaluation of the lira with respect to international currencies and the growing current transactions deficit are factors of short-term vulnerability in the Turkish economy. The fairly high level of public debt, especially the acceleration of internal indebtedness denominated in local currency, heightens this vulnerability. Moreover, the low rate of internal savings and the lack of human capital, by making the Turkish economy susceptible to competition from low-wage countries and emerging countries with greater investment capacity, heighten the risk of long-term vulnerability.

The role of the informal economy in the dynamism of Turkish economy is a controversial topic in Turkey. It allegedly accounts for 30% to 40% of GDP, depending on estimates. The OECD estimates that in the parallel economy, productivity is low and work conditions mediocre, but administrative rigidities and the weight of social contributions encourage economic actors to stay in it. According to other analysts, the family SMEs that make up the informal economy fit into the world economy by positioning themselves as subcontractors. These small, highly flexible structures make up the heart of "Turkish-style post-Fordism". But by helping to worsen the welfare deficit, the informal economy has a negative impact on the state budget and the quality of social welfare services. In the face of competition from China, a major challenge for Turkish governments is to foster the absorption of the informal economy into a dynamics of growth more based on high added-value products.

The weight of the agricultural sector and its lack of productivity constitute the other weak point. Agricultural activity, which has been plummeting in recent years, continues to employ slightly less than 30% of the active population whereas it only contributes 10% of GDP. It is too often carried on by small family farms. Rural-urban drift is pushing up the number of the jobless in big cities (over 10%), an unemployment rate that economic growth has not managed to stem. Even if nearly the entire jobless population is covered by universal health insurance, only a minute portion of the jobless (about five per 1,000) receive payments from the unemployment insurance fund. The particularly low female unemployment rate (28%), atypical among emerging countries, also reduces the effects of the demographic window of opportunity.

Lastly, Turkey suffers from high energy dependence. Energy represents 20% of its imports and increases the trade deficit. One dimension of Turkey's foreign policy is to ensure the security of energy supplies by bilateral agreements with its neighbouring gas and oil suppliers and by a platform country strategy for the delivery of Caucasian and Iraqi gas and oil (the port of Yumurtalik has become a nerve centre of the Eastern Mediterranean). This strategy also puts Turkey in a position of rivalry with Russia. Along with the ambitious programme to control water resources, which kindles tensions with the countries bordering the Tigris and Euphrates and poses environmental problems, the government is also considering undertaking a highly controversial programme to build nuclear power stations starting in 2010.

The slow demise of economic and political life

Despite strong economic growth in these past few years, several factors diminish the mean term predictability of the Turkish economy: growth was beginning to sputter towards the end of 2007, while political instability in the region (uncertainties about the future of Iraq, questions over the status of Iraqi Kurdistan, the growing tension between the US and Iran), the doubts expressed in Turkey about pursuing the strategic alliance with the United States, and more recently the threat of Turkish military intervention in the north of Iraq, have heightened risks of instability. Lastly, the uncertainties dawning in the past two years about the outcome of the EU accession talks have diminished the transformative capacities of the accession process. In fact, the pace of reform has slowed considerably since 2005, and Euroscepticism is gaining ground in Turkish society.

In the first half of the 2000s, the foothold in Europe provided most of the impetus for the explosion of political modernization. Sovereignty-concerned, nationalist and conservative resistance was weakened by the strength of the pro-accession social dynamics. But with this enthusiasm on the wane, the primary factors of internal tension have returned to the fore. Contrary to what supporters of the privileged partnership believe, limiting Turkish-EU relations to the economic sphere may revive domestic social and political tensions that would undermine growth, as they did in the 1990s.

During that decade, growth was highly cyclical: high-growth periods were followed by equally strong recessions. Political instability, exacerbated by cobbled-together government coalitions, was in part responsible for the great economic instability. It must be admitted that the political stability following the November 2002 elections won by the Justice and Development Party has done much to promote the current stable economic growth.

On a domestic level, growing inequality in both social and regional terms is stirring social tensions. In 2005, one-fifth of the Turkish population was living below the absolute poverty threshold. That same year, the poorest 5% of the population earned 0.8% of the income as opposed to 23% for the richest 5%. Lastly, the gap between average incomes in the wealthy western provinces and the poor eastern provinces remains very high. The failure to resolve the Kurdish conflict condemns the eastern regions to underdevelopment and in the medium term risks spreading tensions related to the Kurdish problem across Turkey (increased terrorist action in the cities, multiplication of local interethnic conflicts, etc.). Added to that are the spasms caused by social and political change, of which the growing tension between the conservative (Muslim-liberal) and secular (secular-Republican) camps is a direct product. This tension reproduces the conditions that enable the Turkish Army to position itself as a political actor and compounds the uncertainties that weigh on Turkish political stability in the medium term.

For the past two decades, Turkish society has been experiencing the convulsions of its integration into the world economy. Today, as yesterday, the incapacity of the political class to normalize democracy and rebalance relations between state and society remains its Achilles' heel. The continuation of Turkey's emergence, however, depends on making improvements in both these areas. The contrast between the mediocre economic performance of the 1990s and the considerably more vigorous achievements of the 2000s is the best proof of the existence, in the case of Turkey, of a close relation between political development and economic development.

Bibliography ·····································

Insel, A. (ed.) (2003). *La Turquie et le développement.* Paris: L'Harmattan.

Insel, A. (2003). "The Justice and Development Party and the Normalization of Democracy in Turkey". *The South Atlantic Quarterly* 102 (2-3).

OECD (2006). *Economic Survey of Turkey 2006.* Paris: OECD.

Pérouse, J.F. (2004). La Turquie en marche. Les grandes mutations depuis 1950. Paris: La Martinière.

Vaner, S. (ed.) (2005). *La Turquie.* Paris: Fayard.

Turkish Statistics Institute (TUIK) data.

South Africa:
A Power Only in the Eyes of Others?

Dominique Darbon

Since apartheid came to an end in 1990-94, South Africa has been asserting itself as an emerging country poised to take a significant place in the new international economic order. This claim, based on its status as "Africa's economic giant" (one-quarter of the African continent's GDP; one-third of the GDP of Sub-Saharan Africa and three-quarters of the GDP of the SADC, Southern African Development Community), is not self-evident. In some regards the country belongs to the developed, even rich, world (per capita GDP and the weight of its tertiary sector) and to the level of countries such as Greece, Thailand or Argentina, whereas its size and regional importance bring it closer to other large emerging countries such as India, China, Mexico, Russia and Brazil. Moreover, the social dualism and major social problems affecting nearly 50% of its population jeopardize and hinder its emergence, bringing it to share similar sets of issues to those the poorest countries must face.

If South Africa appears "naturally" as an emerging country, it is because of its preponderant economic position on the continent combined with the appeal of its experience and political trajectory. This combination makes the country a "useful power" in the new world order. South Africa contributes a sub-Saharan African presence to international debates and offers its own path of development, integrated nevertheless in the process of globalization, to a continent faced with underdevelopment, instability and marginalization. What other country besides South Africa could properly represent sub-Saharan Africa today in the major international forums with the same economic and organizational features and the same democratic political track record? This situation has become a fundamental resource for the country. South Africa has been using its "usefulness" as a trademark that it tends to export well beyond the African continent. Its appeal lies in its capacity to bring into play very different economic, social and political actors, all concerned at once with efficiency, profitability and access to new markets and with forming a pole of stability and a reliable intermediary to play a part in a sub-Saharan Africa characterized, conversely, by a high degree of volatility. South Africa thus imposes its usefulness by building an ideological and political model highly in tune with the issues of globalization for the African and developing world, thereby reinforcing its emergence strategy and confirming its economic choices.

South Africa combines the characteristics of a middle power, with considerable resources and a real but limited capacity to influence, and those of a semiperipheral state that depends largely on dominant powers to be able to exist as a major partner in the new international order. The country's specific emergence strategy draws on the association of these two positions.

Exploring the options and resources

Its colonial history and apartheid constructed a country that combines a protected modern sector, formed on the Western model and essentially benefiting a white racial minority, contrasting with a massive economically and politically marginalized population. The end of apartheid inaugurated considerable challenges. Integration of the marginalized population, the conquest of an underexploited domestic market to endow the poor populations with greater spending power, modernization and enhancement of the competitiveness of the production apparatus and development and redeployment of collective infrastructures—such are the considerable reforms that South Africa, a society undergoing rapid expansion, has had to set in motion.

Since the early 1990s, the South African economy has been painfully rediscovering the virtues of liberalism and opening up to international competition of which the policies of apartheid and protectionism had deprived it. Its economic transformation takes root in the combined efforts of the political authorities and social and economic actors within forums of negotiation such as NEDLAC (the National Economic Development and Labour Council). In these forums, the role of private entrepreneurs who possess real capacities for management and negotiation via their professional organizations and the country's major multinationals is fundamental. The South African state is thus essentially a developmentalist state that intervenes in order to strengthen the production capacities of private actors and infrastructures while striving to orient them in such a way as to benefit the poorest segments of the population. This creates considerable tensions, but the state has clearly opted for a liberal policy that favours investment aiming to strengthen the production apparatus, to the detriment of a policy of social redistribution, abandoned in the early 1990s. In the framework of the GEAR (Growth, Employment and Redistribution) programme from 1996 to 2006, replaced since January 2006 by the Accelerated and Shared Growth Initiative (ASGI-SA), such modernization of the economic apparatus, marked in particular by deregulation, the opening of markets, budget and monetary stabilization and the end of exchange restrictions, has translated into economic revival evidenced by continual growth (3.2% per year from 1994 to 2005, compared with 0.8% from 1983 to 1993) which is currently accelerating (5% in 2006) to reach the 6% per annum objective required to accelerate the deep structural changes in the economy. South Africa has gone from a closed economy basically focused on mining and agriculture to an open, manufacturing economy largely reliant on services (the tertiary sector now represents two-thirds of GDP). The abundant and diversified sources of energy—even if bad management causes shortages and cuts—and the exploitation of significant mineral and agricultural wealth guarantee sizeable revenue (10% of GDP), particularly with the skyrocketing prices of raw materials. Today, manufacturing, despite structural problems of low competitiveness, and certain key sectors such as automobiles, telecommunications, banking, insurance and tourism, buttressed by high-power multinationals, are plainly at the heart of the country's economic expansion.

These economic transformations are indivisible from the redistribution and empowerment policies conducted by the South African state in favour of the groups most marginalized by apartheid, particularly the blacks. They aim to correct the economic, social and territorial distortions and reduce the considerable social inequalities and extreme poverty that characterize South African society. This catching-up policy has three main directions: systematic support for the modern production sector to provoke a trickle-down effect; the modernization of less efficient economic activities; a redistribution policy based on investment in healthcare, education and social infrastructure and social aid programmes helping marginally but progressively to improve the fate of the poorest citizens; and, last, an affirmative action policy in all areas ensuring access for all former marginalized groups to jobs and management positions. This last direction is evidenced by the emergence of a new social category of affluent black managers contributing to the expansion of a better-trained middle class with considerable spending power. The series of Black Economic Empowerment programmes in particular enables black managers to attain corporate leadership positions and gradually increases the share of business capital controlled by blacks, thus contributing to the "normalizing" of the private sector, albeit very slowly. A black middle class is developing, helping to support the rapid expansion of domestic consumption. The catching-up effect has nevertheless been curbed by the economic austerity policy conducted until 2006 to the detriment of public investment and modernization of the production apparatus, which is very costly in terms of jobs. Since ASGI-SA in

figure 37: **South Africa's foreign trade, 2007**

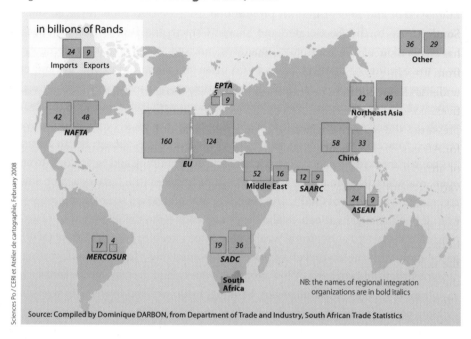

Source: Compiled by Dominique DARBON, from Department of Trade and Industry, South African Trade Statistics

2006, and with the 2010 soccer World Cup in sight, public investment expenditure has risen significantly.

Economic expansion, however modest by comparison with other emerging countries, is steady and accelerating, buoyed by dynamic domestic consumption as well as the redeployment abroad of certain activities. International trade accounts for about half of GDP and positions the country among the major expanding economic regions.

figure 38: **Annual growth of South Africa's foreign trade, 2006-2007**

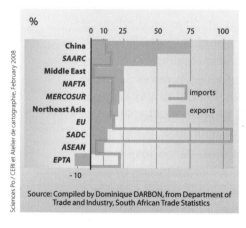

Source: Compiled by Dominique DARBON, from Department of Trade and Industry, South African Trade Statistics

South Africa thus has a strong commercial foothold in the world's major economic regions. At the same time sub-Saharan Africa seems to be the natural area for its expansion and action. South African development cannot accelerate without a stabilized and prosperous "hinterland", just as South Africa cannot be stabilized in the long run without an eventual decrease in its neighbours' instability.

South Africa is now one of the main investors in Africa and is establishing itself as the sole practicable gateway to the continent, at the risk of running up against competition from other emerging countries, China in particular.

The strategy of multiple interfaces: playing the 'usefulness' card

South Africa's emergence is taking advantage of the political aura that the country has enjoyed since it successfully managed its transition process. But it also benefits from its political stability and its capacity to suggest options for solving crises and underdevelopment in poor countries, particularly those in Africa. These alternatives, combining Africanist assertions (African Renaissance), developmentalist pressures and an active role in the global political order (the New Partnership for Africa's Development, NEPAD), are buoyed by the country's economic power of attraction as well as by a political activism that reverberates throughout the various regions of the world via the various communities (national, linguistic and religious) that make up the country (Africans, Europeans, Indians, Anglophones, Portuguese-speakers, Muslims, Christians, etc.). South Africa appears in international debates as an "honest broker" that can legitimately serve as a bridge between the richer states and the most destitute states and populations. These qualities, the real organizational capacities present in the country and the lack of a better alternative have prompted great world leaders seeking an African interlocutor to recognize South Africa as the only African country in a position to act as a leader and representative of Sub-Saharan Africa or even all Africa.

That does not mean that South Africa settles only for playing the "usefulness" card. It optimizes its position by using the stands it takes and policies it conducts to claim its place as an indispensable continental intermediary. The emergence of South Africa thus results largely from its capacity to play a part in different spheres and take advantage of each of its roles to reinforce its overall position. It has become a privileged economic and political partner of emerging or established major powers, benefiting from AGOA (the US African Growth and Opportunity Act) since 2000 (renewed in 2002), a special trade agreement with the EU since 2000 (Trade Development and Cooperation Agreement), and a special alliance with India and Brazil (IBSA since 2003). It ensures a leadership role within several groups of emerging or poor countries (G20 since Evian in 2003, G33, G8+) but can also take a lead in disputes, for instance within the WTO over the marketing of certain drugs and services. It is present as a mediator on new international issues, such as United Nations reform, peaceful conflict resolution and interposition between belligerents, and has had its role as essential African partner confirmed in international organizations, including the FATF (Financial Action Task Force), over which it presided until 2006, as well as the WTO, the IOC (International Olympic Committee) and the UN. At the same time it has constantly multiplied initiatives on the continent either to renovate the pan-African organization, now the AU (African Union), whose parliament it hosts, to initiate new development projects such as NEPAD, to relaunch an

figure 39: **Economic weight of South Africa in Sub-Saharan Africa, 2006**

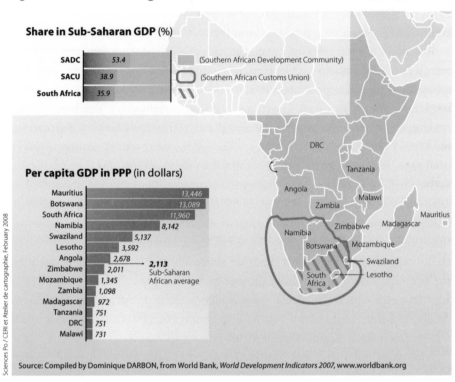

Source: Compiled by Dominique DARBON, from World Bank, *World Development Indicators 2007*, www.worldbank.org

Sciences Po / CERI et Atelier de cartographie, February 2008

overall renewal project for Africa of which the "African Renaissance" is a particular example, or to strengthen its role within the SADC, now with 14 member
states and involved in the creation of a free trade area by 2008. It is stabilizing
the SACU (Southern African Custom Union) countries, helping to federate its
regional area of influence, without being economically bound by it, and is trying
to gain acceptance as continental leader.

In short, South Africa is endowed with an ideological apparatus borne by an
intense international activism that positions it as the indispensable actor in the
new world order, not necessarily because its power imposes it as such, but because
it is the only country on the African continent capable of acting as a role model,
able legitimately to represent the poorest countries' demands and give them a
strong resonance. These political resources are thus the best amplifier of its economic achievements, which in turn reinforce the former.

The pitfalls of a limited power strategy

South Africa is thus likely to pursue its current expansion and emergence strategy,
which should make the country a significant actor in the new world order. There

remain, however, a series of internal and external challenges largely tied to the legacy of apartheid that will continue to weigh heavily on its economic expansion in the next ten years.

Regarding the rise in domestic consumption, partly due to expansion and the overall rise in the standard of living, investment remains insufficient. National savings are very low, FDI remains too limited and especially too fluctuating, while South African companies that see more advantageous investment opportunities opening up abroad and particularly elsewhere in Africa tend to export their capital and know-how. For lack of sufficient domestic investment, unemployment remains at an extremely high level (30% to 40% of the active population) and companies in the informal sector are not managing to emerge; this reinforces the feeling of frustration of over 50% of the population that lives in poverty contrasting with an ever richer minority (South Africa is ranked second on the Gini Index). Social and criminal violence runs very high. The xenophobic riots of early 2008 fuelled by some prominent leaders of the Contralesa (Congress of Traditional Leaders of South-Africa) and populist politicians, are but one form of violence caused by growing social discontent. In these prevailing economic and social conditions, the rise in consumption is partially ensured by an increase in imports from emerging countries, particularly China and India, more than by a rise in national produc-tion—all the more so since economic competitiveness, especially in the manu-facturing sector, is still crippled by fairly high salaries for an emerging country, the relative rigidity of the labour market, an insufficiently trained workforce, the departure of young managers abroad and the dramatic impact of AIDS on the workforce. South Africa differs from other emerging countries in that, since 2003, its current account balance is occasionally in deficit. The ASGI-SA, by launching a vast programme to invest in infrastructure and the fight against poverty, and by making the enhancement of the economy's competitiveness a priority, particularly in high-tech sectors, hopes to address all of these problems.

AIDS is a specific challenge to the country. With a rate of prevalence hanging around 31% of the adult population, particularly high among the younger genera-tions, the financial, economic and social costs to meet are considerable and likely to jeopardize the country's expansion as well as that of all the southern zone of Africa.

At the same time the emergence of South Africa is partly limited by the "tox-icity" of the African continent. While the latter constitutes a considerable politi-cal and economic resource for South Africa and is at the very heart of its defini-tion of useful power, it is just as likely, owing to the rivalries running through it, its bad habits and the new appetites the major powers have acquired for it, to affect South Africa's potential for expansion. Unlike other emerging countries that have strong domestic markets and an area for expansion made up of rela-tively stable and expanding neighbours, contributing to the strengthening of the

figure 40: **GDP, economic growth and population of SADC states**

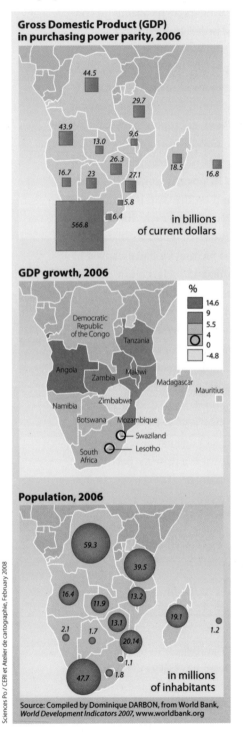

Gross Domestic Product (GDP) in purchasing power parity, 2006

44.5

29.7

43.9

13.0

9,6

26.3

18.5

16.7   23   27.1   16.8

5.8

6,4

566.8

in billions
of current dollars

GDP growth, 2006

%

14.6
9
5.5
4
0
-4.8

Democratic
Republic
of the Congo

Tanzania

Angola

Zambia   Malawi

Madagascar

Mauritius

Namibia   Zimbabwe

Botswana   Mozambique

Swaziland

South
Africa   Lesotho

Population, 2006

59.3

39.5

16.4

11.9   13.2

2.1   1.7   13.1   19.1   1.2

20.14

1.1

47.7   1.8

in millions
of inhabitants

Source: Compiled by Dominique DARBON, from World Bank,
World Development Indicators 2007, www.worldbank.org

Sciences Po / CERI et Atelier de cartographie, February 2008

growth trend, South Africa is extremely isolated at the tip of the African continent and its natural area for expansion seems for the moment hardly conducive to the development of real economic and financial partnerships. The SADC zone constitutes an interesting but still economically very weak and fairly unstable neighbourhood (Zimbabwe, the Democratic Republic of Congo, Burundi, Zambia).

At the same time, the exasperation of several African countries with regard to South Africa's dominant and moralizing positions is being expressed more and more openly, and it contributes to the fostering of new rivalries likely to affect South African expansion, and already hinders the continent's revival. Aside from Nigeria, whose emergence is old news since the country's independence, other oil-producing and resource-rich countries such as Angola are conducting competing policies likely to benefit from the support of Brazil, for instance, which may opt for historic and Portuguese-speaking solidarity. The presence and ambition demonstrated by the major emerging countries in Africa, including China and India, added to the new economic aspirations of other major powers, is a factor also likely to thwart South African expansion on the continent and thus limit the country's ability to rely on a neighbouring growth area.

South Africa is thus engaged in an emergence race in which it must manage to reconcile contradictory expectations on both the domestic and the external level. Its position as an interface between several international interest groups enables it to draw resources from all its partners and assert itself as an international and not merely an African medium power. This position is likely to help regulate the new appetites generated by a sub-Saharan Africa rich in mineral and energy resources as well as new markets. Faced with what more than ever resembles an economic "scramble for Africa", South Africa will be in a strong position as long as it can convince these other powers and the African states that the continent needs a strong leadership that can help structure it. That will require demonstrating its own capacity to consolidate its stability and successfully integrate its poor population.

Bibliography •

Alden, C. and G. Le Pere (2004). "South Africa's Post Apartheid Foreign Policy: From Reconciliation to Ambiguity". *Review of African Political Economy*, Vol. 31 (100), pp. 283-97.

Bond, P. (2004). "The ANC's 'Left Turn' and South African Sub-Imperialism". *Review of African Political Economy*, Vol. 31 (102), December, pp. 599-616.

Daniel, J. et al. (2004). "Post Apartheid South Africa's Corporate Expansion into Africa". *Review of African Political Economy*, Vol. 31 (100), June, pp. 343-8.

Darbon, D. and M. Foucher (2000). *L'Afrique du sud, puissance utile?* Paris: Belin.

Vale, P. (2003). *Security and Politics in South Africa: The Regional Dimension*. Boulder, CO: Lynne Rienner.

Wa Kabwe-Segatti, A. and L. Landau (2008). "Migration in post-Apartheid South Africa: Challenges and Questions to Policy Makers". Paris: AFD.

Russia: Emerging or Re-Emerging?

Panel discussion with Geoff Barnard, Gilles Favarel-Garrigues, Jérôme Guillet, Christophe Jaffrelot and Anne de Tinguy.

Can Russia be classed as an emerging country?

Jérôme Guillet: An emerging country is one that Western multinationals can invest in, a country where New York and London banks can do business with Western multinationals as well as local businesses. Secondly, it has cheap labour, which encourages Western companies to relocate and enables them to keep up the pressure on wages at home. Thirdly, emerging countries are treated with condescension by the West, which is prepared to extend a helping hand to allow them to catch up. Russia does not really qualify as an emerging country according to any of these criteria, but it has a great deal of money which the bankers are keen to get their hands on. And so it has been classified as a BRIC country as it represents a potential financial market.

Russia's emergence is often portrayed in a negative light, as Russia is not open to Western multinationals. The country is seen as a market but not as an investment or development centre, nor as an offshore platform, as China and India are. At the same time, Moscow makes no secret of the fact that its economic relations are governed by politics, which is also out of keeping with international models. The Russians follow other people's rules when it suits them, and keep to their own when they so wish. Consequently they are seen by the West as troublemakers and a threat.

figure 41: **Foreign direct investment in Russia, 1990-2006**

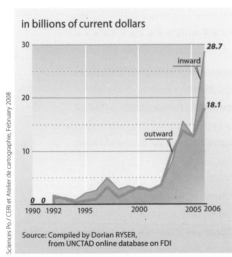

in billions of current dollars

Source: Compiled by Dorian RYSER, from UNCTAD online database on FDI

Sciences Po / CERI et Atelier de cartographie, February 2008

Geoff Barnard: The term "emergence" entered the lexicon in the 1980s in the context of the phrase "emerging market". That generally is taken to mean three things: the country in question has a low or medium level of per capita income, it is experiencing rapid growth and converging towards advanced country income levels, and it is integrating into the global economy. It could be argued that Russia is now *re*-emerging, since by the 1950s, per capita GDP in the USSR had attained two-thirds of the Western European level, having rapidly increased since the 1920s. At that point the USSR was a middle-income country converging towards the income levels prevailing in the West, and could in that sense have been seen as an emerging economy. But the USSR's relative living standards then eroded gradually until 1990, and they then plummeted during the first years of transition, so that by 1998 GDP per capita was only 25% of the average level in Western Europe. Now, with rapid growth (partially but not entirely driven by high oil prices) we are again witnessing convergence in income levels, but this time there is also—a new factor—financial and economic integration. So the current facts seem to fit the usual definition of emergence well, and it is probably best to see the Russian economy as emerging for the first time.

Gilles Favarel-Garrigues: Many Russians would find it hard to understand how their country could be described as "emerging"! They aspire—as the government is well aware—to regaining what they see as their rightful status as a major global power, which they associate with the Soviet past. They feel that too often the West treats them with condescension and is only interested in Russia when it is in difficulty. This climate of mistrust can be explained by military factors, and also by the damage that has been done by American and European policies promoting democracy, the market economy and the rule of law. Under cover of moral righteousness, these policies have often masked expensive but ineffective, even dangerous undertakings, in that they endorsed the legitimacy of power circles that are now condemned. This applies for example to some technical aid programmes in CIS countries instigated by the European Commission from the 1990s till after 2000. The result is a climate that foments nationalist rhetoric, as happened in Russia in the mid-1990s. The political exploitation of this issue reflected a renewed interest among Russians for national history and contemporary geopolitics.

That said, the Russian government has adopted the status of an emerging economy, since it wants to be a member of the BRIC club, which gives it legitimacy and guarantees its continued status as a major power in the multipolar world that it hopes for.

Anne de Tinguy: Russia does indeed have ambitions of power and even grandeur, insofar as it seeks recognition as a driving force for what it calls a more "just" international order. Its positioning alongside emerging powers such as Brazil, India and

China is key to this and has been at the core of Vladimir Putin's foreign policy. This positioning is linked to Moscow's analysis of the international situation, which it perceives as being in a state of major change: Russia sees a weakening of the United State's geopolitical role, a permanent withdrawal of the European Union into itself, new sources of influence as a result of globalization, a shift of power in the world towards new actors, emerging countries and those that own natural resources, the growing importance of fossil fuels in the world, etc. Moscow sees this new order as a tremendous opportunity which its positioning alongside the emerging countries enables it to exploit. This effectively reinforces its analysis of a multipolar world in which it sees itself as a major player and redefines Russia's relationship with the United States and the European Union. In order to be seen as one of the major players on the international stage, Russia is pursuing a policy it describes as "independent", prompting it to differentiate itself from the Western countries. Vladimir Putin refuses to allow his country to be seen as the junior partner of a Western world which he considers to be losing momentum. Positioning itself alongside the major emerging countries allows Moscow to reinforce the idea that the West's days are over. That is the message Russia was trying to get across in stating that the G7, "the club of Western powers"—now the G8—has become more representative thanks to Russia, and also in the summer of 2007 when it supported a rival candidate to the one chosen by the United States and the European Union for the position of Director of the IMF. That said, Russia is "the small one" within the BRICs, in terms of both its demographic and economic weight. The growing gulf between Russia and China is now huge. In 1990, the two countries were more or less equal in terms of GDP. Today the ratio is one to three in China's favour, which means that Moscow could be Beijing's junior partner... whereas Russia has strengthened its partnership with China in order to stand up to the USA.

Can a country that has a rentier economy be described as an emerging country? In principle, a country that lives on its income does not invest. Can an emerging economy that does not invest ever "emerge", or will it remain "emerging"?

Jérôme Guillet: Russia's relations with the rest of the world and its emergence are fundamentally bound up with its role as an energy-exporting country (oil and gas, and, to a lesser extent, metals). Russia exports chiefly raw materials and in recent years its economy has benefited massively from the oil price boom, which means that it is no longer totally dependent on the goodwill of its creditors (unlike in the 1990s when rescheduling the debt was a key issue), and has also given it the means to aspire to power and step up its military investments. Energy prices reflect a new imbalance between supply and demand. It is now a producers' market rather than a consumers' market, which gives Russia a stronger political and geopolitical influence.

figure 42: **Gazprom gas sales in the European countries, 2006**

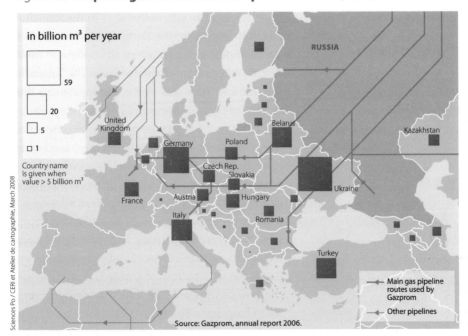

Source: Gazprom, annual report 2006.

Sciences Po / CERI et Atelier de cartographie, March 2008

Growth in Russia is mainly the result of the rise in oil prices, and Moscow has been lucky in that until now this increase has been steadily linear. So far, there has been a beneficial effect each year and this pattern looks set to continue for some time, since tensions in the energy market are growing with prices continuing to rise. I still maintain that Vladimir Putin was lucky, as there is so much money in Russia that even the oligarchs can't grab it all, and some of it ends up in the pockets of the population. With this boon, even Boris Yeltsin would have managed to restore Russia's power. Money has made both consumption and the reconstruction of some industries possible. And so the question of whether Russia can ever "emerge" remains, but it is not being asked—and will not be asked for a long time—as a matter of urgency.

It is uncertain whether Russia is aggressive because it can afford to be, or, more likely and in my view, as a reaction to the West which is alarmed by this new state of affairs. In a nutshell, Europe's energy policy comes down to "What's our gas doing beneath your tundra?" The assumption is that we should be able to consume as much gas as we like and that it should not be expensive; the Russians must therefore provide. Added to the current price rises is the fact that Britain has recently become an importer whereas it used to be an exporter. The British, incidentally, being the Europeans with the greatest influence on EU policy at present, especially on issues of liberalization and deregulation, are spearheading this debate. The provocation is coming from the West rather than from Russia.

figure 43: **Natural gas trade in European countries, 2006**

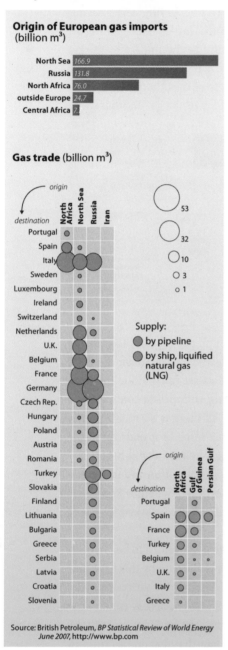

Origin of European gas imports (billion m³)

North Sea	166.9
Russia	131.8
North Africa	76.0
outside Europe	24.7
Central Africa	7.2

Source: British Petroleum, *BP Statistical Review of World Energy June 2007*, http://www.bp.com

Sciences Po / CERI et Atelier de cartographie, March 2008

The gas situation is one of intense co-dependence, but neither side can exploit it: the Russians can stop supplying the Europeans with gas, but the Europeans can stop buying it. Europe buys 25% of its gas from Russia whereas the Russians sell 100% of their gas to the Europeans. So the dependency is not necessarily all that it seems.

It is easier for a country to blame others for its energy policy's failings than to find fault with itself. It is easy to bow to market forces when there is a surplus in supply. Up until three or four years ago when the Russian oligarchs were allowed to enter into partnerships with Western oil companies, they were our friends. But now things have changed: some are in prison, and some companies have been nationalized or sold to Gazprom, while the position towards BP and Shell is becoming more hard-line. As a result, Vladimir Putin is no longer our friend, and we are rather more concerned about human rights than we were when we had access to oil. We have rediscovered that the Kremlin has authoritarian leanings and we are protesting. There is an overdetermined discourse that Russia is no longer fulfilling its treaty obligations and is provoking the West by warning against the anti-missile shield, but we have forgotten the Anti-Ballistic Missile Treaty. Russia's reactions are seen as acts of aggression towards the West. Furthermore, Vladimir Putin plays into the West's hands as he gives knee-jerk reactions, is capable of taking a very hostile line and is pursuing a power-seeking policy. He maintains an atmosphere of confrontation that ultimately suits everyone since it is always easy to get elected by rallying the country around oneself rather than tackling problems.

But are Russian energy investments sufficient?

Geoff Barnard: To a large extent Russia is a rentier economy, but that does not preclude achieving rapid sustainable growth, and the current situation appears quite promising in that respect. The rise in oil prices has certainly led to an increase in Russian consumption but Russians are also saving a good part of the windfall. Along the lines of the Norwegian example, Russia has set up institutions (an oil price stabilization fund, which was recently split into a reserve fund and a savings fund) to invest some of the oil revenues. The Russians have also managed to curb the real appreciation of their currency so as to minimize the impact of the rise in oil prices on the non-oil tradeables sector. If there is indeed a "resource curse" that makes resource-rich countries grow less quickly than the others, so far Russia has been able to avoid it, in part by implementing effective macro- and microeconomic policies.

You mention savings and consumption, but what is Russia's investment strategy, if it has one?

Gilles Favarel-Garrigues: In government circles, there is a growing awareness that Russia must make the most of the financial boon to try and ensure its long-term development. Numerous colloquia and discussions are held to decide which sectors should be developed with the idea that Russia must find its own niche, as China and India have done. In 2008, for example, a major nanotechnology agency was established. However, Russia is still paying the price from the 1990s in that the industrial infrastructure is old and needs modernizing, and there is a growing shortage of skilled labour because the university training system has collapsed. The Russian elites are now trying to find the magic formula that will enable them to make the profits from the current growth lasting and sustainable.

Some people say that Russia's investments in energy are insufficient to modernize the infrastructure…

Jérôme Guillet: That is a very biased viewpoint. Russia is the country that has seen the strongest growth in its oil production in the last decade. That is the result of short-term investments. For the medium term, it is harder to predict. In the gas sector, the Russians have attempted to minimize their production for the domestic market since domestic consumption does not

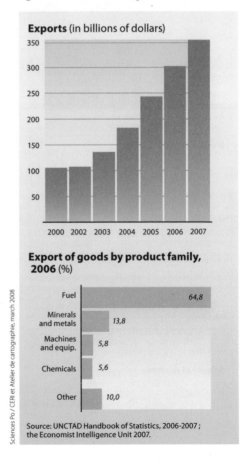

figure 44: **Russian exports, 2000-2007**

Exports (in billions of dollars)

Export of goods by product family, 2006 (%)

Fuel	64,8
Minerals and metals	13,8
Machines and equip.	5,8
Chemicals	5,6
Other	10,0

Source: UNCTAD Handbook of Statistics, 2006-2007 ; the Economist Intelligence Unit 2007.

Sciences Po / CERI et Atelier de cartographie, march 2008

133

pay, which means that Gazprom's interests conflict with those of the political authorities since they want to keep the electorate happy by charging as little as possible for gas, while Gazprom of course wants to produce as little gas as possible for the unprofitable domestic market. So Gazprom has created an impression of shortages so as to be able to deliver less gas, pay lower taxes to the Russian state and be able to say "raise domestic prices". This is an internal ploy. The Russians invested what was necessary to maintain production at the level that enabled them to maximize their revenues, which is Rule 1 of the capitalist economy. They export as much as they can. If they don't sell more, it is because Europe doesn't want to buy more. For the last fifteen years people have been saying that the Russians can't carry on producing in this manner, but that is the line pushed by politicians keen to give opportunities to BP or Shell, rather than an industrial fact.

figure 45: **Russia's balance of current account, goods and services, 2000-2006**

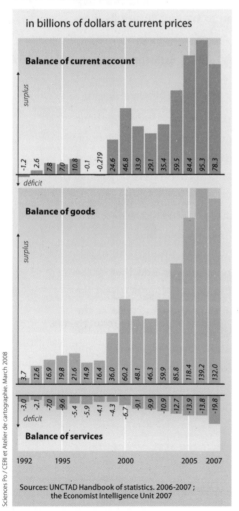

in billions of dollars at current prices

Balance of current account

surplus

déficit

-1,2 2,6 7,8 7,0 10,8 -0,1 -0,219 24,6 46,8 33,9 29,1 35,4 59,5 84,4 95,3 78,3

Balance of goods

surplus

deficit

3,7 12,6 16,9 19,8 21,6 14,9 16,4 36,0 60,2 48,1 46,3 59,9 85,8 118,4 139,2 132,0

-3,0 -2,1 -7,0 -9,6 -5,4 -5,9 -4,1 -4,3 -6,7 -9,1 -9,9 -10,9 -12,7 -13,9 -13,8 -19,8

Balance of services

1992   1995   2000   2005 2007

Sources: UNCTAD Handbook of statistics. 2006-2007 ;
the Economist Intelligence Unit 2007

Sciences Po / CERI et Atelier de cartographie. March 2008

Geoff Barnard: For some years now observers have been saying that production is going to peak or that it is about to begin falling. In 1999, they were already saying that it would take years before production capacities could increase. Since then, output has nearly doubled. So the Russians have been able to find the means, but perhaps they are beginning to run out of options and probably only a massive investment programme can avert a decline in production. But it is hard to be sure. More generally, investment has risen by 10%-15% a year over the last nine years, which is not negligible, but economic growth has mainly reflected increases in total factor productivity rather than the accumulation of capital. With the drop in production in the 1990s, the rebound began from a position of ample excess capacity. That will not always be the case, however, so that investment will have to rise if the rapid economic growth rates that we have seen are to continue. There are in fact signs that this is happening: in 2007, investment grew very rapidly, particularly in infrastructure, which badly need to be upgraded. There was also heavy investment in services.

If you had to identify the actors in this investment strategy and the type of institution with

which they are associated, how would you do so? What is the relative importance of private versus public enterprise? Are we faced with a new variety of capitalism rising from the ruins of the Communist system?

Geoff Barnard: Until recently, we had, oversimplifying somewhat, a pure and simple capitalist model. Within the government, for a long time it was the liberals who steered economic policy. Then, from the Yukos episode onward, we have seen the growing influence of the *siloviki*,[1] who favour taking control of some strategic areas, in particular the energy sector. Hitherto, the overall strategy has remained market-driven. However, things are changing, and there is certainly a danger of a move towards more of a statist model, with an attendant risk of inefficiency, waste and corruption, and therefore weaker growth and slower convergence with Western living standards.

Jérôme Guillet: Russia is a country where the legal entity does not really exist and where you don't talk to the boss of Yukos but to the man who is the boss of Yukos, you don't talk to the Energy Minister but to the man who is entitled to sign documents as Minister. Personal and individual interest is often a determining factor in many decisions.

In Boris Yeltsin's day, companies dictated their terms to the state, and the active partner in corruption dictated his terms to the passive one. Under Vladimir Putin, the relationship has been reversed: the *siloviki* are in power. They were poor, and when they saw those billionaires trying to dictate their terms, they managed to wrest control and to capture most of the financial flows. The passive partner gained the upper hand over the active one. Increasingly one had to deal with virtual legal state entities rather than virtual private-sector personalities.

There is acceptance of the formal rules of the market, but things are pre-approved; individuals make deals but it is on behalf of the state more than of private companies. Their job is to defend Russia's national interest and that of the Russian population. Suddenly there is a huge lack of understanding between the Russians and the West as investment decisions do not obey the same criteria: the Russians overdetermine the very short term and manage to concentrate on the very long term—Gazprom functions very well in the short term (a few weeks) and in the very long term (30 years) but not at all in the medium term (1 to 5 years)—whereas the Western capitalist markets operate on more of a medium-term basis, investment decisions covering three- to five-year periods.

---

1   *Silovik* (from a Russian word for *force*) is a Russian politician from the old security or military services, often the officers of the KGB, the FSB, the Federal Narcotics Control Service and military or other security services who came into power under Presidents Boris Yeltsin and Vladimir Putin. The term derives from the fact that these people come from "power ministries", which under Yeltsin and Putin formed a *de facto* higher level inner cabinet.

Does this return of the state represent a risk for the emerging economy?

Jérôme Guillet: In my view a strong state is a good thing for coordinating invest-ments and infrastructure planning. All the countries that have developed have done so thanks to heavy state interventionism, direct or indirect, through legisla-tion. The American middle classes are the children of the New Deal and govern-ment legislation. But the state must be competent and that is the question that arises with regard to Russia. The country is fortunate to benefit from this boon, a large proportion of which goes into the public sector, which should be seen as a good thing. Is this linked to the present economic climate, or might it last? It is hard to say today, but the state plays a strategic role even if it is led by individuals whose motivations are sometimes more personal than political.

Gilles Favarel-Garrigues: Owing to the lack of transparency surrounding political power, most observers develop a "Kremlinological" analysis. For years, the liberals have been seen as the opponents of the *siloviki*, but I believe we should question this view, as I am not convinced they represent two consistent camps, and I wonder whether reducing the political rivalry to a clash between these two camps isn't masking the real issue. For twenty years, the individual path to enrichment has been based on three pillars: managerial skills, adminis-trative resources (that is, special relations with senior government officials) and access to protection services. Vladimir Putin is the perfect embodiment of these conditions.

Now it is the state that dictates its conditions to business. The lack of an inde-pendent judiciary, in both criminal and commercial law, is a major problem. All the actors are of the opinion that access to the courts is never impartial, though recent years have seen a growing number of successful individual cases against state norms. The battle against corruption, mirrored by that against money laun-dering in the private sector, serves to control the elite civil servants who are seek-ing to challenge the presidential authority. Holding economic intelligence con-stitutes a fundamental power asset. It is enough to look at the number of private agencies taking the place of bailiffs to ensure court decisions are implemented; it is former police officers and secret service agents who are now working in the private economic intelligence sector.

Jérôme Guillet: These days there are no more liberals. There are different clans among the *siloviki*, often represented by different administrations, tax depart-ments, police forces, etc. There are several centres of power and when one becomes too dominant, another one is set up to curtail its power. Vladimir Putin is finding it difficulty to control the conflicts between the various depart-ments.

Is the appearance of an entrepreneurial middle class, able to operate independently in Moscow and the regions, the effect of emergence?

Gilles Favarel-Garrigues: Russia's tertiary sector has grown considerably in recent years. Employees in the banking, insurance, media and IT sectors could form a relatively homogeneous social group, and are of the same generation. Today's political and administrative elites were born after World War II, up to the 1960s. They experienced the frustrations of the final decades of the Soviet Union and their work practices were formed in this context. Within ten or fifteen years, there will be a completely new administrative and political elite, and also a completely new generation at the helm of the major Russian economic groups.

Does Russian society see itself as moving towards both increased prosperity and increased inequality, which often go hand in hand, especially in emerging countries?

Geoff Barnard: Until the late 1990s, the Gini coefficient showed growing inequality, but since then the figures have levelled off, even fallen. Insofar as the figures are reliable, they show a decrease in inequality.

Jérôme Guillet: The Gini coefficient tends to be stable, even to show an improvement. A number of public services have been maintained in Russia. Gazprom has managed to keep the country on its feet for the last ten years by supplying the population with heating and electricity almost free of charge, the education system is still functioning even though fees are continually rising, and the same is true of transport services and the health system. Running the public services is the state's prime responsibility and the boon of recent years has made it possible to make up for the backwardness of the past, for example by paying nurses and teachers who, for a while, were no longer paid.

Gilles Favarel-Garrigues: Social policy was one of the priorities for the 2008 presidential election. For some years Dmitri Medvedev's name has been linked to "national projects", those huge investment projects in four key sectors: health, education, housing and the agricultural sector. For the moment, there is no social movement, though embryonic action by strikers, the retired and the poorly housed is being closely watched by observers. Those who adhere to theories of relative frustration believe that in the current climate of economic growth, the discontent could lead to a broader social movement.

Jérôme Guillet: One of the rare times when Vladimir Putin had to climb down was when he asked the Russians to pay for public services at their true cost. The fact that Gazprom provides heating and electricity at a very low price constitutes

figure 46: **Russian demographics, 1950-2050**

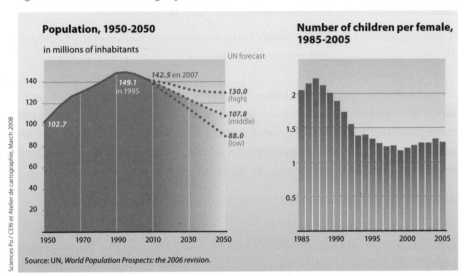

Sciences Po / CERI et Atelier de cartographie, March 2008

Source: UN, *World Population Prospects: the 2006 revision.*

a real social policy instrument, and ultimately the high cost of this operation is a minor disadvantage compared with the social advantage it represents.

How can a country that is ageing so fast plan for the future?

Jérôme Guillet: This question and the issue of growth are the alpha and the omega of any economic policy and must enter into long-term thinking. Furthermore, Russia isn't the only country asking itself this question. China has similar problems. A stable, even declining demography is likely to prove an asset in a few years' time. If there is a shortage of labour, it will become more expensive, and the issue becomes the division between salaries and profits. It will therefore be determined by the investors and not by the population.

Geoff Barnard: True, the demographic trends are worrying from some points of view, but they do not imply a lack of dynamism or convergence towards the standard of living in advanced countries, nor do they prevent Russia's gradual integration into the global economy. Demography may be destiny, but it is not emergence, which remains possible even if the population is ageing and declining. Growth depends on the increase in the factors of production and on increases in the efficiency with which factors are used. If the work force shrinks because of demography, there will be lower growth than otherwise but not necessarily lower growth per capita. Russian growth is robust now even though the population has already been decreasing for a few years. As for the comparison with China, the latter's performance is certainly impressive and in absolute terms, the Chinese economy is already much larger than Russia's, but we should perhaps remember that GDP per capita in Russia is still three times that of China. Furthermore, China has its own demographic problems.

Is it appropriate to talk of the creation of a rouble zone in the former Soviet region, which would mean that the currency is strong not only in Russia but also in a whole hinterland corresponding to the former Soviet region?

Geoff Barnard: It is possible that the rouble is beginning to be used more and more in the region but it is hard to see it becoming a reserve currency on the scale of the dollar or the euro. The least that can be said is that it would take a long time, since Russia currently represents only 3% of the global economy.

Jérôme Guillet: The rouble's stability facilitates trade in this region as the currencies of the other countries are even less reliable and Russia remains the preferred partner, but I don't think a rouble zone could go beyond this region.

Could it be said that on Russia's borders there is a sort of periphery where Moscow's expansionist policy is coming up against a fierce demand for independence?

Anne de Tinguy: Yes, the two phenomena—the desire to expand and the desire for independence—both exist, but in a complex way and to varying degrees from one state to another. Vladimir Putin has frequently claimed that he has no neo-imperial ambitions, as he said on 25 February 2000 in his "Open letter to the Russian Electorate"; he also denied any desire for hegemony or pressure on the CIS. Furthermore, he declared that Russia did not aspire to an exclusive position in this region. In 2001, when the American military presence was set up in Central Asia as part of the intervention against the Taliban in Afghanistan, he even acknowledged that such an operation might serve his country's interests. Vladimir Putin remains convinced, however, that Moscow retains a special place in the region, which is a "sphere of vital interests dictated by history". "Russia," Sergei Lavrov (Minister for Foreign Affairs) recently said, "is the natural centre of this region." His policy, which is far from rational with respect to some of Russia's partners, in particular Ukraine and Georgia, is in keeping with this line. In the Russian perception of this region, there remain "red lines" which cannot be crossed either by CIS member countries or by countries outside this zone. The potential for NATO membership to be extended to CIS countries remains one of Moscow's "red lines", which it will go to any lengths to avoid (particularly in the case of Ukraine and Georgia).

The new independent states' positioning vis-à-vis Russia varies enormously. Some, like Belarus, Armenia, Kyrgyzstan and Tajikistan, have remained close to their powerful neighbour on which they are dependent. Others, like Kazakhstan, have distanced themselves from Moscow while retaining close ties. Others again—

Ukraine, Georgia and to a lesser extent Azerbaijan and Moldova, in other words the GUAM countries—are focusing on the Euro-Atlantic space, taking different approaches. In my view, Ukraine unquestionably seems to be the most determined: its Euro-Atlantic focus, which it has continuously asserted since the collapse of the USSR, reflects a profound drive. For a long time there has clearly been a huge gulf between Ukrainian discourse, which has often been lacking in substance, and reality. Furthermore, Ukrainian development has been chaotic. The country's political instability causes some observers to say that the Orange Revolution was only incidental. I am not of that opinion. I see the Orange Revolution and its aftermath—and I am not alone in this—as the stages of a process of democratization and the inclusion of Ukraine in the Euro-Atlantic space. This is a very thorny issue for Russia, as its positions within the post-Soviet space and vis-à-vis the European Union will be very different according to whether or not it is supported by a Ukrainian neighbour that was the jewel of its former empire for more than three centuries.

One of the criticisms that can be made of Vladimir Putin's foreign policy is that he has not modernized his policy towards this space: he has not sped up what I call the "exit from the empire"; he has not tried to create modes of thinking that would enable Russia to relinquish its relationships based on a dominant-dominated model and find a new way of convincing its partners that it is beneficial for them to link their futures to cooperation with Russia. The strong and disproportionate animosity expressed by Moscow for years towards "little" Georgia is exemplary of this policy.

Jérôme Guillet: The ties never really loosened. They are just overdetermined by the infrastructure. The Soviet Union has a fairly strong specialization exemplified by the nuclear power stations; uranium mainly came from the Central Asian Republics, initial processing used to be carried out in Ukraine, enrichment in Russia, and then the uranium was returned to Ukrainian power stations. Each of these plants had an absolute monopoly. On independence, the breaking of ties led to chaos. Some succeeded in setting up local replacements; others pragmatically reinstated the links. Nowadays, there is a tendency towards increasing interdependence rather than the contrary.

Is it more fitting to speak of interdependence or dependence?

Anne de Tinguy: There are dependences that have survived—Russia is still a key player in some sectors—and in some cases these are indeed interdependences: Turkmenistan cannot dispose of its gas without Russia, but Russia needs Turkmenistan to fulfil its commitments and its own needs. Ukraine needs Russian gas, but Russian gas is exported to Europe via Ukraine. However I disagree with Jérôme Guillet's view that "the ties never really loosened". He may be right, at least up to a point, concerning the economic sphere. But that is not everything. To echo the words of the Russian political scientist Alexander Nikitin, "It is time to acknowledge the end of the post-Soviet space." That does not mean that the influence of "Sovietism" has disappeared, but that this region no longer forms a geopolitical entity. Since the early 1990s, the centrifugal forces have been very powerful. They have led to the fragmentation of this formerly unified space and an erosion of Russia's position in numerous areas. An emblematic illustration of the changes: in 1985, 86% of international flights from Russia were to countries in what is now the CIS; in 1997, a decade on, this proportion had fallen to 34% (Vladimir Kolossov). Georgia's Rose Revolution (November 2003) and Ukraine's Orange Revolution (November-December 2004) were milestones in the dismantling of this space. They revealed the attractiveness of other development models. And the Orange Revolution confirmed that Ukraine and Russia have different identities and political trajectories.

Jérôme Guillet: The West has a desire for absolute control and does not want to manage interdependencies; it prefers power struggles in which it can assert itself as dominant. Today, the West feels it can no longer dictate the terms of the deal and has to negotiate on an equal footing. Meanwhile the Russians are very prickly about being treated as equals and being able to defend their interests. Now they feel they are in a position to do this and are doing so emphatically.

Discussion chaired by Christophe Jaffrelot.
Translated by Ros Schwartz

A Flight of Wild Geese:
Regional Integration and
Emergence of Asian Economies

Françoise Lemoine

Many Asian countries have followed a path to catch up with rich countries. In the past 20 years the emergence process has spread to the demographic giants, for which globalization provides a powerful growth accelerator. Their dynamism takes root in internal reforms that aim to liberalize the economy and build a modern state, as well as in their increased opening up to and participation in international exchanges. Emerging economies thus differ from "rentier" economies whose growth depends mainly on the rise in raw material prices.

Dragons, tigers and giants

Meteoric growth brought Japan to the rank of second largest economic power in the late 1960s. When it surpassed Germany in terms of GDP, it already had a per capita income that placed it among the club of rich countries. Subsequently, cases of rapid growth multiplied throughout Asia. Hong Kong, Taiwan, South Korea and Singapore formed the first generation of "newly industrialized countries" (NICs) or so-called Dragons. The per capita income rose sixfold in three decades (from 1960 to 1990) and they, too, entered the club of high-income countries. Since then, the city-states Singapore and Hong Kong have even surpassed Japan in terms of per capita income. Even if their belated industrialization sometimes still

figure 47: **Per capita GDP compared to Japan, 1960-2005**

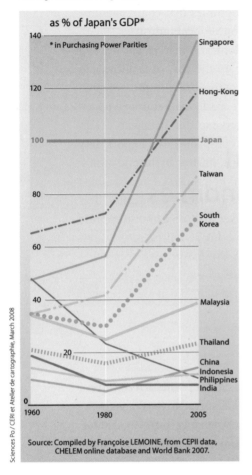

as % of Japan's GDP*

* in Purchasing Power Parities

Singapore
Hong-Kong
Japan
Taiwan
South Korea
Malaysia
Thailand
China
Indonesia
Philippines
India

1960   1980   2005

Sciences Po / CERI et Atelier de cartographie, March 2008

Source: Compiled by Françoise LEMOINE, from CEPII data, CHELEM online database and World Bank 2007.

places them in the emerging economy category, they have clearly emerged. A second generation of NICs—Malaysia, Thailand, the Philippines and Indonesia—appeared in the 1980s. These tigers are on a catching-up trajectory, but they still have a much lower income level than rich countries. The growth of these economies, although brutally disrupted by the 1997-98 financial crisis, now stands above the world average. China started to emerge in the early 1980s, and its income level now exceeds that of the Philippines and Indonesia. Ten years later, India entered the race.

From the early 1960s to the end of the 1980s, South Korea and Taiwan recorded growth in per capita GDP (around 7% and 8%) that was comparable to China's since 1980. But these Dragons were not large enough to destabilize the world economy for long and were easily "absorbed" by it. The case of China and India differs both from that of Japan and the dragons, because these two demographic giants rose to become major economic powers well before becoming rich. In 2005, China, with 5.5% of the world's GDP, and India, with nearly 2%, ranked respectively 4th and 12th in the world's economies, but with a per capita income that was respectively 10% and 5% of that of the United States.

An Asian model

A World Bank report in 1993 (World Bank 1993) analyzing the reasons for the success of Tigers and Dragons underscored the crucial role played by the state, which first ensured the fundamental conditions for takeoff (competitive markets, macroeconomic balances, legal and institutional framework), and secondly intervened selectively to promote high-growth industrial sectors. Already, then, its analysis implicitly recognized that economists had learned more from Asia than the continent had learned from them and that the pragmatism of Asian economic strategies had caught the conventional wisdom of various schools of thought off guard, a conclusion found again in a 2006 report from the same institution.

The evolution of the Chinese economy provided another example. China's reform and opening-up policy followed a specific rationale due to the country's size, its history and the international context. But the country also borrowed elements from successful experiments in the region. Its economic opening-up policy in particular drew on that of East Asian economies that combined promotion of export-oriented industries and protection of local industries (South Korea, Taiwan). Trade policies that protect the domestic market usually end up putting a damper on export: protection drives up the cost of facilities and imported semi-finished goods needed to develop competitive export-oriented industries. They also drive domestic prices up above world market prices, which makes producers steer away from export. To overcome this handicap, Asian countries established special export zones where companies can import duty free. China significantly expanded this selective policy: starting in the mid-1980s, it exempted from customs duties imported goods to be processed or assembled for export as well as capital goods imported by foreign-owned companies. This preferential system was remarkably successful. Over half of Chinese exports are related to international assembly and subcontracting activities, mainly conducted by foreign affiliates. The advantage given to these exporting companies was all the more substantial in that tariffs were relatively high before China joined the WTO in December 2001 (the average tariff of 37.6% in 1994 dropped to 16.2% in 2001) (Lemoine 2006).

'Wild-geese-flying pattern'

"A wild-geese-flying pattern" is the image that the Japanese economist Akamatsu (1961) used to describe the model by which development propagated throughout Asia, in which new techniques spread quickly to industrializing countries that follow in the wake of more advanced countries to catch up gradually to them. The leading countries, in this case Japan, first brought in tow the Asian Dragons, then the Tigers. In many respects the emergence of China, and later Vietnam, fitted this pattern.

Thus Japan in the 1970s, and then in the 1980s the first NICs (dragons), in general deserted labour-intensive traditional industries (textiles) to specialize in new technologies. The rise in wages pursuant to the reevaluation of Asian currencies (after the Plaza Accord in 1985) prompted many companies to shift low added-value production to second-generation NICs (tigers) and to China, by finding subcontractors or setting up affiliate companies. These newcomers developed their specialization in traditional industries and later moved to the new technology sector, the tigers in the 1980s and China in the 1990s.

The wild-geese-flying model explains the considerable interdependence in Asia between emerging economies and emerged economies. The two are linked by strong intersectoral complementarities, trade and investment flows and technology transfers.

figure 48: **Share of Asian countries in world exports, 1980-2006**

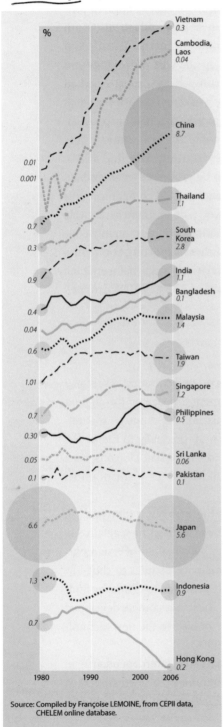

Source: Compiled by Françoise LEMOINE, from CEPII data, CHELEM online database.

Sciences Po / CERI et Atelier de cartographie, March 2008

The pattern also implies a hierarchy among the most advanced economies, which must renew their comparative advantages and innovate to maintain their leadership, and the others. The globalization process that gained speed in the 1990s gave a new twist to the Asian dynamics. A deeper division of labour has taken place, strengthening the interdependences, accelerating China's rise and finally challenging the existing hierarchy among countries.

Globalization accelerates reconfigurations

Since the 1990s industries have been organized on a global scale because of the international fragmentation of production processes. Different countries are increasingly involved in the various stages of manufacturing one and the same product. This is true of Nike sports shoes, Barbie dolls and the iPod. Multinational companies choose to locate successive production stages according to the advantages offered by the various countries. Production stages that require skilled labour and investments in R&D (product design, component manufacturing, marketing and sales) are usually handled by the most advanced countries. The newcomers specialize in activities requiring large amounts of low-skilled labour (assembly). The value created in China represents about 10% of the price of an iPod assembled and exported by China; and the product was designed in India.

The electronics sector lends itself particularly well to this type of organization, because manufacturing processes can easily be fragmented, transport costs are relatively low compared to the product price, and economies of scale are particularly high. Companies in advanced Asian countries (especially Taiwan) that often act as suppliers for US companies organize production through a network of affiliates and subcontractors scattered over several countries in the region.

The international segmentation of production processes is at the heart of productivity and efficiency gains made in Asian industries. It has profoundly reshaped the pattern of Asian trade in the course of the past decade. The most advanced countries (Japan and NIC1s) now share their industrial production capacities with China, whose position is rapidly expanding. The growing wave of trade in parts and components (which has risen from 20% to 31% of intra-Asian trade in manufactured products) is a perfect reflection of this division of labour (Gaulier, Lemoine and Unal-Kesenci 2007).

China at the heart of the division of labour

Thanks to its infrastructure and the quality and quantity of its workforce, China has become the world's largest hub for export-oriented production. Chinese factories are now an essential link in the world added-value chain. The assembly trade accounts for the huge trade surplus ($250 billion in 2007) of the world's workshop.

figure 49: **China's share of exports from other Asian countries, 2006**

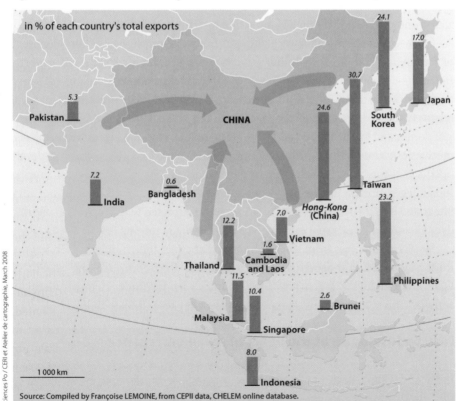

in % of each country's total exports

Pakistan 5.3
India 7.2
Bangladesh 0.6
Thailand 12.2
Cambodia and Laos 1.6
Vietnam 7.0
Malaysia 11.5
Singapore 10.4
Brunei 2.6
Indonesia 8.0
CHINA 24.6
Hong-Kong (China) 30.7
Taiwan 23.2
South Korea 24.1
Japan 17.0
Philippines

Source: Compiled by Françoise LEMOINE, from CEPII data, CHELEM online database.

Sciences Po / CERI et Atelier de cartographie, March 2008

China mainly exports finished goods, most of which are consumer goods. Chinese electronic products, which have made a particularly remarkable breakthrough on the world market, are now the main export item. In 2007, China produced 600 million mobile phones (half the world production) and exported more than 400 million of these products (almost all of which are foreign brands: Nokia, Motorola, Samsung, Ericsson, etc.). Most Chinese imports of semi-finished goods, especially electronic components, come from Asia. China has become the fulcrum of the division of labour on the continent. Its integration in the region has made it a world trade power and the largest in Asia (one-fifth of all the region's exports). It has far surpassed Japan as the main market for Asian manufacturing industries and has almost caught up with it as a regional supplier of manufactured goods.

The demand for agricultural and industrial raw materials and for energy has risen sharply, reinforcing complementarity with Asian producer countries. Indian exports to China multiplied eight times between 2000 and 2005, iron ore deliveries accounting for half of this increase.

India, the other giant in the international division of labor in Asia

Lagging behind China by about 10 years, India adopted a new economic liberalization and international opening-up strategy in the early 1990s.

Its development model is very different from the industry-based development of East Asian countries. In India, services drive economic growth and exports. Industrial development was hindered by domestic regulations, a lack of sufficient transport infrastructure and an electricity shortage. Indian industry remains a relatively underdeveloped sector (it contributed about 20% of the GDP in 2006), still dominated by the main traditional areas (textile, steelmaking, petrochemicals, mechanics). The pharmaceutical industry is the exception. The sector has developed a first-rate world production of generic drugs, taking advantage of specific Indian legislation on intellectual property that existed until 2005. India is not very integrated into the Asian division of labour but is attracted to the region's economic dynamism, and its external exchanges are increasingly turning towards Asia.

Services suffer less from the hindrances that affect Indian industry. This is the most powerful and most dynamic sector of India's economy, making up 54% of GDP and employing a quarter of the country's labour force. High-productivity activities (finance, telecoms, computing) play a key role (Boillot 2006).

New technologies at the heart of Asian emergence

India and China have made the most remarkable breakthroughs in activities that grew out of the technological revolution of the late 20th century. This, combined with globalization (increased capital mobility and opening of markets), has prompted companies to relocate (through affiliates) and/or outsource (by using subcontractors) segments of their activities beyond borders, especially in emerging countries. Globalization—understood as a worldwide reorganization of the production of goods and services—has offered China and India the possibility of short-circuiting certain stages of modernization by adopting cutting-edge technologies. China has become a world production hub for electronics products and the world's foremost exporter of them, with 17% of the world's exports in 2005 (televisions, DVD players, cell phones, iPods, etc.). India is an international centre for computer and information services and the world's largest exporter with 21% of the world's exports. China and India, both major economic powers until the early 19th century when they missed out on the first industrial revolution, have mastered the new information and communication technologies (ICT) and managed to position themselves in very dynamic sectors of world demand (Gaulier, Lemoine and Unal-Kesenci 2006). They have developed competitive production capacities in new sectors much faster than they have been able to renovate obsolete facilities and management methods in the traditional sectors of their economies. In both countries, the boom in new sectors relies on quality labour that is highly productive and paid at a low rate. The efficiency in implementing new technologies explains the strengths of India's and China's comparative advantages in these sectors and the appeal these two countries have for multinational corporations and foreign capital.

Consumption: the weak link in Asian growth

Learning from the 1997-98 financial crisis in several East and South Asian countries (Thailand, Malaysia, South Korea and Indonesia) caused by the sudden withdrawal of international capital, East Asian countries have since conducted cautious policies aimed at sheltering their economic growth from another external shock. For this purpose they have given priority to exports and accumulation of currency reserves. In fact, the Dragons and Tigers have returned to the path of high growth, but household consumption has been the weak link of their economies. Currently, China is an extreme case in this regard. Since the late 1990s, its economic growth has mainly been driven by domestic investment, which has reached new heights (45% of the GDP), and more recently by exports. Since 2005, external demand has accounted for about one-quarter of China's growth. Household consumption has increased less quickly than other components of demand. Chinese households in fact have a strong propensity to save, both out of cautious habit and to make up for the lack of social welfare (health, retirement), and in the face of the increase in schooling costs.

The strong propensity to save and invest is characteristic of the East Asian economic development model, where the priority given to competitiveness keeps a lid on wages and consumption. On the other hand, South Asia, particularly India, generally devotes more to consumption. For instance, even if India's per capita GDP is half that of China's, per capita consumption is only 30% lower.

Towards autonomous growth?

Asia is the region that has known the greatest economic dynamism in the world since the mid-20th century. It now contains major emerging powers that are contributing more and more to world growth. Does that mean the Asian economy functions in a truly autonomous fashion, or is it still dependent on the rest of the world? China's rise in power has given new impetus to Asian integration and suggests the idea of delinking of Asian activity from Western economies, especially the United States.

In 2007, China, which represented 5.4% of the world GDP (in current dollars), recorded an 11.5% growth rate. It thus contributed more than the United States (1.9% growth and 27.5% of the world GDP) to world growth. India, which represented 2% of world GDP and had a 9% growth rate, contributed as much as Japan to world growth. If the economy slows down in developed countries, the emerging economies' contribution to world growth should increase. Does that mean they will be able to drive the rest of the world's growth?

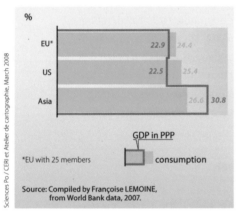

figure 50: **Share of EU, US and Asia in GDP and world consumption, 2007**

*EU with 25 members

Source: Compiled by Françoise LEMOINE, from World Bank data, 2007.

Sciences Po / CERI et Atelier de cartographie, March 2008

The spillover effect of Chinese growth on the US and the EU economies is fairly limited because China remains for both entities a market of only minor importance. It receives 5% of total US exports and 4% of the EU's extra-community exports. India has even less weight than China. The BRICs taken together (Brazil, Russia, India and China) account for less than 10% of EU and US exports.

Chinese growth has spillover effects on the rest of Asia thanks to gains in efficiency related to an intense international division of labour in the region. Asia thus supplies China with two-thirds of its imports. It is not certain, however, that Asian growth has acquired great autonomy from the American continent on which it is still heavily dependent for much of its finished product exports. The "de-coupling" of Asia from the United States runs up against the importance of the American market for Asia: East Asia exports 30% of its finished products (consumer goods and capital goods) to North America and 20% to the European Union.

Only a more dynamic Asian internal demand based on a rise in household consumption can lead to a real "de-coupling" of the region's growth and give the continent a truly driving role with respect to the rest of the world.

Bibliography ································

Akamatsu, K. (1961). "A Theory of Unbalanced Growth in the World Economy", *Weltwirschaftliches Archiv*, 86.

Asian Development Bank (2007). *Asian Development Outlook 2007*.

Boillot, J.J. (2006). *L'économie de l'Inde*. Paris: La Découverte, Repères.

Gaulier, G., F. Lemoine and D. Unal-Kesenci (2006). "Chine: le prix de la compétitivité", *La Lettre du CEPII*, no. 254, March.

—— (2007). "China's Emergence and the Reorganisation of Trade Flows in Asia", *China Economic Review*, Vol. 18, issue 3.

Lemoine, F. (2006). *L'Economie de la Chine*, Paris: La Découverte, Repères.

Maddison, A. (2001). *The World Economy: a Millennial Perspective*, Development Centre Studies.

World Bank (1993). *The East Asian Miracle: Economic Growth and Public Policy*, Washington DC: World Bank.

—— (2006). *An East Asian Renaissance: Ideas for Economic Growth*, Washington DC: World Bank.

Yusuf, S., M. Altaf Anjum and K. Nabeshima (eds) (2004). *Global Production Networking and Technological Change in East Asia*, Washington DC: World Bank.

Central and Eastern Europe Buttressed by the European Union

François Bafoil

T he changes currently underway in Eastern European territories are the product of both the profound transformations made by the imposition of the Soviet model between 1945 and 1989 and the new economic dynamics set in motion since 1989. If the first decade of post-communism was marked by the collapse of the traditional industrial and agricultural milieus, the arrival of foreign direct investment (FDI) in certain sectors and the blossoming of private initiative, the second decade is characterized by the emergence of poles of development hinging on European aid, particularly structural funds. The radical reconfiguration of the production environments inherited from the former regime led to a major reorientation of trade towards the West in the 1990s. The territorial disparities once contained by the communist egalitarian policy widened after 1990 as a result of the polarization of development. The notions of metropolization, cluster and cross-border cooperation that structure economic development in the West have now taken hold in the East as the basic categories for development, sustaining growth rates considerably greater than the EU-of-15 average.

Communist legacies and territorial polarization

Development of heavy industry and incomplete urban development

The Eastern European territories have been deeply marked by the imposition of the Soviet model, for which the size of production complexes and their sectoral and regional concentration were the two major levers of development. In that light, the primary aim was not to wipe out the entire industrial base, as with the

figure 51: **Annual GDP growth rate of EU states, 1998-2007**

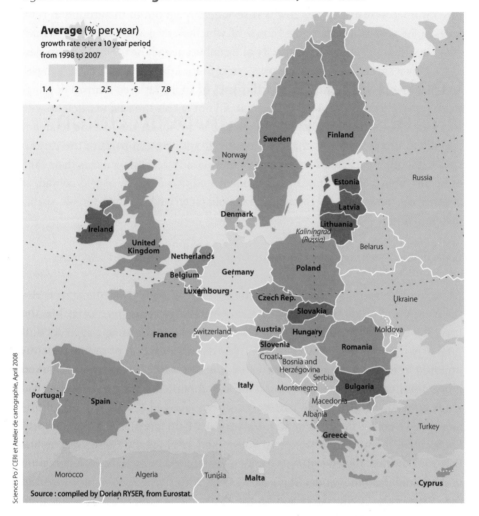

Average (% per year)
growth rate over a 10 year period
from 1998 to 2007

1.4   2   2,5   5   7,8

Source : compiled by Dorian RYSER, from Eurostat.

Sciences Po / CERI et Atelier de cartographie, April 2008

liquidation of the propertied classes. On the contrary, the aim was to reinforce industry where it existed by concentrating activities within huge production units, and to create industries in places where they did not yet exist, particularly in the eastern territories. The former mining and steel manufacturing areas of Lower Silesia and Upper Silesia in Poland, of Moravia and Sudetenland in Czechoslovakia, of northeastern Hungary and of the Jiu Valley in Romania—all legacies of the first and major wave of industrialization that took place in Central Europe in the 19th century, and for regions such as Silesia and Moravia two centuries earlier—were thus largely privileged. It was in these gigantic plants, which often employed over 10,000 workers, that the authorities intended to shape the "new man".

To hasten the process, investment was lavish: it reached considerable sums, about 20% of the total public investment, so that new industrial areas could be created, devoted exclusively to heavy industry at the expense of so-called "light" or consumer industries. New towns rose suddenly up out of the ground in rural areas right next to the factories, some of which were never completed. Examples were the steel manufacturing city of Eisenhüttenstadt near Frankfurt-an-der-Oder, Nowa Huta ("the new steelworks") next to Kraków, Dunaújváros in Hungary and the steel-producing area built at the gates of Sofia. Yet even if urban development experienced a considerable boom, it did not enable the East to catch up with the West. Worse, the new urban ensembles did not invert the historic tendency specific to urban networks that were denser in the western parts of the various countries, often particularly those with a Germanic tradition, whereas their eastern counterparts in the Russian or Ottoman tradition typically lagged behind, as is generally the case with eastern regions characterized by considerable spatial dissemination.

Collectivization of the Eastern European countryside and East/West disparities

Alongside the working-class bastions that were the mines and the steelworks, the energy and utility sectors as well as the metallurgical and mechanical industries, the Communist authorities intended to operate in the same way in agricultural areas. In this case, however, the industrial organization of production was imposed by force via the creation, often *ex-nihilo* as well, of collective farms, even if in several countries the agricultural dualism inherited from past centuries had made large farms part of the Eastern European landscape. This was true of the large Junker estates throughout Mecklenburg and Pomerania, in the once German Pomeranian territory that was now Polish, and in Hungary. Conversely, in the Balkan countries, the end of the Ottoman Empire led to extreme fragmentation of land holdings. The model imposed was the Soviet-type *kolkhoz* developed in the 1930s in the USSR. Very soon, in the 1950s and 60s, technical specialization led large farms to appear, specializing in stockbreeding or crop farming. These farms regrouped several dozens of thousands of workers and sometimes had a farm machinery station added (on the *sovkhoz* model). Lastly, in the vicinity of the state farms, tiny plots of land were left at each family's disposal, parcels that varied in size over the years but whose economic, social and local importance was vital, given that they guaranteed economic survival and more generally the transmission of peasant know-how. The entire area under communist domination was covered by these large industrial agriculture units—cooperatives or state farms—with the notable exception of Poland, where nearly 75% of the arable land remained privately owned, but with the average holding scarcely exceeding 6 hectares in 1989, compared with 1,300 ha for state farms.

The dynamics of territorial development thus underwent considerable upheaval due to such excessive industrialization, all the more as development throughout the continent was conceived simultaneously in terms of an integrated market in the East as well as conflict, even war, with the West. For this reason, areas bordering the now-enemy Western countries were hermetically sealed and dotted with watchtowers, barracks and military training fields, resulting in considerable degradation of the soil, the renovation of which took up the better part of the 1990s. The old territorial balances suffered the effects of Cold War geopolitics, and entire territories were cut off from their traditional hinterlands, such as those lying near the border between the two Germanys but also those situated between Bulgaria and Yugoslavia or between Poland and Germany. The north of the German Democratic Republic, which had never been developed, was rapidly industrialized, particularly to compensate for the loss of ports, all located in the West (Hamburg, Bremen and Kiel) or handed over to Poland (Szczecin). In Czechoslovakia, investment was concentrated in the eastern part of the country (today's Slovakia), particularly for military production. Hungary went through a similar evolution.

Post-1989 dynamics

Starting in 1989, the deep restructuring of Soviet-style economic organization as well as a flow of foreign direct investment upset the balances created over the course of nearly 45 years in Central Europe. These two factors made the countries eligible for European pre-accession funds starting in the year 2000, and for structural funds which, beginning in 2004, made regional development a national priority.

The end of a model, the return of dualism

On a territorial level, the combined impact of opening borders and confronting markets on the one hand, and the radical transformation of the Soviet development model on the other, translated into a serious crisis for formerly privileged sectors—mining, steel manufacturing, energy and mechanics—which few investors, if any, wanted to take over. In that time of rapid transformation, it was imagined that catching up could be achieved not by fitting out the missing technological cycles in sectors affected by radical changes due to exposure to Western capitalist practices, but by liquidating them. Thus, the industrial colossuses of the Soviet era soon became industrial wastelands. The weight of such decrepitude was all the heavier to bear on a local scale since these industries had contributed to shaping entire regions. Simultaneously with this collapse, which caused large pockets of unemployment, a trend developed of starting companies in the vicinity of the large complexes. Tiny family businesses came into being, only a handful of which eventually converted into service providers for business. At the same time, the gap widened between the major regional cities or capitals, certainly hit by the crunch but having their own alternative resources available, and the rural milieus, dotted with small and medium-size towns. These small urban areas were the ones that had to bear the most dramatic effects of the post-1989 transition, first because they had been the first beneficiaries of industrialization in the 1960s and 1970s, when they acted as subsidiaries of major groups which themselves had remained in the large cities; next, because in the wake of this wave of industrialization, they benefited from the creation of major government service agencies, to the extent that some of them became "regional capitals". The severe crisis in the 1990s drove them into an impasse, not only because the industrial subsidiaries were the first to be dismantled, but also because state reforms very often led to the liquidation of their administrative prerogatives, and lastly, because of the collapse of the large community farms.

Very soon, the idea prevailed that the agricultural model now had to conform to the West's, dominated by average-sized family farms. Two public policies gave concrete backing to this model, which had never really existed in the Eastern European countryside: the restitution of land to its former owners (prior to collectivization) and privatization of collective property. The first policy led to a scattering of land ownership and its extreme fragmentation; in many places it was ineffective because of the incapacity of landowners to make their way in the new economic landscape, owing to age or merely incompetence. The second policy, land privatization, was conducted in a highly disorganized fashion in the name of ideological principles: for some, the guiding principle was to obliterate the legacy of collectivism; for others, the main thing was to preserve jobs and local traditions. In this incessant conflict, the state often retained a large share of land ownership, particularly in Romania. These two dynamics resulted in a considerable diversification of rural areas, whether in the practice of leaving large stretches of land fallow, or the reappearance of very large industrial farms managed by former engineers and technicians who managed to rent land that was not cultivated by the new owners, or the emergence of a large number of small farms, often under 10 ha in size. Finally, the dualism historically very present in this part of Europe underwent a revival after 1989, although it did not bring in its tow either the anticipated efficiency or a real privatization of farming activity comparable to that in Western Europe. Thus, contrary to expectations, large estates with often more than 1,000 hectares continued to predominate in the eastern part of Germany and the Czech Republic, while in Estonia, Lithuania, Poland, Bulgaria and Romania, all countries with a strong farming population, farms did not exceed nine hectares on average (3.5 hectares in Romania, 8.6 hectares in Poland) in 2006.

Foreign direct investment

FDI has had a considerable impact on the territorial level, and for this reason largely accounts for new forms of polarization in this part of Europe. Not only has it buoyed up macroeconomic development by boosting exports and stimulating the territories through financial funds and technology, but it has also largely contributed to the employment crisis by drastically reducing the exorbitant number of workers employed in the companies taken over. It was only from the 2000s that greenfield investments replaced brownfield investments and created the anticipated jobs.

First, and throughout the whole 1990 decade, FDI was concentrated on the four countries of Central Europe and there was hardly any, or none at all, in the Baltic countries or the Balkans. In terms of per capita amounts invested, Hungary and the Czech Republic, Slovakia and finally Poland together concentrated nearly 80% of the investment. This superiority was not reduced until the 1990s when foreign investors moved north and especially south towards more politically stable countries certain to join the EU in the long run, even if they were taking a little longer than the first group to enter.

Within each country, FDI created a large gap between cities and rural areas. Several agribusiness industries certainly benefited from large investments, particular in Hungary, Poland (the second largest producer of red fruit in the European Union), and Bulgaria (in the milk products sector). But FDI nevertheless shifted massively to urban areas where the effects of agglomeration were the most palpable, opportunities most obvious and services most developed. The capitals and major regional cities were the first to benefit from FDI, as opposed to medium-sized and especially small towns. It was not uncommon to see more than half of foreign investments localized in capital regions. This explains the importance of another disparity that came to overlap the first: the gap between west and east. Given that the most developed cities were always located in the west (with the notable

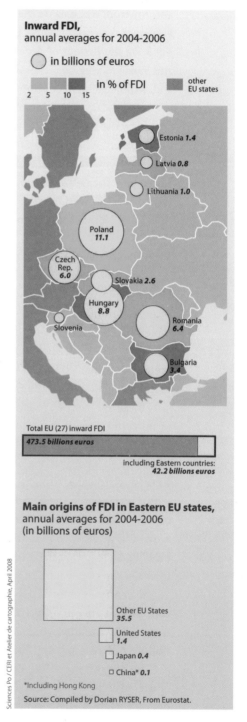

figure 52: **FDI to some Eastern EU states, 2006**

Inward FDI, annual averages for 2004-2006

in billions of euros

in % of FDI   other EU states
2   5   10   15

Estonia *1.4*

Latvia *0.8*

Lithuania *1.0*

Poland *11.1*

Czech Rep. *6.0*

Slovakia *2.6*

Hungary *8.8*

Slovenia

Romania *6.4*

Bulgaria *3.4*

Total EU (27) inward FDI
473.5 billions euros

including Eastern countries: **42.2 billions euros**

Main origins of FDI in Eastern EU states, annual averages for 2004-2006 (in billions of euros)

Other EU States *35.5*

United States *1.4*

Japan *0.4*

China* *0.1*

*Including Hong Kong

Source: Compiled by Dorian RYSER, From Eurostat.

Sciences Po / CERI et Atelier de cartographie, April 2008

exception of Warsaw), territorial development was much more apparent in this part of Central and Eastern Europe. Added to that is the fact that the western regions of some countries are adjacent to highly developed countries (Germany and Austria), whereas on the other hand, the eastern regions border poor or even very poor regions (Ukraine, Belarus, Moldova and Russia). The latter moreover do not have the benefit of decentralized governments, unlike the Polish, Hungarian and Slovakian regions. The concentration of FDI in the countries of Central Europe, and, within them, in developed urban areas adjacent to the territories of the EU-15 states led to the polarizing of growth and development in the quadrilateral represented by the cities of Prague, Bratislava, Vienna and Budapest, with the hope that development would spread to the surrounding areas. It is in this quadrilateral that all the automobile manufacturers of Western Europe, the United States, Japan and Korea have located along with their suppliers. Connected with the developing EU territories, the western regions of the ten countries that recently joined the EU thus stand clearly apart from their largely peripheralized eastern counterparts.

Main lines of development: metropolization, clusters and cross-border cooperation

Under the impact of these various factors, identified early on in the first decade of post-communism, three main lines of endogenous development, largely sustained by European financial aid, have been identified as the structural pillars of the 2000s. The first, on which the "new" member states are massively wagering, is metropolization. Unlike the West, where this term refers to urban units of over one million inhabitants, in the East, although it also refers to capitals of comparable size, these are part of a much looser urban network. With the exception of Poland, in no country does the second largest city exceed 500,000 inhabitants, scarcely 300,000 in Bulgaria and 200,000 in Slovakia or Hungary. Only Poland can actually claim to have a strong urban network with eight large cities—Warsaw, Lodz, Kraków, Katowice, Wroclaw, Poznan, Szczecin, and Gdansk—to which should be added two cities in the Eastern region, Bialystok and Lublin. In any event, the concept of metropolization is used to conceive a type of development concentrated around large cities, due to transport infrastructure capable of supporting worker mobility by fostering the link between urban peripheries and city centres as well as between the centre and its regional hinterland. The prevailing notion here is one of polycentric territorial development organized around cities viewed as regional capitals that are purveyors of services, particularly in terms of the job market and community facilities. And so, associated with the idea of metropolization are the notions of free zones and "industrial parks".

The second main line of endogenous development relates to the notion of cluster which, in the field of sectoral production, is supposed to illustrate the decisive factors for the economic catching-up process, the concentration of resources (material and human), and the potential for diffusion to surrounding areas. Here again, the term is employed in the East in a different sense from the way it is used in the West, where it refers to a central factor of "social capital" in economic geography analyses. This term refers in theory to relations of mutual trust at the basis of local production systems that constitute informal networks in which various employment, innovation and export services are exchanged. Borrowed directly from Putnam, this approach emphasizes the importance of informal relations, the anticipatory capacity of actors and collective initiative in building local milieus. In practice, the term "social capital" refers to the French "local systems," the "second Italy" or "Silicon Valley"—all examples that highlight the innovative capacity of local milieus, largely based on family relations or relations of proximity, which rely more on the "community" than on "society", to use the standard dichotomy.

After nearly a half-century of communist-style organization based on the liquidation of family production, it seems to make little sense to talk about local heritage in the East. What heritage could possibly have been preserved that could revive local production networks, alumni associations, family relations or industrial traditions? Moreover, development deficiencies attest to a glaring lack of cooperation among private and public actors. Everywhere the low level of government commitment to industrial policy can be noted. Despite that, there is a great diversity of clusters on the basis of a very high degree of territorial concentration in certain industrial branches, the development of their innovative capacities and the networking of certain services, particular commercial services. The pre-1989 territorial organization can play a role when it is linked with the introduction of FDI. Rarely are local operators alone responsible for tapping "hidden resources", to use Hirschmann's term, even if such cases do exist, for instance the "Aviation Valley" in southeastern Poland. More generally speaking, Eastern European development since 1989 seems more like a combination—some speak of a hybridization—of local resources and foreign capital, more exactly as the recomposition of an industrial heritage (with strong cultural traditions) that fits with Western development norms.

This is for instance the case in the automobile sector wherever it has developed (particularly in the above mentioned quadrilateral), as well as the pharmaceutical and electronics sectors, particularly in Poland—in Lodz, Warsaw and Kraków— but also in Hungary, and in the region of Ljubljana in Slovenia, in the metallurgical and energy sectors in Moravia, and in the lumber sector in the Baltic countries, Poland and Hungary. Certain clusters have arisen out of the initiative of a few SMEs that have set up in the same location and have generated a regional concentration. Others have been created by cooperatives in reaction against supermarkets. Still others, more rarely, have a specifically agricultural focus, such as the food production cluster in the Polish region of Lubelski.

Sometimes these clusters are located within "special economic zones" that were created after 1990 in declining industrial areas. The aim was to attract both foreign and domestic investors by setting up fiscal incentives on the condition that a minimum amount was invested (from 500,000 to one million euros in Poland), jobs were created, new technology introduced, etc. Given their importance in these regions undergoing conversion, the European Union tolerated them beyond 2004, and some of the zones today have turned out to be major actors in Eastern European development. This is true of the "economic zone" of Wallbrzych in Lower Silesia, Poland, hard hit by the mining crisis in the 1990s, which in 2007 constituted one of the most dynamic regions in Poland. Spread over 18 sites and 14,000 ha, the zone can boast of having attracted some 30 major international corporations, including Toyota, KPMG and Italmetal, for a cumulative amount of 1,505,000 million euros invested and 22,980 jobs created.

The third main line of development has to do with cross-border cooperation, to which the European Union since 2006 has devoted a new development instrument. Border areas represent a major development stake owing to the number of inhabitants in such areas, particularly those in the East adjacent to Russia, Belarus, Ukraine and Turkey, and the backwardness affecting them. Several phenomena have come together to reinforce the peripheral nature of these regions since 1989: the collapse of agricultural complexes, the lack of FDI, the emergence of a vast informal economy, large trade asymmetries due to the centralized nature of the Russian, Belarusian and Ukrainian economies, and the introduction of the neighbourhood policy which deprives states bordering the EU of any hope of membership in the short term. Yet Poland, Slovakia and Hungary are all keen to link their eastern regions to their central poles of development and to do so have implemented assistance programmes all based on the same principles: the strengthening of transport infrastructure between regional cities and border areas, support for local economies, particularly SMEs, and aid for cross-border cooperation in the educational and cultural sectors. The fact nevertheless remains that to attract foreign investment, many of the so-called peripheral regions still rely essentially on the low cost of their labour. In this context, the relevance of certain programmes that seek to enhance innovation where there exists no scientific community is questionable, as is the wisdom of favouring the metropolization process where urban networks are extremely loose.

Are these development characteristics of Central and Eastern Europe likely to provide outlines for an Eastern European "model"? Beyond the differences stemming from their industrial, agricultural and territorial legacies, the ambitions of the political authorities on the whole or the instruments used to further them do not seem very different from what can be observed in the West. EU recommendations regarding economic, social and territorial cohesion have been accepted by all. They constitute the basis for national development programmes, all oriented towards

figure 53: **Unemployment rate for the over 25s, 2006**

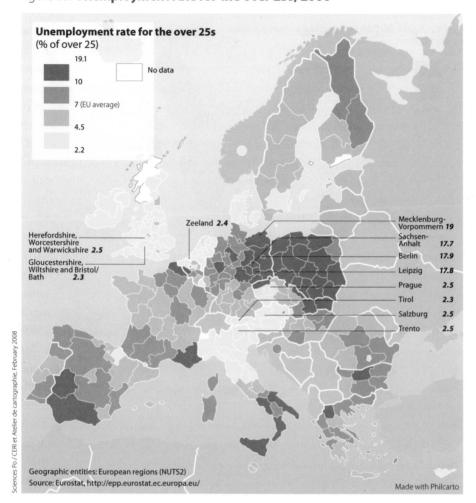

Unemployment rate for the over 25s
(% of over 25)

19.1

10

7 (EU average)

4.5

2.2

No data

Zeeland **2.4**

Herefordshire,
Worcestershire
and Warwickshire **2.5**

Gloucestershire,
Wiltshire and Bristol/
Bath   **2.3**

Mecklenburg-
Vorpommern **19**
Sachsen-
Anhalt   **17.7**
Berlin   **17.9**
Leipzig   **17.8**
Prague   **2.5**
Tirol   **2.3**
Salzburg   **2.5**
Trento   **2.5**

Geographic entities: European regions (NUTS2)
Source: Eurostat, http://epp.eurostat.ec.europa.eu/

Made with Philcarto

Sciences Po / CERI et Atelier de cartographie, February 2008

promoting growth, reducing unemployment and reducing the growing territorial disparities due to the rapid growth all these countries are experiencing.

In all the operational programmes established for the 2007-13 period, regional development is at the top of the list of allocated amounts, ranging from 25% to 30% of the total aid. At the national level, the consolidation of regional and local governance is cited as the mainspring of territorial development in the future. Infrastructure is the primary budget item and the notions of metropolization, cluster and cross-border cooperation are considered as the foundations for development. Lastly, the West's fundamental concerns over energy supply and environmental protection are all the more shared by the East because the dependence of these countries on Russia is much greater than the West's (except for Germany), and the weaknesses inherited from the former regime are immense in this particular area.

figure 54: **Per capita GDP, 2006**

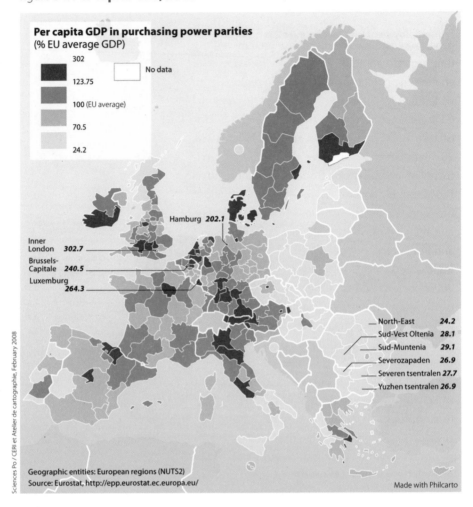

Per capita GDP in purchasing power parities
(% EU average GDP)

302

No data

123.75

100 (EU average)

70.5

24.2

Hamburg **202.1**

Inner London **302.7**

Brussels-Capitale **240.5**

Luxemburg **264.3**

North-East **24.2**
Sud-Vest Oltenia **28.1**
Sud-Muntenia **29.1**
Severozapaden **26.9**
Severen tsentralen **27.7**
Yuzhen tsentralen **26.9**

Geographic entities: European regions (NUTS2)
Source: Eurostat, http://epp.eurostat.ec.europa.eu/

Made with Philcarto

Sciences Po / CERI et Atelier de cartographie, February 2008

The conditions for a balanced development

Nearly 20 years after the fall of communism in Central and Eastern Europe, several development patterns have come to light. These are characterized by polarization and concentration of resources on one hand, and slower development and a low rate of FDI in certain territories marked by rural decline and their peripheral situation, on the other. A dual phenomenon results: growth in the territories taken as a whole with respect to the European average—in other words catching up with the West, evidenced by annual GDP growth rates of more than 6% since 2004 in all the countries—and increasing differences with developed areas.

In these conditions, it is nearly impossible to ensure balanced development, and one that would combine economic growth and territorial cohesion, even if the territorial disparities are not as marked in the East as they are in the West. Actually, between growth and solidarity, national development programmes have opted for the former, hoping that growth will have a domino effect powerful enough to prevent the gulf between regions from widening. In Hungary, differences in regional GDP between Budapest, the capital, and northeastern Borszöls were on a scale of 1:2 in 1988; 20 years later, it was more than 1:3. The territories of northeastern Romania or the central Bulgarian plain show a regional GDP of about one-quarter of the European Union average, and the poorest Polish regions, the Carpathians and Podlasie, about one-third. This is the feature highlighted in the third report on cohesion in 2005 for the member countries of the former EU of 15, when the Commission had identified both a dynamic of convergence of national GDPs and growing disparities within certain countries at the regional level.

Yet, the fourth report published in the spring of 2007 emphasizes the lack of homogeneity of territorial developments in Central Europe with respect to the west of the EU. This points to the major role of structural aids in reinforcing growth by favouring the concentration of funds and preventing territories from going adrift under the effect of growing inequalities.

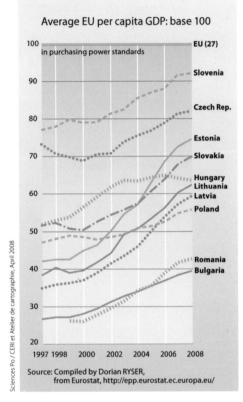

figure 55: **Per capita GDP of some Eastern European states compared to the EU per capita average, 1997-2008**

Average EU per capita GDP: base 100

in purchasing power standards

EU (27)
Slovenia
Czech Rep.
Estonia
Slovakia
Hungary
Lithuania
Latvia
Poland
Romania
Bulgaria

1997 1998 2000 2002 2004 2006 2008

Source: Compiled by Dorian RYSER, from Eurostat, http://epp.eurostat.ec.europa.eu/

Sciences Po / CERI et Atelier de cartographie, April 2008

Bibliography ···

Bafoil, F. (2006). *Europe centrale et orientale. Mondialisation européanisation et changement social*. Paris: Presses de Sciences Po.

—— (2008). *Sub-national Governments in the European Union. Organisation, Responsibilities and France*. Brussels: Dexia.

DEXIA (2007). *Les finances locales de l'UE27*. Dexia.

Mc Master, I., H. Vironen and M. Ferry (2007). "Policies Development in the 12," *Regional Policy Country Reviews*, 2006-7.

OECD (2006), *Business Clusters. Promoting Enterprises in Central Europe.*

European Union (2003). *Second Report on Economic and Social Cohesion*

European Union (2007). *Growing Regions, Growing Europe. Fourth Report on Economic and Social Cohesion.*

Latin America:
Regionalism to No Effect

Olivier Dabène

For the last fifty years Latin America has displayed a remarkably dynamic regionalism. Many integration agreements were signed at the end of the Second World War, and even more during the 1960s. Some of these, in Central America for example, were cited as success stories of South-South cooperation. Many onlookers believed that the dream of a united Latin America—one it had cherished since the era of independence and Simon Bolivar's campaigns—was finally to come true, enabling the continent to occupy a more prominent position in the concert of nations. However, from the 1970s onwards, the situation called for a grim reappraisal: paralyzed tariff negotiations, low increase in intraregional trade, unfulfilled commitments and insufficient government involvement. The 1980s and especially the 1990s saw a strong revival, but this also ended in disappointment. Some of the most commonly voiced criticisms are of overburdened negotiation agendas, institutions not acting in the general interest and not benefiting from any transfer of sovereignty, lack of coordination of macroeconomic policies, frequent trade disputes and very incomplete customs unions.

The 2000s have not really seen a change in circumstances. Political readiness to move the integration process forward is often expressed and sometimes leads to major reforms, but Latin America seems to have real difficulty in arousing collective interest and creating the institutions capable of managing it.

However, could it be said that regionalism in Latin America enables some of its emerging countries, in particular Brazil and Mexico, to gain additional influence on the international scene? This chapter shows that these two countries, for different reasons, are not taking on regional leadership. Only Venezuela, through its oil diplomacy, has managed to lay the groundwork for a new regionalism and

figure 56: **Main regional integration processes in the Americas, April 2008**

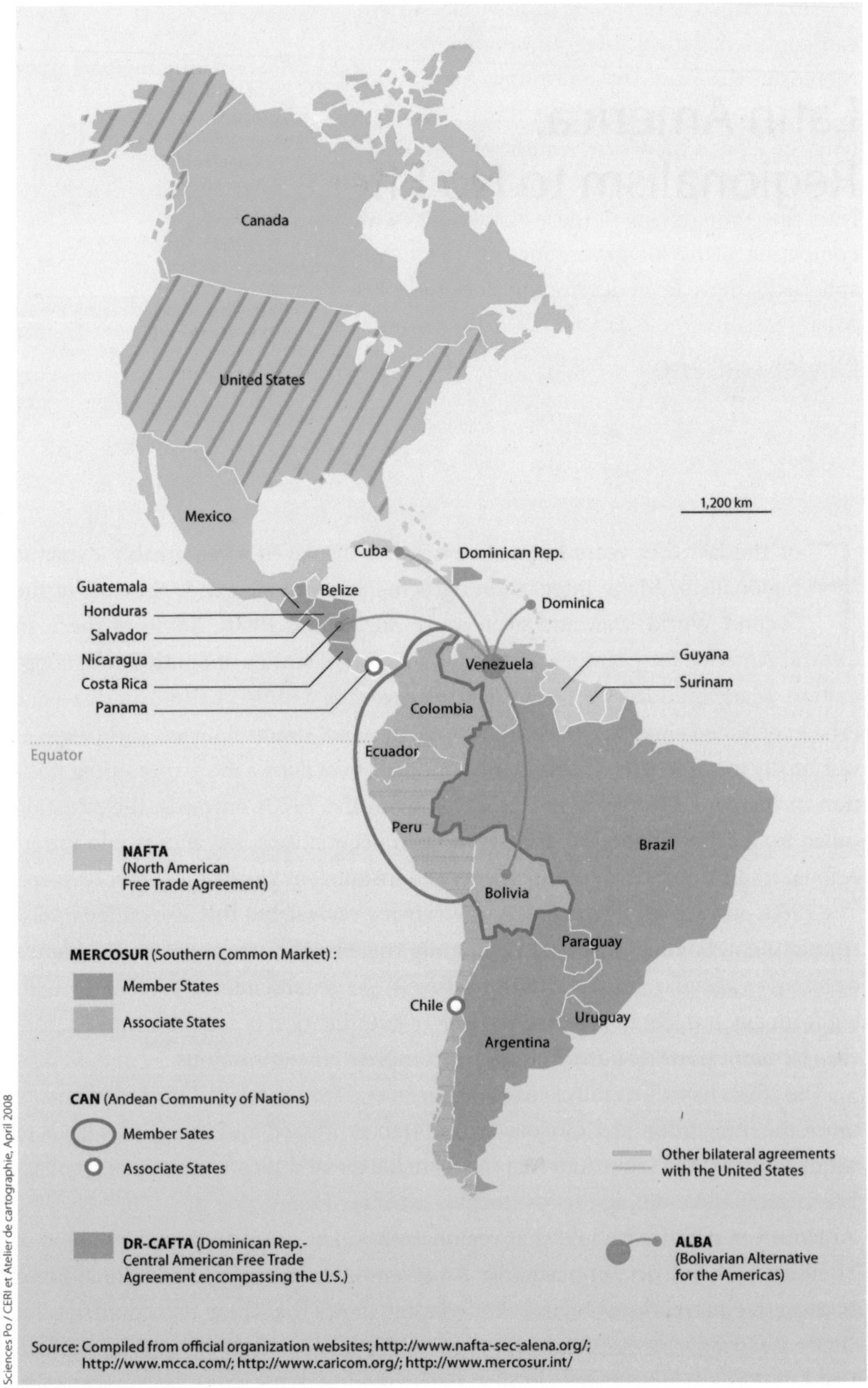

Canada

United States

1,200 km

Mexico

Cuba

Dominican Rep.

Guatemala

Belize

Honduras

Dominica

Salvador

Nicaragua

Guyana

Costa Rica

Venezuela

Surinam

Panama

Colombia

Equator

Ecuador

Peru

Brazil

NAFTA
(North American
Free Trade Agreement)

Bolivia

Paraguay

MERCOSUR (Southern Common Market) :

Member States

Chile

Associate States

Uruguay

Argentina

CAN (Andean Community of Nations)

Member Sates

Other bilateral agreements
with the United States

Associate States

DR-CAFTA (Dominican Rep.-
Central American Free Trade
Agreement encompassing the U.S.)

ALBA
(Bolivarian Alternative
for the Americas)

Source: Compiled from official organization websites; http://www.nafta-sec-alena.org/;
http://www.mcca.com/; http://www.caricom.org/; http://www.mercosur.int/

Sciences Po / CERI et Atelier de cartographie, April 2008

to project itself onto the international scene as leader of the struggle against imperialism.

This chapter takes stock of how the American continent's main integration agreements—Mercosur, the Andean Community of Nations (CAN), the Central American Integration System (SICA) and the North American Free Trade Agreement (NAFTA)—have evolved, then analyzes the compatibility of these agreements with competing plans for governance of the hemisphere that have been developing since the 1994 Miami Summit of the Americas and the proposal for a Bolivarian Alternative for the Americas.

Regional experiments with mixed results

The newest of the Latin American integration processes was immediately considered the most promising, probably because Argentina and Brazil intended to learn from past mistakes. In March 1991, Argentina, Brazil, Paraguay and Uruguay signed the Treaty of Asunción, lending their project for a Southern Common Market (Mercosur) an aura of pragmatism.

Mercosur, its political reforms and the question of its expansion

Throughout the 1990s the process went through highs and lows. Trade increased rapidly but institutionalization remained at a low level and compliance with community norms erratic. Imbalance within the bloc did not make negotiations any easier. Brazil, considering itself a global trader, ultimately gave little regard to Mercosur. In 2001, Mercosur celebrated its tenth anniversary as Argentina was experiencing an economic crisis. So integration was paralyzed, and the trade flows remained at a level comparable to that of 1991.

As often in such circumstances, a crisis gives rise to a common desire to make the integration

figure 57: **Intra-regional trade for NAFTA, MERCOSUR and CAN, 1996-2006**

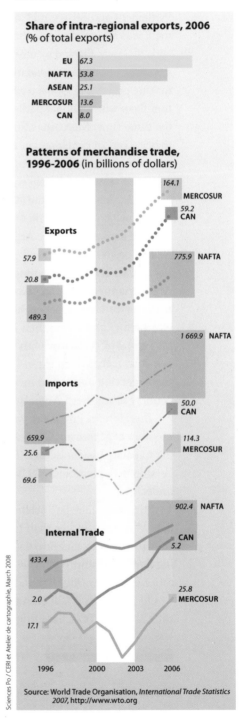

Share of intra-regional exports, 2006 (% of total exports)

EU	67.3
NAFTA	53.8
ASEAN	25.1
MERCOSUR	13.6
CAN	8.0

Patterns of merchandise trade, 1996-2006 (in billions of dollars)

Exports
57.9
20.8
489.3
164.1 MERCOSUR
59.2 CAN
775.9 NAFTA

Imports
659.9
25.6
69.6
1 669.9 NAFTA
50.0 CAN
114.3 MERCOSUR

Internal Trade
433.4
2.0
17.1
902.4 NAFTA
CAN 5.2
25.8 MERCOSUR

1996 2000 2003 2006

Sciences Po / CERI et Atelier de cartographie, March 2008

Source: World Trade Organisation, *International Trade Statistics 2007*, http://www.wto.org

167

process cross a qualitative threshold in order to prevent such incidents. It was time for a fresh start, which came mainly in the form of institutional improvements. Elsewhere I have analyzed the scope and limitations of the two main political reforms, the Parliament and Structural Convergence Funds. The creation of a Mercosur Parliament was designed to give the integration process additional democratic legitimacy and efficiency. Elected by universal suffrage, the Parliament has no power of codecision, but if its recommendations are followed, it helps to speed up the decision-making process. Regional parliaments are moreover expected to act as communication links with national parliaments and mobilize the national political classes. At the same time, Mercosur's Structural Convergence Funds (FOCEM) are supposed to help combat development asymmetries within the regional bloc. A regional fund was set up based on the European model to finance development projects.

These reforms are unlikely to have significant impact in terms of the degree of integration inasmuch as the four countries have taken great care to avoid any transfer of sovereignty. But they still represent substantial progress as they symbolize the will to move forward after the Argentine debacle and in the face of external challenges.

Mercosur must indeed manage its expansion to include Hugo Chávez's Venezuela. The strengthening of that country's ties with Mercosur is largely due to Argentina's need to reduce its debt servicing and find solutions to its energy dependency. As for Hugo Chávez, he chose to turn his back on the Andean Community (see below) and strengthen his connection with Mercosur, taking advantage of his capital of sympathy with the Argentine President Nestor Kirchner. He clearly saw it as a chance to extend his influence in the region, and his offer to buy up the Argentine bonds and finance the construction of a jumbo pipeline linking his country to southern Argentina, was certainly tempting.

Therefore in July 2006, with no preliminary negotiation, Venezuela became a member of Mercosur. Chávez's outbursts and very aggressive diplomacy did nothing to pacify his detractors. The Brazilian Senate still not having ratified its membership in September 2008, Venezuela's legal status within Mercosur was then still undecided.

Mirroring Europe's relationship with Turkey, Mercosur chose to accommodate Venezuela rather than marginalize it. But nothing seems able to calm Hugo Chávez's fervour, and Brazil is proving incapable of standing its ground and imposing any leadership. To those who thought that Mercosur was going to become a tool for empowering Brazil, Luiz Inacio Lula da Silva has shown instead that he would rather go it alone on the international scene and lead the battle in arenas such as the WTO where Brazil could find allies of its standing, India and China.

The Andean Community (CAN) after Venezuela's withdrawal

The situation is not much clearer as regards the CAN (Bolivia, Colombia, Ecuador, Peru), none of which can lay claim to regional leadership. Venezuela has participated in Andean integration for 35 years but has maintained its trade preferences, particularly with Colombia, and Hugo Chávez may yet change his mind. Originally Venezuela pulled out in order to punish Colombia and Peru, guilty in the eyes of the Venezuelan president of having signed a free-trade agreement (FTA) with the United States. The CAN was, however, able to make a speedy comeback under the leadership of the new Peruvian President Alan Garcia, who orchestrated a rapprochement with Chile (which had left the group in 1976) and Panama, the two countries becoming associate members. The opening of negotiations with the European Union in 2007 also guaranteed the lasting stability of this agreement regularly threatened by internal friction.

The Andean Community is in fact divided between supporters (Ecuador, Bolivia) and opponents (Colombia, Peru) of Hugo Chávez, and runs up against the energy issue. The Venezuelan president immediately set up offices representing ALBA (the Bolivarian Alternative for the Americas) in Peru and directly finances social projects in Bolivia, Ecuador and Peru. His country also provides assistance to Ecuador and Bolivia in their reforms aiming to regain control of their natural resources, and Hugo Chávez has even declared willingness to help Evo Morales with military defence in the event of an attempt to destabilize Bolivia. That country tried to renegotiate its gas-exporting contracts with Brazil and Argentina and still refuses to deliver gas to Chile until the matter of its access to the sea is settled. Michelle Bachelet's Chile has proven willing to allow an "almost" sovereign corridor across its northern border, but this, according to Peruvians, ends in their territorial waters. Like the dispute between Argentina and Uruguay over a cellulose factory set up by Uruguay on its shore of the River Plate, the triangular Chile-Bolivia-Peru dispute highlights the limits of regional integration.

Central America faced with the challenge of free-trade (CAFTA) with the United States

On 5 October 2007 Costa Rica approved a free-trade agreement with the United States by referendum. This followed a relentless campaign in which President Arias used every means at his disposal to ensure success.

A political first for Latin America, this referendum revealed a clearly defined bipolarization of public opinion showing noticeable divisions throughout the continent. The media, business and all the conservative forces in favour of free trade were violently pitted against the intellectual and trade union circles who were opposed to it. For Costa Rica the possible dismantling of successful public companies such as the Costa Rican Institute of Electricity (ICE) was one issue at stake. The reforms that will come about as the FTA comes into force are likely to generate social protest movements.

Costa Rica was the last country in Central America not yet to have ratified the CAFTA, a comprehensive trade agreement negotiated separately by each of the Central American countries and the United States. The fact that the region was not able to negotiate collectively reflects both the pressure applied by the United States and the weakness of the regional integration process.

While in the 1960s the Central American Common Market (MCCA) was often cited as an example of successful integration in developing countries, the people of Central America at first vigorously revived the integration process with the end of the regional crisis of 1979-1990 (the Sandinista revolution in Nicaragua), before this momentum ran out and the prospect of negotiation with the United States became the main focus. The Central American Integration System (SICA) is still the most complex of the Latin American integration processes, covering many fields from social to environmental, economic to educational, and political to security. The region has many communal bodies, but these lack an overall view and have little political support. Paradoxically Hurricane Mitch, which devastated Honduras in 1998, was the only event that for a time revived regional solidarity.

Daniel Ortega's victory in the Nicaraguan presidential elections in 2006 reintroduced an element of political polarization in the region that had disappeared since the leader of the Sandinista revolution lost the 1990 elections. His rapprochement with Hugo Chávez is not looked on favourably by his Central American counterparts, traditionally close to the United States. Border disputes, especially with Costa Rica, add to the climate of tension.

North America in the aftermath of September 11, 2001

Since its inception in 1994, the North American Free Trade Agreement (NAFTA) has produced an explosion in trade among its three members, Canada, the United States and Mexico, taking the trade flows between these three countries from $109 billion in 1993 to $622 billion in 2000. The social consequences, however, are very controversial, notably in Mexico where the figure of 1.5 million bankrupt peasants is often quoted. Another great source of concern is the prospect of elimination of the remaining tariff barriers in 2008.

Since the terrorist attacks of September 11, 2001, the security-oriented turn American foreign policy has taken has certainly affected NAFTA. While the United States was already in the habit of disregarding the rules set out in trade agreements, such as those concerning Canadian timber, the Homeland Security Act brought about the closure of the border that NAFTA had contributed to opening.

On the political front, tensions surfaced within the group. Vicente Fox's Mexico courageously opposed the United States during debates prior to the Iraq war in the United Nations Security Council. The new President Felipe Calderón has taken this even further, initiating a noticeable strengthening of ties with South America, in particular with Mercosur. A rebalancing of inter-American relations is definitely on the agenda, at least until the 2008 presidential elections in the United States, which could once again bring about a change in the situation.

Regional governance beyond the failure of the Free Trade Area of the Americas (FTAA)

The post-2001 security orientation also contributed to the paralysis of negotiations for the FTAA, but it was not the only factor responsible. Following Luiz Inacio Lula's arrival in power Brazil, the other main actor in negotiations revealed a preference for global negotiation arenas such as the WTO and set about building new alliances with other major emerging countries such as India, China and South Africa.

The failure of the FTAA must not blind us to other issues. The trade aspect of the negotiations set in motion at the 1994 Miami Summit of the Americas is often the one that grabs media attention, but it is not the only issue. In fact, for about the last ten years, the continent's negotiations have tackled some twenty themes that cover the whole spectrum of international cooperation, from democracy, human rights and justice to security, from trade to infrastructure, from sustainable development to gender issues, from agriculture to labour laws, and from education to cultural diversity and minority rights. The body has been co-chaired since 2001 by a working group made up of the Economic Commission for Latin America (ECLAC), the Inter-American Development Bank (IDB), the Pan American Health Organization (PAHO), the World Bank and the Organization of American States (OAS). Other institutions such as regional banks (Central American, Andean) have recently joined the group.

The summit process has all the trappings of a complex exercise in regional governance, bringing together a number of public and private actors. No supranational decision can be taken, but resources are mobilized and international regimes strengthened. It is certainly a tricky job to understand the advantage gained by the exercise, since the summit process is more a means of harmonizing a set of existing mechanisms

figure 58: **Oil consumption and production in the Americas, 2006**

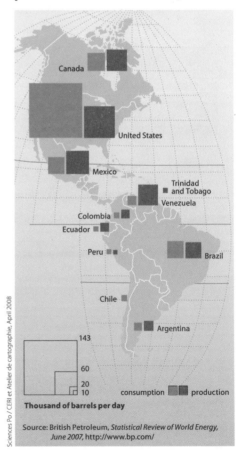

Sciences Po / CERI et Atelier de cartographie, April 2008

Source: British Petroleum, *Statistical Review of World Energy, June 2007,* http://www.bp.com/

than of creating a new structure. Nevertheless, the fact remains that a silent revolution is operating in the region where the inter-American system has proved very disappointing over the last century. Anyway the progress of these negotiations does not seem to be affected by the Venezuelan President Hugo Chávez's competing offer.

The Bolivarian Alternative for the Americas (ALBA): a true alternative?

From the moment he came to power in 1998, President Chávez of Venezuela had luck on his side with the continuing rise in oil prices, and as his predecessors had done in similar circumstances, he was keen to use this windfall to further his diplomatic ambitions.

Hugo Chávez, champion of the Bolivarian revolution in his country, poses as Fidel Castro's heir and endeavours to influence the political developments of the continent. Often proving himself impolitic in his support of like-minded candidates during the wave of elections in 2005-6, he managed to rally only a few countries to his anti-imperialist crusade. In spite of a "shift to the left" in Latin America, only Bolivia and Nicaragua joined ALBA along with Cuba.

Chávez's idea of launching a regional integration process based on channels other than trade is being slow to take shape. However, aid projects have been set up, and most importantly, the map of energy integration has been redrawn. The Venezuelan president is quick to supply his political friends with hydrocarbon resources, keen for the whole of Latin America to profit from his country's oil wealth. His project to build a pipeline that will reach Argentina leaves many an observer sceptical, but Chávez's project for a "Bank of the South", which is intended to enable Latin Americans to do without the International Monetary Fund (IMF), arouses more enthusiasm as the dismal record of the Washington Consensus years lingers on in people's memories.

This does not mean that the whole of left-wing Latin America supports his plan to build the socialism of the 21st century and stand up to North American imperialism. Brazil's Luiz Inacio

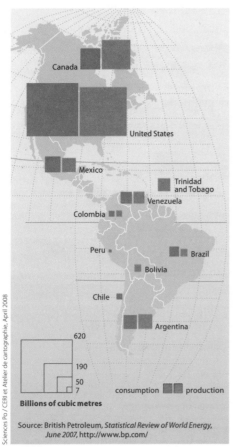

figure 59: **Gas consumption and production in the Americas, 2006**

620
190
50
7

consumption production

Billions of cubic metres

Source: British Petroleum, *Statistical Review of World Energy*, June 2007, http://www.bp.com/

Sciences Po / CERI et Atelier de cartographie, April 2008

Lula, in particular, has often said that confrontation is a thing of the past and that inter-American cooperation is the way forward. The Chilean President Michelle Bachelet is equally doubtful and advocates a mature relationship with the United States. Did Chile not oppose the Iraq war while negotiating a free-trade agreement with the United States?

Towards a conciliation of inter-American relations?

During his second term George Bush has generally turned a deaf ear to Hugo Chávez's outbursts. Latin America, as was often the case throughout the 20th century, was not on the American president's foreign policy agenda. The difficulties he met with while trying to get the free-trade agreements ratified by a Congress dominated by the Democratic Party dissuaded him from taking on new negotiations in the last year of his term of office. Although Colombia is the United States' closest ally in the region, the treaty with that country was blocked because of President Alvaro Uribe's supposed links with the paramilitaries and drug cartels, in particular that of Pablo Escobar.

The relative abandonment of Latin America could turn out to be salutary in as much as it allows each of the countries of the region to gain political leeway. But a constructive and not overly "ideologized" attitude on the part of the United States administration has always defeated many of its principal opponents' arguments, something George Bush has not managed to do with Hugo Chávez. A more pragmatic approach would enable the consensus on common regional values to move forward. It would also allow the United States to make a comeback on the Latin American scene and further throttle Brazil's and Mexico's vague ambitions for regional leadership.

Nevertheless, for the time being integration agreements in Latin America are going through difficult times and the major emerging countries, Brazil and Mexico, are not able to use them as springboards to gain access to the international scene. Brazil is going it alone and neglecting its background team on the continent. Mexico is just barely turning back towards Latin America. Only Venezuela is benefiting from the paralysis of regional integration to construct an alternative regionalism, financing social projects in many countries on the continent. ALBA may have only a few members but the hyperactivism of Hugo Chávez' oil diplomacy and his inflammatory outbursts, picked up in many countries by the "Bolivarian circles", have earned him the stripes of an important player in international relations.

Bibliography ••••••••••••••••••••••••••••••

Dabène, O. (1998). "L'intégration dans les Amériques. Economie politique de la convergence". *Les Etudes du CERI*, 45, September.

—— (2005). "La relance du Mercosur. Le temps des réformes politiques". *Critique Internationale*, 26, January.

Santander, S. (2008). Le régionalisme sud-américain, l'Union européenne et les Etats-Unis. Bruxelles: Presses de l'Université de Bruxelles.

PART 3

A NEW WORLD OUTLOOK

Emerging Countries and the Changes Implied for Europe

Jean-Marc Siroën

Following the financial crisis of the late 1990s, emerging countries quickly returned to high growth rates. But their economic achievements should not be measured solely in terms of GDP. They are also asserting their financial power, and the largest of them today are claiming a place in the international economic order in proportion to their weight. In contrast, European achievements are far more mediocre, and Europe's status in the world economy is being increasingly challenged.

The option of export-led growth has made emerging countries new competitors with the former industrial countries, starting with Europe. High trade surpluses and highly raw-material-driven growth cause worldwide market upsets. But emerging countries have also become poles of attraction, encouraging the development of new partnerships, though in a changing context in which emerging countries demand recognition for their rank, which automatically has implications for Europe.

Emerging countries as competitors

Does emerging country assertiveness imply the relative decline of former powers, especially "old Europe", whose dynamism is often considered atrophied?

Emerging countries first stand out as trade competitors on both national and world markets. Their share in international trade rose from 21% to 29% between 1995 and 2005.

figure 60: **Share of emerging countries and Europe in world exports, 1995-2007**

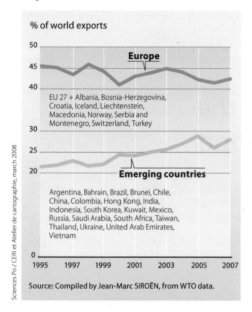

% of world exports

EU 27 + Albania, Bosnia-Herzegovina, Croatia, Iceland, Liechtenstein, Macedonia, Norway, Serbia and Montenegro, Switzerland, Turkey

Argentina, Bahrain, Brazil, Brunei, Chile, China, Colombia, Hong Kong, India, Indonesia, South Korea, Kuwait, Mexico, Russia, Saudi Arabia, South Africa, Taiwan, Thailand, Ukraine, United Arab Emirates, Vietnam

Source: Compiled by Jean-Marc SIROËN, from WTO data.

Sciences Po / CERI et Atelier de cartographie, march 2008

These countries, with their abundant supply of cheap labour, compete with European production in the most traditional sectors. This means that European countries must either opt for sectors requiring highly skilled labour or transform traditional sectors such as the textile industry into capital-intensive high technology industries. However, even in these areas, Europe's position appears fragile. Emerging countries no longer settle for being mere subcontractors and are aiming to work their way up the added-value chain to assembly and finished goods (an example being Airbus in China), while also expecting to benefit from technology transfers. India trains an impressive number of engineers and is asserting its presence in high technology services and industries. Emerging countries also assert themselves in sectors such as petrochemicals, pharmaceuticals, computer engineering, renewable energy and aeronautical construction.

Emerging countries are generally broken down into three broad categories according to specialization: agricultural (Argentina, Brazil) or mineral primary goods (Venezuela, Gulf countries), industry (China, Vietnam) and services (India). This perspective can however be misleading: Brazil has not given up on its industry any more than India has, and China, with Hong Kong, has become the world's third-largest exporter of tradable services.

Emerging countries also seem to be competitors in world capitalism. Their firms are becoming part of world oligopolies by buying up Western and especially European companies. Emerging countries are investing in Europe. Mittal's takeover of Arcelor in 2006 earned the group, chaired by an Indian, first place in the world steel oligopoly in which another Indian firm has also made a breakthrough: in 2007 Tata Steel took over the Anglo-Dutch steelmaker Corus, trumping Brazil's CSN. The incursion of emerging countries into world capitalism is not limited to private actors. Sovereign funds—state-backed and state-controlled investment funds—of certain emerging countries such as Kuwait, the United Arab Emirates, China and Russia may also become more involved in Western firms by increasing their stakes in them and demanding a degree of management control. This change, which also affects the financial sector, has in fact prompted a rise in "economic patriotism" that is no longer characteristic only of France and the United States. Such economic takeovers indeed have a chance of increasing the political influence of certain countries.

These fears should, however, be put in perspective. The increased market share of emerging countries was only marginally detrimental to the European share. Nothing can yet be taken for granted. Emerging countries are far from mastering all techniques. Quality is not always a feature of their products and services. Counterfeiting can lead to sanctions. Low wages are not necessarily enough to offset a lack of labour productivity, which remains low, even if the undervaluation of certain currencies disguises these shortcomings. Distortions are accumulating particularly in the real estate and financial sectors. The effects of the "purge" induced by the financial crisis of the late 1990s are fading, and emerging countries remain vulnerable to crises, whether these stem from their own imbalances or from those in developed countries. They did not for instance escape the summer 2007 subprime mortgage crisis.

Emerging countries as disruptive factors

Emerging countries are often seen as latecomers in a world economic order constructed without them, disrupting, voluntarily or not, the well-honed organization of markets heretofore dominated by the developed countries alone. Today the United States, Europe, and Japan are no longer the only ones that set interest rates, exchange rates and world commodity prices.

New global imbalances appeared a few years after the stabilization plans applied by most of the emerging countries in the late 1990s (Thailand, South Korea, Russia, Brazil, Argentina) to tackle the financial crisis. Restrictive policies, abundant savings, dynamic exports and rising world raw material prices have thus encouraged current account surpluses and the accumulation of foreign currency reserves. However, this spectacular evolution is also the counterpart of the twin American deficits—budget and current account—which can be ascribed to a growth model based on public deficits, consumption and debt. Since 1995, we have observed both deepening of the US current account deficit and swelling of the surplus in emerging countries,

figure 61: **Trade balances of certain economic groupings, 1995-2006**

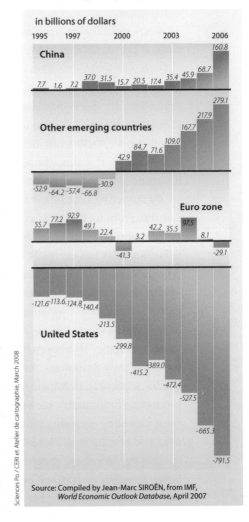

Source: Compiled by Jean-Marc SIROËN, from IMF, *World Economic Outlook Database*, April 2007

Sciences Po / CERI et Atelier de cartographie, March 2008

in particular China. To a lesser degree, the usual Eurozone surplus has been reversed.

This surplus is expressed by an increase in foreign exchange reserves in emerging countries. Between 2000 and 2005, Chinese reserves grew from $166 million to $820 billion. Emerging countries thus quickly turned from debtors to creditors.

Asymmetrical imbalances between emerging countries and the United States have significant implications for Europe. The official reserves are in fact primarily placed in dollars and to a lesser extent in euros or sterling, which buoys the US currency and fosters the undervaluation of the currencies of certain emerging countries, primarily the Chinese yuan. Greater wariness towards the US currency would have undesirable effects in Europe. The collapse of the US dollar, in addition to the financial crisis that it is likely to entail, would mean a transfer to European currencies, thus amplifying their overvaluation to the detriment of European competitiveness.

Responsibility for these imbalances cannot be ascribed to any country in particular. The American model of excessive debt corresponds to the probably too austere policies practiced in emerging countries. Their mercantilist export-driven growth strategy may lead to concentrating attention on foreign demand rather than stimulating domestic demand. An appreciation of the yuan would only reduce these imbalances if the United States reduced its public deficit and saved more. The fact nevertheless remains that emerging countries, just like the United States, make do with this situation as long as growth continues on an upward trend, even if Europe has not drawn all the dividends of these consolidated imbalances.

By attracting the savings from emerging countries and Japan, the United States can thus fulfil its function as world banker by converting a low-interest debt into longer-term and higher-yielding investments. The resulting abundance of international liquidity has certainly stimulated the world economy and trade. It has also reintroduced the risk of global inflation.

For the time being, the rise in world prices is confined to raw materials. The high growth rate of emerging countries and the improvement in their purchasing power have caused a skyrocketing demand for primary goods, the supply of which is anything but elastic. This boom has on the whole benefited emerging countries which, whatever their ambitions, remain economies dependent on the primary sector. It has constituted an unhoped-for windfall for countries that export oil or agricultural products. For a country such as Brazil, this sudden rise in prices has served to reinforce its strategy of giving priority to agribusiness, and vindicate its industrial policy objective of achieving a leadership position in the entire biofuel industry.

This evolution might defuse debates on the future of the Common Agricultural Policy formerly discredited by surpluses and low world prices. For other raw materials for which Europe's self-sufficiency is not conceivable, this evolution could damage competitiveness. However, the price of raw materials remains highly volatile, and phases of higher prices do not rule out a contrasting historic long-term trend, bearish for agricultural produce and bullish for fuels.

Emerging countries as partners

Although emerging country exports in penetrating the European Union's traditional markets (Africa, the Mediterranean, Eastern Europe) may supplant the production of certain former industrial countries, the world market is increasing in size owing to emerging country growth. What is lost on certain markets can be gained in areas of expansion that offer opportunities to the firms of industrial countries: demand for consumer goods (often luxury items), investment and infrastructure goods. Between 1999 and 2005, although the share of extra-European imports from emerging countries rose from 32% to 43.5%, the share of exports also increased, albeit less significantly, from 24% to 31%. This growing asymmetry means that Europe does not take enough advantage of the expansion of emerging countries despite its specialization theoretically adapted to demand: aeronautics and transport equipment, luxury goods, capital goods, etc. All European countries do not have the same specialization and the same market power. They do not all have the same capacity to take advantage of these new opportunities. Although Germany, unlike France, was more affected than other European countries by the financial crunch of the late 1990s in emerging countries, it has also largely taken advantage of their recovery in these past years. One of the biggest economic challenges facing Europe will thus be to increase exports to emerging countries.

Although direct investment in emerging countries is often thought to bring about relocation, it is also a vehicle for European presence in the host country. In addition, it allows the EU to penetrate local markets and often generates exports that are more complementary to them than substitutable. Although investments entering Europe from emerging countries are rising parallel to investments moving towards emerging countries, the latter represent approximately 30% of extra-European investment (compared to a little more than 10% for incoming investment flows).

Europe's breakthrough in emerging countries could be consolidated by trade agreements. Some EU countries are moreover emerging countries themselves. Others, such as Ukraine, Russia, Turkey and other Mediterranean countries, are on Europe's fringe. The European Union has signed preferential trade agreements with Turkey, Mexico, Chile and Egypt. Negotiations are underway with Mercosur and the Gulf Cooperation Council, and the European Commission has been given a mandate to negotiate new agreements revolving around trade and investment with, in particular, India, South Korea, ASEAN and the Andean Community. With China, Ukraine and Russia, trade negotiations may also be engaged in the framework of partnership and cooperation agreements.

The European Union cannot escape this trade agreement race if it aims to consolidate its presence in emerging countries. Indeed, the European Union is in direct competition with the United States, each of them trying to rob the other of its traditional areas: Latin America for the United States, Africa and the Middle East for Europe. Even if India and China assert themselves as regional leaders, to the detriment of Japan, and even if interregional trade is historically increasing, this open battle raises questions about the vision of a tripolar world that had been taken for granted in the 1990s. The United States will have to get used to a European and Asian presence in Latin America, just as Africa will link itself as much (or more?) to the Asian pole as to the European one. At the same time, the proliferation of agreements contributes to sidelining multilateralism. Paradoxically, membership of the WTO, where preferential agreements are allowed, becomes the best way to negotiate bilateral agreements, even if this circumvents the founding principle of non-discrimination between member countries.

Emerging countries, bearers of a new international economic order?

More than 50 years after the Bandung Conference, emerging countries are still demanding their place in global governance. The largest of them expect recognition of their regional leadership status, which would legitimate their active participation in the political and economic condominium of great nations. The positions established after the Second World War are thus being challenged, and the old system is unable to satisfy demand from emerging countries.

Reform of the major international institutions is late in coming. The European Union's place appears excessive: two permanent Security Council seats (United Kingdom and France), and seven of the 24 representatives on the IMF and World Bank executive board. Even after the IMF's 2006 reform that increased the quotas of four emerging countries (China, South Korea, Mexico, Turkey), the European Union still has over 32.4% of the voting rights, compared with 11.5% for Asia (17.1% for the United States); Belgium carries more weight than India or Brazil. The European Union preempts the post of IMF managing director, the United States maintaining its prerogative over the World Bank. Europe has considerable influence over the WTO. The status quo has become all the more indefensible since emerging countries have become net exporters of capital, conduct rigorous macroeconomic policies, enjoy high growth rates and bear no responsibility for the August 2007 financial crisis, which was due to the collapse of US subprime mortgages. The European and American weight is still crushing whereas the world bankers today are Japan, China and Venezuela.

The weakening legitimacy of developed countries has led emerging countries to emancipate themselves and, pragmatically, pave the way for an independent growth model. Heavily indebted to the IMF after the Asian crisis, they recently, rapidly and spectacularly disengaged themselves to the point of leaving the IMF with an abundant liquidity it cannot use.

Such financial emancipation sets the stage for ideological emancipation. The "Washington consensus", which inspired the IMF market-friendly structural adjustment programmes, has become obsolete for lack of new requests for financing.

This evolution is admittedly fragile because it is too bound up with a conjunction of favourable events that are highly unlikely to repeat themselves: exceptionally high growth rates that are probably unsustainable in the middle term, rising raw material prices, a locomotive effect created by the American deficits, and the risk of

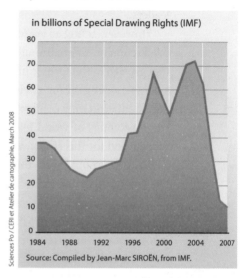

figure 62: **Value of loans granted by the IMF, 1984-2007**

in billions of Special Drawing Rights (IMF)

Sciences Po / CERI et Atelier de cartographie, March 2008

Source: Compiled by Jean-Marc SIROËN, from IMF.

a financial and banking crisis. Countries such as Brazil are just barely coming out of a monetary and fiscal policy that exceeds IMF prescriptions. Others, such as Venezuela, are squandering the oil income windfall to the point of possibly setting the stage for a new financial crisis when oil prices turn around.

The fact nevertheless remains that the state of mind in emerging countries is euphoric. It is a heady euphoria that hints at the establishment of a new international order that would rehabilitate state control as well as populist and nationalistic ideologies. Even if the proposal to set up a "Bank of the South" to compete with international or regional financial institutions is unlikely to take the shape that Hugo Chávez intends for it—who is prepared to substitute Venezuela for the United States and Europe?—the question has nevertheless been raised; many emerging countries, including Russia, India and Brazil, have embarked on a strategy of conquering the keys to "world" power, whether they are in the hands of corporations, financial institutions or international organizations. The reversal has been brutal and swift. It is not certain that the European Union has perceived all of the issues involved.

Yet the European Union was called to order during the Doha Round. Neither before the failure of the Cancún Conference in 2003 nor, perhaps, even afterwards have European negotiators accepted the idea that the emerging countries of the G20, given their highly incompatible trade interests, could band together to defeat the US/EU duopoly. For emerging countries, one important issue is certainly to engage in a test of strength that would enable them to obtain more from developed countries, in other words a greater opening of agricultural markets in the European Union in exchange for less opening of industry and services markets in emerging countries. Another is to show the former powers that nothing can be done in the future without reckoning with the emerging countries or at least their leaders.

However, acting as leader also involves accepting more than one's share in the production of "international public goods". Emerging countries can certainly argue that growth in the former industrial countries was based on child labour and considerable disregard for environmental consequences. But such a line of populist argumentation only confirms the reluctance of emerging countries to assume the responsibilities of world leaders and thus, probably, the impossibility of gaining recognition for this status, at least in the near future.

In the coming years, there is no reason for the rivalry between Europe and the emerging countries to soften. As shown by the suspension of negotiations with Mercosur, trade agreements will be difficult to negotiate with core emerging countries such as Brazil, China, India and Russia. Internal European Union compromises, on agriculture in particular, moreover narrow the room for negotiation. The export-led growth strategy adopted by emerging countries will come up against European demands for "fair" competition, close monitoring of counterfeiting, sanitary norms, environmental and social concerns and dumping. Takeovers of European corporations will be all the more scrutinized when they emanate from sovereign funds. However exorbitant they are, the European Union will surrender its prerogatives all the less easily since the United States does not appear any more willing to make concessions.

But the assertiveness of emerging countries should also encourage European leaders to intensify their coordination. A more coherent macroeconomic policy that pays more attention to exchange rates should prevent the resolution of imbalances between the United States and emerging countries leading to an unjustified appreciation of the euro. Without any suggestion of a European industrial policy, which would be more likely to offer greater protection to declining sectors than to promote forward-looking activities, European education, research and infrastructure policies should be strengthened and made more coherent to get beyond mere allusion to the Lisbon strategy. Institutional progress should also allow the Eurozone, if not the European Union, to act as such in the international financial organizations.

Bibliography

Aglietta M., and L. Berrebi (2007). *Désordres dans le capitalisme mondial*, Paris: Odile Jacob, March.

Artus, P. (2005). *La résolution des crises dans les pays émergents*, Paris: Economica, November.

Bénassy-Quéré, A. (2007). "FMI: des quotes-parts mal taillées", *La Lettre du CEPII*, 238, June-July. http://www.cepii.fr/francgraph/publications/lettre/pdf/2007/let268.pdf.

Longueville, G. (2007). "Panorama 2006-08 des pays émergents: une croissance soutenue à l'épreuve de la durée", *BNP Paribas, Conjoncture*, August. http://economic-research.bnpparibas.com/applis/WWW/RechEco.nsf/navigation/FrameMainInter?OpenDocument&Lang=FR&Mode=6.

Mathieu, E. (2006). "Les investissements des grands pays émergents en Europe et en France, Notes et études de l'AFII (Agence française pour les investissements internationaux)", 2006/11, 18 October 2006, www.investinfrance.org/France/ChoosingFrance/Statistics/research_2006-10-16_fr.pdf.

Santiso, J. (2003). *The Political Economy of Emerging Markets*. New York: Palgrave Macmillan.

Chinese and Indian Multinationals Out to Conquer the World

Jean-François Huchet and Joël Ruet

Indian and Chinese companies have emerged in large numbers on the international scene in the past few years, investing more and more heavily in the four corners of the globe. Having a strong presence in the raw materials sector already because of the two Asian giants' high degree of energy dependence, they are also found today in the steel, telecommunications, biotechnology, distribution and household appliances sectors. Such multinationalization of Chinese and Indian firms is a result both of the rapid maturing of their domestic economies (growth rate, domestic market, technological development, profit accumulation) and the globalization of the world economy, which obliges them to invest abroad to continue on the road to catch up with multinationals in industrialized countries. Despite similarities in their multinationalization processes, Chinese and Indian firms still remain strongly influenced by their countries' economic history, devising different strategies and facing different types of obstacles in their internationalization process.

A sharp rise in Chinese and Indian FDI

Regarding Chinese companies, their first foreign direct investment (FDI) operations were made in the 1980s in Hong Kong while it was still under British rule, mainly in the banking and commercial sectors. But it has primarily been since the early 2000s that Chinese FDI has really taken off, particularly in the energy and raw materials sectors. Official figures[1] in fact indicate that Chinese firms entered in

---

1   It remains difficult to gauge Chinese FDI precisely from official Chinese government statistics. Many operations transit through Hong Kong and are not listed. Moreover, only investments over $1 million appear in the official statistics; this conceals all private firm operations, particularly in Guangdong province, which is beginning to invest in Southeast Asian countries.

2001 a new phase in their internationalization, which has rapidly accelerated since 2005 with $12.3 billion, then $21 billion in 2006.[2] Chinese FDI stock certainly remains at a moderate $78 billion, only 0.6% of the world total. But the Chinese authorities predict a strong increase in annual FDI flows, which could soon exceed $30 billion. By the end of 2006, the Chinese Ministry of Commerce had inventoried slightly over 5,000 Chinese companies that had made investments abroad, establishing nearly 10,000 overseas firms in 172 countries.[3]

As regards Indian investments abroad, a few major groups such as Tata, Kirloskar and Birla started investing in the 1960s in neighbouring Sri Lanka and in Africa. But it was during the 1990s that the number of Indian multinationals exploded. Pradhan (2004 a, 2007) reckons that the number of Indian firms with branches abroad has multiplied over 40 times in the space of 20 years between 1986 (208) and 31 March 2006 (8,620). From 1995 to 2006, FDI stock went from $212 million to $8,181 million.

The buyout of the Anglo-Dutch steel manufacturer Corus by Tata in 2007 for $11 billion could usher in a new phase for Indian FDI. Many analysts have traditionally identified two phases in the takeoff of Indian FDI. Before 1990, FDI (by a few private groups allowed to invest abroad) was primarily directed towards the manufacturing, energy and raw materials sectors. Most of this FDI was by the major state-owned corporations. After 1991, a three-faceted tendency took shape: a high rise in amounts invested, sectoral diversification and the arrival of new actors from the private sector, which would soon become the main source

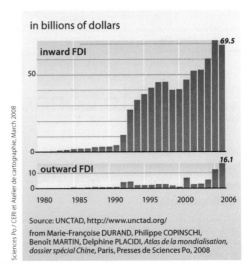

figure 63: **Chinese Foreign Direct Investment, 1980-2006**

Source: UNCTAD, http://www.unctad.org/
from Marie-Françoise DURAND, Philippe COPINSCHI, Benoît MARTIN, Delphine PLACIDI, *Atlas de la mondialisation, dossier spécial Chine*, Paris, Presses de Sciences Po, 2008

table 3: **Outward FDI per annum, China and India**

	China	India
1990-2000 average	2.1	0.1
2005	11.3	2.5
2006	17.8	9
2007	26	10

Source: Economist Intelligence Unit, 2007.

2 Ministry of Commerce of the People's Republic of China.
3 *China Daily*, 17 September 2007.

table 4: **Annual flow of Indian FDI (US$ billions)**

	India
2003-04	2.2
2004-05	2.5
2005-06	9.7

NB: the Indian fiscal year runs from April 1 to March 31
Source: UNCTAD, *World Investment Report*, 2007

table 5: **Mergers and acquisitions by foreign companies in India and Indian companies abroad (US$ millions)**

	In India	Outside India
2004	1760	863
2005	4210	2649
2006	6716	4740

NB: the Indian fiscal year runs from April 1 to March 31
Source: UNCTAD, *World Investment Report*, 2007

of Indian FDI. But it is probably wise to subdivide the second phase, with a cutoff point around the years 2001-2. Before this turning point, the major Indian industrial groups had undergone a long decade of refocusing on certain core trades after being forced to diversify for nearly 40 years because of investment regulations[4] set up after independence in 1947. Not yet very competitive internationally, in the 1990s these groups preferred to remain on the national market, which was still highly protected. After 1995, the "reverse brain-drain" of returning Indian expatriates gave rise to a very dynamic information technology industry. Some of these companies worked their way fairly quickly up the value chain (Bomsel and Ruet 2001) and ventured into foreign investment during the late 1990s. Companies in the biotechnology and pharmaceutical sectors then followed suit (Huchet, Richet, Ruet 2007). It was not until after 2002 that the major Indian manufacturing groups would truly begin their internationalization process. The restructuring of their activities during the previous decade provided them with considerable financial reserves, and they partly anticipated the pressure of foreign competition on the domestic market, which they knew was bound to grow with the opening-up measures instituted by various governments since 1991.

With all the FDI operations, mergers and acquisitions increased. But until 2006 they remained to the advantage of foreign firms, although Tata Steel's exceptional bid for Corus, followed by Suzlon's smaller-scale but still significant bid for Repower, might foreshadow a new stage.

Investment sector diversification

Regarding Chinese firms, the energy and raw materials sectors continue to account for nearly half of the total amount of Chinese FDI in 2006. China's colossal energy needs[5] prompted the Chinese government in 1995 to start restructuring the major state-owned firms operating in these sectors. Then, starting in the early 2000s, the

---

4   Known as the "Licence Raj".
5   In the year 2006 alone, five new 300 MW power stations came into service every week in China, new production in one year amounting to total French production. See Reuters, 23 March 2007. China became a net importer of oil in 1993.

state encouraged them to invest abroad in order to secure supplies overseas. Activity by Chinese firms in the oil sector has been intensive in Africa, Central Asia[6] and the middle east to the point of feeding obsessive fears that the Chinese firms will oust US and European operators from the African market. Despite an increase in FDI flows from Chinese oil giants, we can expect to see their presence increase even further in the years to come, as the external supply of oil from fields controlled by Chinese firms only amount to 15% of China's total imports.[7] Since 2005, other sectors, such as telecommunications, information technology, consumer electronics

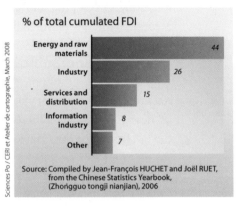

figure 64: **Distribution of Chinese FDI by sector, 2002-2005**

% of total cumulated FDI

Source: Compiled by Jean-François HUCHET and Joël RUET, from the Chinese Statistics Yearbook, (Zhōngguó tongji nianjian), 2006

and automobile manufacturing have grown rapidly: they now represent nearly 35% of total Chinese FDI. Three firms—Huawei, Haier and ZTE—are particularly active in these sectors. In less than a decade, Haier has for example set up 13 production units, 8 design centres, 22 trade companies and nearly 4,600 retail stores outside China.[8] Chinese FDI is also rapidly increasing in the commercial sector. Chinese industrial firms that do subcontracting for European, US and Japanese multinationals are now trying to work their way up the added-value chain in order to capture a larger share of the profits made on consumer sales in developed countries.

The constraints of internationalization related to growing competition on national soil are reflected in the sectoral makeup of Indian FDI today. For instance, in the panorama outlined by the Boston Consulting Group report on the 100 emerging giants, which compared criteria including company size, growth rate and business model performance, 44 Chinese firms and 21 Indian firms are listed. Among the latter are Infosys, Satyam, Tata Consultancy Services and Wipro in the field of information technology in both low added-value activities, such as business processing outsourcing, and high added-value areas, such as organizational consulting and virtual industrial design. Cipla, Dr. Reddy and Ranbaxy in the pharmaceutical industry are making rapid headway in their international strategy by filing numerous patents abroad. The automobile and automobile parts and accessories sectors are multiplying their subsidiaries abroad with Bajaj, Bharat Forge, Mahindra & Mahindra, Tata Motors and TVS Motor Company. Engineering is not far behind with Crompton Greaves and Larsen & Toubro. Many operations

---

6   China National Petroleum Corporation bought PetroKazakhstan in 2005, for $4.2 billion, the biggest ever operation by a Chinese firm abroad.

7   The remaining 85% were bought on the international market, Kenneth Lieberthal and Mikkal Herberg, "China's Search for Energy Security: Implications for U.S. Policy", *NBR Analysis*, vol. 17, no. 1, April 2006.

8   *China Daily*, 13 March 2007.

have also taken place in steelmaking, energy and raw materials with Hindalco (nonferrous metals), Tata Steel and the Reliance conglomerate (energy), without forgetting ONGC (oil and gas). Foreign investments in the oil and gas sectors accounted for 19% of the Indian FDI stock in 2006.

Changing geographical patterns in FDI distribution

Asia remains the primary destination for Chinese FDI. Hong Kong still soaked up nearly 48% of all Chinese FDI in 2004 (28% in 2005). If investments made in the tax havens of the Cayman Islands and the Virgin Islands are added, in 2005 the three territories culled a little over 80% of the total amount of Chinese FDI. It thus appears difficult to get a precise grasp on the establishment strategy of Chinese firms abroad since the three territories, acting as they do as tax havens, are often merely a stopover destination. A few notable trends can nevertheless be detected that corroborate the sectoral distribution of FDI with the strategic needs of Chinese firms. The African continent, Australia, South America, Russia, Central Asia and Indonesia are territories coveted today by the major Chinese firms in the energy and raw materials sectors. Since 2003 the search for new technologies in the information industry and new markets in consumer electronics, the automobile sector and commerce has led to a steady increase in Chinese FDI in South Korea ($5.9 billion in 2005, or 4.8% of the total amount), the United States ($2.3 billion, or 1.9%), Europe and Japan. A World Bank (2006) study of Chinese firms' foreign investment plans for the next five years indicate a change in choice of geographical territory: South East Asia, Africa, Northern Europe, Latin America, Eastern Europe and South Korea are the big winners, whereas East Asia, North America, the Middle East and Australia should see a slowdown.

As regards the destination of Indian FDI, a radical change is observed that is clear evidence of an overhaul of the industrial strategies of Indian groups. Before 1990, to mention only those territories for which the share exceeded 5% of the total, the destination countries were, in decreasing order of total FDI stock, Thailand, Singapore, Kazakhstan, Senegal, the United Kingdom, the United States and Indonesia. Developing countries thus were the major beneficiaries. After 1991, the UK was in the lead with nearly 27% of the total, while the US received 25% and the tax haven of Mauritius (which serves as a platform for reinvestment in India) nearly 10%. Although Indian concerns initially sought to secure energy resources and conquer external markets in a context where their growth on the domestic market was tightly controlled, recent dynamics mainly reflect a search for strategic assets: technology, market shares in developed economies, brands and new R&D skills. Like Chinese firms, they are seeking to improve their initial cost advantage on the domestic market by moving up the added value chain. It is thus interesting to note that in the year 2004, for instance, the sectors in which

figure 65: **Chinese Foreign Direct Investment, 2005**

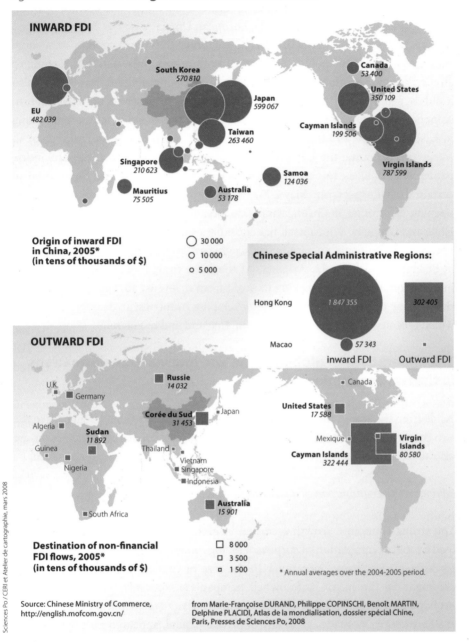

INWARD FDI

South Korea
570 810

Japan
599 067

EU
482 039

Taiwan
263 460

Singapore
210 623

Mauritius
75 505

Australia
53 178

Samoa
124 036

Canada
53 400

United States
350 109

Cayman Islands
199 506

Virgin Islands
787 599

Origin of inward FDI
in China, 2005*
(in tens of thousands of $)

○ 30 000
○ 10 000
○ 5 000

Chinese Special Administrative Regions:

Hong Kong   *1 847 355*   *302 405*

Macao   *57 343*

inward FDI   Outward FDI

OUTWARD FDI

U.K.
Germany

Russie
14 032

Corée du Sud
31 453

Japan

Algeria

Sudan
11 892

Guinea

Thailand

Nigeria

Vietnam

Singapore

Indonesia

Canada

United States
17 588

Mexique

Cayman Islands
322 444

Virgin
Islands
80 580

Australia
15 901

South Africa

Destination of non-financial
FDI flows, 2005*
(in tens of thousands of $)

□ 8 000
□ 3 500
□ 1 500

* Annual averages over the 2004-2005 period.

Source: Chinese Ministry of Commerce,
http://english.mofcom.gov.cn/

from Marie-Françoise DURAND, Philippe COPINSCHI, Benoît MARTIN,
Delphine PLACIDI, Atlas de la mondialisation, dossier spécial Chine,
Paris, Presses de Sciences Po, 2008

Sciences Po / CERI et Atelier de cartographie, mars 2008

Indian firms concentrated their FDI in the US were information technology (80%), chemicals (7%) and pharmaceuticals (7%). On the other hand, only 19% of the FDI in the European Union targeted information technology, the rest going to pharmaceuticals (17%), electronics (10%), transport (9%), chemicals (7%) and metal products (6%), the remaining 30% going to a wide variety of other sectors (Milleli

2007). These figures are a very accurate reflection of the industrial specialization of the economies concerned, but also of targeted knowledge and sectoral interaction between Indian industry and the European Union.

The reallocation of Indian FDI destinations thus corresponds to a large extent to a search for new technological skills and brands, naturally leading to an increase in the weight of developed economies among them. But there is also a purely geographical trend due to the need to get closer to the customer, in computer-outsourcing sectors for instance. Thus Indian companies are investing in Eastern Europe and the Maghreb to reach Western European markets, or in Mexico to penetrate the US market. In so doing, Indian firms today are anticipating what is likely to be a major industrial evolution with the digitization of certain design aspects. In May 2007, Tata Consultancy Services announced the opening of an office in Guadalajara. Tata already employs 5,000 people in Brazil, Chile and Uruguay. Wipro itself has subsidiaries in Saudi Arabia, Canada, China, Portugal and Romania, to name a few. Cognizant Technology Solutions has offices in Shanghai and Phoenix, Arizona. At the same time, Indian companies in the information industry are seeking to profit from their cost advantage to dominate the growing outsourcing industry in developing countries: an example is Infosys, which recently bought up back offices in Thailand and in Poland.

The imperatives of globalization and internal transformations in the two economies

Aside from the search for outside energy supplies, factors related to changes in the two countries' domestic economies, and the growing influence of globalization, are also at the root of rapid growth and FDI from Chinese and Indian corporations.

Savings and accumulation of financial capacities

The strong economic growth recorded in each of the two countries has generated a rapid accumulation of corporate savings and reserves that can be mobilized for foreign investment operations. In the case of China, the largest investments are made by the major state-owned companies, especially those operating in monopolized sectors such as energy, raw materials and telecommunications. Only the Lenovo group, made up mostly of private capital, appeared on the list of the 20 largest Chinese investors abroad in 2005. The major Chinese companies, the majority of which are state-controlled, are the most thrifty in Asia, saving about 33% of their profits, compared with 17% for the rest of Asia. Until 2006 they distributed few dividends to the state and even if their profit margin remains slim, the high growth recorded since 2000 has enabled them to accumulate a considerable cushion of financial resources to back their international ambitions. Moreover, the monetary context is particularly conducive to anything that favours getting capital out of Chinese territory. In the face of international pressure for China to revalue its currency because of the unprecedented accumulation of foreign exchange reserves (nearly $1,700 billion), the Chinese government has considerably reduced the restrictions imposed on Chinese firms in their investment operations abroad.

The macroeconomic financial context is fairly different for Indian companies: monetary reserves are much lower and the country has a trade deficit. On the other hand, the structure of the Indian stock market plays a positive role that off-sets this disadvantage. Indian companies benefit from their stock market value, linked to their rapid and steady growth (according to an elementary stock market mechanism, which gives them greater value than their Western competitors for an equal turnover because anticipated gains are higher). For instance, the largest acquisition operation made by an Indian group—Tata Steel's takeover of the Anglo-Dutch Corus for $11 billion—was partly made possible by the presence of Tata Consultancy Services in the Tata group,[9] which increased Tata Steel's borrowing capacity. The rising prices on the Mumbai stock exchange for the moment enable Indian groups to issue shares and raise the capital required for their future expansion.

Opening up and competition on national markets

Along with external factors, the increasing globalization of the world economy has obliged Chinese and Indian firms to go international. The opening up of the two economies spells increased competition for their companies on their domestic markets, which were once long protected by high customs tariffs. After WTO accession talks were accelerated (China became a member in 2001), China agreed to drastically lower its customs tariffs, which went from an average 25% in 1997 to 7% in 2005. Chinese groups are now in direct competition with foreign groups heavily investing in China. It is thus no accident that the sectors in which the increased internationalization of Chinese firms is speeding up today are also the sectors in which FDI entering China is the largest (telecommunications, electronics, vehicle manufacture). The search for new overseas markets is by far the primary factor explaining the keenness of Chinese firms to increase their investments abroad.[10]

Indian companies, like their Chinese counterparts, are increasingly exposed to direct competition from major international groups on their own soil. The latter will also benefit increasingly from the same price structures related to the cost of labour in Chinese and Indian territories. These changes will affect both

---

9   At the time when it took over Corus, Tata Consultancy Services accounted for 50% of the Tata Group stock market value while representing only 16% of its turnover.

10 *China's Outward Foreign Direct Investment*, op. cit.

production and product design. The major Indian groups thus find themselves in a probably more exacerbated situation than their Chinese counterparts in several key industrial sectors. In the vehicle sector, for instance, joint venture arrangements are prevalent in China. In India, the groups that position themselves in car manufacturing know that even if they can sometimes count on joint ventures, these are not long-term partnerships supplanting their own production. Such groups must develop their own models in the long run. Indian groups (Tata and Mahindra & Mahindra) are faced with having to sell vehicles abroad to offset the foreign competition they face. In the field of electronics, it is another reason that prevails. The geographical competence clusters of companies, and their number, are much more limited than in China. Companies face competition from Europe, the United States and Japan as well as China. Indian industry is trying to build competitive clusters outside the computer services or pharmaceutical sector, but competition is stiff in these areas. To tackle it, Indian groups nevertheless have an advantage over Chinese companies. The structure of their capital, which is mainly private, enables them to move faster than Chinese groups in the merger and acquisitions market.

The need to scale up technology and build brand names

In this context of increased competition on their domestic markets, Chinese and Indian firms must also continue to accumulate technological skills and build recognized brand names that free them from segments with the lowest added value in the international division of labour. Lenovo's takeover of IBM's personal computer division, TCL's takeover of Thomson's TV division, and Haier's failed attempt to acquire the US refrigerator manufacturer Maytag are all examples of this strategy. The increase in Chinese FDI in commerce also indicates the Chinese firms' desire to reinforce their presence in international distribution channels and capture a larger share of the added value on products sold to consumers. Galanz, for instance, world leader in microwave ovens with nearly 40% of the world market, supplies its products to nearly 250 firms that resell under their own brand name. Galanz today is seeking to establish its own brand and invest in the distribution and marketing phase, where the larger share of profits is made. The same pattern is found in many industrial sectors, such as the textile and garment industry, shoes, electronics and toys, of which the Chinese have become major producers through subcontracting without managing to reap large profits.

Indian industrial corporations, less numerous but larger than their Chinese counterparts, have generally begun the process of brand building. Brand promotion nevertheless remains confined to a rather small number of countries. To remedy this problem, already well-known brands are seeking to strengthen their recognition abroad. In addition to the computer groups and pharmaceutical firms already known on the international scene, new brands are also beginning to emerge. Some traditional groups such as Tata and Reliance are gradually acquiring a reputation in the infrastructure and energy sectors; others such as Jet Airways in air transport, Suzlon in renewable energy, Bharti in telecommunications and DLF in real estate are following suit.

The risks of these development strategies

While there can be no doubt about the capacity of Chinese and Indian groups to become serious competitors in the long run, they nevertheless suffer from a certain number of deficiencies or disadvantages likely to limit their competitive potential in the short and medium term. Chinese groups suffer from a lack of internationally trained managers, limited knowledge of the European and American legal and administrative environments, a lack of flexibility to put together complex financial operations for mergers and acquisitions, and considerable deficiencies in their system of governance. This last point is perhaps the most worrisome given the size of Chinese FDI in the tax havens of the Virgin and Cayman Islands (52% of the total in 2005). In contrast to the Indian groups, to a large extent privately owned, the fairly inefficient state control over the major Chinese groups that are crumbling under the weight of liquidity could encourage certain Chinese firms to undertake investment operations abroad for prestige or, worse, to facilitate the personal enrichment of company managers.

These weak points are not shared by the major Indian groups. But the stiff competition among the country's firms clearly offers advantages to those who position themselves first in new sectors, new business models and new production niches. This early-bird premium probably justifies the high share price of these companies. As long as the Mumbai stock exchange remains on an upward swing, it will offer significant means to finance expansion abroad. In the event of a drop in confidence on the stock market, the consequences could be harmful for the internationalization strategies of these companies. The channelling of the currently high liquidity of the world financial economy has so far been beneficial to the major Indian groups, but to continue to benefit from it, they will have to demonstrate great precision in their development strategy.

Bibliography ·

Accenture (2005). *China Spreads its Wings. Chinese Companies go Global.*

Battat, J. (2006). *China's Outward Foreign Direct Investments.* Washington DC: Foreign Investment Advisory Services, Firm Survey, World Bank/IFC.

Bomsel O. and J. Ruet (eds) (2001). *Digital India - Report on the Indian IT Industry*. Paris: Cerna-Ensmp, June.

Huchet, J-F., X. Richet and J. Ruet (2007). *Firms and the State: Industrial and Administrative Models for Globalisation in China, India, Russia,* especially Ch. 13, pp. 285-310, "Asset Specificity, Partnerships and Global Strategies of Information Technology and Biotechnology Firms in India". New Delhi: Academic Foundation India.

—— (eds) (2006). "Globalisation and Opening Markets" in *Developing Countries and Impact on National Firms and Public Governance: The Case of India*. CSH-LSE-NCAER-ORF-Cerna report.

Liberthal, K. and M. Herberg (2006). "China's Search for Energy Security: Implications for U.S. Policy". NBR Analysis 17(1).

Milleli, C. (2007). "International Expansion by Indian Firms: what of European Market Entry?" in *The Indian Economy in the Era of Globalization*, Geneva: CAS Occasional Papers, no. 26, Center for Asian Studies, June 2006.

Pradhan, J. P. (2004), "The Determinants of Outward Foreign Direct Investment: A Film-level Analysis of Indian Manufacturing". *Oxford Development Studies*, 32 (4), pp. 619-39.

—— (2007), *Trends and Patterns of Overseas Acquisitions by Indian Multinationals*, working paper no. 2007/10, October, Institute for Studies in Industrial Development, New Delhi.

Ruet, J. (2007). "Emergence des firmes multinationales du "Sud" et lecture du capitalisme" in *Annuaire de relations internationales*. Paris: IFRI, pp. 802-825.

The Boston Consulting Group (2006). *China's Global Challenges. How 100 Top Companies from Rapidly developing Economies are Challenging the World*.

World Bank/IFC (2006), *China's Outward Foreign Direct Investment*, Foreign Investment Advisory Services, Firm Survey.

Emerging Countries and International Cooperation

Jean-Jacques Gabas

E merging countries, which have come to the fore of the international economic scene in recent years, are also highly involved in the sphere of development cooperation. For some, this represents a re-emergence (Russia, new EU members in Central and Eastern Europe, China); others, such as South Africa, India and Brazil, are newcomers to international development financing. The methods of intervention that these new actors use is currently altering the field of international cooperation, affecting the practices of DAC (Development Assistance Committee)[1] member country donors and multilateral institutions as well as the countries and regional cooperation organizations that benefit from this development aid.[2]

Having become, or again become, purveyors of aid, emerging countries have more or less explicitly developed cooperation policies with several countries in Africa, Asia, Latin America and Eastern Europe. But most of them remain recipients of aid from DAC/OECD member countries and international financial institutions, even if the aid received represents only a minute portion of their development financing.

---

1 Specific OECD cooperation programmes are currently in place Brazil, China and Russia. The OECD also conducts a number of specific activities with other non-member countries, for instance Chile, India and South Africa.

2 In speaking of international cooperation, this article refers only to international cooperation for development. Economic, commercial and military cooperation will therefore not be discussed.

figure 66: **Official development assistance (ODA), donors and recipients, 2006**

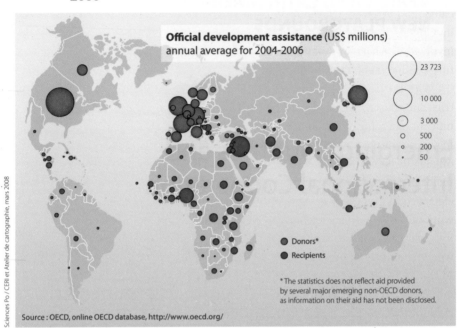

Sciences Po / CERI et Atelier de cartographie, mars 2008

Source : OECD, online OECD database, http://www.oecd.org/

This dual status of recipient and donor adds complexity to international relations (Tubiana 2007, Severino 2006). For in this historically very unique context, non-emerging developing countries, particularly the least developed countries (LDCs), will radically alter the rules of international negotiation for development financing; the functioning of the fora that coordinate aid, international bodies such as the OECD, the World Bank and the European Commission, will be similarly altered.

Emerging countries as donors

A historical overview

The involvement of emerging countries on the international development cooperation scene is not a new phenomenon. During the 1950s, over 95% of public development aid was supplied by the "founders" of the DAG (Development Assistance Group working within the OEEC (Organization for European Economic Cooperation), precursor of the DAC/OECD). The only donor that rivalled these founding countries (the United States, France, Germany, and Belgium in particular) in the Cold War context was the Soviet Union, with the financing of the Aswan Dam in Egypt. During the 1960s, aid from COMECON (Council for Mutual Economic Assistance) member states was sent to countries having the same political orientation (such as Mali, Guinea, etc.), while students—particularly African ones—were educated in European Communist countries and in China, then a nonaligned country already involved in Africa in building urban infrastructure (stadiums, public buildings etc.).

With the first oil crisis in 1973, OPEC countries and their financial institutions became significant emerging actors in development financing, accounting for nearly 30% of the world's official development assistance (ODA). Some major projects, such as the irrigation and hydroelectric dams on the Senegal River in the framework of OMVS (the Senegal river basin authority), were mainly financed by OPEC funds, as were major highway projects south of the Sahara. In the 1970s IFAD (International Fund for Agricultural Development) was founded to finance agricultural programmes. During the 1980s and 1990s, over 95% of world ODA was again supplied by DAC member countries and those belonging to the international financial institutions. Cooperation between emerging countries and developing countries has only really been affirmed or reaffirmed since the early 2000s.

Statistical monitoring of the flow of aid on an internationally harmonized basis—the only real way to gauge actual development initiatives—remains very difficult, but a few avenues can nevertheless be mapped out. As regards non-DAC OECD donor countries, statistics show that a country such as South Korea or Turkey supplies significant volumes of aid by comparison with other DAC donor countries (Greece and Portugal) and OPEC countries (Kuwait), even if these volumes remain lower than aid from all the other donors.

The volumes of aid from China, Brazil, India and even South Africa are not counted by the DAC, as these countries do not report their figures or use harmonized definitions of statisti-

figure 67: **Official Development Assistance (ODA) by non-DAC member donors, 2001-2005**

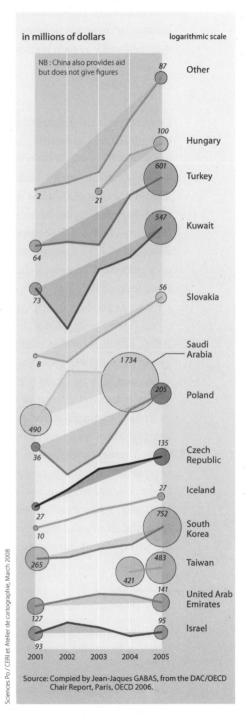

Source: Compiled by Jean-Jaques GABAS, from the DAC/OECD Chair Report, Paris, OECD 2006.

Sciences Po / CERI et Atelier de cartographie, March 2008

cal categories. Only more or less reliable estimates are therefore available: some data reflect annual payments, others reflect pledges to finance over an unspecified number of years. Financial conditions generally remain confidential since aid policy continues to be considered a strategic element of foreign policy. As for the specific content of these aid policies, the often very vague outlines of what may be implemented locally in each state have to be filled in by surmise.

China in Africa

Development aid disbursed by China remains obscure, the various statistics being difficult to compare as they are incomplete and the sources are unreliable. According to the 2003 and 2006 editions of the *China Statistical Yearbook*, total Chinese aid amounted to about US$970 million in 2005, compared with $650 million in 2002 (Lancaster 2007). But for many observers and analysts, the flows are actually much higher, varying between 1 and 2 billion US dollars. Official Chinese statistics apparently only take into account Foreign Trade Ministry data.[3] The portion allocated to Africa apparently amounts to 30%-50% of the total. These overall and very uncertain estimates show the scope of aid and make China a donor on the same level as Belgium, Switzerland, Austria and Denmark.

China's strategy in Africa[4] is particularly interesting in that it is a reflection of a real public policy constructed around a set of highly coherent actions (Gabas 2006). Africa is and has always been a major diplomatic issue between Beijing and Taipei (Taylor 1998). Any cooperation agreement between an African country and China can only be made if it breaks with Taiwan. The primary basis for cooperation is not a partnership in the sense spelled out by the DAC in March 2003 in its Principles for Effective Aid, but reciprocal advantages with more or less clear compensation in terms of economic or trade advantages upon signature. Cooperation agreements are systematically presented as a win-win venture between the two parties. The compensation materializes as access to mineral raw materials and forest concessions (Coussy & Gabas 2007) and aid liaison.

China, in its dealings with Africa, observes a policy of non-interference in domestic affairs and thus in questions of governance. This attitude contrasts with the principles of intervention set out by donors such as the World Bank or the European Union, which allocate aid according to the criteria of "good govern-

---

3 The Chinese authorities seemed to want to model their practices on administrative and political forms of aid management. They are pondering the creation of a specific agency and have made contacts with the DFID (Department for International Development) in the United Kingdom, the Swedish International Developmemt Agency, the Canadian government and USAID (United States Agency for International Development) (Lancaster, 2007).

4 Chinese foreign policy aiming to guarantee its supply of raw materials and open its markets does not only apply to Africa. In fact, Latin America, the second-largest destination of Chinese FDI after Asia, which receives 60% of it, received nearly 16% of Chinese FDI in 2004 (Santiso, 2006). Conversely, Brazil is also investing in China.

ance". China is only interested in a country's political stability, seen as conducive to economic exchanges. This orientation enables it to maintain relations with pariah states such as Sudan, practice arms policies that contravene Western rules, reject the universal application of human rights principles, and advocate non-interference as the foundation of foreign policy initiative. The six main themes of Chinese foreign policy (Gabas 2006) shed light on the country's strategy in Africa: securing oil and raw material supplies; establishing more and more private companies involved in infrastructure construction; providing incentives for establishing a diaspora; signing bilateral trade agreements; and an assertive development cooperation strategy, and lastly, military cooperation policy. This situation perturbs DAC donor cooperation policies: their allocation criteria are at odds with China's, and the international consensus on the fight against poverty, i.e. the Millennium Goals, are not shared by the Chinese authorities. As for debt reduction initiatives (Highly Indebted Poor Countries Initiative, HIPC), in certain countries these are accompanied by phenomena of re-indebtedness on an unknown scale. However, in December 2007, China's coming on board as an IDA (International Development Association) donor for the 2008-2013 period can also be analyzed as the sign of the desire for coordination with other donors. But the lack of conditionality that still characterizes Chinese aid to the present day is perceived, rightly or wrongly, by African states as a fundamental aspect that gives them real bargaining power with respect to all donors, which may enable them to break free from historic relationships often perceived as too overbearing, and whose effectiveness, in addition, is widely disputed (Gabas 2002).

Indian uniqueness

India is considering regional or bilateral accords (Comprehensive Economic Cooperation Agreements, CECA) with Japan, Brazil, South Africa, Russia and the European Union. Although the aim of these agreements has to do with increasing trade and investment flows, they nevertheless have effects on development aid policies. The Indian Development Initiative project emphasizes a new lending instrument: India could borrow capital on international markets and refinance projects, particularly in Africa south of the Sahara. Over 85% of these loans— amounting to between $300 million and $400 million, ten times the 2004/2005 amount—would be tied and would thus have to be spent in India. Furthermore, Delhi backs NEPAD programmes to the tune of between $200 million and $500 million in a credit line at Eximbank for West Africa, in the context of its TEAM-9 (Techno-Economic Approach for Africa-Indian Movement) programme. India wants to share with African countries the benefit of its expertise in areas such as information technology, pharmaceutical manufacturing and health care. Nevertheless, aid as a means to finance development is presented with a risk of increased dependence with regard to the donors, which points to the limits of aid as a development factor.[5]

The African situation

South Africa's development aid policy was the focus of debate at an ANC (African National Congress) conference in June 2007. An annual contribution by the South African International Development Agency (SAIDA), an agency based within the Foreign Affairs Ministry or the Treasury, of aid ranging from 0.2 % to 0.5% of GDP was considered. This agency would concentrate on the major issues facing the continent, providing aid to countries in post-conflict situations and on the road to democratization; it would thus be conditional. Such development aid policy is part of South Africa's broader foreign policy, which rests on three pillars: consolidation of the African agenda, and South-South and South-North cooperation. Regarding the latter aspect, South Africa is demanding a strategic partnership with the European Union similar to the one engaged with China, Brazil, India and Russia.

Prior to 1989, Hungary and Czechoslovakia devoted 1% of their GDP to development aid for "brother" countries such as Ethiopia and Angola, from which several thousand students were trained in the universities of Central Europe. In the same way, many Malian and other African students were trained in Russia. These states put an end to their cooperation policy in the 1990s, restarting it in the early 21st century with neighbouring countries, especially those in the Balkans and Ukraine, Georgia and Moldova, and further-off socialist countries like Vietnam. The overall contribution of countries that entered the EU after 2004 remains marginal and only concerns Africa to a very small extent. The Central and Eastern European countries (CEECs) that have expressed the desire to join the DAC are seeking to share their experience of political, economic and institutional transition, and make no secret of the fact that their aid also fits within an international security objective.

All things considered, emerging countries will in the medium term become real actors in the field of development cooperation. The areas of food aid, regional conflict resolution, international debt and relations between the EU and Africa are good illustrations of this new international situation. If the total flow of food aid for the 1998-2006 period is analyzed, one notes a general downward trend with significant inter-annual fluctuations. The total volume went from 8.4 million grain equivalent tons in 1998 to 6.7 million in 2006.

---

5   India refused international emergency aid during the December 2004 tsunami. Aid earmarked for India hardly represents more than 0.1% to 0.2% of its GDP in recent years. But one must keep in mind the subtle game India was playing in the 1960s in its diplomatic relations and cooperation agreements, which enabled it to receive financing both from the United States and the USSR.

In this context, China considerably increased its food aid to reach 576,000 grain equivalent tons in 2005, a significant volume by comparison with European aid, which amounted to 1.6 million grain equivalent tons the same year; in 2006, it dropped back down to 144,000. This aid, basically directed at food emergencies in Asia, particularly in North Korea, only rarely concerns the African continent. If the volumes allocated remain low in certain African countries, they are programmed without any consultation with other donors. But food crisis situations are increasingly complex: conflicts in one country produce effects in the subregion to which it belongs and more generally on the functioning of grain and food markets. Poorly programmed and poorly targeted food aid can have considerable adverse effects on populations.

As regards conflict resolution, South Africa now plays a major role in Africa and in particular in Burundi and the Democratic Republic of Congo (DRC). The latter country, however, has just borrowed $5 billion from China to be repaid in raw materials. The situation is becoming more complex in Africa, where South Africa is devising its own cooperation policy without at all consulting the new donor China.

Now that the credit-worthiness of African countries has been restored through multiple bilateral and multilateral debt foirgiveness initiatives, donors have defined a reasoned process of re-indebtedness in a conditional framework, so as not to fall back into the debt/cancellation cycle, taking into account each state's debt-burden threshold (Djoufelkit-Cottenet 2007). The re-indebtedness process, necessary for development financing, is subject to conditions. But several African states are very tempted to go further into debt than the Debt Sustainability Framework (DSF) allows, with emerging countries—because of the virtual lack of conditionality. Although the latter pay lip service to a need for coordination, they stray from it in practice when it comes to implementing their policies in the various states.

Lastly, as paradoxical as it may seem, emerging countries are at the heart of renegotiation of the Cotonou Agreement between the EU and the ACP (African, Caribbean and Pacific) countries, as illustrated by President Abdoulaye Wade's recent statement: "If Europe doesn't want to form the new EU-ACP partnership, the Chinese will do it faster and cheaper." The President of Senegal also declared: "It's not because there's Darfur that you can't invest in Africa," considering that EU's excessive caution regarding investment in Africa could largely be compensated by emerging country investment, from China in particular. But more basically, the traditional donors believe they hold the key to "good aid practices" and consider that emerging countries must adopt directives from the various international bodies (the DAC, the United Nations, etc.). According to F. Bourguignon,[6] "the World Bank

---

6   He moreover finds that "the duration and interest rates of loans granted by the World Bank to emerging countries are close to market conditions; the attribution procedure is very involved. Some large countries thus decide to do without, such as Mexico which borrowed $29 million in 2007, peanuts compared with the billion dollars that used to be commonly requested. The World Bank might just disappear from these countries." (Le Monde, 13 November 2007).

table 6: **Official development assistance in selected emerging countries**

	South Africa	India	China	Brazil
Volume of ODA* (2003-2005)	650	1100	1500	180
flow behavior	*stable*	*unstable*	*rising*	*stable*
Private transfers *	5000 (in 2005)	5114 (in 2005)	19205 (in 2005)	-764 (in 2003), +20734 (in 2005)
	very unstable	*rising*	*rising*	*very unstable*
Five largest donors	European Commission, United States, United Kingdom, Netherlands, Germany	World Bank, Japan, United Kingdom, Germany, European Commission	Japan, Germany, France, United Kingdom, World Bank	Japan, Germany, France, United States, Netherlands
Population**	45	1094	1300	186
Per capita GDP ***	4900	720	1740	3460
ODA/GNP	0.3%	0.2%	0.1%	0%

Sources: DAC/OCDE data. * = current USD millions, ** = millions of inhabitants, *** = current USD.

currently does a poor job of handing on the experience it has accumulated, because it has a tendency to utter uniform recommendations and doctrinaire formulas."

Emerging countries as recipients of aid

Emerging countries receiving bilateral or multilateral cooperation programmes have rather specific development financing profiles if one takes into account aid volume, private transfers and the main partners.

Depending on the donor, the pace and the degree of intervention can be fairly different, revealing divergences in economic or even geostrategic issues in these countries. On the other hand, most bilateral cooperation takes place in similar areas with an emphasis on the question of global public goods.

In the four emerging countries of South Africa, India, Brazil and China, we note the ongoing involvement of Germany, the United Kingdom and Japan. For various reasons related to their history and foreign policy, these three last countries enter into development cooperation agreements without ever mentioning the word "aid", contrary to what DAC members do with respect to the LDCs.

Germany for instance considers that cooperation with countries such as China should fall within a "strategic partnership", because of attendant environmental issues. The areas of intervention are enlightening. The aim of German assistance is to foster dialogue, build scientific networks and promote staff exchanges between the various administrations in charge of managing aid. But the most original direction involves setting up triangular cooperation programmes between Germany, an emerging country and a developing country, often an LDC. Given the very nature of economic growth in "anchor countries" (China, India, and Pakistan, Thailand, Egypt, Iran, Saudi Arabia, Nigeria, South Africa, Argentina, Brazil, Mexico, Russia and Turkey) and the issue of governance and regional security, taking account of global public goods (primarily environmental ones) constitutes another, more general aspect of its strategic cooperation. German cooperation thus does not consider China (or Brazil, India or South Africa) as mere "recipients" of aid, because these countries have the capacity to build their own poverty reduction policies. In terms of modalities, Germany's financial resources are allocated to China in the form of loans on near market conditions, with Chinese compensation for each cooperation project. The policy of the Canadian International Development Agency (CIDA) is very similar to Germany's, and emphasizes the environmental question as well as individual freedoms in the case of China. The 2005-10 CIDA plan announced a substantial increase in aid without giving figures. With Brazil, cooperation agreements are more focused on reducing inequalities. With Russia, the programmes date back to 1991 and have to do with governance and measures to accompany the transition process.

France has only recently taken an interest in emerging countries.[7] A particular feature of French aid is high concentration in a "priority solidarity zone" (*"zone de solidarité prioritaire"* or ZSP) grouping 55 countries, 45 of which are in Africa. Among the 20 most aided countries, 14 are on the African continent. The Emerging Country Reserve[8] represents 300 million euros out of a total ODA volume which in 2006 amounted to 8,445 million euros. The main themes of intervention presented in the Gaymard report (2006) are higher education, interventions in the field of global public goods and support for private French companies. The report's conclusions, sanctioned by the Védrine report (2007), placed particular emphasis

---

7 The French development agency, the Agence Française de Développement (AFD), was authorized to intervene in Thailand, Jordan, Syria, Turkey, Egypt and China in October 2003, and in Indonesia after the tsunami of 26 December 2004. In 2006, The Interministerial Committee for International Cooperation and Development (CICID) authorized the AFD, whose mandate was broadened in 2001, to intervene in India, Brazil and Indonesia (not only in the context of reconstruction operations) in an experimental capacity as well as in South Africa after the transition in 1994.

8 The following countries are eligible for an emerging country reserve (RPE) according to country specific conditionalities: China, India, Indonesia, the Philippines, Thailand, Kazakhstan, Azerbaijan, Montenegro, Turkey, Egypt, Tunisia, Morocco, South Africa, Vietnam, Algeria, Albania, Armenia, Mongolia, Bolivia, Colombia, El Salvador, Guatemala, Peru, Uzbekistan and Serbia.

on the need for European and US capacities of persuasion to raise social and environmental norms (this point intersects with the issue of funding for global public goods). France's Interministerial Committee on International Cooperation and Development (CICID) moreover considers that exploitation of mineral resources in Africa will take place in a tense international context owing to the growing involvement of emerging countries (Strategic Policy Paper 2007).

The French development agency AFD (Agence Française de Développement) frames its activities in emerging countries in Asia in a development bank strategy. In fact, AFD commitments in Asia reached over 459 million euros in 2005, compared with 119 million the year before. During the same period, by way of comparison, commitments to Mediterranean countries have regularly declined to reach 297 million euros in 2006. AFD loans to fund global public goods, such as the construction of energy-efficient homes and the building of hydraulic infrastructure, wind farms and other innovative renewable energy projects, are all investment opportunities that involve China, India and Brazil, countries whose energy needs in urban and industrial development are considered a threat to the global environment.

In the context of decentralized cooperation, the Rhône-Alpes region experience focused on scientific cooperation with China is an original one, as are the experiments with triangular cooperation initiated by Montreuil (in the eastern Paris suburbs) with Mali and Vietnam. Even if the latter country is not (yet) ranked among emerging countries, this sort of cooperation, albeit on a very limited scale, deserves attention for the economic, social and political repercussions it can have locally (the Cercle de Yélimané in Mali, Hai Duong province in Vietnam).

The European Union in its cooperation with South Africa supports the reform process and stresses the reduction of social and regional inequalities. This is a strategic partnership with a country that has a major influence in Africa and often speaks in the name of emerging countries: "Like Europe, South Africa is committed to countering the proliferation of weapons of mass destruction, to the recognition of the jurisdiction of the International Criminal Court, to the abolition of the death penalty and to combating terrorism. Both share a strong belief in the multilateral system of collective security and in the prime responsibility of the UN Security Council for the maintenance of international peace and security." (Communication from the Commission to the Council and the European Parliament, "Towards an EU-South Africa Strategic Partnership" [COM(2006) 357 final, not published in the Official Journal]).

In East Asia, the EU considers China a key actor in maintaining a regional balance and improving relations with its neighbours: India, Russia, the Central Asian countries and Japan. In this region, security is the main issue mentioned by Brussels (see the Commission policy paper for transmission to the Council and the European Parliament, 10 September 2003, "A Maturing Partnership – Shared Interests and Challenges in EU-China Relations", updating the European commission's communications on EU China relations of 1998 and 2001 [COM(2003) 533 final]).

The European Union and India maintain close relations which have developed exponentially in recent years as regards their philosophy and objectives. The Commission has proposed a new strategy (see the "Communication from the Commission to the Council, the European Parliament and the European Economic and Social Committee of June 16, 2004: an EU-India Strategic Partnership" [COM (2004) 430 final, not published in the Official Journal]). Its objectives are as follows:

- international cooperation through multilateralism, including promoting peace, combating terrorism, non-proliferation and human rights;
- enhanced commercial and economic interaction, in particular through sectoral dialogue and dialogue on regulatory and industrial policy;
- cooperation on sustainable development, protecting the environment, reducing climate change and combating poverty;
- continuous improvement of mutual understanding and contacts between the EU's and India's civil society.

These objectives are however taking a long time to be achieved.

US development aid policy has been substantially reoriented since George Bush's re-election in 2004. Development assistance constitutes the third pillar of his foreign policy after diplomacy and defence. The major orientation is one of "transformational diplomacy". Condoleezza Rice defines this approach as follows: "To work with our many partners around the world to build and sustain democratic, well-governed states that will respond to the needs of their people – and conduct themselves responsibly in the international system..."[9] American aid policy has adopted specific instruments and forms of action according to groups of countries in an overall perspective of democratization and the fight against terrorism. The "emerging country" category does not exist as such for those official US purposes, even if diplomatic missions have been strengthened in these countries as they have been in countries in transition. Numerous attempts to support pro-democratic organizations in China, Russia and Vietnam have moreover been thwarted by these countries' authorities.

Alliances and multiple strategies

In this early 21st century, relations of cooperation between traditional DAC donors and emerging countries are very different from those practiced by the DAC member states and the LDCs. It is more often a question of strategic partnership, and

---

9 Georgetown University, Washington, January 2006.

emphasis is placed on the consolidation of future markets, scientific and technological cooperation and intervention in the area of global public goods. For the
donors, the faster increase in inequalities in emerging countries is the main threat
to their stability. Engagement in this cooperation takes on different forms depending on DAC member states. Germany has been extremely open for a number of
years, whereas in France interest is only recent.

In many newly emerging countries, development financing, although considered as a policy in its own right, remains marginal. Even if China's official
discourse advocates coordination among DAC donors as well as with multilateral agencies, a lack of coordination and harmonization of aid procedures can
be noted in most countries. There can be no doubt, moreover, that China's or
South Africa's strategy in Africa or Latin America, or India's policy with respect
to East Africa, have major consequences on the bargaining power of the recipient
states. Henceforth, states are negotiating with several donors each with different
strategies, and a subtle game is taking hold, based sometimes on alliances but on
competition as well.

Bibliography ·····································

Africa National Congress (ANC) (2005). *International Policy. A Just World and a Better Africa is a Possibility.*

Brautigam, D. (2007). "China's Foreign Aid in Africa: What Do We Know?" prepared for Conference on
China in Africa: Geopolitical and Geoeconomic Considerations, 31 May – 2 June, John F. Kennedy
School of Government, Harvard University.

Coussy, J. and J.J. Gabas (2007). "Les investissements chinois en Afrique: à quel prix?" in *Alternatives
Internationales*, Special issue no. 5, November.

Djoufelkit-Cottenet, H. (2007). "Quelle politique de ré-endettement pour les pays africains après une
décennie de remise de dette?" *Repères* 36 January, Paris: OECD Development Centre.

Gabas, J.J. (2006). "Les politiques de coopération au développement au début du XXIème siècle: essai
d'analyse comparée", in *Interdépendances et aide publique au développement*, Actes du séminaire
DGCID-IDDRI, Paris: Ministry of Foreign Affairs.

Gaymard, H. (2006). "Un nouvel usage du monde." Rapport au gouvernement pour une France plus
active dans les pays émergents, Paris.

—— *Un nouvel usage du monde : propositions pour une France plus active dans les pays émergents.* Paris :
Mille et une nuits, 2007.

King, K. (2006a). "China and Africa: New Approaches to Aid, Trade and International Cooperation", Presentation at the Annual General Meeting of the Comparative Education Research Centre (CERC) 24
March 2006 Faculty of Education, Hong Kong University.

—— (2006b). "China's Partnership Discourse with Africa", University of Hong Kong and University of Edinburgh, mimeo 13 p.

Lancaster, C. (2007). *The Chinese Aid System*, Center for Global Development, Washington: June.

Manning, R. (2006). "Will 'Emerging Donors' Change the Face of International Cooperation?" ODI Lecture, 9 March, London.

Santiso, J. (2006). "Dragons and Elephants in Latin America", *Policy Insights* 28, September. Paris: OECD.

Tull, D. (2006). *China's Engagement in Africa: Scope, Significance and Consequences*, German Institute for International Affairs and Security, Berlin.

Védrine, H. (2007). *La France et la mondialisation. Rapport pour le Président de la République*, Paris, September.

China and Africa:
From Reunion to Illusion

Roland Marchal

The rising price of raw materials, particularly energy, the Darfur crisis, as well as, more subtly, the renewed favour that Africa's rural sector and infrastructure are finding in the discourse of major international institutions, are all disparate events. Yet all more or less directly reflect the emergence of the People's Republic of China (PRC) as a strategic actor on the African continent.

The PRC, which in 1996 still ranked in 83rd place among the continent's trading partners, is today in the front line, ahead of the former colonial powers and the United States. Trade volume has been increasing by about 35% per year since 2000, to reach nearly $55 billion in 2006. Even if it represents only 2.8% of Beijing's foreign trade, the proportion is double Africa's share in world trade.

In November 2006 China organized the third China-African summit in Beijing, attended by senior representatives of 48 states; the level of representation far exceeded the meetings of the African Union or France-Africa summits. A few months later, in May 2007, the African Development Bank (ADB) and its partners met in Shanghai: Beijing used the opportunity to announce it had earmarked $20 billion to finance its action in Africa.

figure 68: **China/Africa trade patterns, 1992-2006**

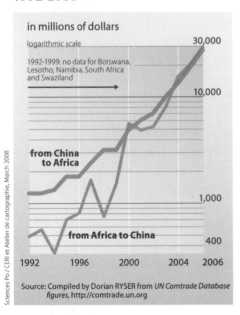

in millions of dollars

logarithmic scale   30,000

1992-1999: no data for Botswana, Lesotho, Namibia, South Africa and Swaziland

10,000

from China to Africa

1,000

from Africa to China   400

1992   1996   2000   2004   2006

Source: Compiled by Dorian RYSER from *UN Comtrade Database figures*, http://comtrade.un.org

Sciences Po / CERI et Atelier de cartographie, March 2008

China has been visibly present in Africa since the beginning of the new millennium, but its presence fits in with a longer timeframe. Moreover, in this case as in others, it is wrong to consider the continent of Africa as unified with respect to Chinese (or Western) interests. On the contrary, China's presence on the African continent heightens differences between countries. And even if in recent years the Asian giant seems to be pulling out all the stops to gain increased access to certain sectors, it should be noted that it is not alone and that China's action does not disqualify more traditional actors (such as the former colonial powers) or preempt the action of newcomers such as India or Brazil. Perhaps the current situation should be considered as transitional, prompting one to think about what new forms the Chinese presence on the African continent might take in the coming years, above and beyond the reproduction of a trading post economy that observers tend to confine it to.

To pursue the analysis, first China's presence in Africa during the period that followed independence will be reexamined. A cost-benefit approach will then be used to highlight the structural differences in the contributions China has made to the African continent. The conclusion takes a look at the probable evolutions of Chinese policy, which often finds itself out of step with the norms of governance defended by its main political and economic partners in the West.

A new focus on old relations

The PRC's interest in Africa cannot be reduced to the quest for markets to assist its own growth. Indeed, the PRC became involved on the African continent as early as the late 1950s. The Bandung conference, the wave of independence, rivalry with the United States: everything worked in favor of a Chinese diplomatic presence on the continent. China back in the 1950s and 1960s already had a tendency to present itself as the *primus inter pares*: a poor, primarily agrarian country having suffered from colonization and now making a comeback. It should however be emphasized that its *modus operandi* was very different from that of the Soviet Union. China has so far never claimed to be a model to follow to become a socialist state or pull out of underdevelopment. Neither has Beijing ever demanded of its partners that they set up a Marxist-Leninist party as a prerequisite to establishing privileged relations, as Moscow did.

African leaders, during the early years of independence, particularly appreciated China's pragmatism. It required no diplomatic convolutions of them and allowed them both to maintain close relations with the former colonial powers and to have access to Chinese development cooperation which, however modest, proved extremely beneficial in some areas. During this period, Beijing constructed buildings that are symbols of sovereignty—presidential palaces, parliaments, stadiums in the capitals—and, last but not least, sent large numbers of the famous barefoot doctors who, unlike the Western aid workers, worked in the countryside in the same destitute conditions as the local population.

This rather positive period for the young African states also enabled the PRC to accumulate support to occupy Taiwan's seat at the UN in 1971. China's popularity, however, suffered from the excesses of the Cultural Revolution and the subsequent tougher stance in relations with the Soviet Union. Although African leaders were hardly interested in the factional fighting that went on in China during the Cultural Revolution, they reacted very negatively when Beijing formed an alliance with South Africa under apartheid and Zaire under Mobutu Sese Seko to support Jonas Savimbi against the MPLA (Popular Movement for the Liberation of Angola) in Angola and its Cuban and Soviet allies. This episode was a resounding failure for Chinese diplomacy because Beijing, unlike Moscow, proved incapable of influencing the outcome of the Angolan conflict and considerably tarnished its image in Africa.

The secondary status was also seen in other areas. China was certainly eager to defy a very inegalitarian capitalist economy and international division of labour, but its means were limited. Certainly, the construction of a railway connecting Zambia's copper mines and the Tanzanian port of Dar es Salaam clearly reflected its desire to challenge the economic domination of Southern Africa by white South Africa, but it would take much more to challenge the economic logics at work in this region.

When Deng Xiaoping returned to power in 1978 and imposed the four modernizations, Chinese interest in the African continent diminished considerably. One reason was that the Chinese message—socialism does not mean shared poverty—was poorly received among African elites who were moreover increasingly subject to pressure from international financial institutions because of their debts. The Chinese leaders themselves also focused more on their domestic problems. Consequently, official visits to the African continent became fewer and farther between and cooperation dwindled.

If the 1980s was for Africa a lost decade for development, for China it was a period of normalization on the international scene. The excesses linked with denouncing the Soviet Union became a thing of the past, as were the most controversial diplomatic postures in the international arena.

Everything changed in the weeks that followed the repression of the student movement in June 1989. The PRC was so isolated internationally that Beijing tried to renew ties with the African countries to avoid new condemnations in international fora. African leaders responded quite favourably to these attempts for at least two reasons. They themselves were often criticized by democratic movements and thus demonstrated international solidarity with disputed elites. Moreover, all of them felt considerable reticence towards the multiple restrictions on national sovereignty imposed mainly by Western donors in the name of human rights, good governance, etc. This renewed contact, which is reflected in an increase in Chinese official visits to the African continent, paved the way not only for broader-based reinstatement of Sino-African cooperation but also for the development of trade relations starting in the middle of the 1990s. The scope of this new dynamic was probably only noticed in the 2000s. Yet the first Sino-African summit in Beijing, despite its success, went relatively unnoticed in Western capitals; however, the first significant Chinese direct investments on the continent since 1970 were not.

But the PRC's interest in Africa has another basis also: the firm application of the "one China" policy. The victory China obtained at the United Nations in 1971 was in fact only one episode in the diplomatic marginalization of Taiwan. At the time Taipei enjoyed ties with Central American and African countries, and the PRC relentlessly encouraged these countries to break off the diplomatic relations with the island in its favour. Naturally, Taiwan could put forward a certain number of arguments: its cooperation could be generous and be applied to useful areas for its partners, beyond mere corruption of government elites (what is politely called "dollar diplomacy").

Yet it would be mistaken to view the African (or Central American) posture as purely lucre-driven. South Africa developed important relations with Taiwan as early as the 1950s. In 1990, the authorities in Taipei were quick to understand the scale of the transformation announced by the release of Nelson Mandela and began to court the main anti-apartheid party, to the point of helping to finance his election campaign in 1994. Nelson Mandela reiterated promises, but diplomatic relations were finally broken off on 1 January 1997. At least three reasons explain such a turnaround. First of all, Pretoria never hid its desire to achieve permanent member status on the United Nations Security Council in the future; it is certain that Beijing would exercise its veto against any country that maintained diplomatic ties with Taipei. Furthermore, most of the trade with China was developed through Hong Kong, which reverted to Chinese control with a special status in 1997. The pursuit of relations with Taipei would have probably created problems for South African economic actors in Hong Kong at a time when South African growth needed to be spurred to offset the costs of reform after apartheid. Lastly, it was obvious already in the mid-1990s that continental China had changed radically and that investments were possible and profitable. Anyway, Taipei has made the best of the situation: it continues to invest in South Africa where it maintains a liaison office.

There are other motivations. For instance, Chad, which had renewed ties with Taiwan for rather conventional reasons (dollar diplomacy), decided to recognize the PRC in July 2006 at a time when its President, Idriss Deby, was confronted with armed opposition backed by Khartoum, also one of China's main African partners. In so doing, Idriss Deby hoped first of all to prevent Chinese support for Khartoum's aid to Chadian rebels and Chinese obstruction at the Security Council.

Moreover, aware of the promises made by some of his opponents to break with Taipei in the event of a regime change in N'Djamena, he preempted the argument and indicated to the PRC that he could be a much more credible partner. In a way, despite the abandoning of agricultural cooperation projects, the Chadian regime came out on top in this rather inglorious episode. Since the summer of 2006, China is neutral in the conflict by proxy between Sudan and Chad and is even striving to lower tensions between them.

In the autumn of 2008, only four African countries still recognized Taiwan: Burkina Faso, São Tomé and Principe, Swaziland and Gambia. As for Senegal, it defected in October 2006 despite Taiwan's generosity towards President Abdoulaye Wade and his regime.

Even if the People's Republic of China has diplomatic relations with the 48 other states on the continent, it would be naïve to believe that they all carry the same weight. The Africa one talks about in China is much smaller. There are, on the one hand, the historic partners such as Guinea and Sudan, which still enjoy warm relations. It is also in this category that Zimbabwe under Robert Mugabe should be classified. In the early 1960s he chose to strike up relations with the People's Republic of China when all the main liberation movements in southern Africa maintained close ties with the Soviet Union (ANC, SWAPO, ZAPU). Robert Mugabe is thus an old friend of Beijing, which is all the more inclined not to interfere in the domestic affairs of Zimbabwe. A second category reflects more the necessities induced by China's current growth. In 2005 nearly 80% of African imports to China came from Angola, South Africa, Sudan, Congo Brazzaville, Equatorial Guinea, Nigeria and Gabon. Chinese exports are directed in similar proportion to South Africa, Nigeria, Sudan, Benin, Ghana and Togo. Except for South Africa, the continent's only real industrial power, all the other countries are producers of mineral or energy raw materials. Africa certainly, but not all of Africa.

figure 69: **Chinese trade with Africa, 2006**

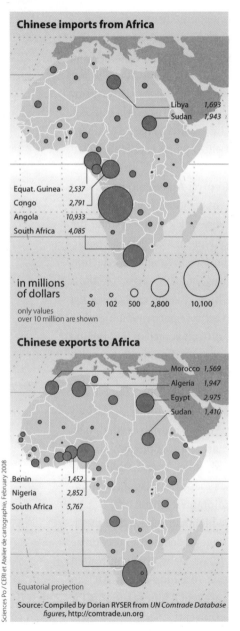

Chinese imports from Africa

Libya 1,693
Sudan 1,943

Equat. Guinea 2,537
Congo 2,791
Angola 10,933
South Africa 4,085

in millions of dollars

50 102 500 2,800 10,100

only values over 10 million are shown

Chinese exports to Africa

Morocco 1,569
Algeria 1,947
Egypt 2,975
Sudan 1,410

Benin 1,452
Nigeria 2,852
South Africa 5,767

Equatorial projection

Source: Compiled by Dorian RYSER from *UN Comtrade Database figures*, http://comtrade.un.org

Sciences Po / CERI et Atelier de cartographie, February 2008

Two remarks should qualify the pervasive image in the media of an absolutely conquering China whose exponential growth feeds on African raw materials. For one, China's presence is in a state of flux. A closer look needs to be taken at the social and economic effects of the considerable Asian/Chinese migrations on the African continent: will this phenomenon produce an economic spillover effect (a sort of "Kenyan debate" revisited) or will these migrants concentrate only on the small distribution sector, thus sharpening competition and autochthonous discourses? Moreover, even if China is always mentioned, attention should be paid to other emerging actors, starting with India and Brazil, but also, probably more discreetly, to the reconfiguration of Japanese and South Korean presence. Moreover, the growth in trade cannot last long at the current pace. The development that nourishes these flows has extremely negative effects on Chinese ecosystems and social balances. Without indulging in catastrophism it remains conceivable that at some point, voluntarily or not, the demand of China's protection system for African products will have reached a peak. The question is whether it will be industrial, ecological or international considerations that will dictate such a development.

A cost-benefit approach

While Africa's image has been particularly tarnished in Western public opinion, Sino-African relations have reinserted this continent into a global economic framework and no longer merely a humanitarian or exotic one. It is thus interesting to draw up a list of both positive and negative consequences induced by the remarkable exchanges between China and Africa. Of course everything is a question of degree: potentially positive effects can also have more negative aspects and vice versa. No assessment can be made in purely numerical terms; the underlying political dimension often remains decisive.

Sino-African trade has reached a level where it directly influences the price of raw materials on a world level. It is not the only explanation for the historic upturn in prices, but it accounts for much of it. Potentially, such an effect can only be beneficial for producer countries (African or other), but all the African countries cannot be put in this category. For many producer countries, such revenue constitutes a means of restoring good relations with the Bretton Woods institutions and negotiating substantial debt cancellations. This is particularly what happened with Nigeria in 2006. Yet this extremely positive aspect should be qualified in at least two ways.

For one, the availability of substantial financial resources does not automatically increase development potential. In the 1960s and 1970s, when the price of raw materials was also high, the resources obtained were used in a dubious manner dictated by profiteering, corruption and strategic errors: development was very limited except as regards the kleptocracy. The social situations in Angola and Sudan lead one to believe that the worst is often probable in countries characterized by mediocre governance. Moreover, China itself remains a supplier of raw materials. The activity of energy companies beyond national borders should be analyzed, because it may not only correspond to ensuring a secure supply. International trade may for instance be valued by these companies because domestic prices are controlled (as are, consequently, any profits) or because it is the Chinese government and not the companies themselves that pay the costs of internationalization. It is also important to examine more generally the latent possibilities the Chinese authorities have of manipulating world prices by playing on the country's strategic reserves.

China is able to implement its development assistance projects considerably faster than Western counterparts. One of the reasons is that Chinese aid is tied (that is, Chinese companies manage the projects), which avoids long delays inherent in the bidding process. As a Kenyan minister reportedly said, "When western donors promise to build a road, they stop work a few yards in to ask us about the human rights situation or corruption. The Chinese come in and do the job." China also places emphasis on infrastructure projects, out of fashion among Western donors for over a quarter-century but nevertheless vital to development.

This capacity to build imposing infrastructures in a relatively short time frame is thus a positive aspect, but the ambiguities must also be measured. These projects are designed as tied aid: even if Chinese companies are believed to be generally competitive in the sector today, nothing indicates that they are for all projects. It is no longer uncommon to see Chinese construction criticized by African oppositions: its quality is (or is said to be) substandard; substantial gifts are allegedly made to regime notables; this infrastructure is said to be primarily to help facilitate exports of raw materials by China. Another factor deemed to be very negative by the Bretton Woods institutions pertains to the macroeconomic implications of reimbursing Chinese aid. Contrary to long-established OECD rules, for instance, repayment is based on delivery of raw

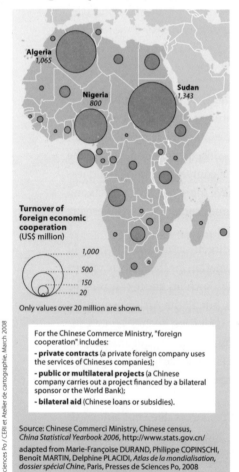

figure 70: **China's "foreign cooperation", 2006**

Algeria
1,065

Nigeria
800

Sudan
1,343

Turnover of foreign economic cooperation
(US$ million)

1,000
500
150
20

Only values over 20 million are shown.

For the Chinese Commerce Ministry, "foreign cooperation" includes:
- **private contracts** (a private foreign company uses the services of Chineses companies);
- **public or multilateral projects** (a Chinese company carries out a project financed by a bilateral sponsor or the World Bank);
- **bilateral aid** (Chinese loans or subsidies).

Source: Chinese Commerci Ministry, Chinese census, *China Statistical Yearbook 2006*, http://www.stats.gov.cn/
adapted from Marie-Françoise DURAND, Philippe COPINSCHI, Benoît MARTIN, Delphine PLACIDI, *Atlas de la mondialisation, dossier spécial Chine,* Paris, Presses de Sciences Po, 2008

Sciences Po / CERI et Atelier de cartographie, March 2008

materials and the conditions for awarding aid are hardly transparent: Western donors are striving to contain debt whereas China is increasing it.

It should also be pointed out that political conditionalities are not always as absent as Beijing claims. For instance, when Charles Taylor was ousted during the summer of 2003, the interim government in Liberia decided immediately to break off relations with Taiwan and recognize the PRC. Why? The UN was to discuss the swift deployment of a multilateral force to stabilize and rebuild the country and any Chinese misgivings had to be quickly allayed.

One of the most talked-about aspects of Chinese development assistance to the continent is the presence of Chinese workers. Initially they came in the framework of major infrastructure construction projects, but today they come on their own (to Cameroon and Angola, for instance). Rumours are circulating about them: they are said to be convicts who are granted reductions in sentence by working in hostile lands, etc. Although the hypothesis is not the most likely, it is not implausible. The Chinese state would not be the first to use such methods: Europeans deported convicts to their distant colonies in the 19th and 20th centuries (the British to Australia, the French to New Caledonia). Yet beyond these legitimate questions regarding forms of *laogai*, this raises questions as to the impact such practices have on local employment, as well as the lack of technology transfer that implementing aid in this way implies.

A third aspect of Chinese action in Africa is its implicit criticism of Western policy. The lack of interest Western developers have in infrastructure has already been mentioned, but in deference to the struggle against (urban) poverty, the considerable neglect of rural areas that the same Western development workers have displayed for the past two decades must also be mentioned. Still in the name of the struggle against poverty, Western cooperation has also hesitated to back local elites but has rather placed emphasis on grassroots programmes (even if the reality on the ground is more complex than that). From this standpoint, China has a very elitist approach that is not necessarily devoid of positive effects, because these African elites can prove to be genuine economic actors.

The donors finally woke up: in 2007, for the first time in many years, the World Bank focused its annual Development Report on rural areas, and the European Commission decided to refresh its thinking about African infrastructures. In a way, the mere fact of reopening the debate, and obliging the various parties to recognize that there is indeed a crisis in development paradigms, is a very positive (even if unintended) aspect of Chinese action on the African continent.

Yet, questions remain about the conditions in which Chinese aid projects are discussed, evaluated and implemented. One of the reasons that prompted Westerners to give up on major construction works was that infrastructure maintenance too often remained an impossible feat. Moreover, such huge projects may be a good channel for rent-seeking, embezzlement and other ruinous corruption practices. The gamble the Chinese have taken on African elites may be understandable, but it at least must be controlled to some extent so that it does not become an additional opportunity to generate clientelism and patrimonialism. Certainly, the lack of interest the Chinese show for local civil society comes as no surprise because that is also what happens in China, except very marginally and only in certain niches. But by excluding these potential interlocutors, China is forming in Africa an opposition that is very critical of its way of doing things and its choice of partners.

Now it is possible to discuss the more potentially negative aspects, while qualifying them. First of all, the current structure of Sino-African trade reinforces an international division of labour that remains structurally disadvantageous for the dark continent: Africa exports raw materials and imports manufactured products (with the notable exception of South Africa). Even if this is true, one must show some degree of realism, because at this stage of development, there is no real alternative. Particular attention should thus be given to the way in which the financial resources obtained by the export of raw materials are mobilized for development.

It is important to stress that this does not mean a revival of the trading post economy, as some radical analysts would have us believe. Indeed, unlike the colonial situation, prices are set on a world market and not by the colonial homeland. By the same token, purchases of manufactured products are unhindered by the very strict conditions of control that prevailed during the colonial period. If China sells more, it is because it sells products that are accessible to larger numbers.

Another aspect has been pointed out countless times in southern Africa. It has to do with the de-industrialization provoked by competition with the PRC. After a free trade agreement was signed with the United States in May 2000 (under the African Growth and Opportunity Act, AGOA), the textile industry developed rapidly in several African countries, particularly in southern Africa, thanks moreover to Chinese investment. The end of the Multi-Fibre Arrangement in January 2005 after 30 years of existence had very negative effects on the African industrial sector. In the space of a few months, South Africa lost nearly 80,000 jobs before China agreed to negotiate and offered a semblance of compromise to the South African authorities.

The situation did not affect all the potentially concerned countries in the same way. Mauritius came out better, almost well, and it is possible to perceive therein the effect of positive national regulations as well as ties between Mauritian operators and Chinese investors. Beijing in any event has continued to claim that China was only following international WTO trade rules (Soares de Oliveira, Large, Alden 2008). Even if the textile sector suffers considerably from Chinese competition, thanks to China the price of industrial goods has fallen. The real question is thus one of ratchet mechanisms, and it appears that the island of Mauritius is better endowed than a country like Nigeria with its large domestic market.

The PRC is accused of backing authoritarian regimes in Africa. Such diplomatic support enables them to resist the virtuous pressures of the West and possible sanctions. Sudan and Zimbabwe are the two cases mentioned most often. The truth of these allegations is undeniable. However, the hypocrisy of the West must at the very least be highlighted. For instance, criticisms of the authoritarian regimes in Angola and the Congo are few and far between, yet these countries keep their populations in deplorable conditions that meet none of the basic conditions required by Western democracies. It should also be remembered that Zimbabwe and Sudan have enjoyed and continue to enjoy cordial relations with many democratic countries (South Africa, France, Spain, Germany, United Kingdom).

The issue thus has more to do with the selectiveness of Western democratic passions. When the Ethiopian regime arrested its entire parliamentary opposition and over 15,000 other people, the European Union protested meekly because Meles Zenawi is a good friend of Tony Blair and George Bush. When Joseph Kabila's army massacred several hundred people in the southwestern Democratic Republic of Congo, the French and the Belgians solemnly explained that Joseph Kabila is the only possible option.

Criticism of Chinese pragmatism will only carry real weight if it is accompanied by criticism of the other major powers for abandoning their democratic agenda in Africa. China at least is coherent in its positioning. It has also shown that it is capable of changing (maybe owing to the threat of a boycott of the 2008 Olympic Games): in Sudan, it was Beijing that convinced Khartoum to agree to a hybrid force of 26,000 troops; in Zimbabwe, the Chinese ambassador no longer denies the scale of the crisis, whereas Pretoria is dragging its feet about doing the same.

If the analysis outlined above is valid, several lessons can be drawn from it. First of all, contrary to the Chinese diplomatic discourse, there is little hope that Sino-African relations will take place in a "win-win" context, any more than by "harmonious" development. These relations in fact underscore the importance of certain countries at the expense of others and produce, as did the former colonial powers, new inequalities between African countries. Although raw material producers can boast of newfound prosperity, others will pay more dearly for products of absolute necessity. This analysis has nevertheless underlined the fact that Chinese interests, like those of the former colonial powers, are not dictated by economic considerations alone.

In China's growing presence in Africa, there is, however, reason for cautious optimism. This presence reminds the Western world that its hegemony is not total and that its policies must be more effective if they hope to carry the day over newcomers. Moreover, this presence benefits certain African countries. The question of the macroeconomic consequences of an increasingly visible Chinese presence on the African continent thus remains open.

Western countries seem very ambivalent about this new situation. From an ideological and political standpoint, China does not represent an alternative (Sudan has borne this out), but its influence makes Western pressures and conditionalities less effective in the short term and highlights the distance that separates the reality of relations between the West and Africa from the rhetoric about partnerships. On the economic level, things are more difficult to measure, because Western countries do not take advantage of their presence on the African continent in the same way. In some sectors (energy, telecommunications, major construction projects), competition is heavy despite the continuing relative technological superiority of the West. In others, such as the banking sector, China today lags far behind. This explains partly why France, still very present in this latter field of activities, has a different attitude to China's impact on the continent.

Another source of relative optimism is the fairly rapid evolution of Chinese policy with respect to certain vital questions for Africa. Perhaps it is an optical illusion created by Beijing's fear of sanctions during the Olympic Games, but between 2005 and 2007, Chinese diplomacy agreed to become involved in certain African crises, participate in peacekeeping operations on the continent and discuss the problems created by its procedures for aid to Africa with its Western counterparts. This is far from a Copernican revolution, but the Western states have not been any more capable of a meaningful *aggiornamento*, as President Nicolas Sarkozy's first steps in Africa illustrate for example.

It is fairly easy to draw up a list of questions that traditional donors and China might discuss: crisis prevention and management, environmental questions (on which Chinese companies do not enjoy good press) which will become essential for the future of the continent as well as China, and the interoperability of international development assistance for the continent.

Although the topics for debate are numerous, one reality that the current discourses tend to minimize must nevertheless be taken into account: the Africans (elites and others) will not remain indifferent as their place on the world chequerboard is reconfigured.

Bibliography ·······································

Alden, C. (2007). *China in Africa*. London and New York: Zed Books.

Cieniewski, S. (2006). "Les relations économiques entre la Chine et l'Afrique." *Lettre de Chine (MINEFI-DGTPE)* (177), pp. 1-3.

Cunningham, E.A. (2007). "China's Energy Governance: Perception and Reality". Working Paper of the MIT's Industrial Performance Center.

Delefosse, O. (2007). "La Chine, nouveau moteur de l'Afrique." *La Lettre des Economistes de l'AFD* (15), pp. 5-7.

Evans, P. and E. Downs (2006). "Untangling China's quest for oil through State-backed financial deals." Policy Brief (The Brookings Institution) (154).

Godement, F. (2007). Searching for energy security: the European Union and China. EU-China Relations. Ponte de Lima: European Strategy Forum.

Kurlantzick, J. (2006). "Beijing's Safari: China's Move into Africa and its Implications for Aid, Development and Governance." Policy Outlook (Carnegie Endowment for International Peace), pp. 1-7.

Marchal, R. (2008). *Afrique Asie: une autre mondialisation*, Paris: Presses de Sciences-Po, 2008.

Mengin, F. (2001). "La politique chinoise de la France, ou le mythe de la relation privilégiée." Critique Internationale, (12), pp. 89-110.

Soares de Oliveira, R., D. Large and C. Alden (eds) (2008). *China Returns to Africa. A Superpower and Continent Embrace*. London: Hurst.

Snow, P. (1988). *The Star Raft: China's Encounter with Africa*. London: Weidenfeld and Nicolson.

Taylor, I. (2006). *China and Africa: Engagement and Compromise*. London and New York: Routledge.

Tull, D. (2006). "China's Engagement in Africa." *The Journal of Modern African Studies*, 44 (3), pp. 459-79.

The Impact of China and India on Latin America

Rolando Avendaño and Javier Santiso

C hina's integration into world trade represents a fundamental episode in the current economic dynamics[1]. With an average growth of 9.5% per year since 1978, China today occupies third place in the world economy. In mid-2007 the country became the leading world exporter, ahead of Germany.

China's boom has partly eclipsed that of another giant: India. Although the latter's contribution to world growth is less than that of China, the effects it has on the world economy should not be underestimated. Since the mid-1990s, India has in fact logged an average growth rate double the world average. This growth moreover goes hand-in-hand with the integration of Indian companies into world markets. They are even managing to compete with the major multinationals of developed countries on their own soil.

Most Latin American countries are not particularly threatened by China and India, and might even be able to enjoy an increase in their revenue given the rising prices of the commodities they export. But these countries also run the risk of growing too dependent on those exports, which in the long run could turn out to be problematic for the entire economy.

Competition and the makeup of commercial exchanges

The remarkable growth of these two Asian giants influences both industrialized and emerging economies, including Latin America. To gauge the effects, we

---

[1] This chapter mainly draws its inspiration from the *Latin American Economic Outlook* 2008 report put out by the OECD Development Centre, presented in Paris on 29 November 2007 at the Maison de l'Amérique Latine. For more information on the Centre's activities, see the www.oecd.org/dev website, and on the topic of the Asian giants' impact on Latin America, the http://www.oecd.org/document/8/0,3343,en_2649_33731_38434504_1_1_1_1,00.html. website.

compared the trade structures in China and India with those of Latin America in order to identify possible areas of competition and then pinpoint complementarities and trade opportunities.

The contribution of China and India to the growth in world production is exceptional: in 2007, 27.9% of the world's growth could be ascribed to China and 7.9% to India. These trends in China and India have major repercussions on other emerging markets. Indian and Chinese companies are flocking to Africa and Latin America, attracted by raw materials (Santiso 2006; Goldstein *et al.* 2006). Chinese investors are also interested in Latin America: in 2004, this region was the destination for nearly 50% of China's foreign direct investment (FDI).

The increase in Chinese and Indian exports has sometimes aroused apprehension. Their gains in market shares, particularly China's, have led certain Latin American countries to worry about their own exports. Some fear that Chinese growth will occur at the expense of other emerging countries (Lora 2007). Moreover, in Latin American opinion polls, China appears as the least desirable foreign investor (Latinobarometro 2007). Exports of Chinese manufactured products are moreover hit by relatively steep tariffs in this region.

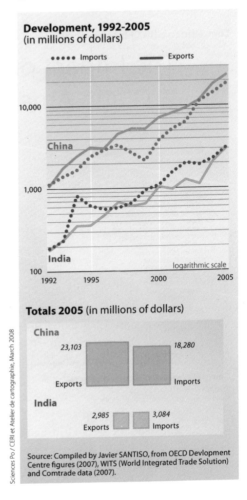

figure 71: **China's and India's trade with Latin America, 1992-2005**

Development, 1992-2005 (in millions of dollars)

Source: Compiled by Javier SANTISO, from OECD Devlopment Centre figures (2007), WITS (World Integrated Trade Solution) and Comtrade data (2007).

Sciences Po / CERI et Atelier de cartographie, March 2008

Is Latin America really in competition with China and India?

A more in-depth study of trade structures provides a means of gauging whether this perception of Chinese and Indian commercial activities is justified. By comparison of trade structures, strengths and weaknesses can be identified in each sector as well as the opportunities that are taking shape. Nevertheless, the composition of trade does not explain everything, because the Asian giants have direct effects, via rising demand, but also indirect ones, via rising prices. The structure of trade nevertheless constitutes an important departure point for this analysis.

The effect of intensified Asian competition and local companies is an important question for Latin America. Our analysis shows that most of the countries

figure 72: **Latin America Trade Competition vs. China and India, 2000-2005**

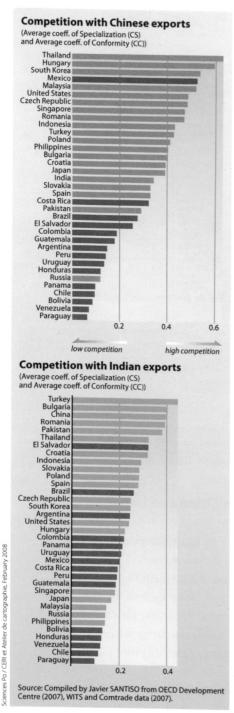

Source: Compiled by Javier SANTISO from OECD Development Centre (2007), WITS and Comtrade data (2007).

Sciences Po / CERI et Atelier de cartographie, February 2008

on the subcontinent have little to fear from the intensification of trade with China and India.

Chinese exports represent competition for some other emerging countries and Latin America. To measure this competition, we compare the composition of each country's trade with that of China.[2] A high indicator, as determined by their specialization and conformity coefficients, reflects a similarity in export structures. When the structures are similar, export competition is considered to be intense. For most of Latin America, however, few elements support the idea of a threat from China and India. Other emerging economies such as Thailand, Hungary and Malaysia have much more to fear from stiff competition with Chinese exports. Competition with India is also relatively moderate.

Encouraging export destinations for Latin America

The boom of China and India can also be perceived as an opportunity, for countries subject to intense competitive pressure among others. To measure this possibility, modified specialization and conformity coefficients have been calculated, to compare the exports of Latin American countries with imports from China and India. The rapid development in the domestic markets of these two latter countries has gone along with a rise in the standard of living, which is a good sign for exports.

At first glance, the results do not seem to indicate the existence of a very strong complementarity between China and India on one hand and

2   The specialization and conformity coefficients (CS and CC) help to estimate the level of trade competition between two countries by comparing their export structures. If two countries (i, j) have exactly the same structure, then the two indexes are equal to 1 and their potential trade competition is high. In the opposite case, the two indexes are equal to zero.

most Latin American countries on the other. The economies of Southeast Asia—Korea, Thailand, Japan and the Philippines—display much greater complementarity with China. This situation cannot be explained by the lack of commercial opportunities, but rather by the fact that the trade potential is concentrated on a relatively limited basket of products.[3]

Furthermore, for countries benefiting from the greater potential for trade with India and China, inter-industrial trade possibilities prove to be numerous. Mexico for instance is a big exporter of telecommunications equipment and electric circuits, which China and India import in large volumes, but for which trade is not currently very regular.[4] In the case of Brazil, beyond the vast potential represented by commodity exports, other sectors are also promising for trade with China: aircraft, telecommunications equipment and motor vehicle parts. In its relations with both India and China, Colombia enjoys considerable trade potential due to its natural resources (particularly oil and coal) but also its manufactured products. Argentina finds its main export opportunities in its natural resources, but in future it could also take advantage of significant possibilities in the processed foods sector.

Agriculture and agri-business in fact count among the most promising areas for Latin American trade with China and India. Latin American exporters in the sector may be able to take advantage of the changing behaviour of Chinese and Indian consumers as long as they move up the added-value and product quality chains, diversify, build brands and innovate.

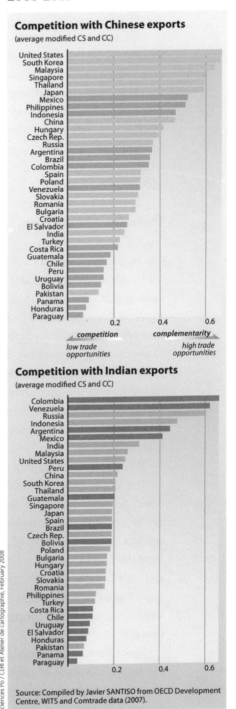

figure 73: **China's and India's trade opportunities with certain states, 2000-2005**

Source: Compiled by Javier SANTISO from OECD Development Centre, WITS and Comtrade data (2007).

Sciences Po / CERI et Atelier de cartographie, February 2008

3   For a more detailed study on trade opportunities between China and Latin America, see *Latin American Economic Outlook 2008*, OECD Development Centre, 2007.

4   These trade opportunities were identified by determining the sectors in which large shares of exports from Latin America corresponded to large shares of imports from China.

Argentina, Brazil, Chile and Uruguay all have agricultural sectors with a good potential for expansion. These countries should also benefit from open access to the agricultural products markets of the Asian giants, which they might negotiate collectively.

Our findings indicate that until now Latin America has little reason to feel threatened by the growth of these Asian giants. On the contrary, it could even draw significant commercial opportunities from it, including opportunities in the more "sophisticated" segments of the value chain (i.e. the agrifood business). Trade complementarity and opportunities between Latin America and Asia have an effect not only on the commercial imbalances but on the entire economy of the subcontinent, which must be careful not to become overly specialized in commodities and must take advantage of synergies between the development of trade and infrastructures.

The risks of excessive specialization in natural resources

Out of the 19 principal Latin American and Caribbean exporters, 11 specialize in commodities (Mulder 2006), while both China and India are prime importers of these goods. The sector thus represents significant export opportunities for Latin America. Despite overall favourable perspectives, countries whose export structure relies primarily on commodities run the risk of finding themselves driven to concentrate on resource industries and neglecting the development of other sectors. The boom in commodity exports and the exceptional revenue it has generated involve a certain number of risks: the literature devoted to the "natural resource curse" sheds light on these dangers, some of which are related to macroeconomic performance, others to the low level of social development (Sachs and Warner 1995, Gylfason 2001, Auty 2001).

We observe the degree of commodity concentration in Latin American exports for the years 2001 and 2006 (a period corresponding to the emergence of the Asian drivers), calculated using the Herfindahl-Hirschmann index. This measure of concentration considers each commodity exported as a portion of total exports. When the share of a specific commodity is high, the index value rises. Here the index seems to indicate that raw material exporting countries could be in jeopardy because of their specialization in commodities. With a few exceptions, in particular Argentina and Costa Rica, most Latin American countries currently show a higher level of concentration of their exports than at the beginning of the century.

Specialization in natural resources highlights the need to innovate. Whereas the lack of diversity of commodities and the low proportion of intra-industrial trade could limit growth in the long run, Latin America displays modest results in terms of innovation. According to the ranking of global competitiveness by the

figure 74: **Export concentration of certain Latin American states, 2000-2005**

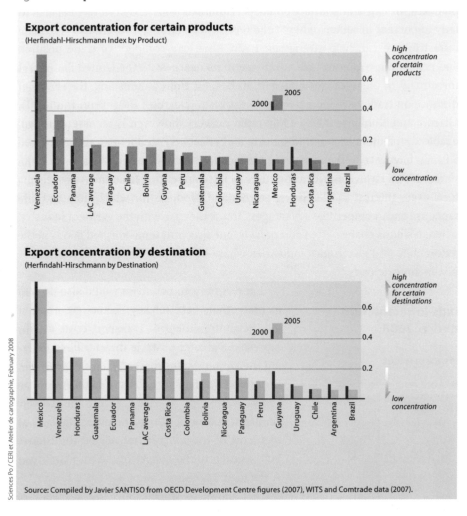

Export concentration for certain products
(Herfindahl-Hirschmann Index by Product)

Export concentration by destination
(Herfindahl-Hirschmann by Destination)

Source: Compiled by Javier SANTISO from OECD Development Centre figures (2007), WITS and Comtrade data (2007).

Sciences Po / CERI et Atelier de cartographie, February 2008

World Economic Forum in 2006, the region is located at the bottom of the ladder. Only Costa Rica, Brazil and Chile stand out, yet with fair to middling overall performances. Furthermore, Latin America concentrates most of its R&D efforts on basic research, with a fairly low level of private sector participation. Lastly, raising the level of education is a priority today in all the countries of the subcontinent, including those exhibiting the best performances, if only to strengthen the contribution of R&D.

Infrastructure: a necessary development

One of Latin America's main assets is its relative proximity to its main markets, especially for the countries closest to the United States. Not only do Chinese exporters have to bear high transport costs, but the distance also implies delays that raise freight and transaction costs (Hummels 2001). This aspect is particularly important in sectors where time represents a strategic advantage. Adequate infrastructure can help strengthen Latin America's competitive trade position and enable the region to take advantage of its nearness to the United States. Yet investment in this area is insufficient. In fact, far from diminishing, the effects of distance on trade have increased in recent years (Deardoff 2004, Brun *et al.* 2005, Glaeser and Kohlhase 2003). Only rapid delivery, however, is an asset that will enable distributors to respond quickly and effectively to fluctuations in demand without having to bear the cost of holding large stocks (Evans and Harrigan 2003, Oman 1996). Latin American countries facing competition from the Asian leaders have every interest in identifying sectors and products for which time and distance are truly competitive advantages. This is the case with the garment industry, where fashions change often and quickly, but also with semi-finished goods in the automobile and electronics industries where lighter production systems impose just-in-time delivery.

figure 75: **Trade infrastructure in Latin America, 2006**

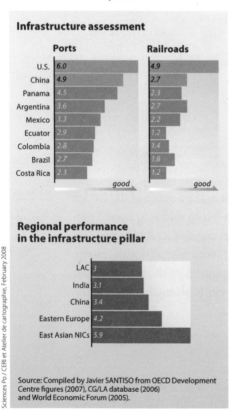

Source: Compiled by Javier SANTISO from OECD Development Centre figures (2007), CG/LA database (2006) and World Economic Forum (2005).

Sciences Po / CERI et Atelier de cartographie, February 2008

Latin American countries would also do well to place their bets on key sectors by improving their infrastructure. Transport costs usually represent a greater obstacle than tariffs to entering the United States market (Clark *et al.* 2004). Paradoxically, transport costs of Latin American countries, except Mexico, are on the average similar to those of China, or even higher. The high cost of transport is not related to distance but basically to the quality of the infrastructure. A detailed analysis of shipping costs to the US market shows to what extent the efficiency of ports is a decisive factor (Clark *et al.* 2004). In the case of Mexico, neighbour to the United States, if the efficiency of its ports was brought up to a level comparable with that of France or Sweden, transport costs could be lowered by about 10%, and by more than 15% for Brazil and Ecuador. Competitiveness indicators highlight the great disparity in performance among Latin American countries. The region's geographical advantage does not show up in the data, with China's performance seeming to outstrip that of most Latin American countries. Commodity-reliant economies such as Chile and Venezuela concentrate their investments on transport infrastructure, whereas countries that depend more and more on the secondary sector, such as Mexico, invest more in energy needs. On the whole, it is estimated that for coastal countries, about 40% of the anticipated transport costs are linked to the quality of overland infrastructure (Limao and Venables 2000).

The main explanation for infrastructural weakness resides in the lack of sufficient investment and inadequate project implementation. Even if Chile's and Colombia's successes show how important it is to convert a rising growth rate into a rise in the infrastructure investment rate, most Latin American countries have not followed their example. The modernization of infrastructure is made difficult by unsuitable regulations, a lack of long-term planning and poor project management. A solid partnership between the public and private sectors is essential in this endeavour. Chile, and to a lesser extent, Colombia, have managed to make the best use of this type of partnership and have invested heavily in infrastructure since the mid-1990s (Calderón and Servén 2004). Despite huge efforts, Mexico has not managed to stimulate solid investment in this area. Similarly, Brazil has shown no notable improvement in the field of transport. It is particularly vital for Mexico and the Central American countries—the most exposed to competition from China and India—to build infrastructure that will reinforce their commercial efficiency and enable them by the same token to capitalize the extraordinary competitive edge that their proximity to the United States, still the world's leading economy, gives them.

A growing role for foreign direct investments

China's and India's growth has had repercussions on the trade relations of all Latin American countries. Even if the surge in exports from the Asian giants has given some cause for concern, the conclusions of the present study show that they pose little threat to most of the region's economies. On the contrary, they could derive considerable benefits from it, both directly by stepping up trade and indirectly by the rise in export prices of Latin American commodities as a result of these countries' rapid growth. However, even if the growth of China and India does not present an immediate threat to most of the Latin American countries, it draws attention to certain difficulties that the subcontinent is confronted with. The development of trade with China and India should increase markets for most Latin American states. Exports are, however, likely to be concentrated on commodities. So Latin American countries should by all means encourage innovation in relation to commodities, pursue diversification of their economies and invest in their infrastructure.

Bibliography ··································

Avendaño, R., H. Reisen and J. Santiso (forthcoming). "The Macro Management of Asian Driver Related Commodity Induced Booms," *Working Papers*, Paris: OECD Development Centre.

Blázquez-Lidoy, J., J. Rodríguez and J. Santiso (2007). "Angel or Devil? China's Trade Impact on Latin American Emerging Markets", in J. Santiso (ed.), *The Visible Hand of China in Latin America*, Paris: OECD Development Centre.

Collier, P. (2007). "Managing Commodity Booms: Lessons of International Experience," Oxford University, Centre for the Study of African Economies, Department of Economics, article presented to the Consortium for Economic Research in Africa, Yaoundé, March.

Goldstein, A., N. Pinaud, H. Reisen and X. Chen (2006). *L'Essor de la Chine et de l'Inde: quels enjeux pour l'Afrique?* Paris: OECD Development Centre.

Lederman, D., M. Olarreaga and G. Perry (2006). *Latin America and the Caribbean's Response to the Growth of China and India: Overview of Research Findings and Policy Implications*. Washington DC: World Bank.

López-Córdova, E., A. Micco and D. Molina (2007). "Competing with the Dragon: Latin American and Chinese Exports to the US Market", in J. Santiso (ed.), *The Visible Hand of China in Latin America*, Paris: OECD Development Centre.

Maddison, A. (2006). *L'économie mondiale: Statistiques historiques*. Paris: OECD Development Centre.

OECD (2007). *Perspectives Économiques de l'Amérique Latine* 2008, Paris: OECD Development Centre.

Santiso, J. (ed.) (2007). *The Visible Hand of China in Latin America*, OECD Development Centre, OECD, Paris.

Santiso, J. (2007). "La Chine et l'Inde en Amérique Latine et en Afrique: du réalisme magique?" *Monde Chinois*, no. 10, Spring-Summer.

The Role of Emerging Countries in the United Nations

Alexandra Novosseloff

G iven the universal nature of its composition, the United Nations has historically been the first organization to grant a place, a voice and a tribune to emerging countries. They have in return profoundly transformed this world organization over time into something that no longer merely brings together the victors of World War II as it did in 1945. This change, which began when the newly decolonized countries joined the UN, has not been without turmoil or resistance.

Today, emerging countries are not only the recipients of international aid and UN interventions, or the "targets" of Security Council decisions; they increasingly influence the decisions of the main UN bodies. Their voice counts, and Western countries can no longer ignore it, particularly when emerging countries are knocking at the Security Council's door.

Once spectators, now actors

The construction of the United Nations Organization in 1945 addressed a certain number of concerns: to prevent the resurgence of enemy states, associate the Soviet Union with the future organization, maintain the preeminence of the major powers and their alliance during the war, help reconstruction and reestablish peace

figure 76: **Number of UN member states, 1945-2006**

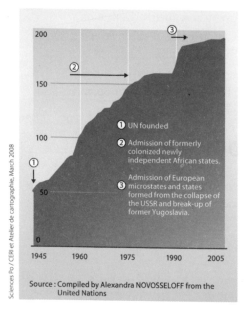

Source : Compiled by Alexandra NOVOSSELOFF from the United Nations

Sciences Po / CERI et Atelier de cartographie, March 2008

among nations. To that was added the desire to achieve, as regards international security as well as crisis and conflict resolution, a more positive result than what the League of Nations managed to accomplish by giving more weight to the new organization (particularly in military matters). The UN, founded in April 1945 in San Francisco, was clearly dominated by the victors of World War II which became the five permanent members of the Security Council: the United States, the United Kingdom, the USSR, Chiang Kai-shek's China, and France, which owed its last-minute admission into this very closed club to Winston Churchill. South Africa, Brazil, Chile, India, Mexico and Turkey, even if they were among the original signatories of the United Nations Charter, on the international scene were only allies of the United States and the United Kingdom at the time, or dependent on them in the case of India. President F. D. Roosevelt is said to have envisaged a permanent seat for Brazil, a faithful ally during the war. The emerging countries moreover expressed themselves little during the San Francisco negotiations, as opposed to Australia and New Zealand for instance. In 1945, Africa had only four independent states, South Africa, Liberia, Ethiopia and Egypt, all charter members of the UN.

This situation did not last long, and decolonization radically altered the postwar landscape. Between 1955 and 1960, 41 additional states joined the UN, a majority of them newly independent African states. The number of member countries doubled in five years. 27 other states joined between 1960 and 1970. To reflect this increase, the number of non-permanent Security Council members went from 11 to 15 between 1963 and 1965. The increase in the number of member states changed not only the nature of the institution but also its field of action.

Designed as a peacetime alliance of five major anti-fascist powers, the UN became a universal organization in the mid-1950s. It went from being an alliance built around a few states to a structure that could only function by consensus and deal with low-intensity conflicts.[1] Within this framework, the United States no longer commands an automatic majority or a blocking third enabling it to prevent adoption

---

1 As Edward Luck wrote, instead of becoming a strong-arm organization of collective security as the Americans expected, the UN has evolved into a subtle and hidden "maker" of peace that is reluctant to use force. Edward Luck, "Peacekeeping Plus: The UN and International Security", in Edward C. Luck and Gene M. Lyons, *The United Nations: Fifty Years After San Francisco: A Conference Report*, 1995, Hanover, Dickey Center, Dartmouth College, p. 28.

of a resolution by the General Assembly. The large-scale entry of newly decolonized, non-aligned developing countries changed the UN during the 1970s into a special platform for anti-Americanism. In the eyes of the Americans, their organization "was being turned against its founders and diverted from its original rationale and principles" and this came as a shock: "children" had turned against their "parents".[2]

In parallel with this evolution in the General Assembly, the Security Council agenda continued to deal with crises and conflicts: from the question of Spain to the question of Iran and the India-Pakistan question, from the question of Palestine to the response to aggression against the Republic of Korea, from the question of Cyprus to that of the Congo, from the question of Indonesia to that of apartheid in South Africa and the situation in Southern Rhodesia. Each gave rise to resolutions and vetoes. In the Security Council, emerging countries were not yet full-fledged actors.

Actors of change or hindrances to adapting the UN system?

Numbers are not everything. Newly independent countries gradually organized within the General Assembly to use their weight and if need be to form a blocking majority. The Assembly enabled some to launch initiatives and projects. Thus, regional groups—the Groups of African States, Asian States, Latin American States, Eastern European States, Western European States and Other States—were formed for the purposes of geographical distribution of positions in the various UN bodies, plus broader interest groups within the General Assembly, such as the Nonaligned Group (or NAM) and the Group of 77 developing countries. The Group of 77, created in 1967 by the Charter of Algiers, currently has 130 member states with a group president elected yearly by geographical rotation between Africa, Asia, Latin America and the Caribbean. It was originally more oriented towards problems of an economic nature and has liaison offices with all the international institutions in Paris, Nairobi, Rome, Geneva, Washington and Vienna.

The Nonaligned Group has 118 members and was initially focused on political issues. These groups and other more regional organizations (Organization of African Unity/African Union, Mercosur, G20, ASEAN, etc.) have become institutionalized. They have not only campaigned for better representation of their regions in all the UN bodies, they have also helped to define voting strategies and mutual support in important negotiations within General Assembly committees and commissions.

Emerging countries want to have a voice that matters in the concert of nations. Their influence constitutes a stronger leverage for partnerships of South-South cooperation. Aside from regional and subregional organizations, the UN is practically

---

2   Edward Luck, *Mixed Messages – American Politics and International Organizations (1919-1999)*, 1999, The Century Foundation, Washington, DC: Brookings Institution Press, p. 108.

figure 77: **Group of 77**

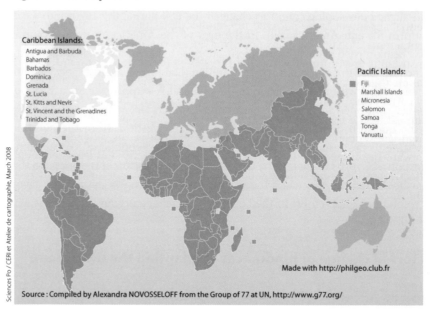

Source : Compiled by Alexandra NOVOSSELOFF from the Group of 77 at UN, http://www.g77.org/

the only place where they can make themselves heard on a world level, lobby on certain topics and criticize the consequences of certain policies. It is also the place where
they can block progress, especially on human rights issues. The UN Human rights
Council at Geneva is increasingly polarized and dominated by regional groups. More
worrying is a tendency within the Council to question the universality of human
rights. Some emerging countries (particularly China, India, South Korea and Brazil)
have also become donor countries with an aid ethic that is sometimes at odds with
current principles and practices of good governance. In Africa, these non-traditional
donors and their no-interest loans tend to wreak havoc with the rules of international aid by exercising less scrutiny than others regarding the respect certain governments have for human rights. On 16 and 17 May 2007 the African Development
Bank Board of Directors meetings were held for the first time in Asia, in Shanghai,
and for the second time outside Africa.

A blocking minority in the Security Council?

There are two categories of emerging countries within the Council: the permanent
members, China and Russia, and the non-permanent members.

The first category plays a highly important role because of its capacity to block
the decision-making process with its veto: Kosovo for Russia, Burma or any other
internal state situation such as Kashmir, Zimbabwe, North Korea or Sudan or any
question regarding Taiwan. On 12 January 2007, China and Russia vetoed a US

draft resolution concerning the situation in Burma. During the September 2007 crisis, the two countries demonstrated a more open attitude that enabled a presidential statement to be adopted in October, not condemning the Burma junta's brutal repression but "strongly deploring the use of violence against peaceful demonstrations in Myanmar." China has threatened to use its veto every time an issue has anything even remotely to do with Taiwan and the recognition of that country by certain states. Thus on 15 February 1999, it did not hesitate to block a resolution extending the mandate of the Preventive Deployment Force in the Former Yugoslav Republic of Macedonia (UNPREDEP) after the latter had recognized Taiwan. In one month, UN forces thus had to pack up and leave, although the effectiveness of its preventive action was unanimously recognized. More recently, China threatened to veto an extension of the United Nations Stabilization Mission in Haiti (MINUSTAH), because the newly elected authorities there expressed a desire to develop relations with Taiwan. China thus prevented Haitian authorities from making an official visit to Taiwan. On the Kosovo question, China remained cautious because Russia has come to the fore. No replacement for Resolution 1244 (1999) has been found and following a meeting on 19 December 2007, certain members of the Security Council publicly stated that it was impossible for the Institution to take a unified stance on this issue.

In this power game among permanent members, the non-permanent members, despite their lack of experience, play the role of gatecrashers, more and more often refusing to merely vote on texts previously negotiated between permanent members. Mexico and Turkey have only sat on the Security Council three times since 1946, the Republic of Korea and South Africa only once, India not since the early 1990s. Turkey is a candidate for the 2009-10 session. Only Brazil has sat on it regularly (until 2005). On all the major issues dealt with by the Council (Iraq, Iran, African crises), the non-permanent countries have played a little publicized but crucial role in the decision-making process. They are often courted by the permanent members and thus constitute a significant "minority" (representing seven of the 15 Security Council members or of the ten non-permanent members of the Council if one sets aside the non-permanent members of the "Group of Eastern Europe States and Other States" that also includes Israel, Australia, New Zealand and Canada). Together they sometimes amount to a collective veto. That was the case during the Iraqi crisis in 2003. Before securing the veto of a second resolution (the one that would have authorized the Anglo-American intervention), the two camps, the first organized around France, Germany and Russia, the second around the United States and the United Kingdom (with Spain and Bulgaria), courted the "undecided" (Pakistan, Mexico, Guinea, Angola, Cameroon, Chile) to secure their vote. But despite the pressure on them, the latter refused until the end to take a clear stand. This refusal thus in a way constituted a blocking minority that prevented the second resolution from being passed.

In this context, the role of South Africa, which entered the Security Council for the first time in 2007, should be examined briefly. A charter member of the UN in 1945, later banished from the international community and deprived of its voting rights on account of its policy of apartheid, the country was elected on 16 October 2006 as a non-permanent member of the Security Council for the 2007-8 period to replace Tanzania. South Africa, consecrated by a crushing majority vote in the General Assembly, is an example of renewed international legitimacy and recognition for both its political and economic weight, but also its exemplary democratic transition. Everyone expected this country to act as a vote-bearer for the African states, but it played this role for the nonaligned states as well, demonstrating its diplomatic capacities on three issues: the situation in East Timor, the relationship with the African Union and promotion of the New Partnership for African Development (NEPAD), and the situation in Somalia (by chairing the Sanctions Committee for that country). Involved in the resolution of many African crises, particularly those of Burundi and Côte d'Ivoire, South Africa aims to embody the new African politics which implies African management of African problems. With 1,800 soldiers deployed mainly in the Congo (MONUC), it is also one of the main contributors to peacekeeping operations on the continent. Concerning Zimbabwe, South Africa has been the most violent opponent of the inclusion of a specific point on the agenda of the Security Council relating to this situation. South Africa along with China, Russia, Libya, Indonesia, Burkina Faso, and Vietnam consider the conduct of the election as outside the Council's remit. According to the States, the Security Council should not pronounce on the internal situation of States so long as there is no threat to regional or international peace. However, faced with international pressure, the Council publicly declared on 23 June that it condemned the actions of the Zimbabwean government and the campaign of violence and intimidation visited on the regime's political opponents.

figure 78: **Participation of selected emerging countries as non-permanent UN Security Council Members, 1946-2008**

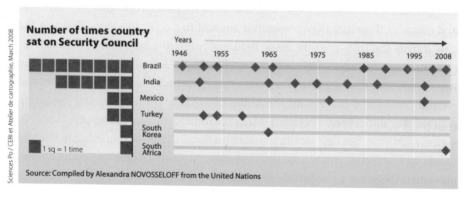

Source: Compiled by Alexandra NOVOSSELOFF from the United Nations

Emerging countries, pillars of UN peacekeeping?

Even if emerging countries are not the main deciders in the field of international peace and security, they have become the main contributors of troops for peacekeeping operations created by the Security Council since the mid-1990s with the disengagement of Western countries after the failures in Bosnia-Herzegovina, Somalia and Rwanda. Southern countries in a way supply UN peacekeeping operations with cannon fodder, whereas the North finances them (the United States, Japan, Germany, the United Kingdom and France are the five biggest financial contributors to the peacekeeping budget of about $7 billion).

There is thus an uneven distribution of risk that maintains a divide between North and South. Indeed, today, the largest contributors of troops are Pakistan with 10,600 police and military personnel deployed, Bangladesh with 9,000, India with 8,800, Nepal with 3,700 and Jordan with 3,000. With respect to the needs of new peacekeeping operations (UNAMID in Darfur with numbers planned up to 19,000 military and 3,700 police personnel, UNMIS in South Sudan with 9,400 soldiers and 600 police, MONUC in the Congo with 17,400 soldiers and 900 police, MINUSTAH in Haiti with 7,000 soldiers and 1,700 police), Southern countries have become the backbone of UN peacekeeping, with Western countries contributing occasional and often rare capacities (logistics, swift reaction, first entry, training for African countries). There too, the Southern countries want to be consulted and listened to: the Security Council and Secretariat have thus regularly organized "troop contributor meetings" since early 2000 before extending the mandate of operations in which they participate. The Special Committee on Peacekeeping Operations (or C-34), a General Assembly committee, each year offers them a forum to negotiate the evolution of peacekeeping operations and doctrine.

The reasons for this "surplus" are numerous: lack of interest among Western countries; payments for UN troops that offer emerging countries the means to help finance their armies while keeping soldiers outside a country's borders; new arguments in favour of a permanent Security Council member seat; assertion of the role of regional powers; involvement in areas having considerable strategic

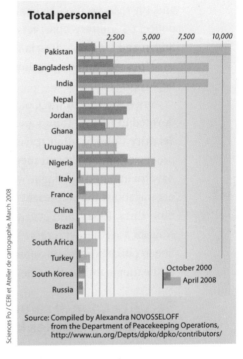

figure 79: **10 largest troop contributors to UN peace operations, 2000-2008**

Total personnel

Sciences Po / CERI et Atelier de cartographie, March 2008

Source: Compiled by Alexandra NOVOSSELOFF
from the Department of Peacekeeping Operations,
http://www.un.org/Depts/dpko/dpko/contributors/

October 2000
April 2008

237

and energy interests. China has decided to become increasingly involved in peace-keeping operations. For the first time, one of its generals has been appointed to lead a peacekeeping operation, MINURSO in Western Sahara. From 1971 to 1981, the country abstained from voting on the creation of any operation, refusing to send troops or pay its share of the budget. During the 1980s, China reconsidered this policy by sending military observers to certain operations and, in 1988, by demanding a seat on the Special Committee on Peacekeeping Operations. It was at the end of the Cold War that China decided to participate more actively and on a larger scale in UN peacekeeping. The operation in Cambodia was the first in which it took an active part, sending 400 engineers and 49 observers between 1992 and 1994. Today, Beijing has 1,900 men engaged in peacekeeping operations (193 police, 66 military observers and 1,700 soldiers), mainly in Liberia, the Congo, Sudan and Lebanon. Russia is pursuing a similar policy and is currently involved in all peacekeeping operations, though to a lesser extent (300 soldiers and police deployed).

Since the end of the Cold War, 70% of the Security Council's work has been devoted to Africa. Things are no longer conducted in a vacuum: not only does the Security Council often travel—the 15 ambassadors go on site to support peace processes underway and meet all the parties involved—but the Security Council has also initiated a dialogue with African countries and the regional or subregional organizations that represent them. On 18 and 19 November 2004, for the fourth time since 1952, the Security Council met exceptionally outside New York, in Nairobi, together with representatives of the African Union, to try to advance the Sudan peace process. In September 2007, peace and security in Africa was chosen as the theme for the third Security Council summit, at the level of heads of state.

Security Council reform:
emerging countries knocking at the door

The first enlargement of the Security Council took place on 10 December 1963, increasing the number of members from 13 to 15. When the ten non-permanent members were elected, five were chosen among African (three) and Asian (two) countries, one from Eastern European states, two from Latin America and two from Western European countries. This enlargement reflected the exponential number of new UN member states after decolonization. In the 1980s and 1990s, as the UN underwent another major increase in the number of its members (37 admissions between 1980 and 2000), the question of reform of the Security Council, more precisely its enlargement, was tabled once again and has been debated ever since. The Council today in fact represents less than 8% of the Organization's 192 member states. It is thus entirely legitimate that emerging countries are knocking at the door of the Security Council. The absence of an African country is now felt by the

figure 80: **Per country participation in United Nations peacekeeping operations, 2007**

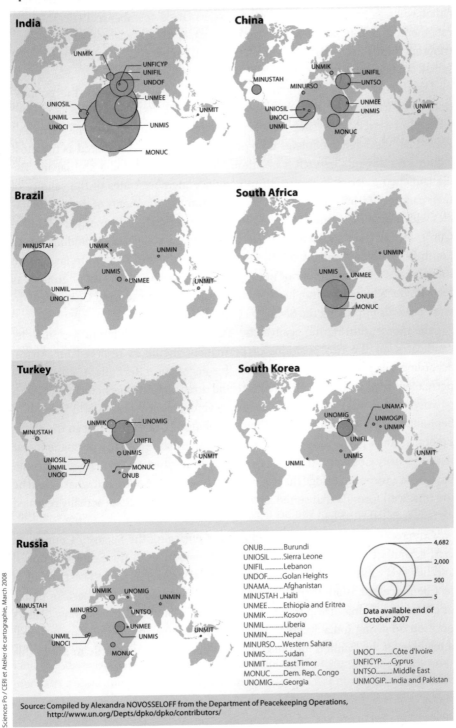

ONUB .... Burundi
UNIOSIL .... Sierra Leone
UNIFIL .... Lebanon
UNDOF .... Golan Heights
UNAMA .... Afghanistan
MINUSTAH ..Haïti
UNMEE .... Ethiopia and Eritrea
UNMIK .... Kosovo
UNMIL .... Liberia
UNMIN .... Nepal
MINURSO ..... Western Sahara
UNMIS .... Sudan
UNMIT .... East Timor
MONUC .... Dem. Rep. Congo
UNOMIG ...... Georgia

UNOCI .... Côte d'Ivoire
UNFICYP ...... Cyprus
UNTSO .... Middle East
UNMOGIP .... India and Pakistan

4,682
2,000
500
5

Data available end of October 2007

Source: Compiled by Alexandra NOVOSSELOFF from the Department of Peacekeeping Operations, http://www.un.org/Depts/dpko/dpko/contributors/

Sciences Po / CERI et Atelier de cartographie, March 2008

states on this continent, to use the words of Senegal's President Abdoulaye Wade, as an "historic injustice done to Africa". Similarly, Latin America is not represented either, whereas Brazil could have become a permanent member in 1945. The largest emerging countries (India and South Africa), just like the largest financial contributors (Japan and Germany) and military contributors (Pakistan, Bangladesh and India), are queuing up for a permanent seat on the Security Council.

Discussions on the enlargement process got a fresh start with the publication of reports by the High-Level Panel in December 2004 and by the Secretary-General in March 2005. They were kept going throughout 2005 by the "Group of Four" (G4), declared candidates for a permanent seat and considered as the most legitimate claimants to such a position: Germany, Brazil, India and Japan. The G4 launched a veritable campaign to convince member states of the validity of their candidacy. This pressure awakened the group of opponents of these candidacies which took the name of "United for the Consensus" (or formerly the "Coffee Cup"), led by Italy, Pakistan, Mexico and Argentina and also including Spain, South Korea, New Zealand and Sweden. The members of this group favoured a mere increase in the number of non-permanent members. One more group was formed, the S5 (Switzerland, Liechtenstein, Jordan, Singapore and Costa Rica), to work towards improving the Security Council's work methods.

The momentum ran up against the African Union's inability to designate its candidates for the two positions of permanent members reserved for Africa, according to a formula used as the basis for negotiation (formula A, creating six permanent seats without the right of veto and three new non-permanent seats with a two-year mandate), and its insistence on a veto. Following the World Summit of September 2005, the reforms lost their momentum due to the African deadlock. Emerging states perceived as having the most legitimate claim to a permanent seat in the Security Council had trouble convincing others, whereas enlargement could have been a means to bridge the gap between North and South. But what would be the (magical) formula that suited all member states? This debate actually revealed certain regional rivalries.

China was one of the main opponents of enlarging the Security Council. In fact, it wants to remain the only Asian representative on the Security Council and has every interest in seeing Japan's candidacy rejected. Japan's seat would in fact be perceived as another US seat and one more step in the American policy of containing China.[3] Despite the improvement of Sino-Indian relations, China's position on giving India access to the Council remains ambiguous. South Korea, a member of the "United for the Consensus" group, has very little to say in this

---

[3] Among the declared candidates, Japan is probably the country that wishes the most strongly to gain admission to the restricted circle of permanent members, which would enable it to have a "return on its investment" from its financial contribution (19%).

debate, and even less since the arrival of Ban Ki-Moon in the post of Secretary General of the UN.

For Africa, it was decided that it was up to the African Union to designate the two candidate countries for a permanent seat. On 7 and 8 March 2005, the African Union member states adopted a common position on the reform of the UN known as the "Ezulwini consensus". It stipulated that full representation of Africa at the Security Council must involve attribution of two permanent member seats having a veto right and five non-permanent seats. The African Union would select the representatives for Africa. Three countries have long claimed to legitimately fulfil these functions: South Africa, Egypt and Nigeria. Alongside the two Sub-Saharan candidacies, Egypt has played the role of gatecrasher, claiming to represent North Africa and the Arab-Muslim world. Egypt is a leading figure in the Arab League but cannot speak in the name of North Africa because of competition with the Maghreb countries, or for the Middle East because of its specific policy towards Israel, and even less for black Africa, which in no way feels represented by an Arab country perceived as distant. Owing to a lack of consensus within the African Union, the candidate countries seem to have understood today that they would improve their chances better by campaigning individually than by going through their regional organization. The question is, do they have the means, the energy and the will to differentiate themselves in an Africa that is seeking to strengthen its unity day by day?

Latin America is also divided on the issue of Security Council enlargement, even if the various countries' positions seem reconciliable. Brazil, owing to its economic weight on the continent, its market of 180 million consumers and the wealth of its subsoil, hopes to become a privileged spokesman for its neighbours and play a leading role on the international scene in the South-South dialogue and spokesman for emerging countries. Brazil seems more concerned with maintaining its rhetoric in its quest for a permanent seat than really engaging with the international arena (for instance by contributing to UN operations in Africa). Argentina, backed by Colombia and Mexico, has campaigned against the G4 project, but seems to admit the legitimacy of the Brazilian claim behind closed doors.

Are the emerging countries the future of the United Nations?

Since the failure of 2005, the bargaining process has fallen back on the indecisiveness of the working group for the General Assembly in charge of this issue. In fact, the machine seems to have trouble getting started again, antagonisms do not seem to have budged, and the status quo seems the best solution for the moment. However, some members are also in favour of an intermediate solution (semi-permanent members with a ten year mandate). Is the question of enlarging the Security Council ripe for consideration? In other words, do UN member states consider it as essential in order to legitimate the Council's decisions? Are emerging states the future of the UN and can they instigate a better balance in world affairs and crisis management?

The UN must adjust to the world and reflect its diversity. Its various bodies should be representative of all continents and the most important states from the demographic, economic, political and strategic standpoint. They must also soften the fractures, divisions and rivalries. Probably this representativeness should also be extended to the international economic organizations (World Bank, IMF, WTO). The past 60 years have shown that emerging countries today want to take their rightful place on the Security Council. But still, to do so they must manage to overcome their regional rivalries so that a South-South paralysis does not replace the East-West paralysis. In order to do so, they must collectively take on the responsibilities (political, military, economic) for the region.

All things considered, is the time really so ripe for enlarging the Security Council to the new powers of the 21st century? The lack of consensus sows doubt. Should the idea of reinvigorating its authority by making it more representative be shelved? The Security Council's legitimacy lies in its capacity to make all UN member states enforce its resolutions (article 25 of the Charter), without discrimination, to reduce the current gap between deciders and contributors and make needs and means converge. It was indeed according to a logic of responsibility and capacity, and not of representativeness, that the Security Council was founded in 1945, and it is to this logic that the Security Council member states, and first of all the five permanent members, should return. Such a process cannot dispense with a renewed political commitment of the 192 member states to respect for the Charter's principles, the central role of the Security Council in matters of peace and security, the effective implementation of all of its resolutions and collective crisis and conflict management.

Emerging countries are increasingly involved in UN peacekeeping missions; they have won their independence from countries of the North. Their responsible attitude regarding world affairs and their role as mediators and negotiators from a political and economic standpoint will eventually lead them to join the permanent members of the Security Council. How long from now remains to be seen.

Bibliography ··

Centre for Conflict Resolution (South Africa) (2006) *The United Nations and Africa – Peace, Development and Human Security*. Policy Seminar Report, Maputo, 14-16 December.

Lecoutre, D. (2005). « Des voix du Sud au Conseil de sécurité : l'Afrique et la réforme des Nations Unies ». *Le Monde diplomatique*. July : 17.

Luck, E. C. and G. M. Lyons (1995). *The United Nations : Fifty years after San Francisco, A Conference Report*. Hanovre : Dickey Cener, Dartmouth College.

Megan, D. (2006). *South Africa on the UN Security Council : The Mouthpiece fo the Developing World*. New Haven (Conn.) : Globalist Foundation.

Mourad, A. (ed.) (2006). *The Group of 77 at the United Nations*. Oxford : Oxford University Press.

Novosseloff, A. (2003). « Les missions spéciales du Conseil de Sécurité des Nations Unies ». *Annuaire français de droit international* : 165-175.

Pondi, J.-E. (ed.) (2005). *L'ONU vue d'Afrique*. Paris : Maisonneuve et Larose.

Seitenfus, R. (2006). « Le Sud devient le Nord : fondements stratégiques de l'actuelle diplomatie brésilienne », in Stéphane Monclaire and Jean-François Deluchey. *Gouverner l'intégration*. Paris : Pepper.

Emerging Power Strategies in the World Trade Organization

Cornelia Woll

E merging countries have become central to multilateral negotiations in the World Trade Organization (WTO). Since the end of the Uruguay Round, their participation has shaped the evolution of the talks, as developed countries had to acknowledge during the Ministerial Conferences at Seattle and Cancún. After all, current negotiations have been labelled the "Doha Development Round" to acknowledge explicitly the link between trade and development. In recognition of the collective trading power of emerging economies, we now speak of the BICS to refer to Brazil, India, China and South Africa (see for example Hurrell 2006; Chakraborty and Sengupta 2006). However, these countries rarely act as a coherent bloc, but rather within a set of changing coalitions. We have to understand how emerging countries have come to speak on behalf of developing countries and how they have been able to impose their demands through this flexible geometry, in order to explain why the United States and the European Union find themselves on the defensive on crucial issues such as agriculture. What strategies do emerging countries employ in multilateral trade negotiations and how have they been tested and revised over time?

This chapter examines the coalition patterns of developing countries under the General Agreement on Tariffs and Trade (GATT) system and within the WTO, to understand how emerging economies have succeeded in incorporating their demands into the trade agenda. Initially, developing countries had criticized the inequalities in trade arrangements agreed, but remained relatively passive in multilateral negotiations owing to their weak positions. Emerging countries first made a concerted effort to counter the agenda of developed countries during the Uruguay Round. Yet, the G10, organized around Brazil and India, failed in its attempt to block service trade negotiations. Other coalitions, such as the Café au Lait coalition or the Cairns Group of agricultural exporters, developed integrative bargaining strategies that proved more successful than pure resistance.

For the current Doha Round, emerging countries have copied these success formulas and developed them further. New coalitions now submit detailed proposals on procedure and content of negotiations and are no longer defined by their common level of development, but rather by the issues they seek to address. In particular, the G20, which formed around India, Brazil and China, but also the Like-Minded Group and a myriad of issue-specific *ad hoc* coalitions, are examples of these new strategies. In many cases, membership is overlapping, but the changing alliances have allowed emerging economies to advance their issues on multiple battlegrounds. Owing to their combined market power, the need to incorporate the demands of emerging economies has risen sharply and has given them room to criticize both the procedures of WTO negotiations and the equity of agreements reached. In this chapter I will study the historical weakness of developing countries in multilateral trade negotiations, before examining the rise of the emerging economies, first in the Uruguay Round and then all the more noticeably in the Doha Development Round, where they were able to exploit the lessons from previous coalition failures.

Historical weakness of developing countries in the WTO

GATT came into force in 1948, after attempts to create a more ambitious International Trade Organization (ITO) had failed. Negotiated between 23 countries in 1947, the GATT instituted a procedure for negotiating tariff reductions based on non-discrimination and reciprocity. Under the most-favoured nation principle, concessions made to one country had to be extended to all other signatories of GATT. As a system of consensus decision-making, the GATT promoted procedural equality. This ran counter to the demands of developing countries, which had previously sought to introduce the notion of economic development into the ITO, claiming that they should be treated differently in order to facilitate their economic development.

Eleven of the GATT signatories were developing countries and their number soon swelled to a significant majority. With each country entitled to one vote, this majority could have given a great advantage to developing countries. Interestingly, as Narlikar (2006) points out, they never actually tried to make use of this advantage, since decision-making was not based on majority voting but on consensus, which implies that no member present at negotiations formally objects to a proposal. This procedure put developing countries in a weak position for several reasons. First, some of the least developed countries lacked a permanent delegation in Geneva and could not ensure a continuous presence at meetings. Second, voting was not secret and developing countries feared that formal opposition would lead to informal retaliation. Passive resistance, however, does not work under the GATT system, where silence is interpreted as consent. Third, preparatory meetings, the so-called "Green Room" meetings, often required invitation by the Director General, and developing countries found themselves excluded from many of the key discussions.

Still, developing countries adhered to the GATT system, as rejecting or leaving multilateral trade negotiations would have had a very high cost. Despite the tension between the procedural equity advocated by the GATT system and the equity in outcomes that was dear to developing countries, they therefore remained members of what they frequently called the "rich man's club" (Narlikar 2006: 1015). Differentiating between forums and issues, they advanced on the question of economic development within other organizations. In 1961, the General Assembly of the United Nations launched the first UN Development Decade and instituted in 1964 an organization charged with reviewing and evaluating the interplay between trade and economic development, namely the United Nations Conference on Trade and Development (UNCTAD). At the same time, developing countries established the G77, a loose collective attempt to advance common economic interests and to provide an alternative to the G7, the intergovernmental forum of the world's major industrialized democracies, which has now become the G8.

The new initiatives did not go unnoticed. Within GATT, the Committee on Trade and Development was established and a new part on Trade and Development was added to the founding text in 1965, which explicitly recognized the principle of non-reciprocity for developing countries. In the 1970s, GATT allowed a waiver to the most-favoured nation principle through a Generalized System of Preferences (GSP), under which countries can offer preferential trade conditions to developing countries as long as they are generalized and non-discriminatory. Although these changes were significant, they did not alter the fundamental principles of the GATT system, still less as developed countries were under no obligation to establish a GSP. The Informal Group of Developing Countries, dominated by countries like Argentina, Brazil, Egypt, India and the former Yugoslavia, was a weak and poorly visible coalition in comparison with developing country groups in the UN system.

Playing the game

During the Uruguay Round, which lasted from 1986 to 1994, the strategies of developing countries changed. To begin with, many developing countries felt a need to negotiate adequate trade agreements to respond to the economic downturn and the agricultural crisis of the 1980s. The benefits of the GSP were not sufficient to compensate for the imperfections of the trading system and non-tariff barriers proved particularly difficult to deal with. Economic liberalization was seen as a necessity and the multilateralism of the GATT system promised to protect developing countries against the "aggressive multilateralism" employed by countries such as the United States (Bhagwati and Patrick 1991).

And yet developing countries were deeply divided about the negotiation agenda proposed by the industrialized countries in the early 1980s. The Informal Group of Developing Countries had insisted on the need to include agriculture and textiles in the GATT agenda and sought to secure standstill and rollback commitments on non-tariff barriers. At the same time, they were opposed to the inclusion of services and intellectual property rights. This opposition to the US agenda contributed to the delay in launching the Uruguay Round, but eventually split the group itself (Narlikar 2003). Some developing countries were willing to debate the implications of a possible services agreement and met under the leadership of Colombia's ambassador Felipe Jaramillo. The Informal Group's big five, Argentina, Brazil, Egypt, India and the former Yugoslavia, initially attended these meetings, but soon refused to continue discussions. Working with like-minded countries under the name of G10, these hardliners developed their own proposal for the new round which made no mention of services, and they even refused to consult with other developing countries. Countries participating in the Jaramillo process therefore formed their own group, which later coalesced into the Café au Lait coalition (whose name refers to the joint Colombian-Swiss leadership) (Narlikar, Tussie 2004). When the Uruguay Round was launched in 1986 with an explicit mandate

figure 81: **G10 and Informal Group, 1980**

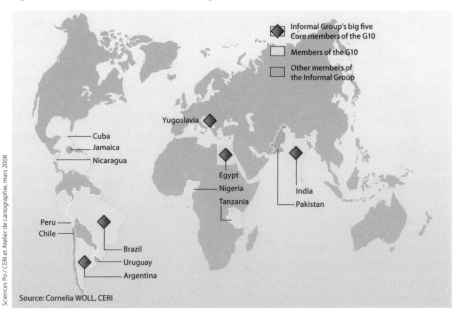

Source: Cornelia WOLL, CERI

Sciences Po / CERI et Atelier de cartographie, mars 2008

for services negotiations, the failure of the G10 had become evident. Moreover, the Punta del Este Declaration that kicked off the new round relied heavily on the draft provided by the Café au Lait coalition (Narlikar and Tussie 2004: 958).

The failure of the G10 provides several insights into the evolution of the trade diplomacy of developing countries, and valuable lessons for future coalitions. First of all, the bloc-style diplomacy based on ideology and distributive demands had proved inadequate. As Narlikar and Tussie (2004) emphasize, the issue-based structure of the Café au Lait coalition was based on research and information-sharing and allowed members to engage in value-creating strategies. Moreover, the Café au Lait coalition was unprecedented in bringing together countries from the industrialized and the developing world.

The Cairns Group of agricultural exporters took this model even further (Tussie 1993). Under the leadership of Australia, non-subsidized agricultural exporters met in April 1986 to coordinate their positions and to respond to the subsidies war between the US and the European Communities. For the participating countries, the inclusion of agriculture in the new round was of the utmost importance, as the unsubsidized middle-income agricultural exporters were increasingly unable to compete with European and American products. When the Punta del Este Declaration confirmed that agriculture would be included, the Cairns Group became an important negotiating coalition. It built its expertise on rigorous studies and developed many detailed proposals during the course of the negotiations, which went a long way to establish a meeting ground for the United States and

figure 82: **The Cairns Group, end of the 1980s**

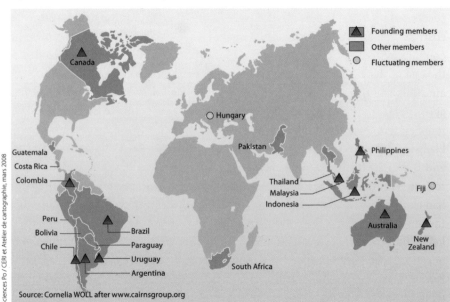

Source: Cornelia WOLL after www.cairnsgroup.org

the European Communities. They were furthermore instrumental in pressing for continued talks on the issue when negotiations threatened to break down in 1988 and 1990, by announcing that several members would use their veto on all other issues if no progress on agriculture was made. Even though a crucial compromise on agriculture was reached between the US and the European Communities in the Blair House agreement in 1992 without members of the Cairns Group, the momentum they were able to create was inspirational for many coalitions that followed them. As with the Café au Lait coalition, the issue-focus, the North-South alliances and the constructive contribution of detailed studies had proved to be a very promising strategy.

The evolving coalition patterns and modes of participation during the Uruguay Round demonstrated that developing countries had started to play the game of multilateral trade talks in order to defend their own interests. After the failure of the old-style bloc diplomacy of the G10 that was reminiscent of the Third-Worldist rhetoric employed in forums such as UNCTAD, new strategies relied on constructive proposals and broad coalitions. By combining the market power of several developed countries, emerging economies and developing countries, these crossover coalitions allowed developing countries to participate on a more equal footing with the trading superpowers that had previously dominated multilateral trade negotiations.

This participation marked a substantial change in the rhetoric and trade position of emerging countries. By insisting on the need to include agriculture and textiles in GATT negotiations and contributing to negotiation on services, they had for the first time worked to reinforce the multilateral framework rather than calling for the abrogation of GATT on the grounds of economic development. The successful participation in the Uruguay Round therefore came at a considerable cost: developing countries made many concessions and bound themselves to a complex system of rules. Moreover, with the creation of the WTO concluded by the end of the Uruguay Round, they faced a reinforced dispute settlement system and thus the threat of being penalized if they could not comply with the new agreements. Even though developing countries' participation in the dispute settlement system increased under the WTO, these countries were also five times more likely to be the target of a complaint now than under the GATT system (Reinhard and Busch 2002). In the aftermath of the Uruguay Round, developing countries realized that the costs of fulfilling their commitments were much higher than they had expected. Although they did not return to the calls for distributive justice that they had employed in the 1960s and 1970s, negotiators for developing countries, led by the emerging economies, realized that they needed to address fundamental questions of equity in procedures and outcomes, rather than simply play by the rules of the world trading system that the industrialized countries had developed (Narlikar 2006: 1020-1021).

Putting development on the international trade agenda

At the Seattle Ministerial Conference in 1999, delegates from African, Caribbean and Latin American countries opposed the launch of a new round by arguing that the negotiating system did not allow them to wield influence comparable to that of developed countries. While proponents of the system argued that the one-country-one-vote rule produced fair outcomes, developing countries pointed to the various informal decision-making procedures, in particular the Green Room meetings, to show how weaker countries were marginalized on key issues. In the aftermath of Seattle, many produced detailed proposals on institutional reform and thereby signalled their willingness to participate in WTO negotiations, while at the same time challenging the fairness of the present system.

Other countries went further and criticized both procedures and substance of the past trade negotiations. The Like-Minded Group, formed in 1996 by Cuba, Egypt, India, Indonesia, Malaysia, Pakistan, Tanzania and Uganda, was vehemently opposed to a new round until developed countries were willing to address the costs of implementing the Uruguay Round, which represented a heavy burden for developing countries. They furthermore opposed the inclusion of competition policy, investment, transparency in government procurement and trade facilitation, the so-called Singapore issues, that the EU had been pushing since 1996. As the Like-Minded Group offered few concessions in its opposition to the launch of a new round, the developed countries began making partial offers to subgroups within the coalition. In return for withdrawing opposition to the Singapore issues, industrial tariffs and environmental concerns, a WTO waiver was established for the EU agreement with the Africa, Caribbean, and Pacific countries. In addition, developed countries began working on aid packages and assistance for capacity-building in the most marginalized countries. When India and South Africa complained about penalization of the use of generic medicines under the WTO intellectual property rights regime (TRIPs), developed countries agreed to issue a declaration on "TRIPs and Public Health" (Chakraborty and Sengupta 2006: 48). Simultaneously, diplomatic relations were used to work against hard line ambassadors. As the coalition became fragmented, several countries felt that it was becoming unwise to continue their resistance and the influence of the Like-Minded Group declined. At the Doha Ministerial meeting on 14 November 2001, India stood alone in its opposition (see Odell 2006). The new round was launched, but signalled commitment to the concerns of developing countries, notably by naming its negotiation the Doha Development Agenda.

Several small coalitions worked to ensure and follow up on the proposals made in 2001 and to press for examination of new issues. Country groups included the African Group, the African Caribbean Pacific Group and the Group of Least

Developed Countries and Small and Vulnerable Economies, while other coalitions focused on specific trading issues, such as the Core Group on Singapore issues, the Coalition on Cotton and the Alliance on Strategic Products and Special Safeguard Mechanisms (for discussion, see Narlikar and Tussie 2004). Through their persistence, these groups succeeded in linking the discussion on intellectual property rights with public health concerns, improving market access in non-agricultural products, securing special and differential treatment for developing countries and obtaining capacity assistance. On the downside, implementation issues and the Singapore issues were linked with the Doha Development Agenda, instead of simply being discarded, as the developing countries had asked; this will most likely imply future concessions.

After many missed deadlines and fruitless discussions on a number of contentious issues in 2002, the preparation of the Cancún Ministerial Conference in 2003 turned out to be a watershed in the strategies of the emerging countries. Whereas they had previously sought to form alliances of sympathy around issues of mutual concern, the joint US-EU declaration on agriculture on 13 August 2003 drove all emerging countries into the opposition. Prior to the US-EU declaration, the Cairns Group members were looking to the US to support their demands, while protectionist countries hoped to side with the EU. When they realized that the US and the EU had jointly prepared a highly unsatisfactory text, Brazil and India drafted a response together with other developing countries. After China joined the group, it had become one of the most important alliances of the Doha

figure 83: **G20, 2003**

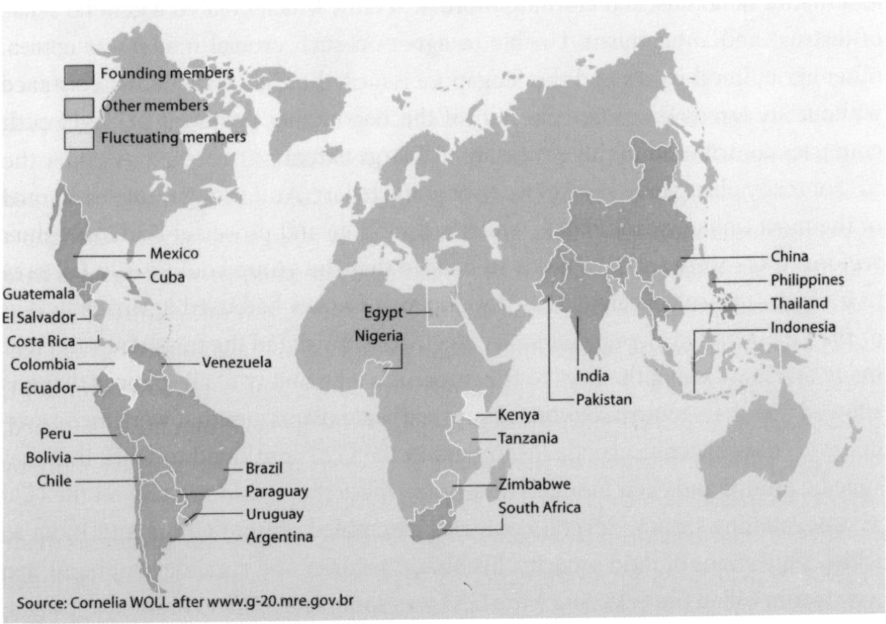

Source: Cornelia WOLL after www.g-20.mre.gov.br

Sciences Po / CERI et Atelier de cartographie, mars 2008

Development Round. The signature of the text on 2 September 2003 marked the birth of the G20, a coalition driven by all the emerging powers from the developing world that could not be ignored.

In contrast to the Like-Minded Group, and much like the Café au Lait coalition and the Cairns Group, the G20 had a proactive agenda. It demanded more substantial cuts in domestic support from both the US and the EU and greater commitments from developed countries on non-agricultural market access, and proposed a differentiated formula for the elimination of export subsidies. References to special and differential treatment were made throughout the proposal. Consultation between the G20 and several of the other small groups was excellent and helped to ensure the cohesion of developing countries' demands (Narlikar and Tussie 2004). Several of the coalitions from poorer developing countries were furthermore coordinated to become the G90 in an effort to show the breadth of support on crucial issues such as cotton.

Neither the developed nor the developing countries were willing to give ground at the Ministerial Conference in Cancún in September 2003. The ministerial draft text, called the Derbez Draft, did little more than restate the joint EU-US proposal in the eyes of the G20, while the EU and the US felt that it went too far on domestic support. On the Singapore issues, the Core Group insisted that consensus was required to commence negotiation on modalities, but several countries pressed for an agreement on all four of the issues. For the least developed countries, cotton was an issue of great concern and four Central and West African countries had demanded a complete phasing out of subsidies in the developed world. The Derbez text, by contrast, leaned close to the US position by dealing with cotton as a matter of textiles and clothing more generally, which created a general sense of distrust and antagonism. Unable to agree on such crucial matters as cotton, other agricultural issues and the Singapore issues, the Cancún meeting collapsed without an agreement. The cohesion of the negotiating positions of developing countries contributed to this stalemate to a large extent.

For many observers, the G20 was not going to last. As it brought together some of the most unlikely candidates, which are all large and powerful leaders of their regions, there were many reasons to believe that the group could easily fall prey to a divide-and-rule strategy that developed countries had used against the G10 or the Like-Minded Group. Yet so far, the G20 has avoided the fragmentation that many foresaw. One of the keys to this success is a flexibility of allegiances that has allowed members to turn to other groups for particular issues that were incompatible with the collective agenda. Members of the G20 continued to work in issue-specific groups and even founded new ones where they could not rely on the G20 as a negotiating forum. Several countries assembled around China and India to address questions of food security, livelihood security and rural development in a new forum called the G33. Since the G33 was somewhat defensive in its approach to agricultural policy, offended G20 members such as Brazil or South Africa did not join (Chakraborty and Sengupta 2006: 53). Throughout these negotiations, consultation between different blocs was maintained.

A breakthrough in negotiations

Brazil and India furthermore cooperated with Australia, the EU and the US in an attempt by the "five interested parties" to move beyond the deadlock in the multilateral negotiations. The two-week discussions in Geneva in July 2004 finally resulted in a draft text known as the July 2004 Package. It presented a compromise signalling that both sides were willing to make concessions in order to get the multilateral talks back on track. In particular, the July Package postponed the deadline for the Round's completion to an unspecified date and dropped all the Singapore issues except trade facilitation, for which it made concessions based on the capacity and infrastructure of the country needing to implement it. In response to the demands of both the G20 and the G33, cotton was treated as a separate issue. The annex on agriculture proposed a "tiered" formula approach for phasing out domestic subsidies and noted that reduction requirements and market access commitments would not be the same for developed and developing countries. Furthermore, both groups of countries could designate sensitive products and developing countries could name "special products" to avoid tariff cuts where food security or rural development is concerned. A special safeguard mechanism was incorporated, and least developed countries were not required to reduce tariffs. In addition, developed countries committed themselves to making a down payment by cutting their subsidies by 20% in the first year. The July Package thus went a long way to address issues that WTO members refused to consider at Cancún, though it is not certain how significant the concessions made by developed countries are going to be once put into practice. Nonetheless, the draft was important in bringing several of the developing countries' concerns to the negotiating table at the Hong Kong Ministerial Conference in 2005.

The Hong Kong Ministerial solidified some of these demands and brought together the G20 and the G90, which formed the G110 to demonstrate that they were determined not to be used against each other by the EU or the US. Another developing country group with Brazil, India and South Africa as members was NAMA-11, founded to press for the rapid liberalization of market access in industrialized products. Even though the ministerial text indicated that reduction of agricultural subsidies and market access under mode 4 of the service agreement still remained open to negotiation, developing countries heartily welcomed the first amendment of a core WTO agreement: changes to the TRIPS agreement with respect to public health, approved by the General Council on 6 December 2005 (Chakraborty and Sengupta 2006: 56). The Hong Kong declaration established a deadline for modalities on agriculture and non-agricultural market access in April 2006 and for submitting comprehensive draft schedules by July 2006. Only the EU submitted a detailed proposal, but India and Brazil were unwilling to make concessions as long as the US refused to bring down its agricultural subsidies. On 23 July the WTO Director General Pascal Lamy suspended the negotiations, which were reopened in early 2007 in Davos. In order to finish the Round by the end of 2007, to avoid postponing it until after the presidential election in the US, trade negotiators consulted intensely in the course of 2007. On 17 July 2007, the chairmen of the WTO negotiating committees on agriculture and industrial market access published their new proposals which are currently being studied.

Even though negotiations were still ongoing at the time of writing, it appears that emerging countries have become key actors in multilateral commercial negotiations. What is certain even before the conclusion of the Doha Development Round is that emerging economies have become key players in the multilateral trade talks. Brazil and India are as central as the EU, the US, Japan or Australia for explaining the evolution of the negotiations started in 2001, and the presence of South Africa or China in a group increases its weight considerably. A key to the emerging countries' success is the flexible use of "shifting coalitions" (Narlikar and Tussie 2004), which have enabled them to express their views on the most important issues and to impose reconsideration of equity issues between developed and developing countries that arise from both procedures and outcomes of multilateral trade talks.

In the early years of the GATT system, developing countries were largely sidelined and preferred to advance on economic development issues outside the multilateral trade forum through organizations such as UNCTAD or the G77. Their silence in trade talks and their Third World rhetoric gave way to new coalition strategies in the preparation of and the negotiations during the Uruguay Round. With the failure of the G10, which aimed at simply blocking the inclusion of the services in the new round, developing countries learned to form issue-specific coalitions and to advance constructive and well-researched proposals. Both the Café au Lait Coalition and the Cairns Group furthermore increased pressure by allying with developed countries in the pursuit of their goals. However, the implicit acceptance of the GATT system that came with these constructive strategies during the Uruguay Round came at the cost of bearing disproportionate implementation costs and seeing the issues central to developing countries largely ignored. Strategies during the new Round therefore aimed at challenging both the seeming inequality in informal procedures at the WTO and the differential impact of agreements on developed and developing countries.

This new focus on both procedure and outcome equality became possible through the intelligent use of multiple coalitions carried by emerging economies that spoke on behalf of developing countries. Without relying on the distributive rhetoric from the 1960s and 1970s, emerging economies tried to retain a certain degree of bloc identity and insisted on the common interests of countries with similar levels of development, while at the same time focusing on specific issue-areas and elaborating constructive and rigorous policy proposals. The dual negotiating identity was possible without falling prey to divide-and-rule strategies of developed countries, through flexible and overlapping membership in a complex web of coalitions, which all worked to maintain friendly relations. On specific issues such as the reduction of agricultural subsidies or the particular issue of cotton, emerging economies were able to mobilize up to 90 or 110 countries, but this did not need to be maintained over a long period of time, as core groups could fall back on previous alliances when internal cohesion was threatened. The intelligent combination of strategies that had proved successful at different periods from the 1960s to the 1990s thus ensured the rise of emerging economies to the centre stage of multilateral trade negotiations and anchored development issues firmly within the international trade agenda.

Bibliography ·······················

Chakraborty, D. and D. Sengupta (2006). *IBSAC (India, Brazil, South Africa, China): A Potential Developing Country Coalition in WTO Negotiations*. CSH Occasional Paper 18. French Research Institutes in India.

Hurrell, A. (2006). "Hegemony, Liberalism and Global Order: What Space for Would-be Great Powers?" *International Affairs* 82:2, pp. 1-19.

Narlikar, A. (2003). *International Trade and Developing Countries: Bargaining and Coalitions in the GATT and WTO*. London: Routledge.

—— (2006). "Fairness in International Trade Negotiations: Developing Countries in the GATT and the WTO", *The World Economy* 29:8, pp. 1005-28.

—— and Diana Tussie (2004). "The G20 at the Cancun Ministerial: Developing Countries and Their Evolving Coalitions in the WTO", *The World Economy* 27:7, pp. 947-66.

Odell, J. S. (2006). *Negotiating Trade: Developing Countries in the WTO and NAFTA*. Cambridge University Press.

Tussie, D. (1993). "Holding the Balance: The Cairns Group in the Uruguay Round", in Diana Tussie and David Glover (eds), *The Developing Countries in World Trade: Policies and Bargaining Strategies*. Boulder, CO: Lynne Rienner.

● NEW POWER STRUGGLES IN THE OFFING

Human Rights Against the Test of Emerging Countries

Guy Hermet

Represented primarily by the BRICs (Brazil, Russia, India and China), emerging countries owe their common description to their economic achievements rather than their respect for human rights or their attachment to democracy. Certainly, China's and Russia's pathetic performance in these two fields cannot be compared to that of Brazil and India, which seems honourable enough. In fact, Brazil's and India's democracies not only figure among the most significant in terms of number of voters; they also ushered in the era of "poor democracies," today referred to as "emerging democracies".

And yet, in actual fact, this glowing report turns out to be deceptive. In both India and Brazil as well as in China and Russia, what lurks beneath the formal political and legal aspects is a disproportion between the scale of the economic upheavals underway and the inadequate penetration of supposedly universal values dear to Western societies. There is also an obvious gulf between the West's ambitious but dogmatic requirements with regard to human rights and the limited opportunities for disseminating them in environments in which the standards advanced for promoting equality, liberty and justice for victims of despotism past or present obviously exceed the actual possibilities of local governments. Everyone knows this. The priority for the inhabitants of emerging countries is a revolution in practical lifestyles and not one of human rights.

The Pinochet syndrome

The expression "Pinochet syndrome" usefully symbolizes the difficulties that crop up during the first phase in which emerging or pre-emerging countries face the challenges of democratic consolidation and the promotion of fundamental rights. For a long time it was often said in the West that not all societies were prepared for democracy and to respect the values of Enlightenment philosophy. These, more or less, only appeared as a belated cherry meant to decorate the cake of material development when nearly complete. Nevertheless, in view of the sudden political changes that occurred in Mediterranean Europe and Latin America between 1970 and 1985, it came to be admitted that the West basically had to recognize a capacity for unconditional democratization in countries whose leaders of all ilks acted with enough caution not to jeopardize the "transition" from dictatorship to freedom. Democracy was no longer the cherry on top of the development cake, but the product of political strategies applicable all the way down to economically handicapped states.

After the end of the dictatorships in Spain and Brazil, the country that best illustrates this evolution was Chile, an emerging country of medium importance rather than a giant like the BRICs. But as in other countries imitating the leaders of the Spanish and Brazilian democratization processes, those who led Chile's transition were to choose, out of strategic caution, not to enforce justice on those responsible for the military dictatorship, so as not to provoke an army compromised by its criminal misdeeds. This strategic disregard for justice also took into account the ambivalence of a large swathe of the population made wary by the earlier experience of President Allende. In short, they applied the new recipe of "unconditional democratization", based primarily on a clever handling of the calendar for political change and finally relying on a certain degree of connivance between relatively liberal sectors of the former authoritarian government and the more pragmatic elements of the former democratic opposition. In this general perspective, until General Pinochet was arrested in London in October 1998, the prevailing principle had basically involved preserving the political transitions underway since Spain's exit from Franco's dictatorship from the dangers involved in a "revengeful" attitude on the part of the "democrats" back in power. This principle recalled—though nobody realized it—that of King Henry IV's Edict of Nantes (1598) which brought an end to the murderous conflict between Catholics and Protestants in France. "First," the Edict stipulated, "that the recollection of everything done by one party or the other between March, 1585, and our accession to the crown, and during all the preceding period of troubles, remain obliterated and forgotten, as if no such things had ever happened." The same idea prevailed with regard to the societies coming out of dictatorships. It was essential to make a clean break with the past, and the memory of it.

table 7: **Ratifications of main international treaties by emerging countries**

	China	India	Brazil	Mexico	South Africa	Turkey	Russia
HUMAN RIGHTS							
International Covenant on Civil and Political Rights - 1966	Sig. subject to Ratification 1998	Accession 1979	Accession 1992	Accession 1981	Ratification 1998	Ratification 2003	Ratification 1973
Optional Protocol to the International Covenant on Civil and Political Rights - 1966	Not a party	Not a party	Not a party	Accession 2002	Accession 2002	Ratification 2006	Accession 1991
Second Optional Protocol to the International Covenant on Civil and Political Rights, aiming at the abolition of the death penalty - 1989	Not a party	Not a party	Not a party	Accession 2007	Accession 2002	Ratification 2006	Not a party
Convention against Torture and Other Cruel, Inhuman or Degrading Treatment or Punishment - 1984	Ratification 1988	Sig. subject to Ratification 1997	Ratification 1989	Ratification 1986	Ratification 1998	Ratification 1988	Ratification 1987
Optional Protocol to the Convention against Torture and Other Cruel, Inhuman or Degrading Treatment or Punishment - 2002	Not a party	Not a party	Ratification 2007	Ratification 2005	Sig. subject to Ratification 2006	Sig. subject to Ratification 2005	Not a party
Convention on the Rights of the Child - 1989	Ratification 1992	Accession 1992	Ratification 1990	Ratification 1990	Ratification 1995	Ratification 1995	Ratification 1990
Optional Protocol to the Convention on the Rights of the Child on the involvement of children in armed conflict - 2000	Sig. subject to Ratification 2001	Ratification 2005	Ratification 2004	Ratification 2004	Sig. subject to Ratification 2002	Ratification 2004	Sig. subject to Ratification 2001
International Convention on the Protection of the Rights of All Migrant Workers and Members of their Families - 1990	Not a party	Not a party	Not a party	Ratification 1999	Not a party	Ratification 2004	Not a party
WORKERS' RIGHTS							
Right to Organise and Collective Bargaining Convention - 1949	Not a party	Not a party	Ratification 1952	Not a party	Ratification 1996	Ratification 1952	Ratification 1956
Abolition of Forced Labour Convention - 1957	Not a party	Ratification 2000	Ratification 1965	Ratification 1959	Ratification 1997	Ratification 1961	Ratification 1998
Worst Forms of Child Labour Convention - 1999	Ratification 2002	Not a party	Ratification 2000	Ratification 2000	Ratification 2000	Ratification 2001	Ratification 2003

Note: "Accession" is the act whereby a state accepts the offer or the opportunity to become a party to a treaty already negotiated and signed by other states. It has the same legal effect as ratification. Accession usually occurs after the treaty has entered into force.
Source: compiled by Dorian Ryser from UN and ILO conventions and treaties

Already in 1976 in Spain, but even more openly in Chile from the 1990s, the aim was thus to place emphasis on the future rather than the past. Priority was given to guaranteeing consolidation of young reconciled democracies, without winners or losers, rather than to punishing ex-dictators and their henchmen. In this spirit, a sort of political "precautionary principle" seemed to justify paying for the triumph of liberty and rights for future generations by a painful lack of expiation of the crimes committed by the overturned despots, which also implied blotting out, at least on the surface, the suffering endured by the persecuted opponents of the past. This was virtually the rule for both the Spanish and the Chileans and beyond them for the Brazilians, Uruguayans and Argentineans freed from their military governments between 1983 and 1985. Until recent years, there was no real prosecution of putschist generals, torturers or child-kidnapping officers. Moreover, some consider that it made no sense to speak of either national or international justice as long as it applied only in certain circumstances, when Mengistu, Ulbricht or the Communist despots in general were exonerated from it much more than right-wing ex-dictators.

The "Pinochet affair" came at a time when this jurisprudence of shutting out the past as an ingredient for civil peace and a recipe for democratic transition was beginning to wear thin. Long after the precedents of the Nuremberg and Tokyo trials of Nazi and Japanese war criminals in 1945-48, the glory days of international criminal justice began in 1993-94 with the creation of the International Criminal Tribunal for the former Yugoslavia (ICTY) and its counterpart designed to try the crimes committed in Rwanda (ICTR). But the turning point really came about in the summer of 1996, when the magistrates of the Spanish *Audiencia Nacional* and lawyers for the deceased Chilean President Allende undertook to bring General Pinochet to trial; later they achieved his arrest in London in 1998, the very year when the statutes of the International Criminal Court (ICC) were approved in Rome. The prejudice that downgraded respect for the primordial right to justice and recognition of wrongs inflicted, for the sake of durable installation of democracy, was suddenly rejected. The strangest thing was that this reversal was the outcome of a peculiar rapprochement of two long antagonistic circles: on one hand young progressive jurists, for years devoted to doing away with reactionary tyrants; and on the other the real or rumoured Chicago Boys, heralds of neoliberalism and former inspirers of economic doctrines of the Latin American military regimes, suddenly won over to democracy. Consequently, the conditionality of respect for human rights as a prerequisite for approval of fledgling democracies came to take precedence over the priority previously given to unconditional democracy. It was no longer the advent of democracy that led to the gradual implementation of human rights, but the opposite: respect for human rights became the indispensable criterion for authenticating any democracy. The era of transitions governed by caution and modest initial ambitions was over.

Human rights meet the market

Legal specialists associated with NGOs geared to defending victims of dictatorships and bringing military torturers to trial, consequently discovered that they shared certain conceptions and interests with the Chicago Boys (in the literal or figurative sense—all did not necessarily graduate from the Chicago school of economics). Both aspire to the dawn of a world governed by law, the former out of a concern for justice in the strict sense, the latter in order to eradicate world poverty by the hoped-for prosperity of markets finally "regulated" by law instead of being subject to the corruption of a predatory state. In both parties' minds, an overreaching body of law authenticating the democratic nature of states that is supposed to monitor the proper functioning of the market should replace states that set or twist the law as they see fit. The hour of "market democracy" wedded to "global jurocracy" had struck. But that wasn't all. The gigantic scope of the political, economic, social and moral upheaval following the collapse of "democratic socialism" in Eastern Europe far exceeded the fairly circumscribed domains of government institutional change and recognition of political freedoms. Everything became subject to radical reform. And the transformation of communist commanded economies into market economies appeared straight away as the most decisive of these reforms, the democratization process being suddenly brought down a notch.

In the political sphere, two principles came to predominate in the course of the 1990s. For post-communist states in particular, the first was integration into the enlarged European Union as a solution to all democratic deficiencies, without any more thought given to the social, cultural or material preconditions formerly deemed essential to make democratization anything other than a façade. It was forgotten that in Spain, Portugal and Greece in 1974-75, political reform had been the essential task; in the East things had to be reformed from top to bottom. A second principle, applying more to the countries of the South in addition to the turbulent Balkan countries, was that the primary goal of the powers that be, international organizations and global NGOs, was less to extend the realm of democracy as a governmental regime than to enlarge the economic and legal space serving an objective of global organization that could make all sorts of international relations more predictable. It is this perspective that spread the ill-defined notion of good governance, meant for poor societies as a substitute for democracy. It also spawned the development of human rights diplomacy to the detriment of other forms of foreign policy.

In this changed context, which remains topical, reference, however emphatic, to human rights should not mislead. Today's primary goal is to impose the hegemony of a re-thought version of the rule of law, mainly to guarantee a property regime and combat corruption. On the other hand, it is much less work toward expanding political or moral freedoms. In short, this variety of rule of law is in some ways closer to the German Rechtstaat under Chancellor Bismarck than the classic Anglo-Saxon vision, in that it primarily outlines a sort of rule for globalization rather than obeying a liberal doctrine going back to respected and ancient sources. This could be seen in a particularly caricatural fashion in the spring of 1999 in Kosovo, when the American government leapt to the defence of human rights to demonstrate to its allies, as well as its designated adversaries, its determination and ability to strike who it wanted and where it wanted. This would have been an appropriate time to launch the slogan "Be democratic, otherwise I'll bombard you", to accompany the new doctrine under which, in fact, newly established young democracies boiled down to the holding of elections "monitored" by the UN with outcomes that met the expectations of powers and international bodies.

The most insulting constraint imposed on emerging countries is, however, something else. It flows from the pseudo-universalistic fundamentalism displayed by the most advanced states, NGOs and crusaders in stating their unrealistic and almost arrogant prescriptions as regards basic rights. This can be seen, for instance, in the spectacle of indignation by opponents of the death penalty in reaction to executions in Afghanistan. The UN protested via the head of its assistance mission in Kabul, urging Afghanistan "to continue working towards attaining highest human rights standards and ensuring that due process of law and the rights of all citizens are respected." Perhaps this virtuous and perfectionist international civil servant should have been transferred to Switzerland or Denmark. Reality has to be looked in the face.

This reality is no more comforting at the UN level in general than at the level of its Human Rights Commission, which for years remained merely a "diplomatic showcase". In September 2001, a few days before the attacks on the Twin Towers in New York, the Durban Conference on Racism, Racial Discrimination, Xenophobia and Intolerance turned into a forum for hate-filled anti-Israeli propaganda. Then came the scandal of 2003, sparked by Libya's election to the chair of the United Nations Commission on Human Rights, for which 33 votes were cast in favour, compared with 17 abstentions and three No votes (Canada, the United States, Guatemala). Likewise, in 2005 Kofi Annan's attempt to reform this commission came up against the difficulty of setting new conditions for admission to a renovated Council on Human Rights. Should only countries demonstrating "indisputable" merits, signatories to the UN pact on civil and political rights as well as the economic and social rights pact, be admitted? The problem would then have been that in this case, poor countries would not have been the only ones among the excluded. Besides being responsible for the despicable Guantánamo Bay prison, the United States also never ratified the second of these documents, while the very emerging China fully intends never to sign the first and Russia is sagging under the weight of its dismal record in Chechnya. In addition, in 2004-05 at the Security

Council the American government, consistent with its hostility on principle to the International Criminal Court, constantly opposed prosecuting the perpetrators of crimes in Darfur before that court.

In any case, human rights diplomacy is less a matter for diplomats or political leaders than for peripheral agents. It began as, and in many of its actions remains, a matter for non-governmental agencies such as Amnesty International, Human Rights Watch, emergency medical organizations or networks of militant and sometimes megalomaniac legal experts or magistrates. This probably explains why, for the G-7 countries in particular, rights have become those granted under a rule of law as defined above in its new meaning: elements of a regulatory framework of activities and situations falling primarily within the economic order or that of neutral administrative and political "management" requiring no particular designation as to whether the regime is democratic not.

From human rights to the 'Beijing Consensus'

Under such conditions, it is not surprising that this rather particular variety of rule of law only incidentally pertains to civil rights falling within democratic values. This moreover became quite plain in June 2002 in the document that came out of the G-8 meeting held in Kananaskis. This document, entitled the G-8 Africa Action Plan, avoids speaking explicitly of democracy and political freedoms and rights when it explains that the meeting's goal was to focus aid from the rich world "on countries that demonstrate a political and financial commitment to good governance and the rule of law, investing in their people, and pursuing policies that spur economic growth and alleviate poverty." That was a verbatim expression of what was called the "Washington Consensus", as a general framework for recommendations addressed by the World Bank to emerging countries and other developing nations.

But this stage has been passed, since the liberal "Washington Consensus" has run into competition in Asia and even Africa with what some have recently called the "Beijing Consensus". What does this involve? The "Beijing Consensus", which should be interpreted pending further information as a state of mind and not an explicit doctrine, is founded on the idea that the Chinese development model, based on a lopsided liberal logic confined to the economic apparatus and individual consumption but excluding any relaxing of the style of government according to democratic ideas, represents the most promising solution for the countries of East Asia or even sub-Saharan Africa. The method is supposed to have proved itself not only in China but also in Singapore, for instance, in a wholly different ideological and social context. Human rights can wait, they may even be counterproductive. Furthermore, old officially-recognized democracies themselves fear that an overly asserted concern for human rights might have a boomerang effect on themselves.

In this regard, just consider the Belgian law of universal jurisdiction, the lawsuit filed in Brussels against Ariel Sharon, even the possibility of judicial examination of American war crimes committed during the Vietnam war or, more worryingly, of an international court indicting GIs returning from Afghanistan or Iraq. Certainly, that does not mean that prosecution or belated action in the name of the right to justice will cease. But there is no doubt that a turnaround could already be detected in July 2002 at the behest of the main actor, with the US decision to veto the continuation of the UN mission in Bosnia-Herzegovina.

Recent indications of this change are proving to be more and more premonitory. In the early autumn of 2007, during the 17th Chinese Communist Party Congress, Hu Jintao, its secretary-general since 2002, argued loudly and clearly in favour of a "correct political orientation"—in other words a non-democratic orientation, declared in no uncertain terms. In the following days, as if to specify an official objective focused on a variety of rule of law oriented primarily towards economic achievement, the new leaders appointed in the same Congress were especially chosen from among legal experts and economists, instead of engineers and scientists from the preceding generation. Such signs are not only observed in Beijing. It is worth pointing out, for instance, that in October 2007 as well, the very irreproachable government of Seoul refrained from mentioning the problem of basic rights in the framework of its rapprochement with North Korea. Above and beyond this show of "tact", the South Korean Foreign Minister Lee Jae-jung specified, before leaving for Pyongyang, that the question should be interpreted according to "each country's circumstances and characteristics". Actually, the page of Rights with a capital R has virtually been turned. Still in democratic South Korea, during the same period Kim Yun-tae, speaking for NKnet, a local human rights NGO, declared frankly that liberalizing economic activity in North Korea was more essential than doing away with the prison camps that the international community is supposedly so concerned about. "For most of the North Korean population," Kim Yun-tae insisted, "rights is an abstract issue. What it wants is to be able to move freely, buy and sell. The 2002 economic reforms [concerning wages and prices] are not enough. It is this point that any policy of engagement should emphasize.".

Besides, do rights issues continue to matter really to rich countries? The question is worth pondering when one considers that the twin themes of the quest for security and the fear of risk, whether they are political or natural, have gained predominance as the major concerns of advanced democratic societies. Prompted by "oriental" terrorism combined with the influx of undesirable exotic immigrants to our still—but for how much longer? —temperate lands, have these very topical and substantial objectives not relegated the promotion of so-called universal rights to the back burner?

Chronology

1689: Promulgation of the Bill of Rights in England

1789: Declaration of the Rights of Man and the Citizen in France

1791: Enactment of the Bill of Rights in the United States

1948: Universal Declaration of Human Rights adopted in Paris by the 58 members of the United Nations

1950: European Convention on Human Rights adopted by the members of the Council of Europe

1984: UN Convention Against Torture

1990: Universal Islamic Declaration of Human Rights adopted in Cairo by the member countries of the Organization of the Islamic Conference.

Bibliography ·····························

Badie, B. (2002). *La Diplomatie des droits de l'Homme. Entre éthique et volonté de puissancei*. Paris: Fayard.

Bergère, M.-C. (2007). *Capitalismes et capitalistes en Chine. Des origines à nos jours*. Paris : Perrin.

Collectif (1984). *Universalité des droits de l'Homme et diversité des cultures*. Fribourg : Editions universitaires de Fribourg.

Corey, R. (2006). *La peur. Histoire d'une idée politique*. Paris : Armand Colin.

Delsol, C. (2004). *La grande méprise. Justice internationale, gouvernement mondial, guerre juste*. Paris : La Table ronde.

Dezalay, Y. and B. G. Garp (2002). *La mondialisation des guerres de palais : la restructuration du pouvoir d'Etat en Amérique latine, entre notable du droit et « Chicago boys »*. Paris : Seuil.

Gauchet, M. (1989). *La révolution des droits de l'homme*. Paris : Gallimard.

Gillet, E. (1997). « La compétence universelle », in Alain Destexhe (ed.). *De Nuremberg à La Haye e Arusha*. Brussels : Bruylant.

Hermet, G. (2007). *L'Hiver de la démocratie ou le nouveau régime*. Paris : Armand Colin.

Zolo, D. (2002). *Invoking Humanity : War, Law and Global Order*. London : Continuum.

Emergence or Re-Emergence?
The Asian Balance of Powers
as a Long-Term Issue

François Godement

The emergence or re-emergence of powers such as India or China in Asia must be understood from a historical perspective. This emergence is new from a Western viewpoint, but it is generally perceived by Asians as a historical return. The emergence of major actors in Asia is not only a contemporary event, nor is the ensuing uncertainty about the Asian geopolitical balance. The advent of new powers and the concept of a regional power balance began with the arrival of the West. The sailors, explorers and tradesmen brought in tow with them a new dynamism and a challenge to the region's states in the era of Vasco da Gama (Carlo Cipolla). This era saw its lease renewed at the conclusion of the Second World War, when the Pacific became an "American lake". Is this Western-led balance to last for ever, or is it a long historical hiatus now drawing to a close (André Gunder Frank)?

The question is of course fundamental, both on the economic level as well as from the standpoint of civilization. Chinese industrial output has already surpassed that of the United States in value, if not in sophistication; the democratic model, vibrant in South and Northeast Asia, is competing with the Chinese model of authoritarian management. The question of the respective roles of the West and the emerging Asian powers can be read like an open book in the dilemmas of Asian regional integration: the open organizations of the Asia-Pacific (APEC, ASEM, ASEAN), which in words if not always in deeds are striving for a convergence of norms and rules, rub shoulders with groupings from which the United States, and Europeans for that matter, are absent (East Asia Summit), or with

figure 84: **Main regional organizations in Asia, 2008**

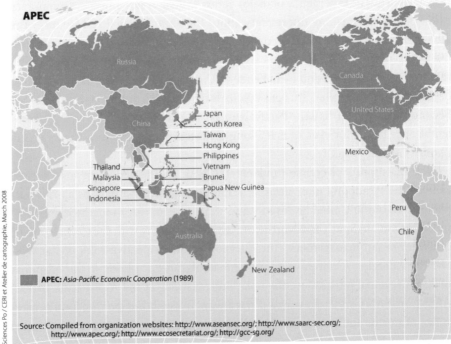

Source: Compiled from organization websites: http://www.aseansec.org/; http://www.saarc-sec.org/; http://www.apec.org/; http://www.ecosecretariat.org/; http://gcc-sg.org/

Sciences Po / CERI et Atelier de cartographie, March 2008

counter-models based on the absolute primacy of nation-states (Shanghai Cooperation Organization).

The West as an emerging actor in Asia

Historically, it was the arrival of British sailors and Scottish merchants off the coast of Canton, and the establishment of Dutch outposts in the straits of Southeast Asia, more than Spanish or French colonization conceived mainly as territorial conquest, that entirely reshaped Asia. The English, the Dutch and later the Americans created an Asian political economy and polarized international relations. They also applied a series of pressures and counter-pressures, in order to stabilize the new Western-led balance of power under challenge from Japan. Emerging next as an industrial and military power, Japan was soon accused of upsetting the existing balance.

China, India and Japan have good historical reason to view themselves as the longstanding embodiment of stable international systems. The existence of global trade flows—the Silk Road, the Calico[1] and Spice Roads—had not transformed local economies and societies so deeply. The descendents of these great ancient states may thus consider the history of their region since the 18th century as an unprecedented phase of instability, caused by the onslaught of Westerners and the emergence of their economic and military dominance. The end of the "Canton system", in fact a more general policy which regulated and limited China's external exchanges, the forced opening of Japan (closed under the Tokugawa since 1632) in 1853, the transformation of Mughal-ruled India into an open market and a springboard towards China, the making of contemporary Southeast Asia by importation of Chinese and South Asian labour to outposts and plantations: all these developments radically altered classic Asia, providing modern Asia and its principal divisions well before the Pacific War and the Cold War.

The West's first stabilization of Asia: 1918-1931

The policy of the major colonial powers, joined by the United States, was at the time both to impose open-door diplomacy—in other words free trade and extraterritorial, i.e. international law—and to establish "stability" and a balance between the major powers, to the detriment of all other newcomers. It was, as Karl Kautsky noted in opposition to Lenin, basically a plan for "imperialist stabilization" that was pursued in the Far East. In the aftermath of World War I, the Treaty of Versailles and later the London and Washington Conferences reflected this dual aim. This was to the detriment of China, which remained subject to co-management by

---

1   Named for Calicut, a center for cotton trade in pre-British India.

the Western powers; of Russia, disqualified from the game by the Bolshevik Revolution; and of Japan, the emerging power of the time. Japan was denied the right to form a "Western-style empire on Asia's doorstep", as the diplomat Inoue Kaoru had wished in 1887. It then raised the banner of Pan-Asianism against the West. As children, both Pandit Nehru and the Vietnamese Catholic doctor Ngo Dinh Diem greeted Japan's naval victory over Russia in 1905 as a promise of Asia's resurrection. The Anglo-American attempt at a "stability pact" persisted, and the Japanese push for demographic and economic *Lebensraum* after 1931 constituted the first historical form of Asian regional unification. The modernity of the Japanese international project, based on educational integration, industrial relocation and a surge in scientific agriculture, was as remarkable as Japan's militarist and racial ravings and its invention of counter-guerrilla tactics.

The 'American lake' and neutralist or Asian reservations, 1945-97

What Wilsonism could not accomplish at the end of World War I, Roosevelt's diplomacy would. The Pacific Ocean became an "American lake" and thus by definition an area of stability over which the United States had absolute control. US policy—transformational diplomacy before the term itself was coined—democratized both Japan and Germany, superseding the domination of the European colonial powers. The US forged Bismarck-style imperial relations—or to use modern jargon, hub-and-spoke relations—with allies that were both aid recipients and subcontractors for mutual security, but in no way equals. This situation served postwar Japan well, leaving it free to ensure its economic boom without bearing the burden of defence. Southeast Asia assimilated the benefits of an unequal alliance so well that it extended the doctrine of neutralism and non-intervention well into the ASEAN era (i.e. after 1967). Unlike Taiwan and South Korea, which were divided nations, the founding members of ASEAN were primarily domestic security states. Young nations with ill-defined borders, they sought to create a stability zone—or, as they proclaimed emphatically, "an area of peace, freedom and neutrality"—protected from the intervention of superpowers, seen as destabilizing. Of course the term then referred more to China or the Soviet Union than to the United States or Japan. After the Japanese model of the "co-prosperity sphere", ASEAN represents the second historical attempt at regional integration: a group of small countries who clubbed together in wariness towards any outside interference. Nationalism and anti-Americanism were strong ferments and anti-Chinese and anti-Japanese demonstrations were also common.

At that time, the largest of the "small" Southeast Asian countries, Indonesia, best exemplified the idea of the emergence of powers after colonized countries gained independence. In 1955 it hosted the first Afro-Asian conference in Bandung, the founding event of what was to become the Nonaligned Movement. At Bandung, not only were Zhou Enlai and Nehru, King Sihanouk and U Nu of Burma present, but also Japanese diplomats who were ensuring their country's return to Asia. In so doing, they hedged the Japan-American Alliance against a pragmatic and open regional diplomacy. In 1964, Indonesia's President Sukarno would become the spokesman for an emerging and neutralist Asia. At the heart of his "*Konfrontasi*" policy against Malaysia, which was defended by the UK and the US, he even announced the withdrawal of his country from the UN and the founding of a "conference of newly emerging forces" (CONEFO).

The episode came to nothing, because Sukarno was overthrown in 1965, but it was a link between past and future: Asianism was not dead, and the official ideologues of authoritarian states in Southeast Asia, at the height of regional economic success, would later view themselves as spokesmen for "Asian values" on the eve of the huge Asian financial crisis in 1997. Thus the stability ensured by one or more powers outside the region could be challenged by the emergence of new forces. Conversely, the regional balance is often made of adjustments to external constraints. Lee Kuan Yew, the *spiritus rector* of modern-day Singapore, one day remarked that he had sung four national anthems in his life (British, Japanese, Malaysian and Singaporean) and did not rule out having to sing a fifth before he died.

Making room for emerging and remerging powers?

Why go back to this contentious historical legacy? It conjures memories of a bygone world, of self-centred empires devoted to a tributary order, the shock of the West's intrusion and the major powers' scramble for the spoils. The Pacific war

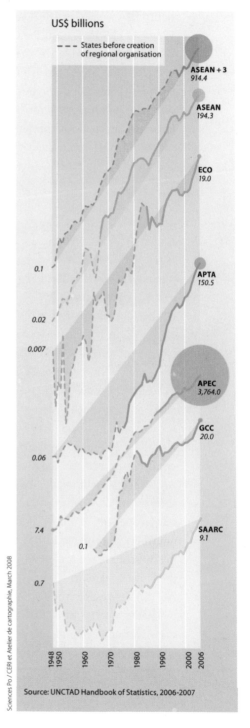

figure 85: **Internal trade among some Asian regional organizations, 1948-2006**

US$ billions

- - - States before creation of regional organisation

ASEAN + 3
914.4

ASEAN
194.3

ECO
19.0

APTA
150.5

APEC
3,764.0

GCC
20.0

SAARC
9.1

0.1
0.02
0.007
0.06
7.4
0.1
0.7

1948 1950 | 1960 | 1970 | 1980 | 1990 | 2000 2006

Sciences Po / CERI et Atelier de cartographie, March 2008

Source: UNCTAD Handbook of Statistics, 2006-2007

figure 86: **Foreign trade of some Asian regional organizations, 1948-2006**

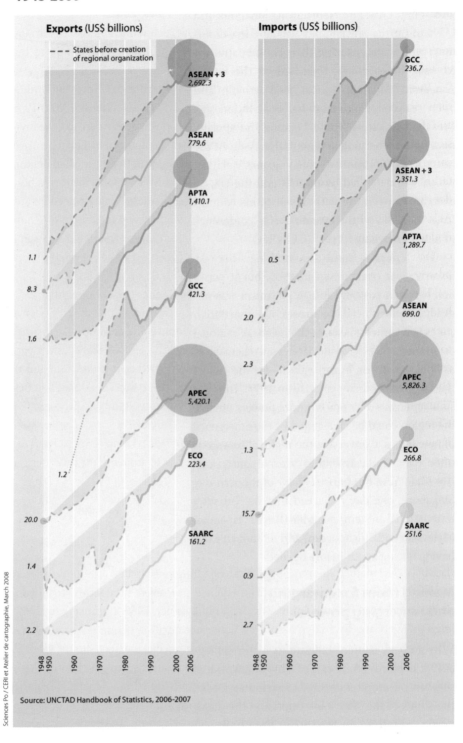

Sciences Po / CERI et Atelier de cartographie, March 2008

Source: UNCTAD Handbook of Statistics, 2006-2007

bequeathed a new order, perhaps a transitory one, when the states of maritime Asia lived under the American umbrella without always sharing its values and missions.

This historical legacy is important because Asia's economic emergence into the forefront of the world economy, with China's rise and India's takeoff now at the core, bring large historical issues back to the fore.

They go well beyond the economic benefits for some due to China's and India's rise, and the losses for others, and well beyond the divisions inherited from 1945 and the Cold War, although the legacy of these divisions matters also, like the division of the Korean peninsula . The situation of Taiwan, colonized by Japan before it came to symbolize the division from the Chinese civil war, the unfinished delimitation of the maritime zones and their resources since 1945, a sub-Himalayan border that remains prey to irredentist conflicts—these are large issues indeed for any Asian agenda. The resolution of these conflicts will both be indicative of a new regional balance of power and revealing of the intention of the major emerging countries, China and India, to adopt behaviour based on either cooperation or power struggles.

The legacy of the past does not stop there. The Chinese policy of giving priority to "peace and stability" and the US pursuit of a partnership with "responsible stakeholders" recall the early 1920s, and the quest then for a compromise in order to achieve stability. The whole question is whether the United States and Japan, established powers, will leave China enough room so that it is not tempted to change the regional rules of the game in its favour. There is no need to claim that "Europe's past is Asia's future" (Aaron Friedberg) to understand the problem that China's emergence poses in particular for Asia. A historical look at a booming Japan after 1918 and its adhesion to international rules, so long as these rules did not work too much against its own interests, helps to understand the question raised by China's rise.

Japan, an example of anticipated adaptation and strategic reluctance

Japan is one major regional power that has long anticipated the emergence of powerful regional competitors, an emergence perceived as a return to history. It has conducted its own China and Asia policy since 1950. Because Japan's foreign policy is usually dual in nature—a native anticipation of contemporary Asian "hedging"—Japan's originality was less apparent during the six years of the Koizumi government, which was intent on securing relations with the United States in order to resist diplomatic and policy pressure from China. Japan's singularity is reappearing today with Yasuo Fukuda. From the maintenance of "special relations" with the PRC starting in 1950 to the Sino-Japanese "trade memorandum" that foreshadowed diplomatic recognition in 1972, and the exemption obtained by Japan in July 1990 from G7 sanctions on China imposed one year earlier, Japan, with a powerful domestic economic lobby in favour of better relations with China, prepared for the end of the Cold War, and also for a regional balance that it could not visibly claim to lead. The same goes for relations with the Southeast Asian countries. The Prime Minister Takeo Fukuda and the "doctrine" named after him granted ASEAN an equal relationship in 1976. They also anticipated publicly the return of communist Indochinese countries to the international fold after the end of the Vietnam War.

The discretion of Japan's initiatives, due to its inability to overcome until now the historical problems of militarism, is only equalled by their diversity. Whether in the energy dialogue with Northeast Asia, concrete projects within APEC or the bilateral free-trade agreements that have proliferated over the past decade, Japan is often "leading from behind" (Michael Green), with the image deficit that such conduct implies but also the resulting capacity for conflict avoidance. Japan's intensified bilateral military relations with Australia and India, its cooperation in maritime surveillance of the straits in Southeast Asia, and its swift and effective intervention after the Aceh tsunami in 2004 also attest to a web patiently woven to contain China's rise without opposing it head on.

In short, what was the first "emerging power" in Asian history perhaps remains—notwithstanding a symbolic and strategic test of will with China from 1998 to 2006 (visits to the Yasukuni Temple, the issue of Japan's possible involvement in a crisis with Taiwan)—the industrialized country that has best prepared its adaptation to China's rise. A portion of Japan's trade surplus has thus been "relocated" to China. The Japanese currency—which the Finance Minister and Bank of Japan refused to internationalize on the European deutsche mark model in the late 1980s—is managed like an instrument in the service of Japanese industrial policy. Even more undervalued than the Chinese yuan, the yen maintains a competitive edge over Asian currencies indexed on the dollar and even more so over the euro. In the field of high technology, Japanese firms know both how to protect their technologies by relocating them within Japan and how to practice regional cooperation in Northeast Asia under the aegis of their government. This is the case for mobile telephony (the future 4G norm), fibre optics, and open software in retaliation against Microsoft's dominant position. Taro Aso, known for his tough attitude toward China as Foreign Affairs Minister in 2006-7, also advocated regional technological cooperation as Communications Minister three years earlier. And he then justified it explicitly by enlisting South Korea and China to compete economically with the United States.

Japan's public diplomacy, embarrassed by its handling of the historic quarrel, has nevertheless evolved under Shinzo Abe's administration in 2006-7. In the Spring of 2007, a Sino-Japanese commission of historians was created after the

model of that which had been set up with Korea, and of course the European reconciliation model. Japan still wavers between a "value-oriented" diplomacy, particularly promoting human rights and democracy, and that of a more pragmatic
competition with China. The alliance of democracies, or the "arc of freedom and
prosperity" according to Shinzo Abe, is appropriate for the democratic regimes in
Northeast Asia but much less so for Southeast Asia, which is at risk of authoritarian regression. By severing most of its historical ties with Burma as Europe
has done (except for humanitarian aid to the population), Japan and the West
have left the country open to regional rivalry between India and China. Neither of
these has an international democratic agenda. India, "the largest democracy in the
world", does little to export democracy. China judges regimes and international
situations solely by the yardstick of international stability and its own interests.
The same indecision can be found in the area of energy security: until October
2006, Japan was in the race for Iranian natural resources in the Azadegan oilfield;
it did not subscribe to the Extractive Industries Transparency Initiative (EITI) for
fear of losing a foothold in the race for extraction contracts in Africa. Japan supports the international development of its oil and gas extraction companies and
has set up a national maritime energy transport programme. The most advanced
country in the world in lowering energy consumption and protecting the environment remains, rightly or wrongly, marked by the fear of an Asian race for natural
resources that would revive the clashes of the 1930s.

Asia, between accommodation and balancing

Japan's divided diplomacy is a good illustration of the dilemma Asia faces with
the emerging power of China. It is drawn to China by the rationale of its firms
and an instinct for compromise or appeasement. But it is also pushed towards
India, Australia and all the major Asia Pacific peripheral partners, which would
put China's influence in perspective. It is also drawn to concrete initiatives for
regional integration that are primarily technological, industrial and corporate
based, much less so to political, institutional or security initiatives. Lastly, it relies
more than ever on the Japan-American security alliance in which it is nevertheless
not considered an equal. For instance, it had to sit back and watch the about-face
the United States made with respect to North Korea in November 2006. Japan's
visible hesitation sits alongside the temptations of its Asian neighbours regarding
China, but also their fear of any conflict with that country.

Indeed, China's own attitude towards Asia remains tainted by an ambivalence
that its rise in power makes even more palpable. The country today participates in
nearly all regional institutions and dialogues, having marginalized Taiwan, against
which it is waging a merciless diplomatic war of influence. China today utilizes
access to its huge market—and its industrial product assembly platform—as a

lever of influence with respect to all of its neighbours: the grand project for a free trade area signed with ASEAN in 2000 is the visible side of this policy. China's "good neighbour" policy contains a wide variety of elements: a policy of trade and military influence over Burma, a so-called "strategic" partnership with ASEAN, a six-way dialogue around the issue of North Korea which is also an asset and a bargaining chip with the United States, "cold peace" with Japan and a Metternich-style organization for Central Asia, where the Shanghai Cooperation Organization hunts down terrorists and dissidents, familiarizes each member with security apparatuses and serves as a collective framework for anti-hegemonic declarative diplomacy. But in contrast, it is important to mention the rapid and continuous rise in Chinese military expenditure and the persistent conflicts not only over Taiwan but also over maritime boundaries with many of its neighbours, in addition to a surprising irredentism toward India. These facts suggest other possible risks: no one really knows, in the era of President Hu Jintao's "harmonious world", if this more worrisome aspect is merely residual or the sign of a hegemony to come.

These reservations also explain the time lag in China's regional integration process in a key area, that of regional preventive diplomacy, if one excepts the signing of a declaration on conduct in the China Sea (2002) and of the ASEAN Friendship and Cooperation Treaty (2003).

While tempted to accept China's policy—reciprocal diplomatic courtesies and mutual economic benefits without significant Chinese military projection or strategic dispute—Asian countries nevertheless subscribe to an insurance policy with the United States. This remains true of South Korea, which today has discarded President Roh Moo-Hyun's populist nationalism; it is also true of Singapore, virtually an American base between the Pacific and Indian Oceans, where conservative politicians nonetheless predict China's superiority over the United States, the obliteration of a powerless Europe and, as a gift of God, the death of Western values (Kishore Mahbubani). These games should not make us

figure 87: **Inward FDI flows into selected Asian regional organizations, 1970-2006**

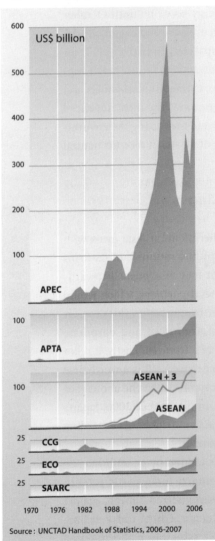

Sciences Po / CERI et Atelier de cartographie, March 2008

Source: UNCTAD Handbook of Statistics, 2006-2007

lose sight of the fact that Asian corporations and professional elites today speak a common language—that of investment and trade, profits and luxury consumerism, the acceptance of growing income inequality throughout the entire region, preference for an ever more economically liberal state unhindered by labour and social organizations. The circulation of capital through offshore financial markets, bank loans, the increase in money supply are again at the record level reached on the eve of the 1997 crisis: the region takes stock in the even more gigantic amount of its sterilized monetary reserves. The emergence of giants like China, and to a lesser extent India, strengthens growth throughout the entire region.

Recourse to India, a window that is not there

Is India a possible recourse for the West, whose value-oriented diplomacy today has been forsaken? Is it also a recourse for maritime Asia in search of a regional complement to the American alliance as well as a counterweight to China's rise and its overly opaque strategy? There is virtually no comparison between the flaring post-combustion phase of the Chinese economic rocket and the steady acceleration of the Indian giant. The former combines state interventionism, direct or indirect control of companies and capitalist mobilization of a labour force atomized by the exit from collectivism. The latter is pursuing gradual liberalization from the Anglo-Indian bureaucratic straitjacket, an internationalization of capital and professional elites, a recreation of regional and global diplomacy after the fall of the Soviet Union put an end to the neutralist posture of Nehru's and Gandhi's India. But it is pointless to credit India with strategic designs based on either the sharing of democratic values or a strategic "axis". Indisputably, Indian military power—which still involves major equipment purchases from Moscow—now follows recipes from the Pentagon and Israel. The 2006 signature of a civil nuclear pact with United States, implying grudging acceptance of the nuclear status of a state which is not a signatory to the NPT, has kindled speculations and probably concerns in China, the big loser in such a deal. The biggest obstacle to this pact, however, was not ratification by the US Congress, but demands from Indian Members of Parliament who were anxious to preserve the future development of nuclear weapons. As for India's role in its own region—the subcontinent and its regional organizations such as SAARC—it hardly serves as an example for regional integration in East Asia. Conflicts over the management of waters from the Himalayan rivers, a burdensome trusteeship over Bhutan, benign neglect—if not a policy of making things worse—in Nepal torn between monarchy, democrats and Maoists, an increased footprint in the generals' Burma, failure to mediate in the conflict in Sri Lanka, absenteeism at the SAARC: India's emergence should not mask the poor state of its periphery, including Bangladesh, today governed by its generals. The persistence of subregional conflicts, the Indian economy's lack of a spillover effect, the contrast between domestic democracy and the growing major power syndrome—all this hardly positions India as an alternative model for Asia.

An adaptive balance, the worst solution except all others

These realistic observations can give rise to several optimistic conclusions. The emergence of a "Chindia", a dream of expatriate financiers but a strategic and social nightmare for old industrial democracies, is highly unlikely. Competition between China and India is not only economic, but is also based on strong mutual strategic suspicions: the increase in bilateral exchanges is stimulating for companies in some sectors but remains an epiphenomenon on the macroeconomic level. The explosion of an original form of regionalism in East Asia—fewer institutions and common rules than in Europe, more ad hoc agreements, prevalence of firms over other actors—is actually at the root of prosperity. But it does not transcend the reality of states and peoples anxious above all to keep their distances, and, if they cannot do that, to ensure their security via a global, and not a regional policy.

figure 88: **Share in intraregional exports, 2006**

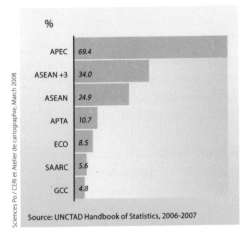

Source: UNCTAD Handbook of Statistics, 2006-2007

The United States, and secondly Europe, still have roles to play. Despite the ageing of its population, and a parliamentary and civic democracy with such complex rules that they tend to override any political programme, Japan remains a step ahead through its technology, corporate models and societal modernity.

China's and India's economic booms do not herald competition between their models as much as is generally believed: the map of Asia is rather being modified by the power wielded by the first, and by the competitive choice that the second offers. American power finds itself tempered and fragmented as a result: with Japan, the military alliance; with China, financial symbiosis that makes the sum of two Chinese and American imbalances the most prodigious overall factor of growth; with India, ASEAN and even certain Central Asian states, a diplomacy of reinsurance and counterweight that is far from encircling China. It is highly unlikely that the emergence of China and India will produce a real upheaval in the regional balance. The terms "rise" and "fall" reflect a geopolitical perception of Asia based on absolute criteria. This vision is primarily historic and Western. Many Asians prefer an image of shifts, adjustments and accommodation or appeasement, which all seem to them preferable to conflict.

Bibliography ·································

Bardhan, P. (2005). *Awakening Giants, Feet of Clay: A Comparative Assessment of the Rise of China and India*, Berkeley: University of California.

Cipolla, C. (1965). *Guns, Sails and Empires*, New York: Minerva Press.

Delamotte, G. and F. Godement (eds) (2007). *Géopolitique de l'Asie*, Paris: SEDES.

Etienne, G. (2007). *Chine-Inde: la grande compétition*, Paris: Dunod.

Frank, A. G. (1998). *ReOrient: Global Economy in the Asian Age*, Berkeley: University of California Press.

Friedberg, A. L. (1998). *Europe's Past, Asia's Future?* SAIS Policy Forum Series, Report no. 3, October, Johns Hopkins University.

Green, M. J. (2001). *Japan's Reluctant Realism: Foreign Policy Challenges in an Era of Uncertainty*, New York: Palgrave.

Jansen, M. B. (2000). *China in the Tokugawa World*, Cambridge, MA: Harvard University Press.

Johnston, A. I. (2008). *Social States: China in International Institutions, 1980-2000*, Princeton University Press.

Countries Emerging, Immersed, Submerged, and Adrift

Pierre Hassner

The term "emerging country" so much in vogue today describes not only a specific phenomenon but even more a broader trend that characterizes the current phase of international relations. The phenomenon that provides a starting point for this volume is economic. It relates to the spectacular growth of a certain number of countries (the most currently accepted version being the BRICs, i.e. the four countries identified by analysts at Goldman Sachs in 2003 as breaking away from the developing Southern countries to become major economic powers that share features of the North and the West without, however, joining their club). These countries call into question the dualist structure of the international economic system. This is clearly apparent in WTO talks: their rhetoric often likens them to Southern countries, but their dimensions and their interests sometimes bring them to hold positions close to those of the North, sometimes competing with them, sometimes investing in them and playing an essential role in their own balance and that of the world economy.

But this phenomenon, revolutionary in itself, in no way describes everything new about today's global landscape. States can emerge in other ways than through their economic power. Iran is emerging, especially since the demise of Saddam Hussein, as a potential regional leader, now promoted by the US to the rank of major threat. Hugo Chávez's Venezuela is emerging as the leader of an anti-American coalition. What is emerging more than anything else is not only the newfound power of certain states: it is a number of problems and tendencies and a general feeling of uncertainty and unpredictability that lend the so-called emerging powers their specificity.

Predictability has certainly never been a major feature of international relations. But since the thirty years of Western prosperity and the end of the Cold War, phases are following in increasingly rapid succession. Furthermore, strong trends that certain figures had identified decades ago, but which until now were moving in opposite directions, are today intersecting, thus giving rise to emergency situations that humanity must address even as it lacks the necessary instruments and consensus to face them. What can be said to be emerging more than anything else are "emergencies", while the new actors, new hierarchies, new solutions needed to replace an increasingly fragile old order are long in taking shape. The relevant question is whether we are going through a period of transition towards new international system or have entered a state of permanent contradiction between uncontrollable mobility of trends and networks and an insurmountable paralysis of institutions and governance.

Successive upheavals and underlying evolutions

Four progressively shorter phases, to simplify things considerably, can be identified in the international landscape since 1945. From the end of World War II to the fall of the Berlin Wall, the world in its East-West dimension was dominated by the Cold War, its North-South dimension by decolonization. The two processes sometimes overlapped, particularly in Asia. From a strategic standpoint, the existence of the atomic bomb deeply transformed war and peace by a balance of terror, to the point of giving its name to "the nuclear age". From an economic standpoint, the establishment of international institutions and the dynamism of Western economies ensured an unprecedented era of prosperity that contrasted with the relative stagnation of communist Europe, China's tribulations and the postcolonial difficulties of the Third World. This produced a similar contrast between an integrated and peaceful centre and a periphery threatened primarily by poverty and conflicts, even if some countries, such as Japan and the Asian Tigers, managed to emerge and join the centre.

The second phase, from the fall of the Berlin Wall to the destruction of the Twin Towers near Wall Street, seems to be on one hand a phase of military unipolarity marked by the triumph of "American hyperpower" and, on the other, one of hope for a "new world order" in which a collective security framework would be guaranteed by the UN and, at least in the eyes of the Europeans, by a concert of both multipolar and multilateral powers, acting to prevent conflicts by discouraging aggression and genocide and keeping the peace. Such optimism, in some respects confirmed by the scale of the anti-Iraq coalition in the first Gulf War, was put to a severe test by non-intervention in Rwanda, the failure of the UN and US intervention in Somalia, the delays, ambiguities and contradictions of the intervention in the former Yugoslavia, the failure of the Camp David negotiations and constant aggravation of the Israel-Palestinian tragedy. However, the idea of a fight for human rights, the advancement of democracy and the duty to interfere has remained a vibrant one. For Western democracies, in any case, globalization rather than war, cold or hot, or nuclear weapons (despite India's and Pakistan's acquisition of them) was the focus of the period and in the long run was supposed to help integrate the East and South into the Western-based world society.

September 11, 2001 changed all that. The eruption of apocalyptic terrorism in the centre (in all meanings of the word) of the international scene threw the fundamental givens of the international system utterly off balance, perhaps for the entire predictable future. First of all, a group of individuals using modern means of communication and destruction in the service of a brand of fanaticism that makes them accept or seek suicide can now inflict on all societies, including the most powerful country in the world, damage of which it was once believed only states were capable. Secondly, the blow was struck from the centre, but its perpetrators came from afar, mostly from an ally of the United States, and their organization and allies or accomplices are spread throughout the world. Differences in nature between imperial power, state power, and the power of sub- or transnational groups were placed in a considerably different perspective by this blow, especially if one pictures those groups in possession of nuclear or biological weapons in the future. The same holds true for the opposition between an integrated and peaceful centre and a divided and violent periphery, and, in the final analysis, for most of the standard geopolitical givens, such as the opposition between land and sea powers, or suggestions of a decisive role for certain geographical situations, such as the *heartland* which, according to Mackinder, supposedly dominates the "World Island", itself supposedly dominating the world.

But these perspectives are valid for the long term. In the short term, it is not the September 11 attacks that changed the world, it is Washington's reactions and the world's reaction to this reaction. The United States, feeling both innocent and vulnerable but at the same time militarily all-powerful, has gone on a "global war on terror" and then on an offensive aiming to do away with tyranny in the world and promote democracy. But this twofold undertaking has only resulted in a spectacular increase in what the reactions to 9/11 had already pointed up: the gap between America's perception of the world and that of almost every other country. Although Western peoples and their governments demonstrated their solidarity with the United States, the sceptical or contemptuous reactions of large swathes of public opinion in the South, especially in Muslim countries, was already striking— displayed in forms ranging from Bin Laden T-shirts to contentment at the punishment inflicted on the arrogance of the powerful, and including dissemination of conspiracy theories implicating the United States or Israel. By lumping together Al Qaeda, the various insurrectional movements of minorities seeking independence and countries in the "axis of evil", starting with Saddam Hussein's Iraq, the

United States war against the latter, its deceitful justifications, its failings and its infringements of human rights in treatment of prisoners, and more generally, its imperialistic attitude reflected in its assuming the right to change other countries' regimes or attack them preventively, have provoked an unprecedented drop in Washington's popularity and credibility, even among its closest allies, from the United Kingdom to Turkey. The more conciliatory attitude adopted after 2004, with plans to promote democracy taking precedence over the war on terror, a greater opening up to multilateral diplomacy, an effort to make progress on the Israeli-Palestinian problem and to reach a common position with the Europeans towards Iran, has certainly relaxed the atmosphere within the West, especially in US relations with France and Germany. But the plan for universal democratization failed in the face of national resistances, the demands of *Realpolitik* and especially the thoughtless reaction to the Palestinian elections, which the US first called for and then contested when the polls handed victory to an adversary of Washington. For the South, the upshot of the second phase is identical to that of the previous one: hypocrisy and powerlessness, even if the excesses of Al Qaeda in Iraq and the rise of Iran give the Americans, at least temporarily, grounds on which to reach an understanding with certain Arab groups and countries.

In short, the crisis in US/world relations seems indeed to lead to the conclusion that the era of American domination and, through it, Western centrality is coming to an end. The United States continues to be by far the most powerful country in the world in terms of "hard power" (if defined by military resources and wealth) and "soft power" (if defined as the preeminence of technology and popular culture). But it now fails to translate either into a political victory.

Since 2003-04, we can consider that we have entered yet a new phase of international affairs, characterized first of all by the crisis of American, and consequently Western, hegemony. This crisis and, we can confidently claim, this relative decline have been greatly hastened and accentuated by the policies of the Bush administration. But other, more general factors, have strongly contributed and made them inevitable. Some pertain to recent political developments: the United States' financial dependence on China, the rise in oil prices, Europe's virtual paralysis as regards foreign policy, especially in energy and military matters (Gomart 2007-2008), Russia's new rise in power and its much more aggressive policy towards Europe and the United States, and China's, India's and Brazil's spectacular economic achievements. The term "multipolarity" can be confusing because it suggests equality and equidistance between poles that are actually very far apart. The fact remains that some countries that have made it their watchword have seen their hopes come true, but often ironically so: for instance, the expected rise in power of Europe and Japan never actually materialized, and they have been replaced by emerging countries, including India and Brazil, whose arrival on the forefront was hardly anticipated in Western assessments (Hassner 2007).

On the whole, however, we have witnessed a spectacular culmination of developments starting a fairly long time ago, and the confirmation of diagnoses that were premature when first formulated. Napoleon Bonaparte in the early 19th century predicted that when China awakened, the world would tremble; Alain Peyrefitte used the expression again in 1980 (Peyrefitte 1980); the prophecy has been fulfilled today. In 1913 Oswald Spengler announced the decline of the West (Spengler 1948) and in 1934 added that the spread of technology would turn against it (Spengler 1934). This diagnosis is more credible today. In the 1950s, it was expected that several dozen countries would have the atomic bomb by 1980. Proliferation has been much slower, but a considerable acceleration is feared today. In 1848, Karl Marx took the world market for granted; in 1970 the Club of Rome announced an energy crunch; today both forecasts have come true or else are realistic. Isolated or minority voices have for decades been warning that if the level of consumption and pollution in developed countries became universally widespread, the planet would not survive (Diamond 2008). Global warming, once ignored or disputed, is now recognized virtually unanimously as a fact that carries major risks, at once physical, human and economic.

Along with US hegemony, globalization is also in crisis. There, too, it is objectively only a relative crisis. Many aspects of globalization, those having to do with the communications revolution, the more general evolution of technology, planetary interdependence, the rise of new producers and consumers, are inevitable and irreversible. The fact nevertheless remains that it increasingly provokes reactions of fear and rejection. The opening up of economies and the primacy of markets lead to a lack of control and overheating, and a quest for immediate profit and a lack of intelligibility that lead to crises such as the subprime crisis; it is virtually impossible to control flows that have become excessive, and this, plus the ineffectiveness of measures against corruption and money laundering, makes predicting the future of the system impossible. In all countries, including the United States, a resurgence of protectionism can be noted, potentially causing conflicts with China, as well as the return of the state via sovereign funds. The latter, which represent a spectacular and healthy reversal, come primarily from the South, naturally arousing concern in the North about their political utilization (Wallerstein 2008).

Here, perhaps, we touch on the most important dimension, which in some respects results from technical, strategic and economic evolutions but which influences them in return at least as strongly. It is the human, cultural and religious dimension. From civil wars to climate change, from famine to identity crises, everything contributes to setting emigrants who can no longer live in their homelands against Northern populations who cannot or do not want to accommodate them or who at best turn them into second-class citizens: suspicious, insecure and uprooted. These emigrants then become the spearhead of another revolt, that of traditional societies destabilized by the invasion or the spectacle of Western customs, which encourages the rise of religious fundamentalism.

If we add to that the rise in ethnic tensions in certain regions of Africa, which challenge the borders established with colonization and long perceived as guarantees of stability, and the rise of religious tensions, particularly in the Muslim world following the Shia awakening, the oppositions between globalization and identity fragmentation and between cultural traditions and modernization collide, producing an explosive mixture. Emerging countries, at least some of them, play a role of moderator in that they are linked to the former Western centre by interdependence and to the periphery by their investments, which are more welcome than those of the former colonizers. But they are also subject to wariness and envy from the outside and social and ethnic tensions on the inside.

Between insufficient governance and unlikely revolution

We should avoid caricature. First, the old order is not on the verge of collapse; US relations with the rest of the world, and in particular with its allies, are less disastrous than they were two or three years ago. Washington's rapprochement with France under Nicolas Sarkozy and Germany under Angela Merkel is notable, as is the strengthening of its ties with India and Japan. All of these continue to count on United States protection for their energy security. In the Middle East, the Sunni monarchies have drawn closer to the United States and Israel out of fear of Iran. That did not prevent the United States' attempt to remodel the Middle East from failing, a symbol of the West's growing incapacity to promote its ideas and interests in the rest of the world. Admittedly, Western societies themselves have not been transformed by the terrorist threat, barring a few exceptions. Above all, the emergence of India, China, Brazil and a certain number of other countries in Latin America, Asia and even Africa symbolizes economic progress and hope for the populations of the South. East Asia seems to be on the way to a peaceful integration. Recession or not, the world economic crisis is unlikely to bring about a collapse comparable to the one that occurred in 1929. Globalization has probably been positive on the whole for most of humanity. Certainly, it is threatened by problems that we have pointed out, and by the explosive situation in entire regions and key countries such as Pakistan, but the accumulation of all sorts of dangers has led to notable progress in gaining awareness of their gravity.

What can be expected to come out of this newfound awareness? Champions of liberal institutions talk about governance, but are less and less in touch with political, economic and social realities. Alterglobalists claim that "another world is possible" but are incapable of investing it with any substance or identifying the means to achieve it.

If the problems are global, solving them usually implies a common authority or a consensus among actors not only regarding the goals and global solutions, but also the hierarchy of emergencies and the distribution of efforts and costs. Now in what could be called either a paradoxical or a dialectic fashion, the more the difficulty of controlling financial or human flows limits the power of states and the impermeability of borders, the greater the emphasis people place on their identity and self-interest and the more governments emphasize their sovereignty. The rise of emerging states only exacerbates this tendency and confirms Karl Deutsch's standard definition of international relations as "that area of human action where interdependence meets with inadequate control" (Deutsch 1968).

In fact, the emerging countries and more generally the large majority of the Southern countries insist primarily on their sovereignty. They consider, with some reason, that the rules of international society and good governance reflect Western conceptions and interests. This is flagrant in the field of human rights, where regional or ideological solidarities take precedence over legal or moral criteria. The Arab League refuses to condemn Sudan, the African Union to isolate Zimbabwe. Russia and China, world powers and permanent members of the Security Council, strive to serve sometimes as arbiters, sometimes as mediators, sometimes as balancers in conflicts that pit the United States and Europe against a given country of the South. Above all, China and Russia take advantage of these conflicts, when they arise from moves for sanctions or imposing of conditions with regard to human rights and their violation, to advance their pawns in the competition for strategic positions or energy resources, taking advantage of their indifference to the nature of existing regimes. Of course, the United States and European Union member states also often grant special treatment to both their clients or allies and their competing partner-adversaries that are too powerful to really feel threatened by them.

The limits of governance and multilateralism, due to differences in approaches and interests, are even more apparent when it comes to managing the world economy or resources such as water, oil or nuclear energy, as well as global problems facing the planet. Two examples are particularly persuasive. The United States refused to sign the Kyoto Protocol because some countries such as China are not subject to the same obligations. China, a mouthpiece for emerging countries, maintains that any new restrictions should first apply to countries that have been polluting for two centuries and should not hinder the development of newcomers. Likewise, Europeans, advocates of development aid, tend to levy duties on products from Southern countries in order to protect their own agriculture, thereby causing a loss of earnings that amounts to far more than the aid they grant.

The example of nuclear proliferation is caricatural. The NPT has a hierarchal or dual structure that favours those who possess nuclear weapons over those who aspire to such status. That does not prevent the former from contravening their own doctrine for political reasons (as in the US-Indian Treaty by which the United States, after inflicting sanctions on India because of its acquisition of the atomic bomb, now grants it cooperation similar to that which NPT signatories enjoy, even though India is still not a party to the treaty) while demanding the imposition of special restrictions on Iran (barring it from enriching uranium) to punish it for having hidden its activities. American strategists who have spent their entire careers dealing with nuclear weapons, such as Henry Kissinger, all of a sudden are calling for their abolition, which the newcomers can only interpret as a measure directed against them. They implicitly reply: "Start by getting rid of yours, or else let us join the club of nuclear powers, and then we'll abolish them together." (Hassner 2007)

The non-proliferation regime is a perfect example of a structure that belongs to another era of the international system, which needs to be renegotiated in a more reciprocal and egalitarian light. At the same time it injects it with an example of an organization, the International Atomic Energy Agency, that provides a precious dose of objectivity and relative independence. The IAEA is nevertheless reliant on states that do not hesitate to criticize it or disregard it, as we have seen with Iraq and Iran. The International Criminal Tribunal for the Former Yugoslavia and the International Criminal Court are other examples of salutary but fragile institutions. In any case, it is this dual imperative—the enlargement and rebalancing of organizations and the creation of and support for technical agencies that are independent (at least in their functioning)—that can increase the credibility and effectiveness of multilateralism.

A dual movement in this direction can be detected, that has unequal chances of success. A rebalancing of the International Monetary Fund and the World Bank that would bring an end to the intra-Western allocation of leadership positions has been announced. The G-8 may well be enlarged in the near future to include China, India and Brazil, ending a glaring anomaly. However, a similar reform of the United Nations Security Council is far more unlikely. The successive projects to achieve this have all run into two obstacles that can be found throughout the international system. The first is the resistance of the permanent members who want to keep their privileges, and particularly their veto that they do not want to see removed or shared. The second is due to the rivalries among candidates whose entry to the Security Council would grant them a role of special representatives of their region of the world. The two obstacles can be cumulative: for instance, Japan's candidacy encounters resistance from China.

Even if these oppositions were overcome, the Security Council could be paralyzed if the veto were extended to all of its members. If instead a new category were created, that of permanent members with no veto right, it would give rise to another inequality and new frustrations. If the veto right were simply abolished, the UN would be less inegalitarian, but cut off from power relations and any ability to act, like the OSCE. States are not about to renounce their privileges in a big jamboree, like the French nobles did in August 1789, any time soon.

What about societies? We have seen earlier that the problem of economic and environmental inequality cannot be tackled seriously without a radical change in lifestyle in developed countries, including emerging countries. But it is sufficient to look at the resistance of the American public to any idea of an energy tax or a voluntary reduction in energy consumption (for instance in the number of vehicles) to understand how utopian any idea of a peaceful and democratic revolution in favour of saving the planet is. The same holds true for world inequality, on the rise in non-industrialized countries and in those without raw materials, especially food, as it decreases in emerging countries. The big conversion, if it ever happens, will only be driven by necessity. This could take the form of a major catastrophe (nuclear war, epidemics, a gigantic natural or economic tsunami) or religious or totalitarian dictatorship which itself could only be established, especially on a world scale, at the price of a catastrophe as disastrous as the one it would prevent.

Today only partial reforms are accessible in certain domains and in certain regions. Of course they are not on a par with the urgency or the gravity of the problems and dangers facing us, but they can serve as examples and bring out convergences. What makes a direct overall or universal solution impossible is that apart from the very nature of the international universe, anarchic for lack of a world authority, there is not only a plethora of often contradictory problems and emergencies, but also the increasingly dire heterogeneity of the system itself. International society can survive without a world government if anarchy is reduced by the recognition of a hierarchical order of powers or a common conception of legitimacy (Bull 1977). But today power as well as legitimacy, those two key elements of any international system according to Henry Kissinger, are fragmented and contradictory. Between the power of states and that of networks or individuals, the power to destroy, seduce and construct, contradictions abound. As for legitimacy, it is seriously disputed and divided between democratic legitimacy, technocratic legitimacy, historic legitimacy and theocratic legitimacy.

A true long-term accord with no ulterior motives on the ultimate goals, and on the role and responsibility of each, hardly seems accessible in the current phase. But in the face of such risk of a general loss of control, we can hope that a minimal working code of conduct will take hold on this side of fundamental convergences to try to establish a fragile, always threatened balance between antagonism and cooperation, heterogeneity and interconnection, inequality and reciprocity.

For John Foster Dulles, brinkmanship was a strategy. For humanity in its current phase, it is rather a destiny.

Bibliography •••••••••••••••••••••••••••••••

Appadurai, A. (2006). *Fear of Small Numbers: An Essay on the Geography of Anger*. Durham: Duke University Press.

Bull, H. (1977). *The Anarchical Society*. London, Macmillan.

Deutsch, K. (1968). *The Analysis of International Relations*, Prentice Hall.

Diamond, J. (2008). "What is your consumption factor?" *New York Times*, 2 January.

L'Expansion (2006). "La mondialisation chamboulée", *L'Expansion*, no. 709, June.

Gomart, T. "L'Europe marginalisée", *Politique Internationale*, 118, Winter 2007-8, pp. 209-26.

Hassner, P. (2007). "Who Killed Nuclear Enlightenment?" *International Affairs*, London, May-June.

Hassner, P. (2007). "L'Europe entre la multipolarité et le multilatéralisme", *Esprit*, May.

Hurrel, A. (2008). *On Global Order*. Oxford: Oxford University Press.

Mahbubani, K. (2005). *Beyond the Age of Innonence: Rebuilding Trust between America and the World*. New York (N.Y.): Public Affairs.

Peyrefitte, A. (1980). *Quand la Chine s'éveillera…*, Paris: Fayard.

Spengler, O. (1934). *Années décisives*, Paris, 1934.

—— (1922). *The Decline of the West*, 2 vols, [*Das Untergang des Abendlandes*. trans. Charles Francis Atkinson], New York: Alfred A. Knopf.

Wallerstein, I. (2008), "The Demise of Neoliberal Globalization". Binghamton (N.Y.) Fernand Braudel Center, 4 Feb. 2008.

PART 4

PERSPECTIVES:
HOPES AND HURDLES

Are Emerging Markets Now Shielded From Financial Crises?

Imène Rahmouni-Rousseau

The 1990s was a decade of major financial crises in emerging markets: sovereign defaults, currency devaluations, plummeting assets markets, sudden halts in capital flows. In 2007 and 2008, ten years after the Asian and Russian crises, the situation appeared in a radically different light: appreciating currencies, net creditor countries, long-term local currency debt markets, rising asset prices and massive inflows of foreign investment.

According to IMF forecasts, emerging countries will grow at a rate of 6.7% in 2008 (after 7.9% in 2007), more than five times the rate of advanced economies (1.3%). The room for manœuvre created by such strong economic growth has been used in recent years to undertake major financial modernization efforts, which tends to bring the financial structures of emerging countries closer to those of advanced countries in various respects: improvement of the debt structure, a broader spectrum of financial markets, investor diversification.

Consequently, the emerging country asset class today is perceived as much less risky and less monolithic than in the 1990s. Investors seem to have taken note of the lowered credit risk in these countries, reflected in less financial market volatility, while maintaining a certain discrimination between them according to their economic fundamentals.

Emerging countries were relatively unaffected by the American subprime crisis. Some observers believed that they even appeared as a safe investment. Does that mean they will be shielded from major financial crises in the future? What is the share of actual progress as opposed to mere catching up, the share of remaining uncertainties and imbalances?

Development and convergence of emerging financial markets

The economic fundamentals of emerging market economies have considerably improved in recent years and their integration into the global economy and international financial markets has intensified. In 2006, net inflows of private foreign capital reached a record level of US$647 billion in these countries, according to the World Bank. Outstanding sovereign bonds issued by emerging countries on the international markets increased fourfold between 1994 and June 2007, from less than $110 billion to more than $407 billion. Bonds thus supplanted bank loans and other sources of capital such as development aid, as the primary source of financing for emerging markets.

This considerable surge in market-based financing has been underpinned by substantial financial efforts to modernize the financial sector, which has enabled emerging countries to offer investors an ever broader and more sophisticated range of financial instruments and thus attract new types of investor. Overall, emerging countries are tending to set up financial structures similar to those in advanced countries.

Improved public debt structure

The debt-to-GDP ratios have tended to decrease over the past 15 years, particularly as a result of more restrictive fiscal policies, at least for a few years, under pressure from the IMF or other multilateral institutions. In some cases, proceeds from privatization or commodity exports have been used primarily to repay the public debt.

At the same time, since the mid-1990s, the financing of emerging sovereigns has increasingly taken the form of securities issuance and less and less that of syndicated loans granted by banks. In the long run, the aim of these countries is to comply with OECD best practice. This institution recommends financing in the form of fixed-rate, long-term domestic debt denominated in local currency, underpinned by a broad base of domestic investors.

Lastly, public debt is generally issued in domestic currency, which reduces currency mismatches and makes States' risk less dependent on exchange rate fluctuations. Thus emerging countries have escaped the curse of original sin—the impossibility of borrowing in their own currency—that had made the crises of the 1990s so costly. In all, according to an IMF estimate in late 2004, the foreign currency debt was down to an average of 16% of the total negotiable public debt of emerging countries (compared with 6% in the OECD) and the short-term debt down to 11% (compared with 16% in the OECD).

With regard to these developments, Latin America appears as a case in point, given the extent of its early repayment of external debt and the use of innovative asset and liability management techniques such as the warrants issued by Mexico in November 2005, by which the dollar debt could be exchanged for a debt denominated in pesos. Thus Brazil, Colombia, Mexico and Venezuela repurchased nearly $30 billion of sovereign debt in 2006, $15 billion of which was for Brazil alone and represented 60% of its external debt in 2005. Other countries, especially among commodity producers (Russia, Algeria, Nigeria), have decided to repay in foreign currency all or part of their external debt to the Paris Club or the IMF, thus proportionally reducing their debt servicing.

Overall, Brady Bonds (special bonds created in 1989 to replace defaulted loans in Latin America), once a symbol of the financial crises in emerging countries, have virtually disappeared. Only $6 billion remained outstanding at the end of 2006, whereas this outstanding debt amounted to $150 billion in the mid-1990s. Conversely, the loans granted by the IMF to emerging countries amounted only to $8 billion in March 2007, as opposed to $100 billion in 2003.

Broadening the spectrum of financial markets

In response to the banking crises in the 1997-2001 period, the structural reforms carried out enabled the banking sectors to restructure and consolidate, financial systems to be opened up to foreign investors, and supervision of financial institutions to be strengthened. At the same time, the share of market-based financing increased with the emergence of new financial instruments.

First there has been a growth in local currency-denominated sovereign bond issuance (see above), as shown by the high capitalization of the new leading index GBI-EM[1] devised by JP Morgan, started in June 2005 ($693 billion), which now represents more than double the capitalization of the former EMBIG[2] benchmark index for foreign currency sovereign bonds ($367 billion).

More recently, private companies in emerging countries have been issuing heavily on the international debt market (bonds and syndicated loans) in a context of abundant liquidity and low risk premia. For instance, in 2006, bonds issued by the private sector in emerging countries ($111 billion) exceeded those of sovereign bonds ($44 billion), a significant change with respect to the early 2000s when private issuance barely represented half the sovereign issuance. This trend was facilitated by the fiscal discipline of States, which borrowed less, thus leaving the field open to the private sector, as well as by a new methodology of rating

---

1 GBI-EM : Global Bond Index – Emerging Markets; index calculated by JP Morgan representing negotiable debt issued in local currency by sovereign emerging countries, including long-term and sufficiently liquid bonds. That is available back to 2002.
2 EMBIG, Emerging Market Bond Index Global, the index calculated by JP Morgan representing assignable debt issued in dollars or euros by sovereign emerging states, including bonds and long-term syndicated and sufficiently liquid films. Data are available as far back as 1993.

figure 89: **Sovereign and private sector bond issuance in emerging countries, 1998-2007**

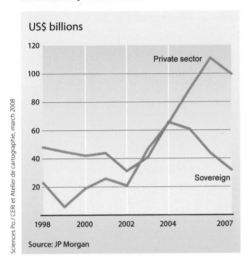

US$ billions

Private sector

Sovereign

1998   2000   2002   2004   2007

Source: JP Morgan

Sciences Po / CERI et Atelier de cartographie, march 2008

agencies, which now authorizes a corporate rating in emerging countries to exceed that of the sovereign State. Likewise, syndicated loans granted to companies in emerging countries in dollars and in euros reached a record $315 billion in 2006, according to JP Morgan.

Furthermore, domestic stock exchanges in emerging countries have gained increasing importance in the financing of local businesses. The intense flow of equity portfolio investment from non-residents reached a record level of $94 billion in 2006, compared with not even $6 billion in 2001-02, according to the World Bank. In the front line of the development of emerging stock exchanges is a small group of highly attractive countries, the BRICs (acronym for Brazil, Russia, India and China), characterized by their heavy economic weight, high growth, the size of their private companies and for some their considerable openness to foreign investment, making them a preferred destination for international investment. The share capital market value of the BRICs (including continental China, but excluding the Hong Kong stock exchange) represents nearly three-quarters of that of all emerging countries.

Finally, derivative markets have shown a considerable boom in emerging countries, enabling investors to better manage their exchange, interest-rate or market risk. Thus foreign exchange futures and currency options, which are very useful to international investors to protect their investments from fluctuations in exchange rates, are now available for most of the major emerging currencies. Securitization has appeared on credit markets. In Latin America it represents nearly 3% of the bond market.

Investor diversification

In this favourable context, since 2002, international investors have turned again to emerging assets in order to diversify their global portfolios. The low level of interest rates over the past four years has also encouraged institutional investors in developed countries (insurance companies, pension funds, mutual funds, etc.) to position themselves on emerging markets with a view to extracting additional yield enabling them to meet their commitments.

All of these factors have fostered the appearance on emerging financial markets of players whose behaviour is more stable and who are likely to hold securities for longer periods. For instance, CalPERS, the largest American public pension fund, increased its share of emerging assets in the funds under its management from

0.6% to 2.4% between 2002 and mid-2007. The Swedish public pension fund AP2 increased its allocation of emerging equities from 3% in 2004 to 5% in 2007. Reputed to be more volatile, the investment flows of mutual funds specializing in emerging countries also recorded very high growth between 2002 and 2007, even if their cumulative outstanding amount accounts for less than 2% of the total assets under management in US mutual funds. Lastly, participation of hedge funds specializing in emerging markets has apparently increased both in numerical terms and in the amounts invested. According to Hedge Fund Research, quoted by JP Morgan (2007), the assets under management of hedge funds specialized in emerging markets have grown twice as fast as total hedge fund outstandings, rising from 2% of the total assets in 2002 to more than 4% in 2006.

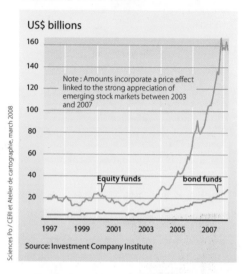

figure 90: **Net assets of US mutual funds specialising in emerging markets, 1997-2008**

US$ billions

Note : Amounts incorporate a price effect linked to the strong appreciation of emerging stock markets between 2003 and 2007

Equity funds

bond funds

Source: Investment Company Institute

Sciences Po / CERI et Atelier de cartographie, march 2008

However, to cover their long-term financing needs, emerging countries still need to develop a broad enough base of national institutional investors (mutual funds, insurance companies, pension funds) to reduce their external vulnerability significantly and durably. In some countries, such development is already under way with the introduction of pension systems based on capitalization, as in Chile, where pension fund assets represented nearly 60% of GDP, or Mexico where private pension funds, which were introduced in 1997, hold the equivalent of $50 billion in peso-denominated government bonds.

An asset class perceived by investors as less risky and more diversified

Lower credit risk

Combined with the often very large-scale accumulation of currency reserves, efforts to consolidate public finances have resulted in an improvement in the ratings of emerging countries, enabling them to recover levels prior to the 1997 financial crisis. The passage of emerging countries from an aggregate situation of current account deficit in the 1990s to a high surplus, and rising rather than depreciating currency trends, have also fostered an improvement in sovereign ratings.

Several emerging countries are thus reaching the "investment grade" category which now represents 40% of the EMBIG index, as opposed to 3% when the index

figure 91: **Rating of foreign currency denominated sovereign debt**

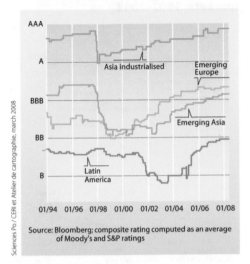

Source: Bloomberg; composite rating computed as an average of Moody's and S&P ratings

figure 92: **EMBI spreads (emerging countries) and US High Yield corporate spreads, 2004-2008**

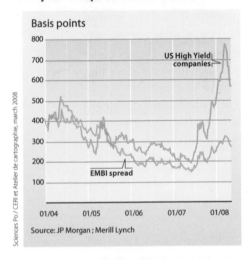

Source: JP Morgan ; Merill Lynch

was created in 1993. This trend has continued recently, as in 2006 rating upgrades have significantly exceeded rating downgrades.

As a reflection of this improvement in the quality of credit, risk premia on emerging bonds have been spectacularly reduced since 2003, reaching historic lows in 2007. Thus, whereas the cost of financing Latin American countries exceeded that of the United States by 10% in 2002, today this gap averages a mere 2%.

Emerging countries are now considered as less risky than American companies in the speculative (high-yield) category, judging by the level of their risk premia. This inversion took place in 2005. This observation holds true if ratings are adjusted: B-rated countries have a lower credit risk premium than American companies with the same rating. Lastly, during recent episodes of financial tensions on global markets, whether in May-June 2006 or in July-August 2007, the re-appreciation of risk premia by investors was lesser and of shorter duration in emerging countries than for risky companies in advanced countries. This tends to accredit the idea that lower risk premia in emerging countries are due more to an improvement in their economic fundamentals than to exogenous factors such as an abundance of liquidity on a world scale and a lowering of international investors' risk aversion.

Lastly, this decrease in perceived risk enables countries that had no access to international borrowing markets to diversify their sources of financing. For example, Ghana became one of the first countries of sub-Saharan Africa to be able to issue bonds on international markets in September 2007, and this despite a market context that was highly affected by the American subprime crisis.

Lower volatility

The decrease in financial risk goes hand-in-hand with a considerable drop in asset volatility across the board in emerging countries in both bonds and shares. A typical

figure 93: **Historical volatility of the EMBI spread and of US government securities, 1998-2008**

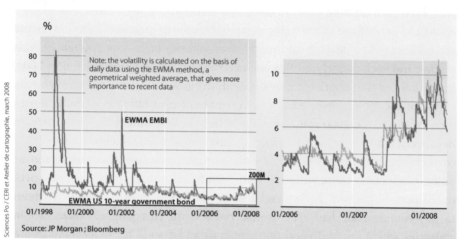

Source: JP Morgan ; Bloomberg

gap in the EMBIG index of emerging sovereign bonds has for instance fallen from 200 base points in the 2000-05 period to 15 base points in 2006 and 7.5 base points in the first quarter of 2007. Similarly, the volatility of the emerging MSCI equity index fell from about 30% in 2002 to 24% at the end of 2003 and nearly 16% in mid-2007.

This drop in volatility is not specific to emerging countries, all financial markets having experienced a period of very low volatility between 2004 and early 2007. But it was larger in scale in emerging markets, to such an extent that in certain cases emerging assets have proven to be less volatile than those in advanced countries—a paradox if one considers that investments in emerging countries remain more uncertain that those made in developed countries. Thus, in 2006, the volatility of the EMBIG index remained constantly lower than that of the US 10-year rate, except for the short episode of May-June 2006.

Besides the drop in risk, lower volatility can be explained by the reduction of macroeconomic volatility in recent years. In fact, GDP fluctuations in emerging countries in these past years have been lower than in preceding decades, a global phenomenon that certain observers dubbed the "great moderation". It could also be that the longer investment horizon in emerging countries (see above), with the appearance of more stable and longer-term investors, has contributed to reducing financial market volatility.

Better discrimination?

The overall improvement in emerging country economic fundamentals conceals a great disparity among most benchmark indicators (particularly growth in GDP, inflation, current account balances, currency reserves, public finances). Thus in order to assess risk in emerging markets, the specific situation of each emerging area, even each country, must be taken into account.

As the percentage of emerging assets increases in their portfolios, investors are encouraged to develop and refine their analysis of factors specific to each market and each country. In this respect, the correction that occurred in May-June 2006 and the subprime crisis since July-August 2007 have, unlike what happened in the 1990s, revealed a certain degree of discrimination among investors. In May-June 2006 the correction affected most emerging stock markets negatively, but to varying degrees depending on their fundamentals. Indeed, the correction affected countries that are most fragile from a macroeconomic standpoint, particularly those suffering from significant public and current account imbalances (especially Turkey and Hungary). The subprime crisis that began in July-August 2007 had very diverse impacts on emerging countries. Some countries which enjoyed good fundamentals and a solid financial sector, such as Brazil, were affected only briefly. On the other hand, countries characterized by strong leverage effects in the financial sector, or by a lack of transparency or weak modes of governance, were noticeably and durably affected. This happened in Kazakhstan and to a lesser extent in the Baltic States and Russia.

All in all, enhanced emerging market transparency, by allowing investors to better manage their risks, has probably fostered this differentiated reaction. This diagnosis was not called into question by the American subprime crisis. Quite the contrary, emerging markets seem to have appeared as a safe haven in the second half of 2007 even though during prior financial crises, foreign investors had immediately withdrawn their capital from the same markets. This lack of contagion is noteworthy. For instance, mutual funds dedicated to emerging equities recorded significant inflows in September and October 2007, after a halt in the month of August. The MSCI emerging equity index also rose nearly by 40% between January and October 2007.

Is this favourable configuration bound to last?

The difficulty of assessing risk

Despite the progress made in recent years, financial markets in emerging countries still have certain deficiencies related to a variety of factors.

First of all, some of these markets are very recent and this makes risk difficult to assess. This is particularly true of bonds issued by private companies. Both rating agencies and investors encountered difficulties assessing and monitoring the risk associated with these debts, due to the lack of reliable historical data on the default of these companies, which display very different characteristics from those of developed countries. Rating agencies thus find themselves undergoing a learning process. As for investors, they often have neither the expertise nor sufficient information in terms of quantity and quality (problems of corporate governance and reporting) to assess risk with any great precision, all the more so since many issuers are not rated by those agencies. The robustness of investor expectations remains to be proven regarding this type of investment, particularly in situations of economic downturn.

Next, the narrowness of emerging markets and their low degree of liquidity (measured by the ratio between transaction flows and assets outstanding) can imply large price fluctuations in the event of even slight portfolio reallocations by international investors. This is all the more true since there is still a significant gap between the size of international investors and the size of emerging markets in which they invest, leaving the possibility of an overly optimistic appreciation of their capacity to exit their positions at reasonable prices

Lastly, given the palpable optimistic mood today on emerging markets, it is likely that investors will be led to overestimate growth potential and so underestimate risk in certain compartments. This could be the case particularly on emerging stock markets, where valuation levels are now higher than those of developed markets. Even if this valuation premium is justifiable by the "growth value" status of emerging companies, it does not take into account the possible sources of fragility of companies in these countries where the structure of governance, sources of financing, international diversification and the experience of competition are probably less established than for a multinational in a developed country.

figure 94: **Valuation multiples of emerging stock markets (PER, Price Earning Ratio)**

Sciences Po / CERI et Atelier de cartographie, march 2008

Source: JP Morgan ; Bloomberg

Accumulation of foreign exchange reserves

World foreign exchange reserves have surged from US$2 trillion in 2001 to an unprecedented $5 trillion in early 2007. Asian emerging countries (notably China) and oil exporting countries were responsible for most of this accumulation.

Initially, accumulation stemmed from an understandable self-insurance motive. In the wake of the financial crises of the late 1990s, when their official reserves rapidly diminished, emerging countries quickly reconstituted their reserve currency holdings to protect themselves against new speculation attacks and strengthen their capacity to cushion sudden stops in capital flows.

However, the academic literature shows that the level of currency reserves today in certain emerging countries is likely to be excessive. This is evident both

figure 95: **Chinese foreign exchange reserves and ratio of reserves to short-term foreign debt, 2001-2008**

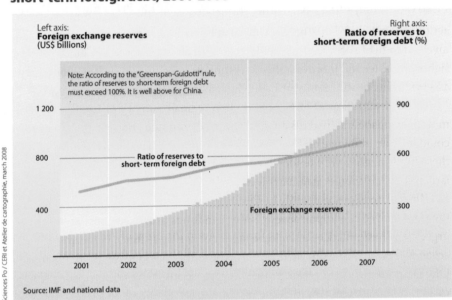

Left axis:
Foreign exchange reserves
(US$ billions)

Right axis:
**Ratio of reserves to
short-term foreign debt (%)**

Note: According to the "Greenspan-Guidotti" rule, the ratio of reserves to short-term foreign debt must exceed 100%. It is well above for China.

Ratio of reserves to short-term foreign debt

Foreign exchange reserves

Sciences Po / CERI et Atelier de cartographie, march 2008

Source: IMF and national data

with respect to simple benchmarks such as the "Greenspan-Guidotti" rule that recommends that reserves should be able to cover the short-term foreign debt entirely, and using more elaborate frameworks of analysis that can compute an "optimal" level of reserves such as that designed by Jeanne and Rancière (2006).

Such hoarding can provoke domestic financial imbalances in countries that practice it (risk of inflation or high capital losses), as well as consequences on the world financial system, particularly in terms of excess liquidity (although this concept remains notoriously difficult to define) or asset price distortions.

Will emerging countries become a source of international financing?

In addition to official monetary reserves, a growing proportion of net external assets in emerging countries is currently invested in the form of sovereign wealth funds. The size of these funds is still limited, between $1.5 trillion and $2.5 trillion, but it is rapidly growing because of elevated commodity prices on one hand, and foreign exchange policies aimed at resisting currency appreciation on the other. In the long run, these funds will become larger than foreign exchange reserves.

The creation of these funds may appear legitimate, for those related to commodities in particular. These are non-renewable resources, and standard economic theory suggests that part of extraction revenue should be saved in order to face difficult periods in the future. The rationale is however somewhat different for non-commodity funds, in that they often result from economic distortions related to foreign exchange interventions and to a financial system whereby the State centralizes the national savings surplus.

In this context, a number of questions arise as to the role and modalities of action of these funds. Whereas official foreign exchange reserves were mainly invested in debt securities, particularly American ones, sovereign funds set their sights on riskier and more lucrative investments in equities as well as in alternative assets such as private equity or hedge funds.

The concentration of large amounts on a small number of funds, which are moreover opaque as regards their asset allocation and most of their positions, could have an influence on the proper functioning of financial markets. Moreover, these funds might have a tendency to make the price of certain assets rise, particularly if they are operating in narrow markets.

The debate is probably only beginning. The G7, in October 2007, for the first time recognized the importance of sovereign funds as international investors and urged that "best practices" should be identified for these funds in the areas of governance, risk management and transparency. The IMF, the World Bank and the OECD are in charge of looking into these questions. Nevertheless, there is a risk of a protectionist reaction in developed countries, all the more so since this issue involves sovereign states as opposed to private companies. The challenge probably involves creating a framework that would enable the emergence of actors in emerging countries, states and businesses as sources of cross-border financing and investment, making sure that they behave as responsible shareholders and investors.

Further financial development

Contrary to the 1990s crisis, the financial crisis of 2007 was not triggered by a currency devaluation or the sovereign default of an emerging country but rather by financial losses on risky housing loans within the very heart of the American financial system, reputed to be the most developed in the world.

This apparent paradox is the result of considerable structural and institutional reforms undertaken by emerging countries in recent years: improvement of the debt structure, broadening of the spectrum of financial markets, and investor diversification. Consequently, the emerging country asset class is perceived today as much less risky than in the 1990s.

However, buoyed by abundant liquidity, high global growth and rising commodity prices, the new strength of emerging countries has not yet been confronted with significant economic downturns in the developed world. This raises a series of challenges which emerging countries will confront in order to deepen their financial development: can emerging financial assets offer investors the necessary diversification if their economic cycles prove to be more dependent than expected on the US cycle? Could the financial imbalances created by their development model, such as the excessive accumulation of currency reserves, threaten their financial stability? Lastly, under what conditions can actors and businesses in emerging countries enter the financial scene as significant investors in developed financial markets, particularly in terms of international governance and international rules of investment?

Bibliography •

Aizenman, J. (2007). "Large Hoarding of International Reserves and the Emerging Global Economic Architecture". NBER working paper.

Chang, J. et al (2007). *Emerging Markets Evolve as an Asset Class*, JP Morgan, Emerging Markets Research.

International Monetary Fund (2006). "Structural Changes in Emerging Sovereign Debt and Implications for Financial Stability", *Global Financial Stability Review*, April.

Jeanne, O. and A. Guscina (2006). "Government Debt in Emerging Market Countries: a New Data Set", IMF Working Paper 06/98.

Newman, G. and L. Arcentales (2007). *Emerging Markets, Emerging Questions*, 18 August. Online publication: http://www.morganstanley.com/views/gef/archive/2007/20070828-Tue.html

Odonnat, I. and I. Rahmouni (2006). "Do Emerging Market Economies Still Constitute a Homogenous Asset Class?" *Financial Stability Review*, Banque de France, December 2006.

Rogoff, K. (2006). Will Emerging Markets Escape the Next Big Systemic Financial Crisis? *Cato Journal*, Spring/Summer 2006, 26 (2), pp. 337-341.

World Bank (2007). *Global Development Finance*. Washington (DC): World Bank.

The Environmental Limits of Emergence

Emmanuel Guérin and Laurence Tubiana

E merging countries arouse fascination. Since the famous but also debatable[1] study published by the Goldman Sachs investment bank[2] the BRICs are everywhere. In the IMF's latest growth forecasts, published in October 2007, growth in the Eurozone (2.5%), even if it is expected for the first time in a long time to exceed US growth (1.9%), remains considerably lower than that of Brazil, Russia or India (4.4%, 7% and 8.9% respectively). China's growth (11.5%) dominates the world economy in pace and in scope. In 2006, 30% of the world's growth could be attributed to emerging economy dynamics.

But emerging countries are also a source of anxiety. Not only because their growth is responsible for a fundamental redistribution of power across the global space, shaking up the existing international order, but also because the environmental cost of their growth poses threats to all. Although the environmental damage caused by such growth is primarily a national problem (20 of the world's 30 most polluted cities are in China),[3] it also spills widely beyond their borders, making it a regional problem, (the US Environmental Protection Agency has found that nitrogen and sulphur oxides in China produce acid rain on the US west coast), and even a global one.

---

1 J.J. Boillot, "La 'grande transformation' de l'économie indienne et ses paradoxes." Paper given at the Futuribles Symposium: "Inde 2025. Scénarios possibles et enjeux pour la France et l'Europe" in 2007; forthcoming in a special issue of *Futuribles*.
2 Goldman Sachs, *Dreaming with BRICs: The Path to 2050*, Global Economics Paper no. 99.
3 World Bank, China Quick Facts, 2007.

figure 96: CO₂ emissions by country, 1995-2005

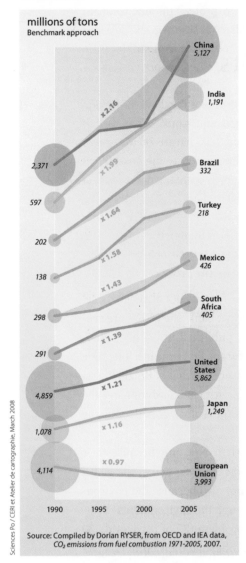

millions of tons
Benchmark approach

China
5,127

India
1,191

×2.16

2,371

×1.99

Brazil
332

597

Turkey
218

×1.64

202

Mexico
426

×1.58

138

×1.43

South
Africa
405

298

×1.39

291

United
States
5,862

×1.21

4,859

Japan
1,249

1,078

×1.16

×0.97

4,114

European
Union
3,993

1990   1995   2000   2005

Source: Compiled by Dorian RYSER, from OECD and IEA data, CO₂ emissions from fuel combustion 1971-2005, 2007.

Sciences Po / CERI et Atelier de cartographie, March 2008

The global nature of environmental risk

The impact of emerging country economic growth on the world's natural resources—energy, mineral raw materials, agricultural and forest products—is obvious and on the rise. China and India already represent 20% of the world's energy consumption. Twenty years from now, these two countries will be the largest importers of oil and coal. China is the second largest importer of timber after Japan.

Beyond the damage related to the rapid industrialization of emerging countries, it is the mass effect linked to their population that makes the environmental question all the more acute. Suffice it to recall Gandhi's famous words: "It took England half the resources of this planet to achieve its prosperity. How many planets will a country like India require?" Access of 2 billion people to a standard of living comparable to that in developed countries will lead to an impasse if the growth and development model relying on the intensive use of natural resources remains unchanged.

Yet not everyone shares this perception of the global nature of environmental risk. Since the Stockholm conference in 1972, developing countries have constantly opposed any definition of environmental policies that would infringe their right to economic growth and prevent their societies from attaining a standard of living equal to the Western world. This position was confirmed at the Rio conference in 1992, leading to the notion of common but differentiated responsibilities. Emerging countries jumped on this bandwagon, but their position has reached its limits. We now know that if the most serious effects of climate change are to be avoided, world greenhouse gas emissions must be halved by 2050 in relation to their 1990 level. This goal means that even if developed countries assume their historic responsibility and cut their emissions by four, emerging countries will also have to make substantial efforts.

China and the other LDCs assembled in the Group of 77 (G77) have so far refused to take part in the international effort to make quantitative emissions reductions, considering with good reason that their development will require increasing them, at least temporarily.

The difficulties of undertaking collective action to protect the environment with emerging countries are related to their intermediary position on the development scale. In fact, although a large segment of their populations is still far from sharing the lifestyle of developed countries, another significant portion lives by European standards.

All emerging countries have ratified the Kyoto Protocol but have not made binding commitments to reduce their greenhouse gas emissions. What we call emerging countries do not form a unified bloc. The very nature of the stakes involved in climate change vary considerably from one country to the next: Brazil for instance faces the problem of protecting the Amazon Forest, whereas China and India have to deal with the problem of industrial and agricultural pollution and rising population pressures which require the development of infrastructure (transport, etc.). In combating climate change, all efforts matter because greenhouse gas emissions have the same impact whatever their source, but they cannot be seen in isolation. They are linked to industrial and energy production systems, means of transport, forms of land use, etc. The highest producers of greenhouse gas emissions thus have a decisive impact on the modification of emissions trajectories for two reasons: first, because much of their infrastructure investment remains to be made and can thus be reoriented, and second, because an agreement on policies to apply in 15 countries (South Africa, Germany, Australia, Brazil, Canada, China, South Korea, France, India, Indonesia, Italy, Japan, Mexico, the United Kingdom, and Russia) could lead to the stabilizing of emissions in the next 15 years.

However, the perceptions of climate risk vary according to country. For the Indian political authorities, climate risk today remains an element of the diplomatic arsenal to claim their country's right to develop. Added to that is the possibility of using this risk as a bargaining chip to attract international investment. Conversely, Indian scientific and non-governmental circles have long been concerned about the negative impacts of climate change. According to IPCC (International Panel on Climate Change) scenarios, India's agricultural revenue could fall by at least 10% in the event of moderate warming ($+2°$ C) and 25% with more pronounced warming (Kumar and Parikh 2001).

Furthermore, the country is particularly exposed to the risk of population displacement due to rising ocean levels as well as climate-related disasters. And drought is now one of the main causes of poverty. So far, Indian civil society has not managed to raise consciousness among the political class of the magnitude of the risk and the need for action on a nationwide scale.

In Brazilian political circles, there is more heightened awareness of the problem. Although 70% of this country's greenhouse gas emissions come from deforestation, only recently has real action been undertaken to fight this process. On the other hand, Brazil's energy model—electricity generation and transport—produces very little greenhouse gas, owing to the intensive use of hydroelectricity and biomass, including alcohol and charcoal.

Brazil has played a constructive role since negotiations for the Kyoto Protocol began. It instigated the proposal to create a fund for clean development in Kyoto, which has become the Clean Development Mechanism (CDM), and it continues to be very active in the G77. The fight against climate change also mobilizes civil society, often consulted by the government to define international policy directions and local policy choices.

China: the stumbling block

If action in all the emerging countries is needed to combat climate change effectively, the international dynamics can only be relaunched if China is prodded to shift into motion.

For the IPCC, China is the second largest producer of greenhouse gas emissions in the world. According to the Netherlands Environmental Assessment Agency, it even became the world's largest producer of CO_2 in 2006.[4] Hence nothing can be done without China's participation. However, the problem is not so much to obtain binding commitments from China as to construct realistic scenarios for transforming its model of development.

In the context of the Kyoto Protocol, negotiations hinged around the central issue of fairness in setting greenhouse gas emissions reduction targets. Kyoto established the principle of binding commitments for developed countries. These targets were relaxed by allowing recourse to market mechanisms. Developed countries could use Kyoto mechanisms to buy carbon credits from developing countries. In practice, this quest for fairness lead to a deadlock: the largest greenhouse gas emissions producer, the United States, did not ratify the Kyoto process and refuses to be party to it unless the new framework contains obligations for emerging countries. The international climate change regime thus rests on integrating the two largest producers of greenhouse gas emissions: the United States today and China tomorrow.

The Kyoto rationale, founded on the idea of burden-sharing, will therefore have to be replaced by a partnership on a new development and growth model and investment to make in order to achieve it. Without eluding the question of fairness, the debate today must be refocused on financing this reorientation and especially the energy transition.

---

4 Netherlands Environmental Assessment Agency (2006). China is now number one in CO2 emissions, the United States in second position.

In this context, China is the essential link in the next climate agreement in the framework of a post-Kyoto regime. China is hungry for energy. The portion of coal in its energy mix is the primary factor explaining its level of CO_2 emissions. Coal represents 63% of its energy consumption, far ahead of oil (19%). It is mainly used to fuel power plants (55%), but it is also used as an energy source in the industrial (26%) and residential (4%) sectors. It accounts for 82% of Chinese CO_2 emissions.[5]

The population mass of China, a continent-sized country (1.3 billion inhabitants, or one-fifth of the world's population), corresponds to different economic and hence energy realities. On the one hand, China's economy is already the fourth largest in the world (5% of the world GDP) and already second in purchasing power parity (PPP) (14.5% of the world GDP).[6] China is also the world's third largest trading power (9% of its exports and 6% of its imports).[7] But per capita GDP is still low (about one-fourth of the OECD average in PPP) and China still has 105 million people (8% of its population) living below the extreme poverty threshold (one dollar per day), as well as 340 million people (26% of its population) living below the poverty threshold (less than two dollars a day).[8] We can therefore only anticipate an increase in the demand for energy and natural resources.

China's demographic weight also accounts for a wide gap between its absolute and relative emissions levels. China produces 3.9 tons of energy-related CO_2 emissions per capita (compared with 7.5 in the European Union and 19.5 in the United States).[9]

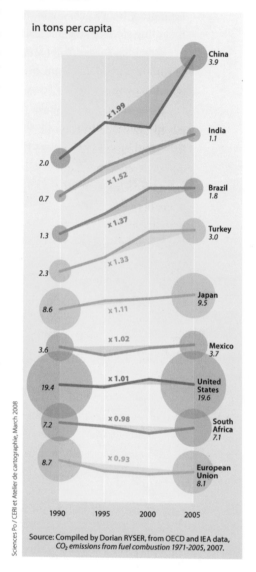

figure 97: **Per capita CO₂ emissions, 1995-2005**

in tons per capita

Sciences Po / CERI et Atelier de cartographie, March 2008

Source: Compiled by Dorian RYSER, from OECD and IEA data, CO_2 emissions from fuel combustion 1971-2005, 2007.

---

5   International Energy Agency (IEA) data.
6   IMF data.
7   WTO data.
8   World Bank data.
9   IEA data.

Last, the country's current contribution to climate change should be seen in the light of its historic responsibility for climate change. Although, according to one estimate, China has become the largest producer of energy-related CO_2 in terms of flows,[10] in terms of stock, climate change remains largely the historic responsibility of OECD countries. The United States and the European Union represented 53% of the total energy-related stock of CO_2 emissions between 1990 and 2005, compared with "only" 8% for China.[11]

These three remarks are important. They will not prevent China from having to offer a certain number of solutions to the question of climate change and its participation in the post-Kyoto regime. Indeed, if nothing is done to stop the current trend, the country will reach a per capita CO_2 emissions level equal to the European Union in 2030 (7.9 tons), and at that time, its total stock of CO_2 emissions between 1990 and 2030 will be close to that of the European Union (about 350 billion compared to 360 billion tons).[12]

By breaking down IPCC greenhouse gas emissions forecasts into subregions, it is possible to compare two scenarios. In the first, the benchmark reference, all states continue to apply the same policies in the fight against climate change. In the second, "alternative" scenario, all states participate in an international effort to reduce emissions according to their level of development. By comparing these two scenarios, we note that even in the event that all other states commit themselves, if China does not, it alone can make the level of emissions rise above what IPCC experts deem an "acceptable" (i.e. emissions leading to a moderate warming of + 2°C).

Sustainable world development is not compatible with extension to China of the energy paradigm that enabled OECD countries to develop. This observation, when made by industrialized countries, is sometimes misunderstood by the Chinese as an attempt to prohibit them from achieving the same standards as developed countries. But deploying the same development model on a world scale based on abundant use of fossil fuels and intensive consumption of natural resources will lead to an impasse. The point is that all countries must adopt another development model that is less energy-driven.

To convince oneself of this, a quick forecasting exercise will suffice.[13] Assuming that Chinese growth stabilizes at an average of 8% per year (knowing that its growth in 2007 was 11.5% and that the IMF predicts a 10% growth in 2008), then China will have caught up with the current level of American per capita GDP in 2031. At that date, if the Chinese economy consumes as many resources per capita

---

10 IEA data.
11 IEA data.
12 IEA data.
13 Earth Policy Institute, *Eco-Economy Update. Learning From China: Why the Western Economic Model Will not Work for the World*, 2005.

as the American economy, China will need 99 million barrels of oil per day (20 million barrels more than the current world production of 79 million); it will also need 2.8 billion tons of coal per year (again above the current world production, 2.5 billion tons).

Chinese introspection: the internal levers for change

Until today, it has been possible to see China as one of the "weak links" in the fight against climate change. The Kyoto rationale artificially assumed two opposed categories of countries, those of the OECD and the LDCs, whereas in 1997 the geometry of negotiations was already triangular. But China could also, paradoxically, be the catalyst for unblocking climate talks. The perception of climate change is in fact changing in China. A conjunction of internal and external factors has placed the question of climate change and environmental protection on the Chinese government's political agenda. The nascent desire to shift goals from maximizing growth rates to striving for more balanced growth patterns could lay the foundation for China's renewed engagement in the post-Kyoto regime.

A new awareness of climat change

The country is undergoing increasing domestic pressure that is making the Chinese authorities aware of the economic and social costs of environmental degradation and prompting them to reassess the potential consequences of climate change.

Water pollution is the primary problem confronting China. Nearly half the major cities do not comply with national standards of drinking water quality.[14] The water is basically contaminated by faecal matter but also by industrial and agricultural pollutants. 110 cities have serious drinking water shortages.[15] According to Chinese experts (Ma Jun 1999),[16] several cities in the northeast of the country could experience a complete shortage in the five coming years. About one-third of China's rivers and streams are very polluted (level 5 or higher); three-quarters of its water bodies and one-quarter of its coastal waters are extremely polluted as well.[17]

Air pollution is also a serious problem in China. Only 60% of Chinese cities larger than the county level comply with national ambient air quality standards. Furthermore, owing to the 13% rise in SO_2 emissions between 2000 and 2004, the proportion of cities subject to very acid rain (pH lower than 4.5) went from 2% to 10%. Coal is responsible for about 70% of SO_2 emissions.[18] According to a

---

14 SEPA, *State of the Environment Report*, SEPA, Beijing, 2006.
15 "Chinese mayors urged to better serve people", *People's Daily*, 24 June 2001.
16 Author of *China's Water Crisis*. China Environmental Sciences Publishing House, 1999.
17 OECD, *Environmental Performance Review of China*, 2007.
18 Ibid.

study conducted in 1997 in 11 large Chinese cities,[19] suspended coal particles are responsible each year for 50,000 premature deaths and 400,000 cases of chronic bronchitis.

In China, these environmental problems were long considered secondary, the absolute priority being given to economic growth. But the effects of environmental damage today largely surpass the limits of "mere" ecological issues. The repercussions on growth prospects and the state's authority have turned the question of the environment into a major governmental concern.

As regards the economy, according to an official report published by the Chinese State Environmental Protection Administration (SEPA) and the National Bureau of Statistics (NBS), pollution problems cost China 3.05% of its GDP in 2004.[20] And this is a conservative estimate: according to a statement by Zhu Guangyao, former deputy director of NEPA, the figure is more likely 10% of the GDP.[21] Water pollution is what has the heaviest negative impact on the economy (about 56% of the total cost), ahead of air pollution (43%) and that of solid waste (1%).

The Harbin catastrophe is an example of how environmental problems can have repercussions on the state's authority.[22] In November 2005, a petrochemical plant accidentally released a large quantity of benzene into a river near the city of Harbin. Local officials at first tried to minimize the importance of the environmental damage, but in the face of sometimes violent public protests, Beijing had to step in to bring about the "resignation" of Xie Zenhua, then director of NEPA. The particularly large popular demonstrations provoked by the scale of the catastrophe were not, however, isolated events. Zhou Shengxian, the new NEPA director, counted 51,000 demonstrations related to pollution issues in the country in 2005.[23]

Given the economic consequences of environmental negligence and their impact on the state's authority, Beijing is gradually becoming aware of the need to take action. In 2005, Pan Yue, deputy director of the NEPA, cautioned that "the economic miracle will soon be over because the environment will soon be unable to keep up."[24]

Internal dynamics in favor of the environment

The 17th Chinese Communist Party (CCP) Congress, held on 16 October 2007, showed that the environment has become a priority on the political agenda. In the

---

19 Beijing, Chengdu, Chongqing, Guangzhou, Harbin, Jinan, Shanghai, Shenyang, Tianjin, Wuhan, et Xi'an.

20 SEPA and NBS, *China Green National Accounting Study Report 2004.*

21 "Pollution costs equal 10% of China's GDP", *China Daily*, 6 June 2006.

22 For a detailed report, see Neil Carter and Arthur Mol, "China and the Environment: Domestic and Transnational Dynamics of a Future Hegemon", *Environmental Politics* 15 (2006), 2.

23 "Wen sets out strategy to tackle environmental protection", Xinhuanet 23 April 2006.

24 Interview with China's Deputy Minister of Environment, *Der Spiegel*, 7 March 2005.

speech he gave on this occasion,[25] Hu Jintao, China's head of state and secretary-general of the CCP Central Committee, described in great detail the notion of "scientific development outlook" and managed to get it mentioned in the Constitution. The concept of "scientific development", which has become integrated into the party line, has three main characteristics: it should be balanced, sustainable and human. Hu Jintao has since expounded the idea of harmonious growth and circular economy on numerous occasions.

This new orientation indicates a major shift in the policy followed up to now. However, despite the centralized nature of the government, measures are not easy to implement and there is a growing gulf between the central government and local officials as to the importance that environmental questions should be given.

Quantitatively, China has made considerable efforts to protect its environment, as can be seen in the increase in environmental investments both in absolute value and in percentage of GDP. These went from about 500 billion RMB (0.4 % of GDP) in 1998 to about 2,000 billion RMB (1.4% of GDP) in 2005.[26]

Qualitatively, China has set up tools for a national governance of the environment. It is progressively moving away from a "command and control" environmental policy and is increasingly making more room for economic instruments and nonstate actors.[27] China does not merely put OECD environmental governance models into practice, it also sometimes comes up with innovative solutions.

The country introduced a "green GDP" index in the city of Chongqing in 2001, and released the aggregated national results for the first time in 2006.[28] The green GDP index has a number of flaws (particularly the limitations inherent in its method of calculation), but it can be a useful instrument to integrate the economic and environmental dimensions of development. If the media are in a position to fulfil their information function properly and the green GDP is published on a regular and transparent basis, then it can be considered as an interesting tool to evaluate the performance of government bodies by comparing economic and environmental criteria. However, the strict control exercised by the CCP over the media does not yet enable the green GDP to fully play this role.

China is the world's largest producer of sulphur dioxide (SO_2), at the rate of 25 million tons per year. According to SEPA, these emissions are more than double the environment's absorption capacity. Since 1998, the Chinese government has established a nationwide threshold for SO_2 emissions: the ceiling sets emissions quotas

---

25 Xinhua English. Full text of Hu Jintao's report at 17th Party Congress 25 October, 2007.

26 Mol and Carter, *China's Environmental Governance in Transition*, 2006.

27 Economy, Elizabeth, "Environmental Governance: the Emerging Economic Dimension", *Environmental Politics*, 2006, vol.15, no. 2, pp. 171-189.

28 World Watch Institute, "China Releases Green GDP Index, Tests New Development Path", 28 Sept. 2006.

figure 98: **CO₂ emissions for $2,000 of wealth produced, 1995-2005**

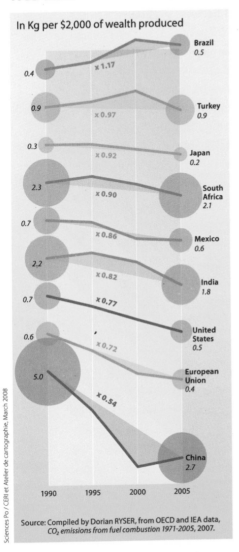

In Kg per $2,000 of wealth produced

Source: Compiled by Dorian RYSER, from OECD and IEA data, CO₂ emissions from fuel combustion 1971-2005, 2007.

Sciences Po / CERI et Atelier de cartographie, March 2008

for each province. Given the relative ineffectiveness of the system, the government has decided, in addition to the quota system, to institute a market for emissions permits. Two pilot projects are currently the subject of experiments in Taiyuan and in Jiangsu province and should lead to setting up emissions permits throughout the country.

Lastly, the development of energy self-sufficient eco-cities modelled on the city of Dongtan (400 projects are on the drawing board) demonstrates China's innovative capacity as regards development and growing recourse to renewable energy sources. China today is the largest producer of solar and wind power.

These domestic pro-environmental dynamics provide important leverage for China to participate in the international emissions reduction effort. In the current context, they are even the best guarantee for an effective commitment.

International levers to engage emerging countries

In the struggle against climate change, better results are to be expected from changes in domestic development models, and thus from policies founded on domestic choices, than from the signing of global and binding agreements. But there are also international levers for change which, owing to the outward-looking nature of economic growth in emerging countries, are potentially very powerful.

The first lever relates to energy security. Growth in emerging countries has been accompanied by a rise in raw materials prices of which they are currently large consumers. This rise in prices has slowed growth in most OECD countries that also import raw materials and particularly fossil fuels, but it doubly penalizes China and India which, because of their relative energy inefficiency, consume more of the expensive energy resources such as oil. The energy intensity of industrial production in China is 20% higher than that of OECD countries.[29] Improved energy efficiency in China and India

---

29 OECD (2007), op. cit.

would entail a decrease in energy-related CO_2 emissions. OECD countries thus have a vested interest in seeing China and India improve their efficiency. They have started contributing to this progress through investment and technological cooperation via carbon markets. This trend will be more pronounced in the future.

Raw materials, once processed, are often re-exported. To justify its emissions levels, China argues that it has gradually become "the world's factory".[30] Developed countries have in fact transferred part of their "ecological footprint" to China. If the share of the total energy consumption devoted to producing goods for export is 6% in the United States and 7% in the European Union, it is 28% in China.[31] Among these exported goods, various industrial products account for 40% of this energy, textiles and clothing for 12%, and chemical products for 10%. Data on the energy intensity reveal that goods exported by China encompass 34% of its energy-related emissions.[32]

A positive image is a considerable asset for emerging countries and their multinational companies; it is all the more important for China since its MNCs conduct most of their activity for export. They therefore cannot take the risk of losing market shares, and seek to protect themselves against environmental catastrophes. The number of ISO 14001 certified Chinese companies[33] rose from nine in 1996 to about 500 in the year 2000 and over 8,800 in 2004.[34]

Meeting international standards

International pressure is also applied in certain sectors via the demand to harmonize technical norms. In Europe, the introduction of greenhouse gas emissions policies has spawned fears of a loss of competitiveness, causing leaders to worry about possible de-localization of industries. In this context, industrialists and governments are considering measures to offset the disadvantages generated by carbon restrictions through border adjustments. Sectoral agreements are being discussed which concern the sectors most vulnerable to international competition, and which are the biggest polluters: cement, steel and aluminium. They should bring together companies in emerging countries and OECD countries as well as the governments of the most affected countries. Several versions are under study. In some of them, the adoption of more demanding technical norms, to be gradually harmonized on a world scale, should lead to the granting

---

30 See Yang Ailun, Greenpeace China climate change specialist, in *USA Today*: "Group: China tops world in CO2 emissions."
31 IEA data.
32 Gill and Kharas , *An East Asian Renaissance: Ideas for Economic Growth: Overview*, 2007.
33 Environmental management standard for organizations.
34 www.iso.org.

of carbon credits that can be traded on the market. Others have examined the possibility of developed countries funding sectoral public policies in emerging countries, resulting in mutual environmental benefits.

This prospect may help the Chinese and Indian leaders to modernize their industrial apparatus while reaping the benefits of a cooperative attitude that will be rewarded by technological cooperation and financing for this modernization.

On 1 July 2007, moreover, China cancelled export credits for 2,800 very polluting or high energy-consuming products[35] (including cement and steel), representing about 40% of the country's total exports.[36] The normalization stimulated by international demands can become an integral part of domestic policy. Indian companies, and particularly Arcelor Mittal, see in this unification of standards a way of escaping the constraints of European carbon regulations.

Protection for market access

The quantitative effects of emerging country participation in world trade are not easy to establish. In most sectors the growing participation of China, India and Brazil in trade liberalization has produced an increase in production, leading to an increase in pollution.[37] But the ecological relocation by OECD countries to countries such as China has not occurred on the same scale.[38] The WTO, via the Dispute Settlement Body (DSB), can provide incentive in cases of environmental disputes. The European Union has for instance imposed trade sanctions on Chinese aquatic products because of antibiotic residuals in the food.[39] These sanctions have forced the Chinese authorities to measure the cost of their environmental negligence and take steps to protect the environment.[40]

Beyond that, the rise of protectionism in most developed countries can instil fear that barriers to the importation of certain products may be raised in both the European Union and the United States in the name of environmental protection. That is the crux of the debate surrounding US and French proposals to make "border adjustments" to even out competition conditions between countries that tax carbon emissions and the others. Protection of market access is thus an element that can modify environmental policies.

---

35 "China cuts export-tax rebate", *Wall Street Journal*, 20 June 2007.

36 "Tax rebates removed, cut to curb exports", *China Daily*, 20 June 2007.

37 OECD (2007), op. cit. Box 7.1: Ecological consequences of WTO accession: CCICED's assessment.

38 World Bank (2005), "Are Foreign Investors Attracted to Weak Environmental Regulations? Evaluating the Evidence from China." *Policy Research Working Paper Series*, 3505.

39 WTO.

40 SEPA.

Towards a global deal?

Emerging countries are more inclined than in the past to engage in the international emissions reduction effort. But China, whose participation is a condition for India's, would only agree to be party to a post-Kyoto regime if a certain number of conditions are met. And the participation of the United States is an essential prerequisite. The two countries together represent more than 40% of greenhouse gas emissions. Beyond the reality of figures, China is engaged with the United States in a power game.

Next, economic incentives must be clear. Indeed, the reorientation of China and India's growth trajectory, and in particular the financing of their energy transition, is costly, at least for the moment, since the benefits will not be reaped for a long time to come. There are solutions, particularly in terms of improving energy efficiency, even if its potential should not be exaggerated. If the fruits of efforts to preserve the environment are to benefit all, it is normal that all, emerging and developed countries alike, bear the costs.

The Clean Development Mechanism (CMD) can no longer remain the only instrument that encourages LDCs to adopt clean technologies in the post-Kyoto regime. Today, about 70 projects are being developed in China, which counts with India among the main beneficiaries of the CMD. The effort is appreciable, but the real impact of projects remains marginal. The CMD hinges on the idea of technology transfer from OECD countries to LDCs. This transfer is no longer sufficient to counter the current crisis and we must consider reforming the CMD to make it a programmatic or sectoral mecanism that could be useful in defining and applying public policies in LDCs. The reasoning in terms of technology transfer must thus be discarded in favour of another, in terms of technology co-development and dissemination.

Lastly, a "global deal", taken as a package that links China and emerging countries to the international emissions reduction effort, is necessary. This package includes a trade aspect: it is by guaranteeing emerging countries that environmental norms are not protectionist measures in disguise that this "deal" can be reached. It is by sharing the costs of energy transition in emerging countries towards clean energy sources that they will become positive actors for the world environment.

Bibliography •

Boillot J.-J., "Inde 2025, les paradoxes de la grande transformation". *Futuribles.*

Carter, N. and A. Mol (2006). "China and the Environment: Domestic and Transnational Dynamics of a Future Hegemon". *Environmental Politics*, vol.15, no. 2, pp. 330-344.

—— (2006), "China's Environmental Governance in Transition", *Environmental Politics*, vol.15, no. 2, pp. 149-170.

Chinese Council on International Cooperation for Environment and Development (CCICED) and International Institute for Sustainable Development (IISD) (2006). *One Lifeboat: China's and the World Environment and Development.*

Dean, J., Lovely, M. and W. Hua (2005). *Are Foreign Investors Attracted to Weak Environmental Regulations? Evaluating the Evidence from China*, World Bank Policy research working paper series no. 3505.

Earth Policy Institute (2005). *Eco-Economy Update. Learning From China: Why the Western Economic Model Will not Work for the World.*

Economy, E. (2006). "Environmental Governance: the Emerging Economic Dimension", *Environmental Politics*, vol.15, no. 2, pp. 171-189.

—— (2004). *The River Runs Black: The Environmental Challenge to China's Future*, Ithaca, NY: Cornell University Press.

Gill, I. and K. Homi (2007). *An East Asian Renaissance: Ideas for Economic Growth*, Washington DC, World Bank.

Ma J. (1999). *China's Water Crisis*, Beijing, China Environmental Sciences Publishing House.

Goldman S. (2003). "Dreaming with BRICs: The Path to 2050", *Global Economics*, Paper no. 99.

OECD (2007). Environmental Performance Reviews: China, July.

World Bank China quick facts http://web.worldbank.org/WBSITE/EXTERNAL/COUNTRIES/EASTASIA-PACIFICEXT/CHINAEXTN/0,,contentMDK:20680895~pagePK:1497618~piPK:217854~theSitePK:318950,00.html,<http://web.worldbank.org/WBSITE/EXTERNAL/COUNTRIES/EASTASIAPACIFICEXT/CHINAEXTN/0,,contentMDK:20680895~pagePK:1497618~piPK:217854~theSitePK:318950,00.html>.

Netherlands Environmental Assessment Agency (2006). China now no. 1 in CO2 emissions; USA in second position: http://www.mnp.nl/en/dossiers/Climatechange/moreinfo/Chinanowno1inCO2emissionsUSAinsecondposition.html <http://www.mnp.nl/en/dossiers/Climatechange/moreinfo/Chinanowno1inCO2emissionsUSAinsecondposition.html>.

SEPA (2006), State of the Environment Report, SEPA, Beijing http://english.zhb.gov.cn/ghjh/index.htm <http://english.zhb.gov.cn/ghjh/index.htm>.

People's Daily, "Chinese Mayors Urged to Better Serve People", June 24, 2001.http://english.peopledaily.com.cn/english/200106/24/enG20010624_73398.html.

Xinhuanet, "Wen sets out strategy to tackle environmental protection", April 23, 2006. http://au.china-embassy.org/eng/xw/t248304.htm.

Xinhua English, "Hu Jintao's report at 17th Party Congress, October 25, 2007", http://www.china.org.cn/english/congress/229611.htm.

China Daily, "Tax rebates removed, cut to curb exports", June 20, 2007 http://www.chinadaily.com.cn/china/20006/20/content_897889.htm.

Globalization and Inequality in Emerging Countries: The Cases of India and China

Pierre-Noël Giraud, Jean François Huchet and Joël Ruet[1]

To analyze the dynamics of inequality induced by the globalization process underway in emerging countries, we will use the concepts devised by Giraud (1996 and 2007), and particularly those of competitive vs. protected individuals on the one hand and nomadic vs. sedentary capitalist actors on the other hand.

Nomadic firms are those that create relations of cooperation and/or competition between individuals in different countries, or "territories" as we will henceforth term them. They can range from firms going global down to the individual entrepreneur. Sedentary firms do the same thing as nomadic firms, but solely within a single territory.

In any territory subject to an opening-up process and put in competition with other territories by nomadic actors, it is possible to distinguish two groups of individuals among the active population: the competitives and the protected. The competitives are those that the nomadic actors place in direct competition with individuals located in other territories. They are thus involved in the production of internationally tradable goods and services. They can only keep their jobs if they are "competitive" on the world market, in the ordinary sense of the term. The protected are put in competition, sometimes an extremely fierce competition, by sedentary firms on the same territory. They are therefore only in competition amongst themselves in the production of goods and services for local consumption.

---

1   Giraud: 2006.

The first level at which to analyze inequality is thus the respective average income trends—for the competitives on the one hand, who confront and take advantage of globalization, and for the protected, on the other. These depend on three interrelated factors: numerical growth and growth of wealth per capita in the competitive group—which depends on their relative competitiveness on the world market—endogenous growth within the protected group, and the exchange dynamics between the two groups, particularly the share of income the competitives are obliged, or agree, to spend on local goods and services.

The second aspect of the evolution of inequality is the way in which average gains are distributed across each group, according to level of education and competence, as well as the monopoly positions some individuals or groups have managed to achieve. But of course, since many competences, especially unskilled labour, can be used by both groups, job markets cause the distribution of competitive and protected incomes to interpenetrate. Certain protected people, generally the most qualified, are drawn upward by the rapid increase in income of the most qualified competitives. Certain competitive people, in particular the least qualified, are drawn downward by the existence of a large mass of unqualified labour in rural areas and the urban informal sector.

The resulting shape of income distribution, a way of measuring social inequality, thus depends first on the intensity of the driving mechanisms operating on average protected income by competitive income, and second on the functioning, of the goods and labour markets. These are what distribute the growth of wealth among groups and within groups. Market imperfections can have classic economic causes, but social ones as well, for instance language barriers or discrimination of any nature: state, social, religious or cultural. These all hinder the "free" working of markets.

The third facet to take into account to understand the dynamics of inequality is the geographical dimension. Legal obstacles as well as costs related to the mobility of people and goods and services—costs that depend on communications infrastructures—naturally fragment both labour and goods markets and hence play an important role in the spatial diffusion of competitives' wealth within their own group and towards the protected. Thus disparities are not only spatially carved out between provinces, and between cities and rural areas, but also within "global" cities themselves. This for instance explains the steadfast preference of poor urban dwellers for slums in the heart of the city rather than project housing 30 km from the centre. Within the city they are much more likely to capture a share of their competitive neighbours' income by sheer proximity to them.

States and their local institutions act in many ways on these intertwined dynamics that contribute to reducing or aggravating inequality: by regulating the functioning of markets, by favouring national nomadic firms or by stimulating concentration among them in order to improve their competitiveness for instance. They also act by supplying public goods ranging from research, education and health care to communication infrastructures. They can also act by making pure transfers: family allowances, unemployment benefits, etc.

If one is willing to admit that market imperfections are omnipresent and that state intervention also has political motivations that cannot be boiled down to a purely economic rationality, then the conclusion must be drawn that it is illusory to claim to establish "general economic laws" for changing patterns of inequality, or even laws applicable only to a subgroup such as emerging countries rapidly on their way to catching up.

Market imperfections are indeed widespread, but to varying degrees within a territory and between territories, in the processes of concentration of wealth—increasing returns on scale, monopoly rents, economies of agglomeration, etc.—and diffusion of it: mobility and substitutability of production factors as well as goods and services, externalities related to the dissemination of knowledge, etc.

It is moreover obvious that states that intervene in these processes do not do so solely according to a single economic goal, for instance to maximize the speed at which they catch up with rich countries (maximum per capita GDP growth) or reduce the absolute poverty index. States also intervene with more specifically political objectives, which themselves depend on historical and social factors, such as the societal degree of "tolerance" for internal inequalities.

In short, the elementary dynamics behind the creation, concentration and diffusion of wealth engendered by globalization and politically influenced by states are beginning to be well understood. However, no generalization can be made about emerging countries as a whole, given the complex intertwining of these dynamics that are acting on a geographical, social and human substratum shaped by the long history of each country. This remains an empirical question that can only be treated in depth through case studies.

This chapter undertakes two such case studies for India and China. Given their population and the types of catching-up processes the two countries have engaged in, the dynamics of inequality within each of them indeed has, as we shall point out in conclusion, significant economic consequences for the rest of the world, which is not necessarily the case for South Africa or even Brazil.

Before that, we will simply gauge the empirical diversity of poor and emerging countries by presenting and commenting on a few figures taken from the World Bank's report on development indicators published in 2007 (WDI 2007).

Growth, disparities and poverty in emerging countries: an overview

The World Bank's 2007 report on development indicators (WDI 2007) gives an overview of changes in per capita income, inequality and the rate of absolute poverty since the early 1980s for a sample of some 60 poor and emerging countries with available data. It takes as an implicit conceptual framework the

figure 99: **Growth / inequality / poverty triangle**

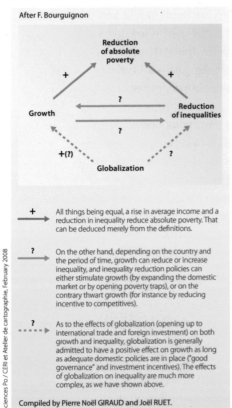

After F. Bourguignon

+	All things being equal, a rise in average income and a reduction in inequality reduce absolute poverty. That can be deduced merely from the definitions.
?	On the other hand, depending on the country and the period of time, growth can reduce or increase inequality, and inequality reduction policies can either stimulate growth (by expanding the domestic market or by opening poverty traps), or on the contrary thwart growth (for instance by reducing incentive to competitors).
?	As to the effects of globalization (opening up to international trade and foreign investment) on both growth and inequality, globalization is generally admitted to have a positive effect on growth as long as adequate domestic policies are in place ("good governance" and investment incentives). The effects of globalization on inequality are much more complex, as we have shown above.

Compiled by Pierre Noël GIRAUD and Joël RUET.

Sciences Po / CERI et Atelier de cartographie, February 2008

"growth-inequality-poverty" triangle made popular by François Bourguignon. This figure provides a simple illustration of the complex links tying globalization to what is henceforth the central objective of development policies: the reduction of absolute poverty.

Below are the most recent income Gini coefficients for a certain number of emerging and OECD countries.

We note a considerable dispersion among income Gini coefficients within emerging countries. Generally speaking, social inequalities are lower in Asia than in Latin America and Africa with the exception of China, which in the last 15 years has reached the level of inequality characterizing some Latin American countries, whereas it began its catching-up process with a Gini coefficient of just over 30, very nearly on a par with India at the same time.

Changes in inequality over the past two decades

Empirically, here are the major trends that emerge from the changes recorded in some 60 poor and emerging countries according to the WDI 2007 report. We note that from the early 1980s to 2004:

- the absolute poverty rate was considerably reduced in East Asia, more moderately in South Asia. In 1996, this rate even started to decrease in sub-

table 8: **Growth, Poverty, Inequality in a selection of emerging and poor countries 1981-2004**

Pakistan (2002)	30.6	Chile (2003)	54.9
Indonesia (2002)	34.3	Brazil (2004)	57
Vietnam (2004)	34.4	South Africa (2000)	57.8
India (2004)	36.8	Norway (2000)	25.8
Russia (2002)	39.9	Germany (2000)	28.3
Mexico (2004)	46.1	Korea (1998)	31.6
China (2004)	46.9	France (1995)	32.7

Saharan Africa, but owing to population growth, the number of poor rose between 1990 and 2004;

- among the 36 countries in the sample that experienced growth in average per capita income, 26 also experienced a rise in inequality;
- in at least six of them, per capita income growth should have reduced poverty, but a rise in inequality overcame it and poverty finally increased;
- inequalities rose in 20 of the 23 countries where average per capita income diminished;
- however, nearly one-quarter of the countries show exceptions to the rise in inequality, with ten countries having an increase in average income and a drop in inequality, and even countries where inequality was reduced despite a drop in average income.

For India and China, which make up part of the sample and which we will discuss in detail further on, here are some additional data.

Growth, particularly in China, has spectacularly reduced the rate of absolute poverty and the number of poor. However, as will be seen in greater detail in the following two sections, such growth has coincided with a sometimes rapid increase in inequality. Thus the reduction in absolute poverty was not as significant as it might have been if the benefits of growth in the catching-up process had been more evenly distributed, unless of course the rise in inequality is itself a condition for the very fast growth of competitives' income. We shall return to this question in the concluding remarks.

In the two countries, inequality among the Chinese provinces or Indian states has increased.

In China and India, how do the legacies of socialist and developmentalist periods fit in with the game of nomadic and sedentary firms in the current trend toward globalization? With what results? This is what the following two sections propose to examine.

China

The Maoist legacy

In 1978, when China engaged in "reforms" and opened the door to economic globalization in which it would become a major actor, the legacy left by the Maoist era was as follows: a centralized and omnipresent party-state with branches all the way down to basic production units; within the party-state, in the general framework fixed by the central powers, relative autonomy at the level of the provinces and large and even secondary cities; a rural industrial tradition drawing its source

figure 100: **Per capita GDP and poverty in China and India, 1981-2006**

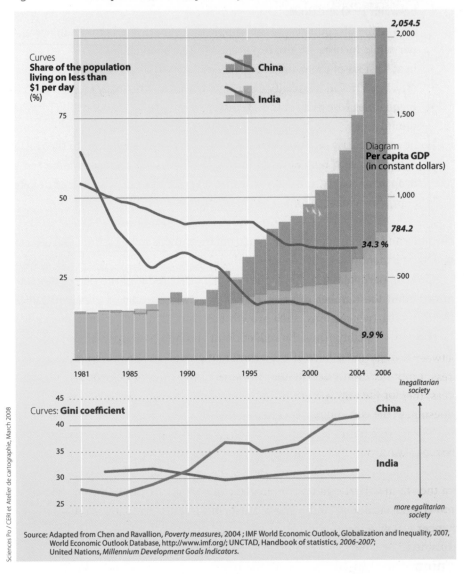

Source: Adapted from Chen and Ravallion, *Poverty measures*, 2004 ; IMF World Economic Outlook, Globalization and Inequality, 2007, World Economic Outlook Database, http://www.imf.org/; UNCTAD, Handbook of statistics, *2006-2007*; United Nations, *Millennium Development Goals Indicators*.

Sciences Po / CERI et Atelier de cartographie, March 2008

in the Great Leap Forward and reinforced by the people's communes; a method of reform proceeding by pilot experiments later applied across the board if success-ful (this method first widens disparities, then reduces them); a multi-millennial concern by the centre about the danger of the country's breaking up; a socialist respect for the worker, the factory, technology; and a basic educational level ini-tially much more egalitarian than in India.

At the end of the Maoist period in 1978, China, like India, had one of the lowest income Gini coefficients of all the Southern countries: between 30 and 35 (more than 60 for Brazil and South Africa). However, stark inequalities remained

figure 101: **Per capita and annual growth by region in China and India, 1978-2004**

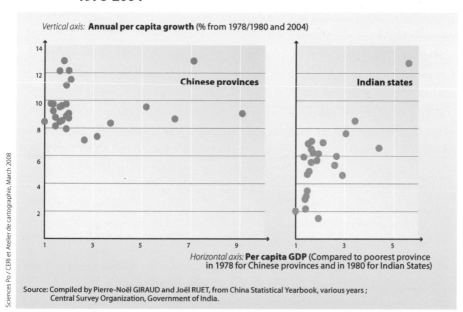

Vertical axis: **Annual per capita growth** (% from 1978/1980 and 2004)

Chinese provinces

Indian states

Horizontal axis: **Per capita GDP** (Compared to poorest province in 1978 for Chinese provinces and in 1980 for Indian States)

Source: Compiled by Pierre-Noël GIRAUD and Joël RUET, from China Statistical Yearbook, various years ; Central Survey Organization, Government of India.

Sciences Po / CERI et Atelier de cartographie, March 2008

between the city and the countryside. 80% of the active population worked in rural areas. Only 22% of the active population were industrial wage-earners in urban areas, thereby benefiting from the socialist system known as the "iron rice bowl" (housing, social welfare), on the eve of reforms.

Inequality since the 1978 reforms

On the whole, "competitives" undeniably had an upward mobility effect on the "protected". Very sustained growth provided for a spectacular reduction in the number of individuals living below the poverty threshold of one dollar per day, as explained in section 2.

Income rose for all quintiles of the population. However, between 1993 and 2004, annual per capita income growth was +3.4% for the 20% poorest, but +7.1% for the 20% richest. Consequently, inequalities among households measured by the consumption Gini coefficient rose sharply in China. Between 1993 and 2004, the coefficient rose by seven points. It was 47 in continental China in 2004, compared with 33 in Taiwan and 32 in Korea. Estimates presented in a recent Asian Development Bank report entitled *Inequality in Asia* (2007) indicate that with the same growth rate, if inequality had not risen, the absolute poverty rate would have dropped below 5% (instead of 10%).

Inequalities between urban and rural areas

The initial reforms applied to the peasantry, as was the case in Korea. They were relatively egalitarian in that peasant families were granted locally well-distributed land-use rights. However, this system allowed significant differences to persist, due to varying degrees of fertility of the regions and distance from town markets. Peasant income increases, which reached a record level during the first half of the 1990s with an annual rate of 14%, ran out of steam from the early 1990s. Competitives involved in industry and services, which have been growing at a rate of 10% or more since the 1990s, have of course only shared a decreasing portion of their income with the protected rural agricultural workers, agriculture thus increasing only by 2% per annum, and rural income by 3%.

In the countryside, the weight of numbers is decisive. The number of peasants doubled between 1950 and 1990 for a cultivated surface area that remained practically stable. Despite higher yields since 1978, the fragmentation of land has reached such a point that it dooms most peasants to low incomes. Out of the 248 million rural households in China, 200 million farm plots of land with an average surface area of 0.6 ha. Over the whole planet, only Vietnamese peasants cultivate smaller plots of land. The French farmer cultivates an average surface area 35 times larger, the American farmer 100 times.

The levelling of incomes between cities and countryside and between industry and agriculture, usually occurs through rural-urban drift. For easily understandable political and economic reasons when one considers the extension of slums in South Asia, that drift is fairly controlled in China. But this undeniably widens the inequality between large cities and the rural milieu.

The difference with city dweller incomes, which narrowed somewhat in the 1980s, has considerably widened since then. Today it is at its highest level since 1949. A rural dweller earns 3.2 times less on average than a city dweller (the lowest divergence to date, reached in 1985, remains 1.8). And this gap is widening for peasants in the interior regions and the far west who earn nearly ten times less than the average annual income of someone living in Shanghai. Even in industrial jobs, for equal skills and seniority, wages in large cities are 50% greater than what they are in average-sized cities in the interior.

Growing inequality in access to public services

Against a backdrop of rising per capita income, the proportion of private funding of once public services has risen sharply, accentuating inequality and causing a slump in household consumption. Moreover, between 1978 and 1994, China organized the phased decentralization of its tax system. The lowest echelons of the administration now manage a large portion of health and education expenditure. The wealthier local governments have the means to redistribute, but not the poorer ones. For instance, tax revenue for an inhabitant of Shanghai is 15 times higher today than for someone living in Guizhou Province, a fact that contributes to widening the inequalities in access to public goods and services.

The difficulty of access to education in rural areas has thus produced a sharp rise in illiteracy in recent years, with a 36% increase between the year 2000 and 2005; it now affects 116 million people, primarily peasant children. Nearly one million peasant children leave the school system each year because their parents cannot afford the cost of education (Rotman 2007).

Widening inequality in the cities

The widening of inequality in urban areas is the result of two phenomena. First, despite the *hukou* system (a sort of internal passport that prohibits a rural dweller from going to work in large cities, legally at least), migrant workers have arrived from rural areas en masse, even though they remain excluded from the urban education, housing and social welfare systems. Second, massive layoffs have been made in the public sector since 1994 to restructure state-owned companies. These have affected between 30 and 50 million people, creating more vulnerability among large segments of the urban population that belonged to the "socialist" system. One worker out of three in the public sector is estimated to have been laid off at some point in 1994. Over two-thirds allegedly found new jobs but in more unstable conditions than those provided by the former Socialist "iron rice bowl".

The development of private entrepreneurship and corruption has also led to the formation of a very wealthy class in the space of some 15 years. It is hard to know the precise figures in a country characterized by mass tax evasion, but their numbers have skyrocketed since 1992, the date when the first Chinese millionaire was counted. A study conducted by a foreign consulting firm estimated that there were 236,000 Chinese millionaires (in US dollars) in 2004, with a rate of increase of about 12% per year. Nearly 2 million Chinese households have available savings of over 100,000 euros.

Towards policies to control inequality?

In China, just as the state claims to be seriously concerned about environmental problems today, growing inequality is also the topic of lively debate. With Beijing's support, cities in the centre of the country such as Wuhan and Chongqing have undertaken to catch up with the coastal cities, which nevertheless continue to grow at an impressive rate.

The "harmonious society" policy advocated by the Chinese Communist Party since 2003 and reinforced during the recent 17th Party Congress is an attempt to refocus growth on domestic consumption, with a rise in purchasing power for the middle classes and rural migrants arriving in the cities. This policy involves reducing inequality in access to public goods, particularly education and health care, which should make possible a decrease in the rate of household precautionary savings and boost consumption. Out-of-pocket medical expenses for the Chinese citizen today are 61% of medical fees (compared to 20% in Thailand, 30% in Brazil and 13% in the United States). As for education, the share of private funding has topped the 50% mark since the early 2000s (it is 1% in Norway).

The first measures aiming to reduce urban/rural disparities were taken in 2004 (Lardy 2006). As regards tax policy, the tax on agricultural produce has been gradually eliminated and peasant income tax has been reduced. The effects of these measures have nevertheless been limited. Tax savings are only about 2% of the rural dwellers' consumer expenses, and moreover, other taxes have been introduced at the same time in the rural milieu. In education, early measures involved waiving tuition for the children of the poorest rural households. These measures were complemented by increased education subsidies at the lowest echelons of the administration, which are precisely the ones responsible for financing these expenditures but are severely lacking in the means to do so.

It is still too early to analyze the repercussions of these measures. As with public health care expenditure, there is a huge lag to make up for. Education expenses today only represent 2.7% of GDP and they are very largely concentrated in the cities. The Chinese government recently announced huge budget increases for education, hoping to reach top the 4% mark in 2010.

India

India has 4,693 communities inventoried by the Anthropological Survey of India (1996), based on self-declared communal membership during a vast anthropological survey conducted from 1991 to 1995 among 25,000 people in over 3,500 villages and 1,000 cities. This gives an idea of the divide and thus the potential inequalities between urban and rural areas, between ethnolinguistic, caste or living communities, and lastly among social-professional categories. Two-thirds of the population live in rural areas. Half of the population earns a living from primary sector activities. To understand the political-economic trajectories, they must therefore be identified at a fairly disaggregated level. In the history of independent India, three distinct political-economic phases should be distinguished, the first two of which (from 1947 to 1971 and from 1971 to 1984) correspond to a closed economy that gradually reduced internal inequality, while the third (from 1985 to today) has gradually engaged the country in the inequality dynamics of globalization.

Inequality over three political-economic phases

From 1947 to 1971, a mixed economic regime was in place, based on the standard tools of developmentalism, around a coalition of "proprietary classes" (capital, feudalism, high caste/class urban intelligentsia), according to Bhardan (1984). In a situation where, in 1947, 85% of the population lived in rural areas with the modern economy concentrated in a few large cities, public financial transfers went from the cities to the countryside. This initiated a nationwide trend towards reduction in economic inequality. Rural development extended the geographical scope of industrial development, which under British rule had been confined to a few industrial cities (Bombay, Calcutta, Ahmedabad). Many inequalities diminished between states, between urban and rural areas, and probably, to some extent, among the thousands of listed communities. When inequality was not reduced, the level of inequality (communal, from one class to another) was at least stabilized. There are two notable exceptions: the aboriginal communities living on the site of major development projects (i.e. dams) and inequalities between Hindus and Muslims. This last exception is rooted in the fact that many of the most affluent Muslims left India in 1947 for Pakistan. Although this trend is purely statistical, the Muslim community nevertheless found itself suddenly orphaned of its elites and was marginalized in the "Congress" system of proprietary classes.

In the 1967 elections, for the first time in the country's history, Congress lost key states. In 1971, Indira Gandhi led the party of Congress to victory again but on a profoundly altered political-economic platform. India entered an era of "mixed socialism". Up to 1984, the political intermediaries in society were shifting. The accumulation of physical capital remained a central model, but with intermediation in the form of social capital constituted by communal ties, class factors, and at the level of the states, which became major actors in negotiation (no longer the federal government alone). The overall dynamics of inequality was still on a downward turn, but new phenomena appeared: the emergence of medium-sized cities as relays for the development-oriented administration; what Gilbert Etienne calls the "overall rural development process", the start of agricultural mechanization creating activities for small local workshops, themselves generating local purchasing power for basic manufactured goods; and especially, state payments to the formerly underprivileged classes via specific development programmes for tribal or aboriginal communities, untouchables or *Dalits*, and specific programmes and administrative bodies set up to help the inhabitants of certain slums. Though not fully able to solve the problems, they did their job of social conversion and redistribution, contributing to the expansion of essential services such as running water, electricity and to a lesser extent sewage treatment. These programmes were complemented by more and more reservations of both local and elected offices, which largely contributed to changing the face of Indian democracy.

These changes stand in contrast with what was, during this period, probably a univocal reduction in inequality. They are the consequence of Green Revolution policies that lifted entire regions out of poverty. In this process, the internal inequalities within the Green Revolution Society increased dependence on the initial capital endowment.

Since 1985, a "liberalization" process was initiated and the political economy refocused on industry and partially on civil society, which gained autonomy from the state reference in a drive toward social modernization. Nationalism, liberalism and economic revival of cities went hand-in-hand. As categories, "competitive" and "protected" have now gained a certain relevance in explaining social realities in India today, although these must be applied with caution.

Globalization, competitives and poverty

The effects of globalization and competitive/protected dynamics are very apparent in India. In the 1993 to 2004 period, 70 million jobs were created in the formal sector, including 13.4 million in manufacturing and 28.8 million in services. The services sector is thus increasingly driving the job market. It is partially made up of export-oriented competitives and brings about the development of related protected sectors (construction services, hotel business, other personal services, etc.). Among the jobs created in the formal sector, 42% are for employees with a medium educational level (incomplete secondary education), compared with a total of 26.9% for people who have secondary education and higher education; in the services sector the figures are respectively 28.1% and 40.5%. Demand in the sector is thus increasing income disparities between skilled and unskilled workers.

During the same period, the income ratio of the 20% richest to the 20% poorest went from 4.85 to 5.22, a 1.18% annual increase in disparity (to be compared with 3.7% for China on the same indicator during the same period). The income of the 0.1% richest rose from 1.2% of the national income for the 1982-83 fiscal year (a historic low) to 4.2 % in 1997-98, that of the 0.01% richest from 0.3% to 1.8% of the national income during the same period. In 2006, India surpassed Japan in the number of billionaires in dollars (36 compared to 24).

From 1993 to 2004, India went from a Gini coefficient of 32.9 to 36.2. The coefficient was higher in urban areas (37.6) than in rural areas (30.5). The impact of this growing inequality is reflected, as in China, in a smaller reduction of the absolute poverty rate (less than a dollar a day) than what could have been achieved if recorded growth had been divided according to the income distribution recorded at the start of the period. The absolute poverty rate today is allegedly 31%, instead of the real figure observed of 34%.

From federal states to metropolises

The inter-state Gini coefficient went from a little over 15 in 1980 to nearly 23 in 1996. This is related to the concentration of investment in a few large states as well as the concentration of remaining large pockets of poverty in only six states. Certainly it is no surprise to find Bihar, Uttar Pradesh, Madhya Pradesh and Rajasthan—given their high population growth and endemic poverty—among the six states. But it is more surprising to find among them Western Bengal, which underwent a major agrarian reform under its communist regime and today is starting to attract investors; more surprising still to find among them the state of Maharashtra, which for a long time was the first destination for both FDI and national industrial investment and which is still among the leading recipients today. Analysis by district would show a high contrast between the very rich western part of Maharashtra and the very poor and isolated northeast, or even the eastern districts of this fairly developed state which is nevertheless threatened by an unprecedented economic and social crisis in agriculture (the Indian rural milieu is experiencing a crisis unknown in human history, with 100,000 suicides among peasants in ten years). This "fracture" in India overlaps a very clear-cut geographical reality, a divide between the country's northeast (except for Punjab, Haryana and Delhi) on the one hand and the west and south on the other. The former group of states is undergoing a process of population growth which, although slowing, is still very high. The literacy rate remains weak, particularly among women. The fertility rate remains very high (usually about 3.5 and often close to or exceeding 5) as opposed to the south (in most districts, it is lower than 3, and often 2), where the literacy rate is very low, especially among women. As a corollary, the capacity to engage in economic development that would "absorb" the demographic transition is very unevenly distributed. This capacity is well measured by the "dependency ratio" (the ratio of nonworking people—children and the elderly—to the working population), with variations as high as 100%. A state such as Bihar, already the most densely populated in India, continues to have a dependency ratio of 0.95, which is characteristic of underdevelopment, compared with states such as Kerala or Tamil Nadu, where the ratio holds steady at 0.56, in other words a rate closer to that of developed countries. The effects of globalization will not bring the absolute poverty rate down in the north; that will require draconian public education and redistribution policies. The relevant echelon for competitive activities becomes the metropolis, even the industrial metropolis, whose numbers have risen in the past 60 years from three to a few dozen (the 2001 census counted 35 cities of over one million inhabitants).

In short, competitives are emerging in information technology and large-scale industry, which has a well-known spillover effect in localized industrial districts but also in conurbations (the cities of Bombay, Thane, New Bombay, Pune and Nasik for instance) and the "industrial corridors" (Bangalore-Mysore and Bangalore-Chennai for instance) that are currently developing. Most of these competitives are employed by large Indian nomadic firms undergoing a rapid process of multinationalization (see the chapter by Ruet and Huchet in this volume). But by comparison with China, the proportion of skilled and semiskilled jobs is greater and the trickle-down effect is less palpable, in terms of both the number employed and geographical scope.

Communal fragmentation, the 'protected', and poverty in the informal sector

Another aspect of inequality specific to India is the economic impact of social fragmentation by caste and religious community. Since independence, the status of a certain number of lower castes has improved, in particular after they achieved political representation at the national and local level through electoral quotas in the more than 600,000 villages in India. 92% of the Muslims (whose number totals 130 million) work in the informal sector, a sector that concentrates 79% of the jobs or activities, and are thus highly vulnerable socially. The Muslim situation is comparable to that of the scheduled castes (SC) (this category includes the erstwhile "untouchables", now also called *Dalits*), and scheduled tribes (ST) or aboriginals, who benefit from positive discrimination measures in public sector jobs. The Muslims are not eligible for this policy, whereas their social and economic situation is also a consequence of discrimination.

Employees in the small-scale sector, which long benefited from "Gandhian socialist" policies protecting them not only from external competition but also from large firms, today find themselves exposed to market competition, primarily from China. India's opening up to globalization is less univocal than that of China. In any event it requires heavy investment in the industrial fabric of small "sedentary" businesses and second stage relocations (relocation of low added value computer industries to Vietnam for instance) are starting to take place.

The protected are found in large numbers in partially opened up rural areas. However, the development of rural road infrastructure and Indian agricultural markets on the internet (*e-choupal*) are putting them more and more in competition, despite their relatively low productivity (public investment in agriculture reached its lowest level between 1997 and 2007 with the Ninth and Tenth Five-year Plans). This is taken all the more seriously today since 200 million Indians are directly involved in agricultural activities (about 40 million households), 70% of the population lives in rural areas (the potential for rural industry also depends on the agrarian economy), the sector's contribution to national growth can be considerably improved, and notably, 170 out of India's 602 districts today are affected by Maoist-inspired Naxalite guerrilla movements; 55 of these districts now receive special development aid. Lastly, there is a strong relationship in India (as in Africa) between alleviating poverty and preserving natural capital for the tribals, hard hit by poverty, as well as other poor peasants living in seriously degraded forest areas and areas that constitute world reserves of biodiversity.

It is hard to draw conclusions regarding the future of public policy and India, but New Delhi is certainly beginning to be convinced that physical, human and natural capital are not perfectly interchangeable and that the country's catching up requires a balanced development of all three. The previous government learned this to its cost in the 2004 general elections. The current government is afraid that this reality will catch up with it in the next nationwide elections to be held in 2009 at the latest.

On the geographical, societal and human substratum handed down by three decades of socialist policy, the creation of wealth in India and China, powerfully stimulated by large nomadic firms—including Indian and Chinese firms—in the process of globalization, has been accompanied by a sharp increase in social and geographic inequality. The dynamics of concentrating new wealth largely prevail for the moment over the dynamics of diffusing wealth. In neither country is the government highly engaged in policies to correct these inequalities so far, even if the governments seem to be showing increasing concern for the problem and have already implemented certain measures toward reducing absolute poverty.

Indeed, to allow inequality to grow or, on the contrary, to reduce it by stringent public policies is one of the fundamental strategic dilemmas of catching up that emerging countries have to confront. To be sure, the current competitiveness of their competitives depends partly on the poverty of the protected. It is thanks to them that an Indian engineer who holds a PhD from Stanford University can actually live much better in Bangalore than in Berkeley with a third of the salary at the current exchange rate. From this angle, the widening of inequalities between a territory's competitives and protected puts the competitives at an advantage in that it improves their relative competitiveness. But it is also true that more self-centred growth, a sort of "Asian Fordism"—not targeting the entire population, of course, but seeking to heighten the emergence of a middle class—could in the long run benefit the competitives just as much or even more, by reducing the disparities with the protected, to whom a large portion of this demand for a rising middle class would be addressed.

Owing to their population size and the economic weight China and India have already achieved, this strategic choice will have all the more consequence in what are today's richest countries. There is indeed no doubt that the current advantage of Indian and Chinese competitives, largely based on the apparently lasting poverty of their protected, is wreaking havoc among the competitives of rich countries. The latter cannot all manage to raise their level of skill or innovation fast enough to remain in the running, and thus find themselves thrown back en masse into the protected group. Thus there are continually more and more of these protected who are seeking to satisfy the demand coming from the "resisting" competitives of their territory, a demand that they have no reason to increase. An increase in inequality is the consequence, which is empirically observable in most rich countries. For some (Giraud 1996 and 2007), the likely outcome of this process is nothing less than the wiping out of the middle class. It is thus plain that there is a long-term objective interest shared by the middle classes of rich countries and those burgeoning in emerging countries. Middle classes of the world... unite?

Bibliography •

Asian Development Bank (2007), *Inequality in Asia.*

Chaudhuri, S. and M. Ravallion (2007). *Partially Awakened Giants: Uneven Growth in China and India.* World Bank. Working Paper.

Giraud, P.-N. (1996). *L'Inégalité du Monde*, Paris: Gallimard, Folio-Actuel.

—— (2006). "Comment la globalisation façonne le monde?" *Politique Etrangère* 4.

—— (2007), "An Essay on Global Economic Prospects," *Constellation*, 14 (1), January 2007, New York.

Lardy, N. (2006). "China: Towards a Consumption-Driven Growth Path," Policy Brief, Institute for International Economics, Washington DC, October.

Rotman, A. (2007). *Harmonious Society, China's Economic & Political Future*, Special Report, CLSA report, May.

World Bank (2007), *World Development Indicators (WDI) 2007.*

Conclusion

Christophe Jaffrelot

S
everal events have occurred during the summer of 2008 that have confirmed the growing influence of emerging countries on the international scene. In the economic field, the WTO's ministerial meeting that took place last July was deadlocked over the agricultural issue. Some of the G20, lead by India, opposed any further liberalization of the agricultural trade as long as Western countries and in particular the United States refuse to revise their own protectionist agendas and to give up agricultural subsidies. Pascal Lamy, director of the WTO, was forced to admit that this impasse might prevent the finalization of the Doha round by the end of the year.

In terms of geostrategy, Russia's military intervention in South Ossetia and in Abkhazia reflected Moscow's intent to reassert itself on the international stage. The Russian troops entered Georgian territory, stopping only forty kilometres from Tbilissi. Moscow pretended to accept the European mediation and to comply with the plan proposed by the European Union. However, as long as the two provinces escape Georgian sovereignty (the Douma recognizing and supporting their claim to independence), international law is flouted. Moscow made it a point of principle to disregard its small neighbour's territorial sovereignty in order to demonstrate Russia's willingness to use force on the rest of the world, and the United Sates and Europe in particular.

Aside from hard power, the Beijing Games, during which for the first time in history China won more medals than the US, has shown that the Middle Kingdom successfully bent this sporting symbol of universalism to its nationalist project. Never before have the games been so imposing, or have so many world political heavyweights been invited to participate in the opening ceremony (and consequently express admiration for China), in effect allowing informal political meetings similar to those that take place in the corridors of the UN. China appeared sure of its increasing power and cultural standing in the eyes of the world, which it previously lacked: notwithstanding the Tibetan crisis, Beijing managed to put the

Olympic Games at the forefront of its strategy which we must recognize as one of soft power.

Despite these recent events, some uncertainties remain as to whether emerging countries can continue to progress on this path.

Although the rising power of emerging countries is in the process of radically altering the international stage, several uncertainties hover over the continuation of their ascent. From an economic standpoint, Imène Rahmouni in the preceding pages is confident that these countries have a capacity to overcome financial crises that in the past had hindered their development. But their growth is particularly unbalanced—as Pierre-Noël Giraud, Jean-François Huchet and Joël Ruet point out, noting that in China and India the gaps are widening between rich and poor, among regions and between urban and rural areas. Such tensions may lead to social unrest, even more so since other variables may hamper growth in the short run: the Euro-Atlantic recession may well penalize exports from countries that depend on them most, such as China, and the ageing of the population and its quest for relative comfort will weigh on public finances because of new demands for social protection (pensions, health care) and on the cost of labour, as wage increases in Asia and Eastern Europe already show; lastly, surging commodity, energy and raw material prices are likely to reduce average purchasing power and further widen the gulf between rich and poor.

This last issue echoes the fundamental question raised by Laurence Tubiana and Emmanuel Guérin in the final chapter of the book: is the development of emerging countries sustainable? These two authors emphasize the scale of the environmental constraints facing these countries due to the rapid increase in their CO_2 emissions. This is a challenge that concerns the rest of the planet just as much, since curbing climate change induced by greenhouse gas emissions is a priority for all of humanity.

The rising power of emerging countries recasts the world situation in other areas as well. First of all, the planet today is faced with new food security risks due to population growth, changes in dietary habits—particularly in emerging countries, where the middle classes are consuming more and differently than before—and lastly the stagnation in food crop production related especially to reduction in cultivated areas (due to rural depopulation and even more so to industrial exploitation of arable land). The contradiction that has arisen from the development of consumption and the stagnation in food-producing crops creates strong inflationary pressure on basic foods. Certain cereal grain prices have exploded: the price of rice and wheat doubled between March 2007 and March 2008. Beyond this effect on prices, the effect noted on food stocks is dramatic: cereal stocks have reached their lowest level in a quarter-century.

Secondly, consumption of raw materials is skyrocketing. Energy is a case in point. Even if oil consumption in rich countries has stabilized or even decreased in recent years, consumption in emerging countries is rising rapidly. It has doubled in 20 years in Brazil, in 15 years in India, in ten years in China. Since production cannot meet demand, the price per barrel is on a constant upsurge. Other raw materials are undergoing a similar trend. With the emerging countries' strong appetite for steel, consumption of iron ore has risen from some 900 million tons in 2001—a level it had already reached ten years earlier—to about 1,300 million tons in 2005. Nickel consumption has leapt from less than 700,000 tons in 1993 to more than 1.3 million tons in 2004, China accounting for one-fifth of world consumption.

Not only do the imbalances thus created have an immediate impact on prices, they also reshuffle the cards of world trade, placing producer countries in a new position of strength, especially when there are few of them (Australia and Brazil together represent two-thirds of iron ore exports; Chile, Peru, Australia and Indonesia are in a similar position as regards copper, etc.). Some raw material producing countries are thus tempted to set up cartels resembling OPEC, even in the agricultural sector. For instance, Thailand, the world's largest rice exporter, has sought to convince Vietnam, the Philippines and Indonesia to form an organization of rice-producing countries.

Beyond that, the rise in the power of emerging countries in the medium term is in danger of hastening the moment when a certain number of natural resources will be depleted—raw materials, or commodities that require no industrial or agrifood processing such as products of the sea. Certain species of fish are already threatened with extinction due to overfishing practiced by some nations, including emerging countries.

All things considered, emerging countries have made extraordinary achievements and also represent an extraordinary challenge. They are proof that it is possible to overcome underdevelopment and achieve a certain degree of prosperity. But at the same time they are adopting lifestyles and following paths of industrialization and urbanization modelled on rich countries that consume huge amounts of raw materials and cause considerable environmental damage, which makes this path more precarious than it would seem, in any case at odds with a rationale of sustainable development. This is probably an additional factor of international instability, as competition for scarce resources—a category in which water must be included as well—may degenerate into open conflict.